Roots of Strategy

Book 4

Roots of Strategy

Book 4

4 Military Classics

Mahan
THE INFLUENCE OF SEA POWER UPON
HISTORY, 1660-1783

Corbett
SOME PRINCIPLES OF MARITIME STRATEGY

Douhet
COMMAND OF THE AIR

Mitchell
WINGED DEFENSE

Edited and with introductions by Col. (Ret.)
David Jablonsky, Ph.D.
Professor of National Security Affairs
Army War College

STACKPOLE
BOOKS

Published by
STACKPOLE BOOKS
5067 Ritter Road
Mechanicsburg, PA 17055
www.stackpolebooks.com

Printed in the United States of America

10 9 8 7 6 5 4 3 2 1

First edition

Cover design by Tracy Patterson
Photographs courtesy of the U.S. Naval Institute Press (Corbett, Douhet); the
U.S. Naval War College (Mahan); and the Air University Press (Mitchell).

Library of Congress Cataloging-in-Publication Data
Main entry under title:

Roots of strategy

   Reprint. Originally published: Harrisburg,
Pa.: Military Service Pub. Co., 1940.
   Includes index.
   Contents: The art of war / by Sun Tzu — The military
institutions of the Romans / by Vegetius — My reveries
on the art of war / by Marshal Maurice de Saxe — [etc.]
1. Strategy — Addresses, essays, lectures
2. Military art and science — Addresses, essays, lectures
I. Phillips, Thomas Raphael, 1892 —
U161.R66 1985   355'.02   84-26826
ISBN   0-8117-2918-4 (Bk. 4)

CONTENTS

PUBLISHER'S FOREWORD

No book series entitled *Roots of Strategy* would be complete without the inclusion of those late-nineteenth- and early-twentieth-century military theorists who addressed—and set the course—for what we today call the joint operational and strategic arenas of warfare. Sun Tzu, Jomini, Clausewitz, Frederick the Great, Napoleon, and other key strategists throughout the ages addressed themselves primarily to land forces. Modern warfare integrates land power, airpower, and sea power. Employment of air and sea power for strategic objectives was seriously addressed at the turn of the twentieth century and thereafter by four "crusaders"—Alfred Thayer Mahan, Julian Corbett, Giulio Douhet, and William Mitchell.

We are fortunate to have the strategic significance of these four writers introduced by the noted author and scholar, Colonel David Jablonsky, Professor of National Security Affairs at the U.S. Army War College. Professor Jablonsky has pulled together the best parts of the writings of the four theorists who have had the greatest influence on the roles of naval and airpower in the past century. Alfred Thayer Mahan's *The Influence of Sea Power Upon History,* Julian Corbett's *Some Principles of Maritime Strategy,* Giulio Douhet's *Command of the Air,* and William "Billy" Mitchell's *Winged Defense* continue to have relevance for students and practitioners of naval and air strategy—and indeed, for students of joint operations and strategy—because their works illustrate the continuity of the fundamentals of strategic thought, even in today's era of great and ubiquitous change.

EDITOR'S FOREWORD

The purpose of the preceding three *Roots of Strategy* books was to make available in compact form the writings of significant strategic theorists throughout history. This volume is no exception. Alfred Thayer Mahan and Julian Stafford Corbett dealt with naval strategy and operational art in a time of great change as navies emerged from the age of sail. The environment of change was even more pronounced for the early air theorists, Giulio Douhet and Billy Mitchell, as they attempted to deal with a new dimension of warfare. In such an environment, it is not surprising that the four theorists were not always correct in their calculations of the relationship of means and ends—the essence of strategy. But the problems they encountered are as important as their successes for the modern strategists who must deal with a future that promises to be marked by both the speed and the ubiquity of change.

My thanks to the following for their help in preparing this volume: Edward Skender at Stackpole Books; teaching colleagues: Donald Boose, Joseph Cerami, James Holcomb, Leonard Fullenkampf, James McCallum, and Richard Mullery; the U.S. Army War College library staff: Jacqueline Bey, Jane Gibish, Kathryn Hindman, Patsy Myers, Mary Rife, and Virginia Shope; the Department of National Security and Strategy staff: Sandy Foote, Jody Swartz and, above all, Rosemary Moore.

INTRODUCTION:
STRATEGY, CONTINUITY,
AND CHANGE

Modern military forces normally work in an environment in which the major dilemma is that of properly matching continuity and change. The answer to this problem lies in the process of what Richard Neustadt and Ernest May call thinking in "time streams." The core attribute for such thinking is to imagine the future as it may be when it becomes the past—a thing of complex continuity. Thus, the primary challenge is to ascertain whether change has really happened, is happening, or will happen. "What's so new about that?" is the operative question that can reveal continuity as well as change.[1]

It is not, however, an easy matter to draw reliable distinctions between the two in advance of retrospect. How, for instance, could Herbert Hoover have known in the spring of 1930 that the accustomed past would not reassert itself? Certainly there was no guide in the experiences of the 1893 to 1897 depression or the financial panics of 1907 and 1921. Nevertheless, such sudden change does not occur often in history; and continuity remains an important anodyne from the past that can inform the present and the future. This is why Thucydides can seem so contemporary—why, for instance, the contest between Athens and Sparta in the Peloponnesian War resonated in the Cold War and why the expedition to Syracuse had overtones for America's "half-war" in Vietnam.

Thinking in time is particularly helpful in peacetime—a period in which military forces normally encounter an environment that is at best indifferent, at worst hostile. This is compounded at the theater strategic, operational, and tactical levels of war, since there is no basis in peacetime for complete feedback—true verification of the interaction of organization, doctrine, and technology. The military at such times, Michael Howard points out,

> is like a sailor navigating by dead reckoning. You have left the terra firma of the last war and are extrapolating from the experiences of that war. The greater the distance from the last war, the greater become the chances of error in this extrapolation. Occasionally there is a break in the clouds: a small-scale conflict occurs somewhere and gives you a "fix" by showing whether certain weapons and techniques are effective or not: but it is always a doubtful mix. . . . For the most part you have to sail on in a fog of peace until at the last moment. Then, probably when it is too late, the clouds lift and there is land immediately ahead; breakers, probably, and rocks. Then you find out rather late in the day whether your calculations have been right or not.[2]

More often than not, these calculations will be wrong. What is equally important, however, is that strategic theorists have been at work asking the right questions, determining what can be jettisoned as ephemeral, what is of continuing validity, and how, in particular, the latter can be reduced to abiding principles. Such questions ultimately separate the variables from the constants—the objective of all scientific thought—and, as a consequence, allow some basis for establishing a capacity to quickly correct doctrinal problems when the moment arrives in which the military discovers that it hasn't got it quite right.[3] The sea and air theorists represented in this volume pose these types of questions.

All four theorists were born in the nineteenth century: Alfred Thayer Mahan in 1840; Julian Stafford Corbett in 1854; Giulio Douhet in 1869; and William "Billy" Mitchell in 1879. Only Mahan, however, actually produced his primary strategic work, *The Influence of Sea Power Upon History, 1660-1783,* in that century. The publication of the study in 1890 was his first effort; and the preface, the introductory, and the first chapter of that book compose the initial selection in this volume. Corbett, on the other hand, worked for many years on a series of historical studies before distilling the essence of his efforts in his 1911 *Some Principles of Maritime Strategy,* extracts of which form the second selection of readings. Giulio Douhet wrote *The Command of the Air* in 1921 and revised it in 1927. The third selection contains most of this work and an additional article, all of which along with two other articles was translated into English and published in 1942 as *The Command of the Air.* The final selection is from Billy Mitchell's *Winged Defense,* a collection of magazine articles and Mitchell's congressional testimony in 1925, the year of his court-martial.[4]

Three of these four theorists were career military officers. Mahan graduated second in his class from the U.S. Naval Academy in 1859 and served in the Civil War on ships patrolling the Confederate coast. For twenty years after that conflict, he served in navy yards, on the Naval Academy staff, and on ships operating in Asia and off the west coast of South America. In 1886 he joined the faculty of the Naval War College and twice served as the president of that institution. In 1889 Mahan organized his lectures into book form, published the following year as *The Influence of Sea Power Upon History, 1660-1783.* The book was instantly acclaimed in Great Britain; and when Mahan, back on sea duty, brought his ship into Southampton in the summer of 1893, he was hailed everywhere, entertained by the Queen and other notables, and presented with honorary degrees from Oxford and Cambridge. In 1896 he retired from active duty and, until his death in 1914, continued to produce an enormous output of books and articles.[5]

Douhet was commissioned as an artillery officer in the Italian Army in 1882 and became an early enthusiast of motor transport for the military. In 1909, however, Wilbur Wright's visit to Italy with a demonstration plane caused Douhet to switch his enthusiasm; he began to write articles on airpower and to urge the establishment of a military aviation branch. In 1912 he assumed command of the first aviation unit in the Italian Army, which he followed by a tour as head of the Army's Aviation Section. In World War I his criticism of government aviation policy resulted in his court-martial for slandering the Italian high command; sentenced to a year in prison, he busied himself with drafting plans for an interallied air fleet of 20,000 strategic bombers. After the debacle at Caporetto, the Italian authorities reopened Douhet's case and restored him to active duty as chief of the Central Aeronautical Bureau. He retired in 1918. In late 1920 Douhet was fully exonerated and, still in retirement, was promoted to brigadier general in 1921, the year he published *The Command of the Air.* He returned briefly to active duty in 1923 as commissioner of aviation in Benito Mussolini's fascist government. From that time until his death in 1930, Douhet revised his book and continued to write articles promoting his concepts concerning airpower and his prophesies concerning future air war.[6]

Mitchell enlisted in the U.S. Army in 1898 at the age of 18 and shortly thereafter was commissioned in the Signal Corps, demonstrating an early interest in the application of radio and motor transport to military operations. In 1916 Mitchell learned to fly and with the U.S. entry into World War I the next year, transferred into the American Air Service, rising steadily to the head of air operations by the closing weeks of the war. After that conflict, there was a tour in Europe to study the status of aviation in the major powers, and from 1921 to 1925 he served in the rank of brigadier general as the assistant chief of the air service. The combination of his zealous promotion of a unified air force, separate from the other services, and his vehement criticisms of policies by the War and Navy Departments resulted in his court-martial in the fall of 1925. He resigned from the Army early in 1926 and devoted the remaining ten years of his life to denouncing the direction of U.S. military and civil aeronautical policies, while promoting the cause of a unified air arm in lectures, writings, and appearances before congressional committees.[7]

Corbett never served in the military. He received a law degree from Trinity College, Cambridge in 1877 and, in the words of his biographer, "spasmodically pursued a legal career until 1882."[8] After some years spent traveling and producing a few indifferent novels, he began to write serious naval history. By 1900 Corbett had produced two important works and, like Mahan at the same age of forty-five, decided to commit himself to the writing of naval history. In 1902 he was invited to be a lecturer at the Royal Naval College and at the same time was drawn into the burgeoning movement for British naval reform led by Second Sea Lord Sir John Fisher. In the ensuing years, Corbett continued to write books on naval history concerning the period between the age of Drake and that of Nelson. The ideas drawn from these writings as well as his lectures and staff work for Fisher were published in 1911 as *Some Principles of Maritime Strategy.* His work continued to have influence in World War I, and he was completing the official naval history of that conflict when he died in 1922.[9]

ENVIRONMENT

The significance of the four theorists represented in this volume lies not so much in the originality of their thinking, but in their being the first to assemble ideas, widely known at the time, into a collected, structured order. They all lived in periods of enormous change, which stimulated not only their thinking but that of other theorists who in turn influenced them.

In such a milieu, Alfred Thayer Mahan drew upon a wide variety of general and specific influences in the 1880s to put together the Naval War College lectures that formed the basis for his first book. First was his father, Dennis Hart Mahan, "old Dennis," a professor at West Point who had provided half the Civil War leaders their education in military engineering and tactics, and in particular had introduced them to the military writing of the Swiss philosopher of war, Antoine-Henri Jomini. Mahan was greatly influenced by Jomini, "my best military friend," who believed that in war "methods change but principles are unchanging."[10] For Mahan, Jomini served as an example of how to integrate structure and system into historical studies in order to create general principles, rules, and conclusions. This structure provided *The Influence of Sea Power Upon History* with a sense of cohesion and universal applicability that was lacking in earlier naval histories and which helped impart a practical, realistic air to the book.[11]

Another major influence at this time, by Mahan's own account, was Theodor Mommsen's *History of Rome,* which he read, during a voyage in 1884, at the English Club in Lima, Peru. "It suddenly struck me," Mahan wrote concerning Mommsen's description of the Punic Wars, "how different things might have been could Hannibal have invaded Italy by sea . . . or could he, after arrival, have been in free communication with Carthage by water."[12] That same year Stephen B. Luce, the founder of the U.S. Naval War College, recruited Mahan to teach at that institution. It was Luce, with his own broad approach to the highest level of naval thought, who introduced Mahan to his ideas and those of the various naval reform groups that had emerged since the Civil War, in particular the pioneering use of historical study in the 1870s by Sir John Knox Laughton.[13] As a consequence, Mahan was well aware by 1890 that with the *The Influence of Sea Power Upon History,* he was embarking on a well-traveled intellectual road. That same year, for example, British Vice Adm. Phillip Colomb published *Naval Warfare: Its Ruling Principles and Practice Historically Treated.* And in the fall of the previous year, even as his manuscript was accepted for publication, Mahan was disturbed by the appearance of an article entitled, "War and the British Empire," by the noted British historian John R. Seeley of Cambridge University. Because the article, in Mahan's judgment, "so epitomized the general drift of my book," he sent it to his publishers who decided nonetheless to proceed with the printing. The Seeley article was a reminder to Mahan, as his most recent biographer concludes, that "*The Influence of Sea Power Upon History* was not an original piece of work from either an intellectual or conceptual standpoint. It was a skillful synthesis of the ideas of others."[14] On the other hand, as another biographer has pointed out, if Mahan "discovered nothing in particular, he discovered it very well."[15]

Many of these same theorists as well as Mahan influenced Julian Corbett as he produced a series of naval histories and lectures between 1898 and the publication of *Some Principles of Maritime Strategy* in 1911. From Laughton, for example, he learned the meticulous use of detailed sources. And from Mahan, he came to appreciate that the use of naval activity minutiae without a constant reference to the primary objectives that caused the activity could distort historical perspective. "For the first time," he wrote of *The Influence of Sea Power Upon History,*

> naval history was placed on a philosophical basis.
> From the mass of facts which had hitherto done duty
> for naval history, broad generalizations were possible.
> The lairs of statesmen and publicists were opened, and
> a new note began to sound in world politics.[16]

Equally important for Corbett was his interaction with Sir John Fisher and other reformers in the navy hierarchy—the so-called "Fishpond." Serving as a War Course faculty member at the Royal Naval College and interacting with a "think tank" for influential naval professionals, enlarged and enriched his perspective as well as his reputation for clear-headed, independent thinking in an environment that almost invariably produced the worst kind of pandering to naval officialdom. At the same time, there was the propitious assignment in 1905 of Captain Edmond Slade as the Director of the War Course—a mentor who was destined to play a role similar to that of Luce with Mahan. Together, the two men took on the strategy curriculum as a joint project, with concepts worked out in close cooperation. One result was that Corbett in consultation with Slade produced the so-called "Green Pamphlet" in 1906, entitled "Strategical Terms and Definitions Used in Lectures on Naval History," which along with a revision in 1909 addressed the concepts and principles that would form the basis for his 1911 masterwork.[17] But Slade's influence did not end there, for it is quite likely that as a linguist and a student of the German wars of unification, he augmented Corbett's reading of Jomini and other war theorists with those of Carl von Clausewitz. In any event, while Corbett's 1904 study of *England in the Mediterranean* was devoid of Clausewitzian thought, the Prussian philosopher was very much in evidence in the "Green Pamphlet," the first section of which began with a paraphrase of Clausewitz's most fundamental dictum concerning war as a continuation of policy.[18]

For both Mahan and Corbett, two trends in the nineteenth century virtually ensured them an audience for their theories of sea power and maritime strategy. The first was the rapid development of naval technology. Steam applied to ships early in the century had been followed within three decades by the advent of the screw propeller followed within a similar period by great innovations in ordnance, armor, and coal consumption. By 1873 the launching of the *Devastation* marked the arrival of a warship similar in its essentials to those of the capital ships early in the next century, with its iron hull, propeller, armor plate, rifled guns, and a mast used only for signaling. This dramatically new technology set the stage for the second trend involving growing global rivalries among the major powers in the late nineteenth century. For these new developments enabled countries like Japan and the United States to establish local naval superiority and thus to challenge the global naval supremacy of Great Britain, just as that country's lead in industrialization was beginning to slip away. Moreover, the 1875 to 1896 global depression caused most of these powers to adopt protective tariffs, which only added to the rivalries that found expression in the seizure of territories held by nations too weak to secure them. These two interdependent trends challenged traditional thinking about navies. Previously, there had been no attempts to intellectualize the subject or to produce any serious professional literature. In this chaotic, fluctuating environment, Mahan and Corbett, dissatisfied with what they perceived as narrow technical viewpoints within their countries' navies, attempted to create "some enduring and steady guide."[19]

The outcome of these trends was not always so self-evident. The history of the accomplishments of the sail-bedecked man-of-war appeared irrelevant as the age of steam began, particularly for enthusiastic navalists who perceived naval change only in the context of the second industrial revolution. Moreover, at the time Mahan was writing *The Influence of Sea Power Upon History,* a naval debate was raging in the United States that demonstrated that neither the Congress nor the public was prepared to accept large naval expansion programs. The European powers were occupied only with themselves; since there appeared to be no external discernable threat to America, there was no rationale to begin a major navalist effort in peacetime. Nevertheless, waiting in the wings was a wide assortment of interest groups ranging from nationalists, manufacturers, and builders of ships, engines, and armaments to ambitious military officers, bankers interested in foreign investment, and merchants searching for colonial markets. These groups, of course, were not unique to the United States; nor was the increased public interest in economic development and international relations, and their relationship to navies. Expansion and reform were in the air.[20]

Air theorists dealt with a faster changing environment and a new technology barely over a decade old when World War I began. That war had a greater impact on the subsequent development of airpower than airpower actually had on the conduct and outcome of the conflict. The American Air Service, for instance, had dropped only 138 tons of bombs and had never penetrated farther than 160 miles beyond the forward edge of the battle area. On the other hand, as David MacIsaac points out, "virtually every theory, attitude, idea, hope, dream, and debate that would mark the course of air warfare a quarter century later had been foreshadowed."[21] But prediction was not the same as implementation; the end of the war frustrated air theorists in all the belligerent countries. In October 1918, as an example, the western forces agreed to form an interallied independent air force that would be capable of a strategic bombardment campaign. The armistice the next month rendered this development inconclusive with no proof that aviation was anything more than an instrument to support armies and navies.[22]

By that time, there had been a liberal cross-fertilization of theories within the allied aviation community. In Italy, Douhet's collaboration with Count Caproni di Taliedo to develop a strategic bomber had resulted by 1917 in successful raids on Austria with as many as 250 of these aircraft at a time. An American mission of aviators and aeronautical engineers, who observed these attacks, left Italy as enthusiastic supporters of the strategic bombardment theories of Douhet, then languishing in prison. Mitchell corresponded frequently with Caproni and certainly was aware of Douhet's ideas. Many of these ideas coincided with those of Major General Hugh Trenchard, the commander of the Royal Flying Corps in France, with whom Mitchell had formed a close relationship even before America's entry in the war. Trenchard, like many of his British colleagues, looked upon air forces as uniquely capable of directly attacking the enemy's strategic heart by means of a "relentless and incessant offensive" that would defeat the nation without the "intermediate step" of defeating the enemy army.[23] This approach was captured in the official Smuts Report to the British government in August 1917, which concluded that

> the day may not be far off when aerial operations with
> their devastation of enemy lands and destruction of
> industrial and population centres on a vast scale may
> become the principal operations of war, to which the
> older forms of military and naval operations may
> become secondary and subordinate.[24]

As a consequence, by the time General John Pershing appointed
Mitchell as the Aviation Officer of the American Expeditionary
Force (AEF) in the summer of 1917, Mitchell had become a strategic bombing enthusiast to the extent that over three decades later,
General Henry "Hap" Arnold could still recall Mitchell's desire at
the time to "blow up Germany."[25] Nevertheless, Mitchell curbed
his zeal because of the AEF's policy focus on the operational and
tactical levels of war; and in the St.-Mihiel offensive in the fall of
1918, he employed 1,481 aircraft, the majority on loan from the
allies, to support U.S. ground forces. That he had not lost his
enthusiasm for strategic bombing was demonstrated by his continued correspondence with Caproni concerning possible acquisitions
of long-range bombers and his continued efforts to assemble target
data on German strategic objectives. At the war's end, Mitchell was
still negotiating with a British firm to procure bombers with a minimum range of 650 miles.[26]

In the interwar years, the Great War continued to exert a
tremendous influence on the environment. To begin with, that
period marked a general decline in the earlier public confidence
concerning technological advances. The old premise of an escape
from the horrors of war through technology had suffered almost
mortal blows in the grim attrition of World War I. Paradoxically,
revulsion against what technology had accomplished in that conflict kept the premise alive in the guise of airpower. For without
some faith in the bomber's expeditious decisiveness, the view
of the future would have been too grim. "The more rapid and

terrifying the arms are," Douhet wrote, "the faster they will reach vital centers and the more deeply they will affect moral resistance. Hence the more civilized war will become." And if all that seemed a bit strained in light of World War I experiences, Douhet acknowledged rather lamely, that cemeteries would grow under the impact of strategic bombardment, "but not as large as they became before the peace signed at Versailles."[27]

The war also demonstrated to both the land and the sea theorists of the 1920s the clear ascendancy of the defense on land over the offense. Firepower, the cause of this change, would only increase in the future, leaving strategic air bombardment as the only solution to the bloody indecisiveness of land warfare. For B. H. Liddell Hart, the key was to attack beyond the enemy's line in order "to strike at the nerve-system of the enemy nation, in which its industrial resources and communications form its Achilles heel." Aircraft, in other words, would enable a nation "to *jump over* the army which shields the enemy government, industry and people, and *so strike direct and immediately at the seat of the opposing will and policy.*"[28]

But for many of the theorists at the time, the effectiveness of strategic bombing would not be due solely to the new technology. Sometimes implicitly, more often explicitly, they created images of how aerial destruction of "vital centers," could bring a nation to its knees. After all, there were the examples of mass panic on the home fronts and mutiny in the trenches during the recent war. Moreover that conflict had demonstrated how susceptible societies were to propaganda and manipulation. In such an environment, the new technology of mass communication would only contribute to the fragility of societies with combinations of bombardment and propaganda working together in adverse synergism to erode the national will. For Douhet, even after four years of proof that public passions and other intangibles could sustain populations at war beyond rational limits, such resistance would still "deny reason itself."[29] Liddell Hart was equally adamant. "Would not the general will to resist vanish?" he asked as he described the destruction of government, factories, and railways.[30] The answer by J. F. C. Fuller was resoundingly in the affirmative as he predicted how enemy air could turn London into "one raving Bedlam" with a government "swept away by an avalanche of terror," ready to make peace on any terms.[31]

All this notwithstanding, the implementation of airpower theories in the interwar years was not an easy matter in most countries. Throughout military history, warfare had been compartmented on the earth's surface between sea and land. With the advent of a new dimension, this separation had been bridged; and in fact airpower was defined in terms of its operation against the surface, whether sea or land. The most immediate practical problem for most governments, then, was to ascertain if independent airpower could win a future war. Here, the conclusions of the new theorists were generally less than convincing, particularly in light of airpower performance in World War I. And if independent airpower could not be decisive, it was understandable that land and sea services in most nations were reluctant to see the segregation of all air assets into a new service committed to its own dogmas and scornful of the future efficacy of armies and navies. In addition, a more fundamental part of the problem was that once the theorists had rejected any sizable aid to surface military forces, then civilian populations were the only practicable targets for independent airpower. The offensive independent air war envisaged by Douhet and the other theorists could be total only in its targeting of traditional noncombatants on the home fronts.[32]

In Italy, because of the geography, the positive wartime experience with strategic bombing, and the more militaristic fascist government after 1921, Douhet's ideas had considerable doctrinal and organizational impact. In the United States, the issue of air strategy was compounded by the rapid reversion after 1920 to a policy of isolationism and continental defense. In this context, as the government-appointed Morrow Board pointed out in 1925, geography would serve as a buffer from foreign bomber threats, if indeed any such threat existed:

> Our national policy calls for the establishment of the air strength of our Army primarily as an agency of defense. Protected, as the United States is, by broad oceans from possible enemies, the evidence submitted in our hearings gives complete ground for the conclusion that there is no present reason for apprehension of any invasion from overseas directly by way of the air; nor indeed is there any apparent probability of such an invasion in any future which can be foreseen.[33]

The findings resulted in a 1926 congressional act changing the title of the Army Air Service to the Army Air Corps with a strength of eighteen hundred planes and appropriate numbers of personnel. But there was no disguising the basic *status quo* conclusions in terms of strategy and command arrangements. The new organization remained firmly under the control of the Army General Staff, the "longbowmen," as Mitchell described them; and Congress would seldom fund the authorized strength of the organization for the remainder of the interwar years.[34]

WAR AND STRATEGY

The approach to war by Mahan and Corbett was fundamentally different from that of Douhet and Mitchell. Both naval theorists essentially saw war in the Clausewitzian sense as a continuation of policy at the grand strategic level. Mahan had not been exposed to Clausewitz when he wrote *The Influence of Sea Power Upon History.* But as Corbett pointed out in terms of Clausewitz, "Jomini, his great contemporary and rival, though proceeding by a less philosophical but no less lucid method, entirely endorses this view. . . . Both men . . . are agreed that the fundamental conception of war is political."[35] It was the influence of both of these war philosophers that led Mahan and Corbett to link military strategy and operational matters to grand strategy and all the elements that compose national power. Equally important, this connection caused the two naval theorists to emphasize the most far-reaching of all strategic questions concerning the nature of a conflict and the idea that limited political objectives could produce limited wars.

For Douhet and Mitchell, the advent of air had fundamentally altered the nature of war. In both their works, the question of political direction was subsumed in the imperative for total war in order to prevent a bloodletting similar to World War I. The irony was that in the search for decisiveness, the two theorists elevated bloodletting to the *sine qua non* of their theories. "The purpose of war is to harm the enemy as much as possible," Douhet wrote, "and all means which contribute to this will be employed, no matter what they are."[36] In such a depiction, if harming the enemy became an end in itself, then war's irrationality could return full circle to the destructive attrition of the Great War. For if the bomber was not immediately decisive in the next war and if nations resisted despite the terror of strategic bombardment, then wars of attrition could emerge in even more brutal form, with entire populations under siege. Such an outcome was characterized by Douhet as "an inhuman, atrocious performance."[37] But like Mitchell, who saw strategic bombing as making war "sharper, more decisive, and more quickly finished," Douhet, did not believe that this would occur and thus did not explore any details of such a scenario.[38]

Mahan

In *The Influence of Sea Power Upon History,* Alfred Thayer Mahan used the naval, military, diplomatic, and commercial events that occurred in the conflicts between Britain and other great powers between 1660 and 1783 to demonstrate that the states that had exercised control of all or important parts of the sea, had dominated history. More specifically, it was the "effect of sea power upon the course of history and the prosperity of nations" that had caused such a broad and decisive effect.[39] And even more specifically, it was this sea power that had allowed Britain to achieve global preeminence. "It can scarcely be denied that England's uncontrolled dominion of the seas, during almost the whole period chosen for our subject," he wrote, "was by long odds the chief among the military factors that determined the final issue."[40]

Mahan addressed two principal subjects in the book. The first was grand strategy, which encompassed for him the relationships of maritime and naval activities with broader political and economic ideas both national and international. This was presented in a relatively straightforward manner with the utilitarian purpose of advancing a political agenda that promoted navalism. The second subject, presented in a more difficult, complex, and elusive manner, was the art and science of command, concerned with operational decision making in wartime. Here, Mahan's objective was to improve naval officer education by providing a series of principles to act as a guide for these professionals. He considered these two elements to be of equal importance and, in fact, interdependent.[41]

The bridge between the two subjects was sea power; a term never clearly defined by Mahan, whose comment in 1897 that it was "at once an abstraction and a concrete fact" did little to clear up the matter.[42] Nevertheless, it was clear that sea power in terms of the operational art and science of command meant command of the sea through naval superiority. Since the sea was both a logistical highway and an avenue of enemy approach, Mahan emphasized, command of sea lines of communications would provide any belligerent with enormous power. Powerful, concentrated fleets organized as units that should never be divided, as history had demonstrated, could attain this command. In that light, commercial raiding was an indecisive, wasteful activity; it could never lead to command of the sea, which could only be attained by a dominant "fleet in being," capable of decisive battles.

Naval power, then, was a subset of sea power—a connection that was an indispensable part of the bridge to the realm of grand strategy. For if the battle fleets were to dominate the sea lines of communication, they would require the capability to range the globe. That had been possible in the self-contained wind-powered ships in the age of sail. But absent widely available coaling and repair stations, this was an impossibility for steam-driven men-of-war. The establishment and defense of such bases, however, meant colonies. And colonies would, in turn, provide the trade necessary for a flourishing merchant marine to travel the sea lines of communications that would have to be secured in wartime by command of the sea. Sea power, in short, consisted of naval power, overseas trade, and colonies—a very attractive combination of power projection and profits in which even in peacetime, a big navy would "pay."[43]

Corbett

The thoughts of Clausewitz permeated Julian Corbett's *Some Principles of Maritime Strategy,* whether the subject was uncertainty and the naval fog of war or the utility and nonutility of theory. Most importantly, there was the Clausewitzian influence in the realm of what Corbett termed "major strategy," which was to be derived from the war's purpose as a whole, encompassing all elements of national power. Britain's success as a great power, he emphasized in this regard, was based on the ability to combine and exploit its entire naval, military, economic, and diplomatic resources in a comprehensive policy.[44] Within the category of major strategy, the maritime component provided the principles governing the relationship of the fleet to policy, to nonmilitary elements of power, and to the actions of political and military forces on land. Naval strategy, a subset of maritime strategy, detailed the operational and the tactical movement of the fleet— "minor strategy" in Corbett's terminology.

Against the backdrop of major strategy, Corbett constantly asserted (throughout a long writing career leading up to his major work) that maritime power was important because of its influence on political, diplomatic, economic, and military operations ashore. In terms of the military, he concluded as early as his 1900 study of the post-Armada period that there was a mutual dependence between land and naval power and that it was a mistake to study separately the histories of British armies and navies. "The real importance of maritime power," he wrote, "is its influence on military operations."[45] And four years later in his study, *England in the Mediterranean,* Corbett demonstrated how both William III and Marlborough used English sea power to influence the outcome of land campaigns against Louis XIV.[46] Finally, there was Corbett's 1910 study, *The Campaign of Trafalgar,* in which he described how the land victory at Austerlitz had confounded the statecraft of Pitt the Younger despite the great operational sea victory in that campaign.[47] Corbett continued this theme the next year in his opening chapter on the theory of war in *Some Principles of Maritime Strategy,* emphasizing that his focus was maritime, not naval,

> for it scarcely needs saying that it is almost impossible that a war can be decided by naval action alone. . . . Since men live upon the land and not upon the sea, great issues between nations at war have always been decided—except in the rarest cases—either by what your army can do against your enemy's territory and national life, or else by the fear of what the fleet makes it possible for your army to do.[48]

Corbett's outlook on the broader aspects of maritime strategy was linked to the concept of limited war—what Clausewitz called "war by contingent"—and the primary policy question concerning the political objective and thus the nature of the war. This idea of limitation brought Corbett's approach to maritime strategy into the

British tradition of using naval strength to assist land allies against any would-be European hegemon. "The army is a projectile," Sir John Fisher commented in this regard, "to be fired by the navy."[49] Acting under this concept and by commanding the sea, Britain would be able not only to isolate any distant objective, but also to prevent invasion of the home territory. In the end, it was a reaffirmation, quoted in Corbett's *Principles,* of Roger Bacon's assertion in Elizabethan times that "he that commands the sea is at great liberty and may take as much or as little of the war as he will."[50]

From this perspective, it was not always necessary to exercise command of the sea in the Mahanian zero-sum sense. For Corbett, the concept was not analogous to territorial conquest, but instead meant "nothing but the control of maritime communications, whether for commercial or military purposes."[51] And this, in turn, meant that decisive battle was not necessarily always the right answer. It was true that winning such encounters was still "the supreme function of the fleet."[52] But if local or temporary control of maritime communications was all that was necessary to achieve objectives, there were other options for navies. What was essential for sea control, then, was not the destruction of the enemy fleet, but the right of passage on the sea. Decisive action against the enemy was only necessary if that fleet was able to render unsafe a friendly fleet's passage. In any event, the presence of a major naval force, a "fleet in being" on the edge of a decisive ocean area might suffice alone to deter an enemy naval force from putting to sea for the purpose of denial or disruption.

Douhet

Giulio Douhet's principal thesis was that the new technology of the air arm had broken the "evolutionary continuity of the character of war."[53] War was now based on the dominance of airpower with its primary proposition that an air force must achieve command of the air to achieve victory. "To have command of the air," Douhet wrote in terms that would not have been unfamiliar to

Mahan and Corbett, "means to be in a position to prevent the enemy from flying while retaining the ability to fly oneself."[54] And only large-scale strategic bombardment could accomplish this. In air warfare, it was a race against annihilation, a fight for national survival based on the destruction of the threatening rival power, "smashing the material and moral resources of a people . . . until the final collapse of all social organization."[55] In the past, enemy blows had fallen on armies and navies, rarely on nations. The land and sea services, as the Great War had demonstrated, had reached a stage of development that consigned them to a purely defensive role in future wars. Those conflicts, Douhet emphasized, would be won instead by the air arm consisting of massive fleets of strategic bombers loaded with high explosive, incendiary, and chemical bombs directed at enemy populations,

> entities less well-organized and disciplined, less able to resist, and helpless to act or counteract. It is fated, there-fore, that the moral and material collapse will come about more quickly and easily. A body of troops will stand fast under intensive bombings, even after losing half or two-thirds of its men; but the workers in shop, factory, or harbor will melt away after the first losses.[56]

It was a scenario of total war, an apparent reversal of Clause-witzian linkage, in which military means in the form of the strate-gic bomber would dominate political objectives. And if war was total, then limitations imposed by law and morality were irrele-vant. As a consequence, Douhet continued to advocate aerochem-ical attacks on cities long after Italy's ratification of the 1925 Geneva Protocol prohibiting such weapons. "It is useless to delude ourselves," he wrote. "All the restrictions, all the international agreements made during peacetime are fated to be swept away like dried leaves on the winds of war. . . . The limitations applied to the so-called inhuman and atrocious means of war are nothing but international demagogic hypocrisies."[57]

Adding to the totality of this approach was Douhet's fundamental belief in the offensive advantages of bombers that was basic to his command of the air concept. "Viewed in its true light," he concluded, "aerial warfare admits of no defense, only offense."[58] From that perspective, surface defenses against aerial attack such as antiaircraft artillery were worse than useless. "How many guns lay waiting month after month, even years," he wrote of the World War I experience, "mouths gaping to the sky, on the watch for an attack which never came!"[59] Nor in the preradar era did Douhet see any great chances for interception, since the infinite approach options of incoming bombers combined with the weak endurance, or "air-keeping" capability of fighter-interceptors, prevented the massing of interception capabilities.

Because there was no defense against air attack, Douhet also emphasized the necessity of an air fleet in being that could begin an all-out attack as soon as the conflict began. Airpower in future wars would not have the luxury of time for mobilization afforded to surface forces. Lack of readiness meant loss of command of the air, which in turn meant defeat. One consequence of this perception of the overwhelming effects of offensive air in which mobilization was not a factor and air defense was impossible, was a situation potentially so destabilizing that preemption might be necessary as the possibility of hostilities increased.

> A belief generally held nowadays is that wars will begin in the air, and that large-scale aerial actions will be carried out even before the declaration of war, because everyone will be trying to get the advantage of surprise. . . . for each side will realize the necessity . . . of ridding the air of enemy aerial means so as to prevent any possible retaliation from him.[60]

All this played a major role in the evolution of Douhet's thoughts on organization. In his original 1921 edition of *The Command of the Air*, he stipulated that the two surface services should be allowed to retain their auxiliary aviation units to assist in their primarily defensive missions, while the aviation arm should dominate the offensive. In his 1927 revision, Douhet acknowledged that a lack of courage prompted his earlier position. By that time, Douhet had also introduced the concept of a "battleplane," a bomber with enough armor and armament to ensure that it could act independently. The proper course, he now insisted, was to provide all air assets to an independent air force to further its essential and decisive mission of commanding the air.[61]

Mitchell

After World War I, Billy Mitchell represented America's different outlook concerning the bomber. He understood the European perspective based on the relative ease with which nations on that continent could reach each other by plane. But in the United States, protected by vast oceans, Mitchell perceived the bomber as a means to strengthen defense by sweeping sea lines of communications to North America and by destroying any sea or air armada that approached the continent. For naval proof, he directed the bombing of a series of obsolete battleships, dismissing the idea that the lack of antiaircraft and other defenses for the surface ships might have detracted from the aerial onslaught's effectiveness. In terms of air, there were the lessons from the recent conflict. "It was proved in the European War," he wrote, "that the only effective defense against aerial attack is to whip the enemy's air forces in air battles."[62] As a result, Mitchell pointed out, interception not retaliation was all that was required, and this in turn meant an air force of fighter and pursuit aircraft as well as bombers—a far cry from Douhet's all-bomber fleet focused on the strategic offense.

But there were also similarities with Douhet in the years immediately after World War I. In his first book, published the same year as Douhet's first edition of *Command,* Mitchell echoed his Italian counterpart by concluding that if a nation achieved command of the air, it was "practically certain to win the whole war."[63] And like Douhet, he relegated land and sea (except submarines) to secondary, defensive roles. Moreover, both men also agreed on the assumption that the current era was one of total war; on the rapidity of change itself in the area of aircraft research and development; and on the importance of civil aviation as a basis during peace for wartime expansion. Finally, Mitchell was as adamant as the Italian about the creation of an independent air force, which in his scheme would be under a "Ministry of Defense" charged with coordinating the functions of the three services as well as their wartime roles. Only a Department of Aeronautics, he insisted, could organize aviation technology development and personnel training. Much of the European perspective in Mitchell's thinking would emerge in starker outline in the late 1920s. In many of his earlier writings, for instance, he described an oceangoing bomber that would have to be in range, size, and accuracy, a plane that could accomplish offensive actions into an enemy's heartland. Opportunities for such attacks by the United States were thinly disguised in his many descriptions of American cities under strategic bombardment, published in his polemics early in the decade and in more detail in 1925 in a series of magazine articles that were eventually included in *Winged Defense*.[64]

The problem was that in the early 1920s, Mitchell's view of airpower matched the public's mood; an inexpensive instrument of war with defensive capabilities against seaborne attack had been dramatized, however unscientifically, to the nation by the bombing tests on the battleships. Airpower, as described by Mitchell in comforting terms, would be a source of cheap security into a future free from the militarism, taxation, and conscription that marked the Great War. For the American people, General Arnold recalled, "Billy and his antiquated bombers were not so much a new weapon as the death knell of weapons. To hell with armament; to hell with everything to do with war!"[65] Unfortunately, Mitchell's plans for American aviation outran the existing technology and thus the prevailing mood of "normalcy," isolationism, and economy. By 1924 he had no issue, which could overcome the bureaucratic morass of interservice and congressional wrangling, to elicit the reforms and support he desired. The next year, he dramatized his case with his own court-martial, convinced that "changes in military systems are brought about only through the pressure of public opinion or disaster in war."[66]

The court-martial in the fall of 1925 was a turning point for Mitchell. Prior to it, his theories were closely tied to both the tactical as well as the strategic realities of air warfare. As late as January of that year, he wrote of strategic bombing as an independently decisive weapon, then added the qualification that ultimately war resolution could only come about on the ground and that the applicability of strategic bombing depended on a nation's geographic position. This schizophrenic approach was captured in *Winged Defense* later in the year, a book that stressed the vulnerability of nations, even the United States, to attacks by bombers, invincible except for an important exception:

> The frontiers in the old sense—the coast lines or borders—are no longer applicable to the air because aircraft can fly anywhere that there is air. Interior cities are now as subject to attack as those along the coast. *Nothing can stop the attack of aircraft except other aircraft.*[67]

After he resigned from the army in 1926, however, Mitchell's predictions concerning airpower became increasingly inflated and more closely aligned to Douhet's "command of the air." "The advent of air power, which can go straight to the vital centers and either neutralize or destroy them," he wrote in 1930, "has put a completely new complexion on the old system of making war. It is now realized that the hostile main army in the field is a false objective, and the real objectives are the vital centers. . . ."[68]

STYLE
The theorists represented in this volume were crusaders. The two naval theorists in the period between 1890 and World War I were bent on promoting navalism, improving naval officer education,

and using lessons from the age of sail to arrive at broad maritime principles based on general theories of war and the proposition that navies exist for national purposes. Both were dealing with a traditional form of warfare in the process of transformation by technology. The use of history and strategy was a reactionary approach that would, nonetheless, prove effective in achieving their objectives in an age of technological revolution. The two air theorists, on the other hand, were dealing with a new form of warfare, not yet completely defined in terms of the new technology. Moreover, they were operating in a different era, separated from the earlier period by the jagged scar of World War I. And their objectives, such as the independence of their respective air forces, posed immediate threats to the traditional services. As a consequence, both men emerged as more strident, but less immediately effective crusaders than their naval predecessors.

For the naval theorists, the utilitarian use of history was essential to their crusade. Mahan dealt with large generalizations and broad syntheses, primarily dependent on secondary sources. But there were problems inherent in his method of coming to predetermined conclusions and then marshaling historical facts as illustrations and proof. Sea power, for example, was certainly a necessary cause of Britain's victories over France in the seventeenth and eighteenth centuries; but it was not, as Mahan maintained, the sufficient cause. Other historical events ranging from military victories on land to diplomatic successes also played a part. In general, Mahan's discrete general thesis dealing with political, economic, and governmental arguments concerning grand strategy was elaborated in a straightforward manner. But his belief that historical narrative and expression of principles were reciprocal approaches made it difficult to get a precise understanding of his operational and professional arguments dealing with the art and science of naval command. The reader of *The Influence of Sea Power Upon History* was often left with detailed narrative descriptions that required close reading for any assimilation of ideas.[69]

Corbett was a self-taught historian who became a strategist. His work was marked by an ability to trace the larger, interconnected significance of historical events and apply his findings to a finely drawn strategic approach. Moreover, his sources were primary in nature for the most part and more extensive than those normally used by Mahan. And since he was less rigidly logical than Mahan, he was less inclined to form conclusions and was certainly more prepared to allow what he called "applied history" to determine his theories.[70] The result in *Some Principles of Maritime Strategy* was a study based on a foundation of rigorous, in-depth research and historical accuracy, which as Donald Schurman points out never deviated from its crusade for reform of British maritime strategy and naval education:

> That such independent work could come from the pen of a man who enjoyed high naval patronage and at a time when subservience to the needs of military men in high places was both common and respectable is a measure of both his character and his accomplishment.[71]

The differences in writing styles between the two naval theorists were equally marked. In *The Influence of Sea Power Upon History*, there were many classic descriptive passages that were marred by long, convoluted sentences and paragraphs. Mahan claimed that the often-wearying style occurred because of his emphasis on accuracy. Whatever the reason, the prose in his first book was sometimes stilted and often difficult. One French admiral commented in this regard that Mahan's style was "ponderous, rambling, ambiguous and cloudy," requiring "genuine courage . . . to persevere to the end. . . ." And even Mahan's son believed that *The Influence of Sea Power Upon History* "could have been considerably shortened to advantage."[72] In a similar manner, Corbett wrote in a somewhat voluble Edwardian style that his War Course students found in lecture form to be "needlessly complicated and obscure as well as killing in its academic austerity and brilliance."[73] But generally, he was a graceful, talented writer who utilized training at the bar and a novelist's temperament to produce in *Some Principles of Maritime Strategy* an energetic style marked by clarity of thought and unobtrusive, informed scholarship.

The historical outlook of Douhet and Mitchell stood in sharp contrast to the naval theorists. For both these men, the airplane's revolutionary nature had transformed warfare and thus rendered history irrelevant. Lessons from the past, Douhet wrote, in particular those concerning the ambiguity of the bomber's performance in the Great War, taught contemporaries "less than nothing."[74] In an environment marked by the ubiquity of change, to consider principles based on the past as "immutable" verged for air theorists on the frivolous if not the irrelevant. And yet Douhet and Mitchell were bound to the experience of the recent past, from which they simplistically extrapolated future results. Both, for instance, derided the *offensive à outrance* mentality of World War I, while elaborating scenarios of air warfare, replete with the offensive spirit and the uncomplicated faith in the offensive capability of the bomber.[75]

Douhet similarly was content to let the recent conflict predict the defensive nature of future sea and land endeavors, in part because new offensive theories of surface warfare involved tactical aviation, the efficacy of which he dismissed out of hand. At the same time, the Italian theorist made no allowance for unpredictability in the evolution of airplanes, negating the possibility that the interplay of defense as well as offense might create its own indecisiveness in the air. Mitchell also never appeared to expect the development of countermeasures in consonance with the developments he anticipated in aircraft. In 1928, for instance, he was correct in assessing the lack of progress in antiaircraft weapons since the armistice. But then typically, there was the all-encompassing conclusion:

> They never can improve much because a missile-throwing weapon needs a point of reference with which to check the strike of its projectiles. There is no such point in the air.[76]

The approach to history was typical for the aviation pioneers who were rarely analytical and never dispassionate about their subject. This was reflected in their visions of how airpower could effect warfare—visions that invariably far exceeded the immediate reality, leaving the converted disappointed and the unbelievers derisive. Both theorists were fluent writers with appealing styles, in Mitchell's case oriented on persuading the public, in Douhet's on a professional military audience. Douhet, in particular, wrote passionately in a broad, eloquent, and dramatic manner that survived the 1942 English translation of *The Command of the Air*. But unlike Mitchell and other writers of the era who tended to glorify air warfare, Douhet's view was decidedly unromantic. There were no passages in his writings that addressed the near mystical, exhilarating experience of flight. There were no comparisons of pilots to chivalrous and dashing knights. Aviators in Douhet's world were simply determined and stoic professionals who matter-of-factly went about their dangerous and deadly business.[77]

In addition, neither theorist was ever exact in his language concerning his vision. In 1930, for example, in a monograph entitled "The War of 19—," Douhet left details of the actual attacks to the readers' imagination, with no suggestion that there were any complicating developments on the ground other than panic and surrender. To have suggested otherwise would have contradicted the basic premise of decisiveness, upon which the promise of airpower was predicated. By that year Mitchell had become an unqualified supporter of strategic bombardment primacy; but like Douhet, he never systematically developed the concept beyond the basic strategic idea.[78]

In the end Mitchell was more an agitator and propagandist for his airpower crusade than a theorist— far removed from the academic retreats in which the sea theorist had operated. In Corbett's time, for instance, there were no examinations on his lectures. And without the feedback of testing his theories in an academic setting, he was dependent on the comments of those who reviewed his books. Even Douhet maintained an attitude of a dispassionate seeker of truth in responses to his opponents. But Mitchell lost his perspective under the weight of his strategic vision of aviation's potential. He began to attack the integrity of an often equally dedicated opposition, attempting, as Trenchard pointed out, "to convert his opponents by killing them first."[79] Equally important, he began to substitute promises for performance, overestimating the rate of technical progress in the near future and exaggerating the possibilities of what was immediately realizable from the technology. "I can say now, definitely," Mitchell wrote in *Winged Defense,* "that we can encircle the globe in a very short time on a single charge of gasoline."[80]

Ultimately, Mitchell was like Woodrow Wilson in his ability to stir his fellow Americans and in his inability to compromise. It was a fatal temperamental flaw. Soon, he was dominated by the publicity that he had courted. And in order to maintain this hold on the headlines, his comments became progressively more reckless in nature and less susceptible to specific proof. In the end Mitchell's crusade foundered, as Alfred Hurley points out, on "his failure to sustain the kind of day-to-day self-effacing effort that builds any institution, whether military or otherwise."[81]

IMPACT

Of the four theoretical works represented in this volume, Alfred Thayer Mahan's *The Influence of Sea Power Upon History,* had the greatest immediate impact. Not since the publication of Harriet Beecher Stowe's *Uncle Tom's Cabin* in 1852, had a book written in nineteenth-century America had such a speedy and profound influence on the nation's direction. Part of the reason was that Mahan's easily assimilated concept concerning command of the sea explained how the larger, more powerful warships of the industrial age could be used. Most telling was his concept of sea power, with its appealing polemical fusion of naval expansion, colonialism, and aggressive mercantilism as a formula to attain or maintain great power status and global influence. The most immediate and direct consequence of the book was reform in U.S. officer education, with Mahan presented as proof of the value of historical perspective, while more up-to-date materials were provided for detailed analysis. At the grand strategic level, however, the popularity of Mahan's initial work was not alone sufficient to convert U.S. policy. Leading political elites like Theodore Roosevelt and Henry Cabot Lodge already advocated navalism by 1890 and used Mahan simply to buttress their arguments. It took a series of international incidents in that decade, ranging from the Venezuelan affair of 1895 to the "splendid little war" with Spain in 1898 to fully launch the United States on a policy of aggressive navalism.[82]

In a similar manner, despite its enormous popularity in Britain, *The Influence of Sea Power Upon History* did little to affect the course of British policy other than to confirm and popularize decisions that had already been made. In fact the book accelerated forces that helped to undermine Britain's maritime supremacy; for by linking sea power to national greatness and imperialism, Mahan stimulated already existing expansionist tendencies in the Far East, the United States, and Europe. The concept of sea power simply strengthened political and economic trends that were already encouraging the growth of navies. Those navies, in turn, generally supported the new imperialism, which then further accelerated the pace of ship construction. As the navies of other nations increased in power, Britain's margin of global maritime supremacy declined.[83]

The impact of Julian Corbett's *Some Principles of Maritime Strategy* was more circumscribed. To begin with, there was the antagonism within British naval ranks to a civilian expert who had never served in the navy. Mahan, of course, had been a mediocre seagoing naval officer who, upon assuming his last command after a stint at the Naval War College, complained: "I had forgotten what a beastly thing a ship is, and what a fool a man is who frequents one."[84] But active duty service and credibility as a theorist went hand in hand; and even Corbett believed that Clausewitz was more valuable as a philosopher of war because he "was no mere professor."[85] In 1911 many criticisms of *Some Principles of Maritime Strategy* were couched simply in terms of Corbett's lack of sea experience. It was a deficiency that Fred T. Jane, author of *Fighting Ships,* soon put in perspective by noting that it would

> be a bad day for historians if the principle ever gets established that unless a man is an actor he is incapable of criticizing the actions of a drama. . . . [T]he contention would work out that "you cannot tell whether an egg is bad or good unless you are a hen."[86]

Corbett's authoritative writings, nevertheless, influenced the public as well as the Royal Navy. The Edwardian period was a time in which there was an insatiable demand on the part of the British public for military books. The patronage of Lord Fisher and Corbett's support of the naval reform movement allowed him to foster close associations with some leading naval officers; nevertheless, Corbett's contentions in his 1911 work on maritime strategy antagonized a whole new segment of the naval hierarchy. In that book, he demonstrated that he understood the limitations of being too defensive minded; but he also emphasized, as he had in his work on Trafalgar the previous year, that there were inherent advantages to the defense in certain circumstances. In earlier years naval officers had accepted the contention in Corbett's lectures that previous naval leaders were so clever that big sea battles were sometimes unnecessary. But they did not like a book by a civilian lecturer that dismissed the idea of grand battle as being decisive in itself instead of a means to an end. It was an approach that ran counter to Nelsonian lore, especially to Nelson's heroic dictum that "no captain can do very wrong if he places his ship alongside that of an enemy."[87]

In World War I Corbett served on various government committees and his services were not only used by Fisher, but Prime Ministers Herbert Asquith and Lloyd George as well. In 1917 he was knighted for that work. In addition Corbett was appointed official naval historian for the war. In this capacity he continued to advise the Admiralty staff and in fact helped draft the overall instructions for Admiral John Jellicoe, who as commander of the Grand Fleet enacted the cautious strategy of exercising sea command outside the North Sea, not risking actions that, as Winston Churchill noted, "could lose the war in one afternoon."[88] It was a measure of his influence that after the battle of Jutland in 1916, one member of the House of Lords blamed the indecisive results on the effect of Corbett's philosophy on main fleet policy and cited his book on maritime strategy as one reason why there had been no major British naval successes in the war. The war's end did not diminish this type of resistance to the principles in that book. In 1922, the year Corbett died, the third volume of the official British naval history dealing with Jutland, was published with a special disclaimer by the Board of Admiralty:

> Their lordships find that some of the principles advocated in this book, especially the tendency to minimize the importance of seeking battle and forcing it to a conclusion, are directly in conflict with their views.[89]

There were no such problems for Giulio Douhet whose dramatic rendering of his ideas in *The Command of the Air* impressed the world within a decade of its initial publication. Nevertheless, the response to his work's first edition in 1921 was fairly muted. The lack of reaction may have been due to the general wave of revulsion to war in the wake of the recent conflict or because of the turmoil concerning fascism that would culminate in the "March on Rome" the following year. In any event, the revised second edition in 1927 with its more extreme views on strategic bombing had a greater effect. In his own country, the book met with considerable resistance. In some nations, the book's influence was mitigated by special circumstances. In Japan, for instance, conservative army and navy leaders controlled the government, and the great distances across the Pacific discouraged interest in strategic bombardment. And in the Soviet Union, the general who had written an introduction to the Russian translation of Douhet's book was purged, a fate, it was rumored, not disconnected from his espousal of Douhet's philosophy. In other countries like Germany and France, Douhet's influence was substantial, bringing together for airpower enthusiasts concepts that confirmed ideas and issues with which they had already been grappling. "Douhet's ideas met with a great deal of approval in Luftwaffe leading circles . . . ," General Adolf Galland recalled of the 1935 German translation. "I still remember clearly a period when the talk was all of strategic bombers and one referred with something of pitying condescension to 'home defense fighters.'"[90] The reception was equally enthusiastic in France where the translation of Douhet's book contained a highly supportive introduction by Marshal Philippe Pétain:

> The study of Douhet is an inexhaustible source for reflection. . . . Let us take care not to treat lightly, as a utopian dreamer, a man who may later be regarded as a prophet.[91]

It was this French translation that provided a more accessible version than the original Italian to U.S. Army Corps officers. By

1933 it had been translated into English, reinforcing an inclination by most American airmen toward a philosophy of strategic bombing. And yet, as the American experience demonstrated, Douhet, unlike Mahan, did not provide commonly accepted principles—a single source from which the enthusiasts of airpower could unlock the mysteries of warfare's third dimension. As a consequence, each major power in the interwar years made separate choices concerning aircraft application. "As regards strategic bombardment," General Arnold recalled in this regard," the doctrines were still Douhet's ideas modified by our own thinking in regard to pure defense. . . . A different attitude from Douhet's toward bomber escort and a very different view of precision bombing resulted."[92]

In contrast to Douhet, Mitchell's impact was primarily limited to his own country, where his controversial stands became part of the political debate over disarmament and military budgets—the latter, of course, a process encountered by all the air prophets and theorists. To start, there was Mitchell's court-martial, a process set in a dingy government building which, as Michael Sherry points out, "suggested his martyrdom by a tawdry and faceless bureaucracy, a replay of old progressive battles pitting the people against the special interests."[93] Mitchell capitalized on this setting, and he was correct to some extent when he appraised his court-martial as a "necessary cog in the wheel of progress, a requisite step in the modernization and rehabilitation of the natural defense of the country."[94] For his statements and writings coupled with that procedure forced the Coolidge administration to reexamine the issue of military aviation and, in conjunction with Congress, proceed with a series of legislative actions that composed the first general aeronautical policy for the United States.[95] In addition, the controversy only increased the readership of Mitchell's popular articles on aviation reform in publications that ranged from the *Saturday Evening Post, Liberty,* and *Colliers* to the *Atlantic Monthly* and various Hearst publications. In keeping with his continual theme in all his writings at the time, one edition of *Colliers* in 1926 even illustrated

Mitchell's article with a picture of an air attack demolishing the New York City skyline.[96] The next year, Lindbergh's transatlantic flight further bolstered Mitchell's career as an aviation publicist.

All this notwithstanding, there were very few immediate political dividends from Mitchell's public travail. The tighter military budgets of the Coolidge administration caused army leaders to increase their resistance to the claims of airpower. Moreover, in his efforts to demonstrate that the more economical and effective airplane had replaced the battleship, Mitchell unwittingly catalysed the creation in naval aviation of a formidable adversary under the skilled direction of Admiral William A. Moffett.[97] And while the spectacle of foundering battleships and quarreling bureaucrats always made good copy, the attention of the press and the public rallied little support from those powerful enough to help his cause. By 1935 Mitchell had lost his public allies among active duty airmen, and he had ineptly cut his political ties to the Roosevelt administration. At the same time, he became increasingly estranged from the popular press who had wearied of his repetitive themes. In the end, Mitchell's fate made very little difference in the short run to U.S. military aviation, which in General Arnold's estimation, "really couldn't have amounted to very much then, even if everybody had agreed with him."[98]

LEGACY

The legacies of the four theorists represented in this volume have much to do with different approaches to thinking about change and continuity. Both Mahan and Corbett were closer to pure theorists than their air counterparts. They systematically created ideas from the past to be authenticated for continuity in the future. To accomplish this, they virtually ignored technology while probing for higher truths from the age of sail—ideas that would be unaffected by change. "Conditions and weapons change," Mahan wrote at the beginning of *Influence;* "but to cope with the one or successfully wield the others, respect must be had to those constant teachings of history . . . in those wider operations of war which are comprised under the name of strategy."[99] In this way, both men, relying on their own particular theorists, produced a large conceptual structure, within which they created the ideas and terminology that still form the foundation for thinking about sea power and maritime strategy. But the key was the lack of technological preoccupation, which as Donald Schurman points out, "lifted the thought above the output of the bric-a-brac 'scientific' lore that passed for strategic thought. . . ."[100]

For the two air theorists, on the other hand, technological change in the infancy of powered flight was the primary issue. "Victory smiles upon those who anticipate the changes in the character of war," Douhet concluded early in his first edition of *Command,* "not upon those who wait to adapt themselves after the changes occur."[101] And in *Winged Defense,* Mitchell observed that "[v]ictory always comes to that country which has made a proper estimate of the equipment and methods that can be used in modern ways."[102] But like the nuclear theorists after World War II, there was little empirical evidence upon which the two men could draw, and who in any case chose to use selectively what little lessons were to be drawn from the Great War. The result was that Douhet and Mitchell were more visionaries than theorists, creating ideas that resisted systematic authentication and were thus more elusive and difficult to assess. It was a curious amalgam of change and continuity that left both men with little apparent grounding in either the past or the future. The significance of visionaries, however, lies not so much in details, as in their ability to inspire others to set new thoughts in train. In this regard, Mitchell and other air theorists were as much the beneficiary of Douhet, as a whole host of future American air leaders would be of Mitchell. "Sometimes visions and even myths," I. B. Holley points out, "are more powerful than the most meticulously and rationally supported theories."[103]

The two different approaches to change and continuity produced errors in both camps that have not stood the test of time.

For Mahan there was his insistence that Britain was great because of her colonies—a reversal of the more accurate cause and effect relationship. And in his period of historical examination, Mahan ascribed a rational, top-down national and global policy to the British government that it only partially adopted under the frenzied imperial scrambles of the late nineteenth century. The major challenge to the structure of maritime dominance, however, emerged in 1904 with Sir Halford Mackinder's geopolitical argument that a new age of continental land powers was replacing the four centuries of European overseas exploration and conquest—the period known as the Columbian epoch. Corbett addressed some of these problems, but like Mahan, he was a blue water determinist who focused his historical examination on a time when the theories of continental geographic dominance appeared not to have great relevance. At the operational level, Corbett modified Mahan's commitment to counterforce, concentration, and decisive battles to argue for a more subtle understudy of the meaning of "command of the sea." But like Mahan, the past for him was a pattern for the future, not a prologue; and, he also failed to appreciate the pace of technological change in the form of submarines and aircraft in the second and third dimensions of warfare that would alter the ways to achieve command of the sea.[104]

For the air theorists, the preoccupation with technological change was understandable in the bid to separate airpower from the other services—with their centuries of history, deeply embedded traditions, slowly evolved doctrines, and fully formed officer education and training systems. One result was the tendency of visionaries like Douhet and Mitchell to make far-reaching claims for airpower, which exceeded the current technology and only exacerbated the skepticism of the traditionally conservative military. This in turn resulted in errors that became apparent in future wars. In Douhet's case, to name a few, he overestimated the psychological and physical effects of strategic bombing; lacked any appreciation for the tactical air war; ignored the necessity of an air battle to determine the command of the air; denigrated the constraints of morality and of international law; and underestimated the future requirement for surface forces. Mitchell also succumbed to many of these errors after his court-martial when he moved away from his commitment to continental defense and tactical employment. Nevertheless, there was always a considerable amount of psychological and geographical distance between Mitchell's ideas and Douhet's stark theory of air bombardment. What linked the two visionaries was a belief that command of the air, however achieved, was a necessity for any nation contemplating war or pursuing national interests.[105]

No matter the approach, visionary or theoretical, both air and naval theorists left a legacy of service parochialism. For Douhet and Mitchell, zealotry was necessary to establish airpower as a revolutionary, unique approach to warfare in the face of stiff bureaucratic opposition. Both men belonged to those crusaders of every age who with their relentless insistence on the correctness of their convictions ultimately undermined what they were trying to achieve. It was this undeviating zeal, however, that also sustained them in their fight against the shortsighted and the uninformed. In a similar manner, Mahan and Corbett were navalists who stressed the principal theme inherent in sea power that dominance of the seas affected the general distribution of global power. Their legacy was the fundamental proposition that fleets provided political and economic security and were thus worth buying and that naval power as a basic component of sea power was worth having.[106]

Naval parochialism in the United States has been dissipated by other intellectual legacies from Mahan and Corbett. To start, both theorists established the linkage of sea power and maritime strategy to a larger strategic concept. In this context, naval theorists no longer claim a dominance of naval power over other forms of military force nor argue that such power can act independently. Instead, naval power is generally perceived as a military instrument within the broader theories of power control; not only is it applicable to national military strategies, but it is relevant to national strategies focused on the use of all elements of national power in international politics. This perception calls for new naval functions in a host of situations short of war, very much in keeping with the historical focus by both men on limited wars. And Corbett, in particular, would understand both the post-Goldwater-Nichols effort concerning jointness and the United States Navy's emphasis on what it can accomplish in support of land operations "from the sea."

There is a similar commitment to jointness on the part of the United States Air Force. Nevertheless, the legacy of both air theorists as crusaders lives on in their vision of the value of an independent air force that could wage and win decisive air campaigns. Neither theorist ever denied that the results of that campaign must ultimately be felt on land. "Of course, everything begins and ends on the ground," Mitchell acknowledged in *Winged Defense*. "A person cannot permanently live out on the sea nor can a person live up in the air, so that any decision in war is based on what takes place ultimately on the ground."[107] But the vision did apply a uniqueness to airpower that surfaced once again in debates after the Gulf War. For land power enthusiasts, that conflict demonstrated that the primary airpower role continued to be the support of surface operations—the only operations that could ensure military victory. Airpower enthusiasts argued that thanks to new technology in the form of stealth and precision attack capabilities as well as information dominance, airpower could now largely determine conflict outcomes, suggesting that at least in high intensity conflict, the primary land power role might be to *secure* a victory rather than to *achieve* it.[108]

One reaction to such debates has been to vent frustrations on the earlier theorists. "Giulio Douhet's conception of airpower and its potential contribution to winning wars," one analyst concluded, "has been rendered obsolete by technological change."[109] This seems a bit harsh for a man of Douhet's vision and intellect who created a work of great scope and audacity. And considering that it took over two millennia of warfare on land and sea to produce Jomini, Clausewitz, Mahan, and Corbett, it also seems somewhat unfair to be overly critical of someone who began writing a theory of air warfare a little more than one decade after the invention of the airplane.

In any event, all this misses the point concerning the ultimate legacy of all four theorists addressed in this volume. Many, if not most of the answers provided by those theorists are no longer relevant because of changes in such factors as technology and the international environment. But if the answers are no longer relevant, the questions they asked from their limited vantage points in times of great change are. All four theorists constantly asked their readers to seriously think about such matters as the meaning of command of the sea or the air; the exercise of that command and its relationship to the other instruments of military power; and, most importantly, the uses of navies and air forces as instruments of national policy. These are questions that link all services to a national military strategy and, together in war and peace, to the entire spectrum of national power that makes up grand strategy. They are, in short, questions that will always help strategists in times of great transformation to arrive at the proper mix of change and continuity.

Capt. Alfred Thayer Mahan

THE INFLUENCE

OF

SEA POWER UPON HISTORY

1660–1783

BY

CAPTAIN A. T. MAHAN, D.C.L., LL.D.

UNITED STATED NAVY

1890

CONTENTS

EDITOR'S INTRODUCTION

This selection consists of the preface, the introductory, and the opening chapter of Alfred Thayer Mahan's *The Influence of Sea Power Upon History, 1660-1783*. The lectures given by Mahan from 1886 to 1888 at the Naval War College served as the basis for his text, which after some refusals and more revisions appeared in book form in May 1890, all 557 pages priced expensively at four dollars per copy. The text initially focused on the improvement of naval professionalism at the strategic and operational level. In the fall of 1899, however, Mahan's publisher suggested that he add a long introductory chapter that would address the current public controversy on future naval construction by discussing the importance of naval strength, the relationship of that strength to a state's development, and how this relationship applied to the circumstances of the United States. These issues were also addressed somewhat in the remaining thirteen chapters of the text in addition to the primary concentration in those chapters on the details of conducting war at sea. But the structure and content of the new chapter, not to mention its lead position, caused the emphasis of the entire book to shift toward the grand strategic, geopolitical theme at the expense of the operational one. It was the material in this opening chapter that drew widespread attention and to a very great degree, as Jon Sumida points out, "has defined the perception of Mahan's writings ever since."[1]

The heart of the first chapter was Mahan's political-economic argument for sea power. Politically, he argued that sea power had exerted a decisive influence upon the development and prosperity of nations throughout history.[2] In the political-economic realm, his basic assumption was that while railways had become the primary transport for the internal economy of a country, ships were and would remain the easier, cheaper, and thus the principal mode of transport for external trade. The first factor in Mahan's argument was that the acquisition of colonies and the concomitant production and shipping that made up maritime economies was essential to a state's prosperity and served as a motivating factor in the policies of a nation adjacent to the sea. The second factor was that history demonstrated the necessity for naval supremacy in protecting national interests concerned with maritime economics—a primary reason for the critical importance of that supremacy in wars among great powers. Finally, the third factor consisted of six "principal conditions" or elements that affected a country's ability to develop sea power: geographical position, physical conformation (to include climate and natural resources), extent of territory, size of population, national character, and character of the government.[3]

The six principles were interdependent. Geographical position addressed nations like Britain and the United States that did not have to divert focus away from the sea for land defense as compared with nations like France and the Netherlands with continental boundaries. Nevertheless, Mahan treated the United States as a continental not an insular power. Like France, he argued, America's productive, land-based economy distracted the government and the electorate from the positive benefits that could be achieved from maritime commercial activity. This geographical characteristic would continue to differ from that of Britain, he maintained, until a Central American canal could connect the seaboards of America's two oceans. Physical conformation focused on the need for any nation aspiring to sea power to have extensive seacoasts, harbors, and rivers combined with "an inborn love of the sea" among its people. Only the latter was lacking in the United States; but Mahan believed that love for and reliance on the sea, a staple of earlier American history, could be rekindled.[4]

The third element of sea power concerned the extent of territory, but more specifically the relationship of the length of coastline and the natural harbors to the size and distribution of the population, the fourth element of sea power. Those two aspects concerning the people must be large and favorable enough to keep a commensurately substantial section of the population following or ready to follow the sea. The key to remedying U.S. problems in this element, Mahan believed in 1890, was to develop a large merchant marine that could engage in external peacetime commerce. This, in turn, tied into the element of national character. For in order that a nation generate and maintain sea power, Mahan emphasized, its people had to generally "love money," that is have an appetite for profitable commercial enterprises combined with a tendency to be materialistically acquisitive. All these were American attributes, he concluded, hindered only in their full manifestation by a government that sponsored "legislative hindrances," and failed both to subsidize the maritime sector of the economy and to acquire overseas colonies.[5]

It was upon the sixth element, the character of the government, that Mahan fashioned his third argument. In this regard, although he perceived sea power as directly tied to all the six principles, he also believed that it required appropriate governmental action concerning naval development to realize the full potential of those principles. "It must . . . be admitted," he wrote,

> that the wise or unwise action of individual men has at certain periods had a great modifying influence upon the growth of sea power in the broad sense, which includes not only the military strength afloat, that rules the sea or any part of it by force of arms, but also

the peaceful commerce and shipping from which alone
a military fleet naturally and healthfully springs, and
on which it securely rests.[6]

In peace, the government by means of its policy could help the
natural growth of industries that deal with commerce, "upon
which alone, it cannot be too often insisted, a thoroughly strong
navy can be based."[7] In war, governmental influence would "be
felt in its most legitimate manner in maintaining an armed navy,
of a size commensurate with the growth of its shipping and the
importance of the interests connected with it."[8] For Mahan, the
history of the Anglo-French conflicts in the previous centuries
demonstrated the importance of these governmental roles and
why it was equally important for his own government to embark
on a more robust maritime and naval policy. "As the practical
object of this inquiry is to draw from the lessons of history inferences applicable to one's own country and service," he wrote, "it is
proper now to ask how far the conditions of the United States
involve serious danger, and call for action on the part of the government, in order to build again her sea power."[9]

All this brought Mahan back to the sixth element of sea power:
the character of government. In this regard, he noted that Britain's
great navy had been built in the eighteenth century by the landed
aristocracy and conjectured on the possible adverse effects on
Britain's sea power of increased democratization in the nineteenth
century:

> Whether a democratic government will have the fore-
> sight, the keen sensitiveness to national position and
> credit, the willingness to insure its prosperity by ade-
> quate outpouring of money in terms of peace, all
> which are necessary for military preparation, is yet an
> open question.[10]

In his opening chapter's last pages, Mahan returned to this theme in order to express his concern that an isolationist electorate in the United States might prevent the government from developing the great navy so essential, he believed, to protect vital political, military, and economic interests in an environment of increased global competition among great powers. This, after all, was one lesson to be taken from the rebuilding of the French fleet after the great defeats of the Seven Years War and the subsequent successful use of that fleet in the American Revolution. "The profound humiliation of France," Mahan warned, "which reached its depths between 1760 and 1763, at which later date she made peace, has an instructive lesson for the United States in this period of commercial and naval decadence. We have been spared her humiliation; let us hope to profit by her subsequent example."[11]

In the remaining thirteen chapters of *The Influence of Sea Power Upon History*, Mahan divided his efforts between expanding on his grand strategic thoughts in the first chapter and addressing principles concerning the art and science of command. Naval strategy was concerned primarily with operational dynamics dealing with naval functions ranging from deployments to logistics and communications. At this level of operational decision making, Mahan pointed out as early as his introduction, technological change had less effect than at the tactical level.[12] Consequently, he argued, the study of history could be used to provide not just examples, but also principles in the form of fundamental truths about the operational dynamics of naval strategy. From this emerged Mahan's focus on concentration of force and other principles and propositions relating to logistics, the desirability of the offense and decisive battle, and the relative ineffectiveness of commerce raiding by cruisers used as a substitute for battleships to maintain control of the sea.[13]

At the grand strategic level, Mahan provided more details from British naval wars to back up his contentions in the opening chapter, presenting his arguments primarily in terms of French failure or success. Using the seventeenth century, Mahan described how France had concentrated on a continental position to the detriment of sea power in various wars, a disastrous overfocus since states "decay when cut off from external activities and resources which at once draw out and support their internal powers."[14] As for the eighteenth century, Mahan believed that England's predominance was due not only to Britain's overwhelming sea power, but to French error as well. The last six of the fourteen chapters were devoted to the Anglo-French naval conflict during the American Revolution. In that war, Mahan emphasized, without European continental entanglements and the concomitant need to field a large European army, France was able to conduct an offensive naval strategy that ultimately compromised Britain's North American position. At the same time, he moved from the grand strategic to his operational principles of naval strategy by pointing out that the French could have destroyed British naval power with more relentless pressure for decisive battles at sea.[15]

In the end, then, the book's political-economic lesson was that a nation like France or the United States with conditions favoring both land and sea development, should choose the sea. The return on the investment in sea power in terms of success in war and larger national wealth was higher. Not following this course had caused France, in Mahan's governmental lesson, to allow British victories in conflicts that would otherwise have been defeats. The brief French adherence to sea power at the end of the eighteenth century had reversed this trend and resulted in the creation of the United States. Finally, in Mahan's viewpoint, these events had resulted in a dominant Britain, a decadent France, and an even stronger United States—all of which for him was the ultimate verification of his central political argument.[16]

THE INFLUENCE OF SEA POWER UPON HISTORY, 1660–1783

PREFACE

The definite object proposed in this work is an examination of the general history of Europe and America with particular reference to the effect of sea power upon the course of that history. Historians generally have been unfamiliar with the conditions of the sea, having as to it neither special interest nor special knowledge; and the profound determining influence of maritime strength upon great issues has consequently been overlooked. This is even more true of particular occasions than of the general tendency of sea power. It is easy to say in a general way, that the use and control of the sea is and has been a great factor in the history of the world; it is more troublesome to seek out and show its exact bearing at a particular juncture. Yet, unless this be done, the acknowledgment of general importance remains vague and unsubstantial; not resting, as it should, upon a collection of special instances in which the precise effect has been made clear, by an analysis of the conditions at the given moments.

A curious exemplification of this tendency to slight the bearing of maritime power upon events may be drawn from two writers of that English nation which more than any other has owed its greatness to the sea. "Twice," says Arnold in his History of Rome, "Has there been witnessed the struggle of the highest individual genius against the resources and institutions of a great nation, and in both cases the nation was victorious. For seventeen years Hannibal strove against Rome, for sixteen years Napoleon strove against England; the efforts of the first ended in Zama, those of the second in Waterloo." Sir Edward Creasy, quoting this, adds "One point, however, of the similitude between the two wars has scarcely been adequately dwelt on; that is, the remarkable parallel between the Roman general who finally defeated the great Carthaginian, and the English general who gave the last deadly overthrow to the French emperor. Scipio and Wellington both held for many years commands of high importance, but distant from the main theatres of warfare. The same country was the scene of the principal military career of each. It was in Spain that Scipio, like Wellington, successively encountered and overthrew nearly all the subordinate generals of the enemy before being opposed to the chief champion and conqueror himself. Both Scipio and Wellington restored their countrymen's confidence in arms when shaken by a series of reverses, and each of them closed a long and perilous war by a complete an overwhelming defeat of the chosen leader and the chosen veterans of the foe."

Neither of these Englishmen mentions the yet more striking coincidence, that in both cases the mastery of the sea rested with the victor. The Roman control of the water forced Hannibal to that long, perilous march through Gaul in which more than half his veteran troops wasted away; it enabled the elder Scipio, while sending his army from the Rhone on to Spain, to intercept Hannibal's communications, to return in person and face the invader at the Trebia. Throughout the war the legions passed by water, unmolested and unwearied, between Spain, which was Hannibal's base, and Italy; while the issue of decisive battle of the Metaurus, hinging as it did upon the interior position of the Roman armies with reference to the forces of Hasdrubal and Hannibal, was ultimately due to the fact that the younger brother could not bring his succoring reinforcements by sea, but only by the land route through Gaul. Hence at the critical moment the two Carthaginian armies were separated by the length of Italy, and one was destroyed by the combined action of the Roman generals.

On the other hand, naval historians have troubled themselves little about the connection between general history and their own particular topic, limiting themselves generally to the duty of simple chroniclers of naval occurrences. This is less true of the French than of the English; the genius and training of the former people leading them to more careful inquiry into the causes of particular results and the mutual relation of events.

There is not, however, within the knowledge of the author any work that professes the particular object here sought; namely, an estimate of the effect of sea power upon the course of history and the prosperity of nations. As other histories deal with the wars, politics, social and economical conditions of countries, touching upon maritime matters only incidentally and generally unsympathetically, so the present work aims at putting maritime interests in the foreground, without divorcing them, however, from their surroundings of cause and effect in general history, but seeking to show how they modified the latter, and were modified by them.

The period embraced is from 1660, when the sailing-ship era, with its distinctive features, had fairly begun, to 1783, the end of the American Revolution. While the thread of general history upon which the successive maritime events is strung is intentionally slight, the effort has been to present a clear as well as accurate outline. Writing as a naval officer in full sympathy with his profession, the author has not hesitated to digress freely on questions of naval policy, strategy, and tactics; but as technical language has been avoided, it is hoped that these matters, simply presented, will be found of interest to the unprofessional reader.

A.T. Mahan

December, 1889

INTRODUCTORY

The history of Sea Power is largely, though by no means solely, a narrative of contests between nations, of mutual rivalries, of violence frequently culminating in war. The profound influence of sea commerce upon the wealth and strength of countries was clearly seen long before the true principles which governed its growth and prosperity were detected. To secure to one's own people a disproportionate share of such benefits, every effort was made to exclude others, either by the peaceful legislative methods of monopoly or prohibitory regulations, or, when these failed, by direct violence. The clash of interests, the angry feelings roused by conflicting attempts thus to appropriate the larger share, if not the whole, of the advantages of commerce, and of distant unsettled commercial regions, led to wars. On the other hand, wars arising from other causes have been greatly modified in their conduct and issue by the control of the sea. Therefore the history of sea power, while embracing in its broad sweep all that tends to make a people great upon the sea or by the sea, is largely a military history; and it is in this aspect that it will be mainly, though not exclusively, regarded in the following pages.

A study of the military history of the past, such as this, is enjoined by great military leaders as essential to correct ideas and to the skilful conduct of war in the future. Napoleon names among the campaigns to be studied by the aspiring soldier, those of Alexander, Hannibal, and Cæsar, to whom gunpowder was unknown; and there is a substantial agreement among professional writers that, while many of the conditions of war vary from age to age with the progress of weapons, there are certain teachings in the school of history which remain constant, and being, therefore, of universal application, can be elevated to the rank of general principles. For the same reason the study of the sea history of the past will be found instructive, by its illustration of the general principles of maritime war, notwithstanding the great changes that have been brought about in naval weapons by the scientific advances of the past half century, and by the introduction of steam as the motive power.

It is doubly necessary thus to study critically the history and experience of naval warfare in the days of sailing-ships, because while these will be found to afford lessons of present application and value, steam navies have as yet made no history which can be quoted as decisive in its teaching. Of the one we have much experimental knowledge; of the other, practically none. Hence theories about the naval warfare of the future are almost wholly presumptive; and although the attempt has been made to give them a more solid basis by dwelling upon the resemblance between fleets of steamships and fleets of galleys moved by oars, which have a long and well-known history, it will be well not to be carried away by this analogy until it has been thoroughly tested. The resemblance is indeed far from superficial. The feature which the steamer and the galley have in common is the ability to move in any direction independent of the wind. Such a power makes a radical distinction between those classes of vessels and the sailing-ship; for the latter can follow only a limited number of courses when the wind blows, and must remain motionless when it fails. But while it is wise to observe things that are alike, it is also wise to look for things that differ; for when the imagination is carried away by the detection of points of resemblance—one of the most pleasing of mental pursuits—it is apt to be impatient of any divergence in its new-found parallels, and so may overlook or refuse to recognize such. Thus the galley and the steamship have in common, though unequally developed, the important characteristic mentioned, but in at least two points they differ; and in an appeal to the history of the galley for lessons as to fighting steamships, the differences as well as the likeness must be kept steadily in view, or false deductions may be made. The motive power of the galley when in use necessarily and rapidly declined, because human strength could not long maintain such exhausting efforts, and consequently tactical movements could continue but for a limited time; and again, during the galley period offensive weapons were not only of short range, but were almost wholly confined to hand-to-hand encounter. These two conditions led almost necessarily to a rush upon each other, not, however, without some dexterous attempts to turn or double on the enemy, followed by a hand-to-hand *mêlée*. In such a rush and such a *mêlée* a great consensus of respectable, even eminent, naval opinion of the present day finds the necessary outcome of modern naval weapons—a kind of Donnybrook Fair, in which, as the history of *mêlées* shows, it will be hard to know friend from foe. Whatever may prove to be the worth of this opinion, it cannot claim an historical basis in the sole fact that galley and steamship can move at any moment directly upon the enemy, and carry a beak upon their prow, regardless of the points in which galley and steamship differ. As yet this opinion is only a presumption, upon which final judgment may well be deferred until the trial of battle has given further light. Until that time there is room for the opposite view—that a *mêlée* between numerically equal fleets, in which skill is reduced to a minimum, is not the best that can be done with the elaborate and mighty weapons of this age. The surer of himself an admiral is, the finer the tactical development of his fleet, the better his captains, the more reluctant must he necessarily be to enter into a *mêlée* with equal forces, in which all these advantages will be thrown away, chance reign supreme, and his fleet be placed on terms of equality with an assemblage of ships which have never before acted together. History has lessons as to when *mêlées* are, or are not, in order.

The galley, then, has one striking resemblance to the steamer, but differs in other important features which are not so immediately apparent and are therefore less accounted of. In the sailing-ship, on the contrary, the striking feature is the difference between it and the more modern vessel; the points of resemblance, though existing and easy to find, are not so obvious, and therefore are less heeded. This impression is enhanced by the sense of utter weakness in the sailing-ship as compared with the steamer, owing to its dependence upon the wind; forgetting that, as the former fought with its equals, the tactical lessons are valid. The galley was never reduced to impotence by a calm, and hence receives more respect in our day than the sailing-ship; yet the latter displaced it and remained supreme until the utilization of steam. The powers to injure an enemy from a great distance, to manoeuvre for an unlimited length of time without wearing out the men, to devote the greater part of the crew to the offensive weapons instead of to the oar, are common to the sailing vessel and the steamer, and are at least as important, tactically considered, as the power of the galley to move in a calm or against the wind.

In tracing resemblances there is a tendency not only to overlook points of difference, but to exaggerate points of likeness—to be fanciful. It may be so considered to point out that as the sailing-ship had guns of long range, with comparatively great penetrative power, and carronades, which were of shorter range but great smashing effect, so the modern steamer has its batteries of long-range guns and of torpedoes, the latter being effective only within a limited distance and then injuring by smashing, while the gun, as of old, aims at penetration. Yet these are distinctly tactical considerations, which must affect the plans of admirals and captains; and the analogy is real, not forced. So also both the sailing-ship and the steamer contemplate direct contact with an enemy's vessel—the former to carry her by boarding, the latter to sink her by ramming; and to both this is the most difficult of their tasks, for to effect it the ship must be carried to a single point of the field of action, whereas projectile weapons may be used from many points of a wide area.

The relative positions of two sailing-ships, or fleets, with reference to the direction of the wind involved most important tactical questions, and were perhaps the chief care of the seamen of that age. To a superficial glance it may appear that since this has become a matter of such indifference to the steamer, no analogies to it are to be found in present conditions, and the lessons of history in this respect are valueless. A more careful consideration of the distinguishing characteristics of the lee and the weather "gage," directed to their essential features and disregarding secondary details, will show that this is a mistake. The distinguishing feature of the weather-gage was that it conferred the power of giving or refusing battle at will, which in turn carries the usual advantage of an offensive attitude in the choice of the method of attack. This advantage was accompanied by certain drawbacks, such as irregularity introduced into the order, exposure to raking or enfilading cannonade, and the sacrifice of part or all of the artillery-fire of the assailant—all which were incurred in approaching the enemy. The ship, or fleet, with the lee-gage could not attack; if it did not wish to retreat, its action was confined to the defensive, and to receiving battle on the enemy's terms. This disadvantage was compensated by the comparative ease of maintaining the order of battle undisturbed, and by a sustained artillery-fire to which the enemy for a time was unable to reply. Historically, these favorable and unfavorable characteristics have their counterpart and analogy in the offensive and defensive operations of all ages. The offence undertakes certain risks and disadvantages in order to reach and destroy the enemy;

the defence, so long as it remains such, refuses the risks of advance, holds on to a careful, well-ordered position, and avails itself of the exposure to which the assailant submits himself. These radical differences between the weather and the lee-gage were so clearly recognized, through the cloud of lesser details accompanying them, that the former was ordinarily chosen by the English, because their steady policy was to assail and destroy their enemy; whereas the French sought the lee-gage, because by so doing they were usually able to cripple the enemy as he approaches, and thus evade decisive encounters and preserve their ships. The French, with rare exceptions, subordinated the action of the navy to other military considerations, grudged the money spent upon it, and therefore sought to economize their fleet by assuming a defensive position and limiting its efforts to the repelling of assaults. For this course the lee-gage, skilfully used, was admirably adapted so long as an enemy displayed more courage than conduct; but when Rodney showed an intention to use the advantage of the wind, not merely to attack, but to make a formidable concentration on a part of the enemy's line, his wary opponent, De Guichen, changed his tactics. In the first of their three actions the Frenchman took the lee-gage; but after recognizing Rodney's purpose he manœuvred for the advantage of the wind, not to attack, but to refuse action except on his own terms. The power to assume the offensive, or to refuse battle, rests no longer with the wind, but with the party which has the greater speed; which in a fleet will depend not only upon the speed of the individual ships, but also upon their tactical uniformity of action. Henceforth the ships which have the greatest speed will have the weather-gage.

It is not therefore a vain expectation, as many think, to look for useful lessons in the history of sailing-ships as well as in that of galleys. Both have their points of resemblance to the modern ship; both have also points of essential difference, which make it impossible to cite their experiences or modes of action as tactical *precedents* to be followed. But a precedent is different from and less valuable than a principle. The former may be originally faulty, or may cease to apply through change of circumstances; the latter has its root in the essential nature of things, and, however various its application as conditions change, remains a standard to which action must conform to attain success. War has such principles; their existence is detected by the study of the past, which reveals them in successes and in failures, the same from age to age. Conditions and weapons change; but to cope with the one or successfully wield the others, respect must be had to these constant teachings of history in the tactics of the battlefield, or in those wider operations of war which are comprised under the name of strategy.

It is however in these wider operations, which embrace a whole theatre of war, and in a maritime contest may cover a large portion of the globe, that the teachings of history have a more evident and permanent value, because the conditions remain more permanent. The theatre of war may be larger or smaller, its difficulties more or less pronounced, the contending armies more or less great, the necessary movements more or less easy, but these are simply differences of scale, of degree, not of kind. As a wilderness gives place to civilization, as means of communication multiply, as roads are opened, rivers bridged, food-resources increased, the operations of war become easier, more rapid, more extensive; but the principles to which they must be conformed remain the same. When the march on foot was replaced by carrying troops in coaches, when the latter in turn gave place to railroads, the scale of distances was increased, or, if you will, the scale of time diminished; but the principles which dictated the point at which the army should be concentrated, the direction in which it should move, the part of the enemy's position which it should assail, the protection of communications, were not altered. So, on the sea, the advance from the galley timidly creeping from port to port to the sailing-ship launching out boldly to the ends of the earth, and from the latter to the steamship of our own time, has increased the scope and the rapidity of naval operations without necessarily changing the principles which should direct them; and the speech of Hermocrates twenty-three hundred years ago, before quoted, contained a correct strategic plan, which is as applicable in its principles now as it was then. Before hostile armies or fleets are brought into con*tact* (a word which perhaps better than any other indicates the dividing line between tactics and strategy), there are a number of questions to be decided, covering the whole plan of operations throughout the theatre of war. Among these are the proper function of the navy in the war; its true objective; the point or points upon which it should be concentrated; the establishment of depots of coal and supplies; the maintenance of communications between these depots and the home base; the military value of commerce-destroying as a decisive or a secondary operation of war; the system upon which commerce-destroying can be most efficiently conducted, whether by scattered cruisers or by holding in force some vital centre through which commercial shipping must pass. All these are strategic questions, and upon all these history has a great deal to say. There has been of late a valuable discussion in English naval circles as to the comparative merits of the policies of two great English admirals, Lord Howe and Lord St. Vincent, in the disposition of the English navy when at war with France. The question is purely strategic, and is not of mere historical interest; it is of vital importance now, and the principles upon which its decision rests are the same now as then. St. Vincent's policy saved England from invasion, and in the hands of Nelson and his brother admirals led straight up to Trafalgar.

It is then particularly in the field of naval strategy that the teachings of the past have a value which is in no degree lessened. They are there useful not only as illustrative of principles, but also as precedents, owing to the comparative permanence of the conditions. This is less obviously true as to tactics, when the

fleets come into collision at the point to which strategic considerations have brought them. The unresting progress of mankind
causes continual change in the weapons; and with that must
come a continual change in the manner of fighting—in the handling and disposition of troops or ships on the battlefield. Hence
arises a tendency on the part of many connected with maritime
matters to think that no advantage is to be gained from the study
of former experiences; that time so used is wasted. This view,
though natural, not only leaves wholly out of sight those broad
strategic considerations which lead nations to put fleets afloat,
which direct the sphere of their action, and so have modified and
will continue to modify the history of the world, but is one-sided
and narrow even as to tactics. The battles of the past succeeded
or failed according as they were fought in conformity with the
principles of war; and the seaman who carefully studies the
causes of success or failure will not only detect and gradually
assimilate these principles, but will also acquire increased aptitude in applying them to the tactical use of the ships and
weapons of his own day. He will observe also that changes of tactics have not only taken place *after* changes in weapons, which
necessarily is the case, but that the interval between such
changes has been unduly long. This doubtless arises from the
fact that an improvement of weapons is due to the energy of one
or two men, while changes in tactics have to overcome the iner-
tia of a conservative class; but it is a great evil. It can be remedied
only by a candid recognition of each change, by careful study of
the powers and limitations of the new ship or weapon, and by a
consequent adaptation of the method of using it to the qualities it
possesses, which will constitute its tactics. History shows that it
is vain to hope that military men generally will be at the pains to
do this, but that the one who does will go into battle with a great
advantage—a lesson in itself of no mean value.

We may therefore accept now the words of a French tactician,
Morogues, who wrote a century and a quarter ago: "Naval tactics

are based upon conditions the chief causes of which, namely the arms, may change; which in turn causes necessarily a change in the construction of ships, in the manner of handling them, and so finally in the disposition and handling of fleets." His further statement, that "it is not a science founded upon principles absolutely invariable," is more open to criticism. It would be more correct to say that the application of its principles varies as the weapons change. The application of the principles doubtless varies also in strategy, from time to time, but the variation is far less; and hence the recognition of the underlying principle is easier. This statement is of sufficient importance to our subject to receive some illustrations from historical events.

The battle of the Nile, in 1798, was not only an overwhelming victory for the English over the French fleet, but had also the decisive effect of destroying the communications between France and Napoleon's army in Egypt. In the battle itself the English admiral, Nelson, gave a most brilliant example of grand tactics, if that be, as has been defined, "the art of making good combinations preliminary to battles as well as during their progress." The particular tactical combination depended upon a condition now passed away, which was the inability of the lee ships of a fleet at anchor to come to the help of the weather ones before the latter were destroyed; but the principles which underlay the combination, namely, to choose that part of the enemy's order which can least easily be helped, and to attack it with superior forces, has not passed away. The action of Admiral Jervis at Cape St. Vincent, when with fifteen ships he won a victory over twenty-seven, was dictated by the same principle, though in this case the enemy was not at anchor, but under way. Yet men's minds are so constituted that they seem more impressed by the transiency of the conditions than by the undying principle which coped with them. In the strategic effect of Nelson's victory upon the course of the war, on the contrary, the principle involved is not only more easily recognized, but it is at once seen to be applicable to our own day. The issue of the enterprise in Egypt depended upon keeping open the communications with France. The victory of the Nile destroyed the naval force, by which alone the communications could be assured, and determined the final failure; and it is at once seen, not only that the blow was struck in accordance with the principle of striking at the enemy's line of communication, but also that the same principle is valid now, and would be equally so in the days of the galley as of the sailing-ship or steamer.

Nevertheless, a vague feeling of contempt for the past, supposed to be obsolete, combines with natural indolence to blind men even to those permanent strategic lessons which lie close to the surface of naval history. For instance, how many look upon the battle of Trafalgar, the crown of Nelson's glory and the seal of his genius, as other than an isolated event of exceptional grandeur? How many ask themselves the strategic question, "How did the ships come to be just there?" How many realize it to be the final act in a great strategic drama, extending over a year or more, in which two of the greatest leaders that ever lived, Napoleon and Nelson, were pitted against each other? At Trafalgar it was not Villeneuve that failed, but Napoleon that was vanquished; not Nelson that won, but England that was saved; and why? Because Napoleon's combinations failed, and Nelson's intuitions and activity kept the English fleet ever on the track of the enemy, and brought it up in time at the decisive moment. The tactics at Trafalgar, while open to criticism in detail, were in their main features conformable to the principles of war, and their audacity was justified as well by the urgency of the case as by the results; but the great lessons of efficiency in preparation, of activity and energy in execution, and of thought and insight on the part of the English leader during the previous months, are strategic lessons, and as such they still remain good.

In these two cases events were worked out to their natural and decisive end. A third may be cited, in which, as no such definite end was reached, an opinion as to what should have been done may be open to dispute. In the war of the American Revolution, France and Spain became allies against England in 1779. The united fleets thrice appeared in the English Channel, once to the number of sixty-six sail of the line, driving the English fleet to seek refuge in its ports because far inferior in numbers. Now, the great aim of Spain was to recover Gibraltar and Jamaica; and to the former end immense efforts both by land and sea were put forth by the allies against that nearly impregnable fortress. They were fruitless. The question suggested—and it is purely one of naval strategy—is this: Would not Gibraltar have been more surely recovered by controlling the English Channel, attacking the British fleet even in its harbors, and threatening England with annihilation of commerce and invasion at home, than by far greater efforts directed against a distant and very strong outpost of her empire? The English people, from long immunity, were particularly sensitive to fears of invasion, and their great confidence in their fleets, if rudely shaken, would have left them proportionately disheartened. However decided, the question as a point of strategy is fair; and it is proposed in another form by a French officer of the period, who favored directing the great effort on a West India island which might be exchanged against Gibraltar. It is not, however, likely that England would have given up the key of the Mediterranean for any other foreign possession, though she might have yielded it to save her firesides and her capital. Napoleon once said that he would reconquer Pondicherry on the banks of the Vistula. Could he have controlled the English Channel, as the allied fleet did for a moment in 1779, can it be doubted that he would have conquered Gibraltar on the shores of England?

To impress more strongly the truth that history both suggests strategic study and illustrates the principles of war by the facts which it transmits, two more instances will be taken, which are more remote in time than the period specially considered in this work. How did it happen that, in two great contests between the powers of the East and of the West in the Mediterranean, in one of which the empire of the known world was at stake, the opposing fleets met on spots so near each other as Actium and Lepanto? Was this a mere coincidence, or was it due to conditions that recurred, and may recur again? If the latter, it is worth while to study out the reason; for if there should again arise a great eastern power of the sea like that of Antony or of Turkey, the strategic questions would be similar. At present, indeed, it seems that the centre of sea power, resting mainly with England and France, is overwhelmingly in the West; but should any chance add to the control of the Black Sea basin, which Russia now has, the possession of the entrance to the Mediterranean, the existing strategic conditions affecting sea power would all be modified. Now, were the West arrayed against the East, England and France would go at once unopposed to the Levant, as they did in 1854, and as England alone went in 1878; in case of the change suggested, the East, as twice before, would meet the West half-way.

At a very conspicuous and momentous period of the world's history, Sea Power had a strategic bearing and weight which has received scant recognition. There cannot now be had the full knowledge necessary for tracing in detail its influence upon the issue of the second Punic War; but the indications which remain are sufficient to warrant the assertion that it was a determining factor. An accurate judgment upon this point cannot be formed by mastering only such facts of the particular contest as have been clearly transmitted, for as usual the naval transactions have been slightingly passed over; there is needed also familiarity with the details of general naval history in order to draw, from slight indications, correct inferences based upon a knowledge of what has been possible at periods whose history is well known. The control of the sea, however real, does not imply that an enemy's single ships or small squadrons cannot steal out of port, cannot cross more or less frequented tracts of ocean, make harassing descents upon unprotected points of a long coastline, enter blockaded harbors. On the contrary, history has shown that such evasions are always possible, to some extent, to the weaker party, however great the inequality of naval strength. It is not therefore inconsistent with the general control of the sea, or of a decisive part of it, by the Roman fleets, that the Carthaginian admiral Bomilcar in the fourth year of the war, after the stunning defeat of Cannæ, landed four thousand men and a body of elephants in south Italy; nor that in the seventh year, flying from the Roman fleet off Syracuse, he again appeared at Tarentum, then in Hannibal's hands; nor that Hannibal sent despatch vessels to Carthage; nor even that, at last, he withdrew in safety to Africa with his wasted army. None of these things prove that the government in Carthage could, if it wished, have sent Hannibal the constant support which, as a matter of fact, he did not receive; but they do tend to create a natural impression that such help could have been given. Therefore the statement, that the Roman preponderance at sea had a decisive effect upon the course of the war, needs to be made good by an examination of ascertained facts. Thus the kind and degree of its influence may be fairly estimated.

At the beginning of the war, Mommsen says, Rome controlled the seas. To whatever cause, or combination of causes, it be attributed, this essentially non-maritime state had in the first Punic War established over its sea-faring rival a naval supremacy, which still lasted. In the second war there was no naval battle of importance—a circumstance which in itself, and still more in connection with other well-ascertained facts, indicates a superiority analogous to that which at other epochs has been marked by the same feature.

As Hannibal left no memoirs, the motives are unknown which determined him to the perilous and almost ruinous march through Gaul and across the Alps. It is certain, however, that his fleet on the coast of Spain was not strong enough to contend with that of Rome. Had it been, he might still have followed the road he actually did, for reasons that weighed with him; but had he gone by the sea, he would not have lost thirty-three thousand out of the sixty thousand veteran soldiers with whom he started.

While Hannibal was making this dangerous march, the Romans were sending to Spain, under the two elder Scipios, one part of their fleet, carrying a consular army. This made the voyage without serious loss, and the army established itself successfully north of the Ebro, on Hannibal's line of communications. At the same time another squadron, with an army commanded by the other consul, was sent to Sicily. The two together numbered two hundred and twenty ships. On its station each met and defeated a Carthaginian squadron with an ease which may be inferred from the slight mention made of the actions, and which indicates the actual superiority of the Roman fleet.

After the second year the war assumed the following shape: Hannibal, having entered Italy by the north, after a series of successes had passed southward around Rome and fixed himself in southern Italy, living off the country, a condition which tended to alienate the people, and was especially precarious when in contact with the mighty political and military system of control which Rome had there established. It was therefore from the first urgently necessary that he should establish, between himself and some reliable base, that stream of supplies and reinforcements which in terms of modern war is called "communications." There were three friendly regions which might, each or all, serve as such a base—Carthage itself, Macedonia, and Spain. With the first two, communication could be had only by sea. From Spain, where his firmest support was found, he could be reached by both land and sea, unless an enemy barred the passage; but the sea route was the shorter and easier.

In the first years of the war, Rome, by her sea power, controlled absolutely the basin between Italy, Sicily, and Spain, known as the Tyrrhenian and Sardinian Seas. The seacoast from the Ebro to the Tiber was mostly friendly to her. In the fourth year, after the battle of Cannæ, Syracuse forsook the Roman alliance, the revolt spread through Sicily, and Macedonia also entered into an offensive league with Hannibal. These changes extended the necessary operations of the Roman fleet, and taxed its strength. What disposition was made of it, and how did it thereafter influence the struggle?

The indications are clear that Rome at no time ceased to control the Tyrrhenian Sea, for her squadrons passed unmolested from Italy to Spain. On the Spanish coast also she had full sway till the younger Scipio saw fit to lay up the fleet. In the Adriatic, a squadron and naval station were established at Brindisi to check Macedonia, which performed their task so well that not a soldier of the phalanxes ever set foot in Italy. "The want of a war fleet," says Mommsen, "paralyzed Philip in all his movements." Here the effect of Sea Power is not even a matter of inference.

In Sicily, the struggle centred about Syracuse. The fleets of Carthage and Rome met there, but the superiority evidently lay with the latter; for though the Carthaginians at times succeeded in throwing supplies into the city, they avoided meeting the Roman fleet in battle. With Lilybæum, Palermo, and Messina in its hands, the latter was well based in the north coast of the island. Access by the south was left open to the Carthaginians, and they were thus able to maintain the insurrection.

Putting these facts together, it is a reasonable inference, and supported by the whole tenor of the history, that the Roman sea power controlled the sea north of a line drawn from Tarragona in Spain to Lilybæum (the modern Marsala), at the west end of Sicily, thence round by the north side of the island through the straits of Messina down to Syracuse, and from there to Brindisi in the Adriatic. This control lasted, unshaken, throughout the war. It did not exclude maritime raids, large or small, such as have been spoken of; but it did forbid the sustained and secure communications of which Hannibal was in deadly need.

On the other hand, it seems equally plain that for the first ten years of the war the Roman fleet was not strong enough for sustained operations in the sea between Sicily and Carthage, nor indeed much to the south of the line indicated. When Hannibal started, he assigned such ships as he had to maintaining the communications between Spain and Africa, which the Romans did not then attempt to disturb.

The Roman sea power, therefore, threw Macedonia wholly out of the war. It did not keep Carthage from maintaining a useful and most harassing diversion in Sicily; but it did prevent her sending troops, when they would have been most useful, to her great general in Italy. How was it as to Spain?

Spain was the region upon which the father of Hannibal and Hannibal himself had based their intended invasion of Italy. For eighteen years before this began they had occupied the country, extending and consolidating their power, both political and military, with rare sagacity. They had raised, and trained in local wars, a large and now veteran army. Upon his own departure, Hannibal intrusted the government to his younger brother, Hasdrubal, who preserved toward him to the end a loyalty and devotion which he had no reason to hope from the faction-cursed mother-city in Africa.

At the time of his starting, the Carthaginian power in Spain was secured from Cadiz to the river Ebro. The region between this river and the Pyrenees was inhabited by tribes friendly to the Romans, but unable, in the absence of the latter, to oppose a successful resistance to Hannibal. He put them down, leaving eleven thousand soldiers under Hanno to keep military possession of the country, lest the Romans should establish themselves there, and thus disturb his communications with his base.

Cnæus Scipio, however, arrived on the spot by sea the same year with twenty thousand men, defeated Hanno, and occupied both the coast and interior north of the Ebro. The Romans thus held ground by which they entirely closed the road between Hannibal and reinforcements from Hasdrubal, and whence they could attack the Carthaginian power in Spain; while their own communications with Italy, being by water, were secured by their naval supremacy. They made a naval base at Tarragona, confronting that of Hasdrubal at Cartagena, and then invaded the Carthaginian dominions. The war in Spain went on under the elder Scipios, seemingly a side issue, with varying fortune for seven years; at the end of which time Hasdrubal inflicted upon them a crushing defeat, the two brothers were killed, and the Carthaginians nearly succeeded in breaking through to the Pyrenees with reinforcements for Hannibal. The attempt, however, was checked for the moment; and before it could be renewed, the fall of Capua released twelve thousand veteran Romans, who were sent to Spain under Claudius Nero, a man of exceptional ability, to whom was due later the most decisive military movement made by any Roman general during the Second Punic War. This seasonable reinforcement, which again assured the shaken grip on Hasdrubal's line of march, came by sea—a way which, though most rapid and easy, was closed to the Carthaginians by the Roman navy.

Two years later the younger Publius Scipio, celebrated afterward as Africanus, received the command in Spain, and captured Cartagena by a combined military and naval attack; after which he took the most extraordinary step of breaking up his fleet and transferring the seamen to the army. Not contented to act merely as the "containing"[1] force against Hasdrubal by closing the passes of the Pyrenees, Scipio pushed forward into southern Spain, and fought a severe but indecisive battle on the Guadalquivir; after which Hasdrubal slipped away from him, hurried north, crossed the Pyrenees at their extreme west, and pressed on to Italy, where Hannibal's position was daily growing weaker, the natural waste of his army not being replaced.

---

[1] A "containing" force is one to which, in a military combination, is assigned the duty of stopping, or delaying the advance of a portion of the enemy, while the main effort of the army or armies is being exerted in a different quarter.

The war had lasted ten years, when Hasdrubal, having met little loss on the way—entered Italy at the north. The troops he
brought, could they be safely united with those under the command of the unrivalled Hannibal, might give a decisive turn to
the war, for Rome herself was nearly exhausted; the iron links
which bound her own colonies and the allied States to her were
strained to the utmost, and some had already snapped. But the
military position of the two brothers was also perilous in the
extreme. One being at the river Metaurus, the other in Apulia,
two hundred miles apart, each was confronted by a superior
enemy, and both these Roman armies were between their separated opponents. This false situation, as well as the long delay of
Hasdrubal's coming, was due to the Roman control of the sea,
which throughout the war limited the mutual support of the
Carthaginian brothers to the route through Gaul. At the very
time that Hasdrubal was making his long and dangerous circuit
by land, Scipio had sent eleven thousand men from Spain by sea
to reinforce the army opposed to him. The upshot was that mes-
sengers from Hasdrubal to Hannibal, having to pass over so wide
a belt of hostile country, fell into the hands of Claudius Nero,
commanding the southern Roman army, who thus learned the
route which Hasdrubal intended to take. Nero correctly appreciated the situation, and, escaping the vigilance of Hannibal, made
a rapid march with eight thousand of his best troops to join the
forces in the north. The junction being effected, the two consuls
fell upon Hasdrubal in overwhelming numbers and destroyed his
army; the Carthaginian leader himself falling in the battle. Hannibal's first news of the disaster was by the head of his brother
being thrown into his camp. He is said to have exclaimed that
Rome would now be mistress of the world; and the battle of
Metaurus is generally accepted as decisive of the struggle
between the two States.

The military situation which finally resulted in the battle of
the Metaurus and the triumph of Rome may be summed up as
follows: To overthrow Rome it was necessary to attack her in

Italy at the heart of her power, and shatter the strongly linked confederacy of which she was the head. This was the objective. To reach it, the Carthaginians needed a solid base of operations and a secure line of communications. The former was established in Spain by the genius of the great Barca family; the latter was never achieved. There were two lines possible,—the one direct by sea, the other circuitous through Gaul. The first was blocked by the Roman sea power, the second imperilled and finally intercepted through the occupation of northern Spain by the Roman army. This occupation was made possible through the control of the sea, which the Carthaginians never endangered. With respect to Hannibal and his base, therefore, Rome occupied two central positions, Rome itself and northern Spain, joined by an easy interior line of communications, the sea; by which mutual support was continually given.

Had the Mediterranean been a level desert of land, in which the Romans held strong mountain ranges in Corsica and Sardinia, fortified posts at Tarragona, Lilybæum, and Messina, the Italian coast-line nearly to Genoa, and allied fortresses in Marseilles and other points; had they also possessed an armed force capable by its character of traversing that desert at will, but in which their opponents were very inferior and therefore compelled to a great circuit in order to concentrate their troops, the military situation would have been at once recognized, and no words would have been too strong to express the value and effect of that peculiar force. It would have been perceived, also, that the enemy's force of the same kind might, however inferior in strength, make an inroad, or raid, upon the territory thus held, might burn a village or waste a few miles of borderland, might even cut off a convoy at times, without, in a military sense, endangering the communications. Such predatory operations have been carried on in all ages by the weaker maritime belligerent, but they by no means warrant the inference, irreconcilable with the known facts, "that neither Rome nor Carthage could be said to have undisputed mastery of the sea," because "Roman fleets sometimes visited the coasts of Africa, and Carthaginian fleets in the same way appeared off the coast of Italy." In the case under consideration, the navy played the part of such a force upon the supposed desert; but as it acts on an element strange to most writers, as its members have been from time immemorial a strange race apart, without prophets of their own, neither themselves nor their calling understood, its immense determining influence upon the history of that era, and consequently upon the history of the world, has been overlooked. If the preceding argument is sound, it is as defective to omit sea power from the list of principal factors in the result, as it would be absurd to claim for it an exclusive influence.

Instances such as have been cited, drawn from widely separated periods of time, both before and after that specially treated in this work, serve to illustrate the intrinsic interest of the subject, and the character of the lessons which history has to teach. As before observed, these come more often under the head of strategy than of tactics; they bear rather upon the conduct of campaigns than of battles, and hence are fraught with more lasting value. To quote a great authority in this connection, Jomini says: "Happening to be in Paris near the end of 1851, a distinguished person did me the honor to ask my opinion as to whether recent improvements in firearms would cause any great modifications in the way of making war. I replied that they would probably have an influence upon the details of tactics, but that in great strategic operations and the grand combinations of battles, victory would, now as ever, result from the application of the principles which had led to the success of great generals in all ages; of Alexander and Cæsar, as well as of Frederick and Napoleon." This study has become more than ever important now to navies, because of the great and steady power of movement possessed by the modern steamer. The best-planned schemes might fail through stress of weather in the days of the galley and the sailing-ship; but this difficulty has almost disappeared. The principles which should direct great naval combinations have been applicable to all ages, and are deducible from history; but the power to carry them out with little regard to the weather is a recent gain.

The definitions usually given of the word "strategy" confine it to military combinations embracing one or more fields of operations, either wholly distinct or mutually dependent, but always regarded as actual or immediate scenes of war. However this may be on shore, a recent French author is quite right in pointing out that such a definition is too narrow for naval strategy. "This," he says, "differs from military strategy in that it is as necessary in peace as in war. Indeed, in peace it may gain its most decisive victories by occupying in a country, either by purchase or treaty, excellent positions which would perhaps hardly be got by war. It learns to profit by all opportunities of settling on some chosen point of a coast, and to render definitive an occupation which at first was only transient." A generation that has seen England within ten years occupy successively Cyprus and Egypt, under terms and conditions on their face transient, but which have not yet led to the abandonment of the positions taken, can readily agree with this remark; which indeed receives constant illustration from the quiet persistency with which all the great sea powers are seeking position after position, less noted and less noteworthy than Cyprus and Egypt, in the different seas to which their people and their ships penetrate. "Naval strategy has indeed for its end to found, support, and increase, as well in peace as in war, the sea power of a country;" and therefore its study has an interest and value for all citizens of a free country, but especially for those who are charged with its foreign and military relations.

The general conditions that either are essential to or powerfully affect the greatness of a nation upon the sea will now be examined; after which a more particular consideration of the various maritime nations of Europe at the middle of the seventeenth century, where the historical survey begins, will serve at once to illustrate and give precision to the conclusions upon the general subject.

CHAPTER I

DISCUSSION OF THE ELEMENTS OF SEA POWER

The first and most obvious light in which the sea presents itself from the political and social point of view is that of a great highway; or better, perhaps, of a wide common, over which men may pass in all directions, but on which some well-worn paths show that controlling reasons have led them to choose certain lines of travel rather than others. These lines of travel are called trade routes; and the reasons which have determined them are to be sought in the history of the world.

Notwithstanding all the familiar and unfamiliar dangers of the sea, both travel and traffic by water have always been easier and cheaper than by land. The commercial greatness of Holland was due not only to her shipping at sea, but also to the numerous tranquil water-ways which gave such cheap and easy access to her own interior and to that of Germany. This advantage of carriage by water over that by land was yet more marked in a period when roads were few and very bad, wars frequent and society unsettled, as was the case two hundred years ago. Sea traffic then went in peril of robbers, but was nevertheless safer and quicker than that by land. A Dutch writer of that time, estimating the chances of his country in a war with England, notices among other things that the water-ways of England failed to penetrate the country sufficiently; therefore, the roads being bad, goods from one part of the kingdom to the other must go by sea, and be exposed to capture by the way. As regards purely internal trade, this danger has generally disappeared at the present day. In most civilized countries, now, the destruction or disappearance of the coasting trade would only be an inconvenience, although water transit is still the cheaper. Nevertheless, as late as the wars of the French Republic and the First Empire, those who are familiar with the history of the period, and the light naval literature that has grown up around it, know how constant is the mention of convoys stealing from point to point along the French coast, although the sea swarmed with English cruisers and there were good inland roads.

Under modern conditions, however, home trade is but a part of the business of a country bordering on the sea. Foreign necessaries or luxuries must be brought to its ports, either in its own or in foreign ships, which will return, bearing in exchange the products of the country, whether they be the fruits of the earth or the works of men's hands; and it is the wish of every nation that this shipping business should be done by its own vessels. The ships that thus sail to and fro must have secure ports to which to return, and must, as far as possible, be followed by the protection of their country throughout the voyage.

This protection in time of war must be extended by armed shipping. The necessity of a navy, in the restricted sense of the word, springs, therefore, from the existence of a peaceful shipping, and disappears with it, except in the case of a nation which has aggressive tendencies, and keeps up a navy merely as a branch of the military establishment. As the United States has at present no aggressive purposes, and as its merchant service has disappeared, the dwindling of the armed fleet and general lack of interest in it are strictly logical consequences. When for any reason sea trade is again found to pay, a large enough shipping interest will reappear to compel the revival of the war fleet. It is possible that when a canal route through the Central-American

Isthmus is seen to be a near certainty, the aggressive impulse may be strong enough to lead to the same result. This is doubtful, however, because a peaceful, gain-loving nation is not far-sighted, and far-sightedness is needed for adequate military preparation, especially in these days.

As a nation, with its unarmed and armed shipping, launches forth from its own shores, the need is soon felt of points upon which the ships can rely for peaceful trading, for refuge and supplies. In the present day friendly, though foreign, ports are to be found all over the world; and their shelter is enough while peace prevails. It was not always so, nor does peace always endure, though the United States have been favored by so long a continuance of it. In earlier times the merchant seaman, seeking for trade in new and unexplored regions, made his gains at risk of life and liberty from suspicious or hostile nations, and was under great delays in collecting a full and profitable freight. He therefore intuitively sought at the far end of his trade route one or more stations, to be given to him by force or favor, where he could fix himself or his agents in reasonable security, where his ships could lie in safety, and where the merchantable products of the land could be continually collecting, awaiting the arrival of the home fleet, which should carry them to the mother-country. As there was immense gain, as well as much risk, in these early voyages, such establishments naturally multiplied and grew until they became colonies; whose ultimate development and success depended upon the genius and policy of the nation from which they sprang, and form a very great part of the history, and particularly of the sea history, of the world. All colonies had not the simple and natural birth and growth above described. Many were more formal, and purely political, in their conception and founding, the act of the rulers of the people rather than of private individuals; but the trading-station with its after expansion, the work simply of the adventurer seeking gain, was in its reasons and essence the same as the elaborately organized and chartered colony. In both cases the mother-country had won a foothold in a foreign land, seeking a new outlet for what it had to sell, a new sphere for its shipping, more employment for its people, more comfort and wealth for itself.

The needs of commerce, however, were not all provided for when safety had been secured at the far end of the road. The voyages were long and dangerous, the seas often beset with enemies. In the most active days of colonizing there prevailed on the sea a lawlessness the very memory of which is now almost lost, and the days of settled peace between maritime nations were few and far between. Thus arose the demand for stations along the road, like the Cape of Good Hope, St. Helena, and Mauritius, not primarily for trade, but for defence and war; the demand for the possession of posts like Gibraltar, Malta, Louisburg, at the entrance of the Gulf of St. Lawrence—posts whose value was chiefly strategic, though not necessarily wholly so. Colonies and colonial posts were sometimes commercial, sometimes military in their character; and it was exceptional that the same position was equally important in both points of view, as New York was.

In these three things—production, with the necessity of exchanging products, shipping, whereby the exchange is carried on, and colonies, which facilitate and enlarge the operations of shipping and tend to protect it by multiplying points of safety—is to be found the key to much of the history, as well as of the policy, of nations bordering upon the sea. The policy has varied both with the spirit of the age and with the character and clear-sightedness of the rulers; but the history of the seaboard nations has been less determined by the shrewdness and foresight of governments than by conditions of position, extent, configuration, number and character of their people—by what are called, in a word, natural conditions. It must however be admitted, and will be seen, that the wise or unwise action of individual men has at certain periods had a great modifying influence upon the growth of sea power in the broad sense, which includes not only the military strength afloat, that rules the sea or any part of it by force of arms, but also the peaceful commerce and shipping from which alone a military fleet naturally and healthfully springs, and on which it securely rests.

The principal conditions affecting the sea power of nations may be enumerated as follows: I. Geographical Position. II. Physical Conformation, including, as connected therewith, natural productions and climate. III. Extent of Territory. IV. Number of Population. V. Character of the People. VI. Character of the Government, including therein the national institutions.

I. *Geographical Position*

It may be pointed out, in the first place, that if a nation be so situated that it is neither forced to defend itself by land nor induced to seek extension of its territory by way of the land, it has, by the very unity of its aim directed upon the sea, all advantage as compared with a people one of whose boundaries is continental. This has been a great advantage to England over both France and Holland as a sea power. The strength of the latter was early exhausted by the necessity of keeping up a large army and carrying on expensive wars to preserve her independence; while the policy of France was constantly diverted, sometimes wisely and sometimes most foolishly, from the sea to projects of continental extension. These military efforts expended wealth; whereas a wiser and consistent use of her geographical position would have added to it.

The geographical position may be such as of itself to promote a concentration, or to necessitate a dispersion, of the naval forces. Here again the British Islands have an advantage over France. The position of the latter, touching the Mediterranean as well as the ocean, while it has its advantages, is on the whole a source of military weakness at sea. The eastern and western French fleets have only been able to unite after passing through the Straits of Gibraltar, in attempting which they have often risked and sometimes suffered loss. The position of the United States upon the two oceans would be either a source of great weakness or a cause of enormous expense, had it a large sea commerce on both coasts.

England, by her immense colonial empire, has sacrificed much of this advantage of concentration of force around her own shores; but the sacrifice was wisely made, for the gain was greater than the loss, as the event proved. With the growth of her colonial system her war fleets also grew, but her merchant shipping and wealth grew yet faster. Still, in the wars of the American Revolution, and of the French Republic and Empire, to use the strong expression of a French author, "England, despite the immense development of her navy, seemed ever, in the midst of riches, to feel all the embarrassment of poverty." The might of England was sufficient to keep alive the heart and the members; whereas the equally extensive colonial empire of Spain, through her maritime weakness, but offered so many points for insult and injury.

The geographical position of a country may not only favor the concentration of its forces, but give the further strategic advantage of a central position and a good base for hostile operations against its probable enemies. This again is the case with England; on the one hand she faces Holland and the northern powers, on the other France and the Atlantic. When threatened with a coalition between France and the naval powers of the North Sea and the Baltic, as she at times was, her fleets in the Downs and in the Channel, and even that off Brest, occupied interior positions, and thus were readily able to interpose their united force against either one of the enemies which should seek to pass through the Channel to effect a junction with its ally. On either side, also, Nature gave her better ports and a safer coast to approach. Formerly this was a very serious element in the passage through the Channel; but of late, steam and the improvement of her harbors have lessened the disadvantage under which France once labored. In the days of sailing-ships, the English fleet operated against Brest making its base at Torbay and Plymouth. The plan was simply this: in easterly or moderate weather the blockading fleet kept its position without difficulty; but in westerly gales, when too severe, they bore up for English ports, knowing that the French fleet could not get out till the wind shifted, which equally served to bring them back to their station.

The advantage of geographical nearness to an enemy, or to the object of attack, is nowhere more apparent than in that form of warfare which has lately received the name of commerce-destroying, which the French call *guerre de course*. This operation of war, being directed against peaceful merchant vessels which are usually defenceless, calls for ships of small military force. Such ships, having little power to defend themselves, need a refuge or point of support near at hand; which will be found either in certain parts of the sea controlled by the fighting ships of their country, or in friendly harbors. The latter give the strongest support, because they are always in the same place, and the approaches to them are more familiar to the commerce-destroyer than to his enemy. The nearness of France to England has thus greatly facilitated her *guerre de course* directed against the latter. Having ports on the North Sea, on the Channel, and on the Atlantic, her cruisers started from points near the focus of English trade, both coming and going. The distance of these ports from each other, disadvantageous for regular military combinations, is an advantage for this irregular secondary operation; for the essence of the one is concentration of effort, whereas for commerce-destroying diffusion of effort is the rule. Commerce-destroyers scatter, that they may see and seize more prey. These truths receive illustration from the history of the great French privateers, whose bases and scenes of action were largely on the Channel and North Sea, or else were found in distant colonial regions, where islands like Guadaloupe and Martinique afforded similar near refuge. The necessity of renewing coal makes the cruiser of the present day even more dependent than of old on his port. Public opinion in the United States has great faith in war directed against an enemy's commerce; but it must be remembered that the Republic has no ports very near the great centres of trade abroad. Her geographical position is therefore singularly disadvantageous for carrying on successful commerce-destroying, unless she find bases in the ports of an ally.

If, in addition to facility for offence, Nature has so placed a country that it has easy access to the high sea itself, while at the same time it controls one of the great thoroughfares of the world's traffic, it is evident that the strategic value of its position is very high. Such again is, and to a greater degree was, the position of England. The trade of Holland, Sweden, Russia, Denmark, and that which went up the great rivers to the interior of Germany, had to pass through the Channel close by her doors; for sailing-ships hugged the English coast. This northern trade had, moreover, a peculiar bearing upon sea power; for naval stores, as they are commonly called, were mainly drawn from the Baltic countries.

But for the loss of Gibraltar, the position of Spain would have been closely analogous to that of England. Looking at once upon the Atlantic and the Mediterranean, with Cadiz on the one side and Cartagena on the other, the trade to the Levant must have passed under her hands, and that round the Cape of Good Hope not far from her doors. But Gibraltar not only deprived her of the control of the Straits, it also imposed an obstacle to the easy junction of the two divisions of her fleet.

At the present day, looking only at the geographical position of Italy, and not at the other conditions affecting her sea power, it would seem that with her extensive sea-coast and good ports she is very well placed for exerting a decisive influence on the trade route to the Levant and by the Isthmus of Suez. This is true in a degree, and would be much more so did Italy now hold all the islands naturally Italian; but with Malta in the hands of England, and Corsica in those of France, the advantages of her geographical position are largely neutralized. From race affinities and situation those two islands are as legitimately objects of desire to Italy as Gibraltar is to Spain. If the Adriatic were a great highway of commerce, Italy's position would be still more influential. These defects in her geographical completeness, combined with other causes injurious to a full and secure development of sea power, make it more than doubtful whether Italy can for some time be in the front rank among the sea nations.

As the aim here is not an exhaustive discussion, but merely an attempt to show, by illustration, how vitally the situation of a country may affect its career upon the sea, this division of the subject may be dismissed for the present; the more so as instances which will further bring out its importance will continually recur in the historical treatment. Two remarks, however, are here appropriate.

Circumstances have caused the Mediterranean Sea to play a greater part in the history of the world, both in a commercial and a military point of view, than any other sheet of water of the sa e size. Nation after nation has striven to control it, and the strife still goes on. Therefore a study of the conditions upon which preponderance in its waters has rested, and now rests, and of the relative military values of different points upon its coasts, will be more instructive than the same amount of effort expended in another field. Furthermore, it has at the present time a very marked analogy in many respects to the Caribbean Sea—an analogy which will be still closer if a Panama canal-route ever be completed. A study of the strategic conditions of the Mediterranean, which have received ample illustration, will be an excellent prelude to a similar study of the Caribbean, which has comparatively little history.

The second remark bears upon the geographical position of the United States relatively to a Central-American canal. If one be made, and fulfil the hopes of its builders, the Caribbean will be changed from a terminus, and place of local traffic, or at best a broken and imperfect line of travel, as it now is, into one of the great highways of the world. Along this path a great commerce will travel, bringing the interests of the other great nations, the European nations, close along our shores, as they have never been before. With this it will not be so easy as heretofore to stand aloof from international complications. The position of the United States with reference to this route will resemble that of England to the Channel, and of the Mediterranean countries to the Suez route. As regards influence and control over it, depending upon geographical position, it is of course plain that the centre of the national power, the permanent base,[1] is much nearer than that of other great nations. The positions now or hereafter occupied by them on island or mainland, however strong, will be but outposts of their power; while in all the raw materials of military strength no nation is superior to the United States. She is, however, weak in a confessed unpreparedness for war; and her geographical nearness to the point of contention loses some of its value by the character of the Gulf coast, which is deficient in ports combining security from an enemy with facility for repairing war-ships of the first class, without which ships no country can pretend to control any part of the sea. In case of a contest for supremacy in the Caribbean, it seems evident from the depth of the South Pass of the Mississippi, the nearness of New Orleans, and the advantages of the Mississippi Valley for water transit, that the main effort of the country must pour down that valley, and its permanent base of operations be found there. The defence of the entrance to the Mississippi, however, presents peculiar difficulties; while the only two rival ports, Key West and Pensacola, have too little depth of water, and are much less advantageously placed with reference to the resources of the

---

[1] By a base of permanent operations "is understood a country whence come all the resources, where are united the great lines of communication by land and water, where are the arsenals and armed posts."

country. To get the full benefit of superior geographical position, these defects must be overcome. Furthermore, as her distance from the Isthmus, though relatively less, is still considerable, the United States will have to obtain in the Caribbean stations fit for contingent, or secondary, bases of operations; which by their natural advantages, susceptibility of defence, and nearness to the central strategic issue, will enable her fleets to remain as near the scene as any opponent. With ingress and egress from the Mississippi sufficiently protected, with such outposts in her hands, and with the communications between them and the home base secured, in short, with proper military preparation, for which she has all necessary means, the preponderance of the United States on this field follows, from her geographical position and her power, with mathematical certainty.

II. *Physical Conformation*

The peculiar features of the Gulf coast, just alluded to, come properly under the head of Physical Conformation of a country, which is placed second for discussion among the conditions which affect the development of sea power.

The seaboard of a country is one of its frontiers; and the easier the access offered by the frontier to the region beyond, in this case the sea, the greater will be the tendency of a people toward intercourse with the rest of the world by it. If a country be imagined having a long seaboard, but entirely without a harbor, such a country can have no sea trade of its own, no shipping, no navy. This was practically the case with Belgium when it was a Spanish and an Austrian province. The Dutch, in 1648, as a condition of peace after a successful war, exacted that the Scheldt should be closed to sea commerce. This closed the harbor of Antwerp and transferred the sea trade of Belgium to Holland. The Spanish Netherlands ceased to be a sea power.

Numerous and deep harbors are a source of strength and wealth, and doubly so if they are the outlets of navigable streams, which facilitate the concentration in them of a country's internal trade; but by their very accessibility they become a source of weakness in war, if not properly defended. The Dutch in 1667 found little difficulty in ascending the Thames and burning a large fraction of the English navy within sight of London; whereas a few years later the combined fleets of England and France, when attempting a landing in Holland, were foiled by the difficulties of the coast as much as by the valor of the Dutch fleet. In 1778 the harbor of New York, and with it undisputed control of the Hudson River, would have been lost to the English, who were caught at disadvantage, but for the hesitancy of the French admiral. With that control, New England would have been restored to close and safe communication with New York, New Jersey, and Pennsylvania; and this blow, following so closely on Burgoyne's disaster of the year before, would probably have led the English to make an earlier peace. The Mississippi is a mighty source of wealth and strength to the United States; but the feeble defences of its mouth and the number of its subsidiary streams penetrating the country made it a weakness and source of disaster to the Southern Confederacy. And lastly, in 1814, the occupation of the Chesapeake and the destruction of Washington gave a sharp lesson of the dangers incurred through the noblest waterways, if their approaches be undefended; a lesson recent enough to be easily recalled, but which, from the present appearance of the coast defences, seems to be yet more easily forgotten. Nor should it be thought that conditions have changed; circumstances and details of offence and defence have been modified, in these days as before, but the great conditions remain the same.

Before and during the great Napoleonic wars, France had no port for ships-of-the-line east of Brest. How great the advantage to England, which in the same stretch has two great arsenals, at Plymouth and at Portsmouth, besides other harbors of refuge and supply. This defect of conformation has since been remedied by the works at Cherbourg.

Besides the contour of the coast, involving easy access to the sea, there are other physical conditions which lead people to the sea or turn them from it. Although France was deficient in military ports on the Channel, she had both there and on the ocean, as well as in the Mediterranean, excellent harbors, favorably situated for trade abroad, and at the outlet of large rivers, which would foster internal traffic. But when Richelieu had put an end to civil war, Frenchmen did not take to the sea with the eagerness and success of the English and Dutch. A principal reason for this has been plausibly found in the physical conditions which have made France a pleasant land, with a delightful climate, producing within itself more than its people needed. England, on the other hand, received from Nature but little, and, until her manufactures were developed, had little to export. Their many wants, combined with their restless activity and other conditions that favored maritime enterprise, led her people abroad; and they there found lands more pleasant and richer than their own. Their needs and genius made them merchants and colonists, then manufacturers and producers; and between products and colonies shipping is the inevitable link. So their sea power grew. But if England was drawn to the sea, Holland was driven to it; without the sea England languished, but Holland died. In the height of her greatness, when she was one of the chief factors in European politics, a competent native authority estimated that the soil of Holland could not support more than one eighth of her inhabitants. The manufactures of the country were then numerous and important, but they had been much later in their growth than the shipping interest. The poverty of the soil and the exposed nature of the coast drove the Dutch first to fishing. Then the discovery of the process of curing the fish gave them material for export as well as home consumption, and so laid the corner-stone of their wealth. Thus they had become traders at the time that the Italian republics, under the pressure of Turkish power and the discovery of the passage round the Cape of Good Hope, were beginning to decline, and they fell heirs to the great Italian trade of the Levant. Further favored by their geographical position, intermediate between the Baltic, France, and the Mediterranean, and at the mouth of the German rivers, they quickly absorbed nearly all the carrying-trade of Europe. The wheat and naval stores of the Baltic, the trade of Spain with her colonies in the New World, the wines of France, and the French coasting-trade were, little more than two hundred years ago, transported in Dutch shipping. Much of the carrying-trade of England even was then done in Dutch bottoms. It will not be pretended that all this prosperity proceeded only from the poverty of Holland's natural resources. Something does not grow from nothing. What is true, is, that by the necessitous condition of her people they were driven to the sea, and were, from their mastery of the shipping business and the size of their fleets, in a position to profit by the sudden expansion of commerce and the spirit of exploration which followed on the discovery of America and of the passage round the Cape. Other causes concurred, but their whole prosperity stood on the sea power to which their poverty gave birth. Their food, their clothing, the raw material for their manufactures, the very timber and hemp with which they built and rigged their ships (and they built nearly as many as all Europe besides), were imported; and when a disastrous war with England in 1653 and 1654 had lasted eighteen months, and their shipping business was stopped, it is said "the sources of revenue which had always maintained the riches of the State, such as fisheries and commerce, were almost dry. Workshops were closed, work was suspended. The Zuyder Zee became a forest of masts; the country was full of beggars; grass grew in the streets, and in Amsterdam fifteen hundred houses were untenanted." A humiliating peace alone saved them from ruin.

This sorrowful result shows the weakness of a country depending wholly upon sources external to itself for the part it is playing in the world. With large deductions, owing to differences of conditions which need not here be spoken of, the case of Holland then has strong points of resemblance to that of Great Britain now; and they are true prophets, though they seem to be having small honor in their own country, who warn her that the continuance of her prosperity at home depends primarily upon maintaining her power abroad. Men may be discontented at the lack of political privilege; they will be yet more uneasy if they come to lack bread. It is of more interest to Americans to note that the result to France, regarded as a power of the sea, caused by the extent, delightfulness, and richness of the land, has been reproduced in the United States. In the beginning, their forefathers held a narrow strip of land upon the sea, fertile in parts though little developed, abounding in harbors and near rich fishing-grounds. These physical conditions combined with an inborn love of the sea, the pulse of that English blood which still beat in their veins, to keep alive all those tendencies and pursuits upon which a healthy sea power depends. Almost every one of the original colonies was on the sea or on one of its great tributaries. All export and import tended toward one coast. Interest in the sea and an intelligent appreciation of the part it played in the public welfare were easily and widely spread; and a motive more influential than care for the public interest was also active, for the abundance of ship-building materials and a relative fewness of other investments made shipping a profitable private interest. How changed the present condition is, all know. The centre of power is no longer on the seaboard. Books and newspapers vie with one another in describing the wonderful growth, and the still undeveloped riches, of the interior. Capital there finds its best investments, labor its largest opportunities. The frontiers are neglected and politically weak; the Gulf and Pacific coasts actually so, the Atlantic coast relatively to the central Mississippi Valley. When the day comes that shipping again pays, when the three sea frontiers find that they are not only militarily weak, but poorer for lack of national shipping, their united efforts may avail to lay again the foundations of our sea power. Till then, those who follow the limitations which lack of sea power placed upon the career of France may mourn that their own country is being led, by a like redundancy of home wealth, into the same neglect of that great instrument.

Among modifying physical conditions may be noted a form like that of Italy—a long peninsula with a central range of mountains dividing it into two narrow strips, along which the roads connecting the different ports necessarily run. Only an absolute control of the sea can wholly secure such communications, since it is impossible to know at what point an enemy coming from beyond the visible horizon may strike; but still, with an adequate naval force centrally posted, there will be good hope of attacking his fleet, which is at once his base and line of communications, before serious damage has been done. The long, narrow peninsula of Florida, with Key West at its extremity, though flat and thinly populated, presents at first sight conditions like those of Italy. The resemblance may be only superficial, but it seems probable that if the chief scene of a naval war were the Gulf of Mexico, the communications by land to the end of the peninsula might be a matter of consequence, and open to attack.

When the sea not only borders, or surrounds, but also separates a country into two or more parts, the control of it becomes not only desirable, but vitally necessary. Such a physical condition either gives birth and strength to sea power, or makes the country powerless. Such is the condition of the present kingdom of Italy, with its islands of Sardinia and Sicily; and hence in its youth and still existing financial weakness it is seen to put forth such vigorous and intelligent efforts to create a military navy. It has even been argued that, with a navy decidedly superior to her enemy's, Italy could better base her power upon her islands than upon her mainland; for the insecurity of the lines of communication in the peninsula, already pointed out, would most seriously embarrass an invading army surrounded by a hostile people and threatened from the sea.

The Irish Sea, separating the British Islands, rather resembles an estuary than an actual division; but history has shown the danger from it to the United Kingdom. In the days of Louis XIV, when the French navy nearly equalled the combined English and Dutch, the gravest complications existed in Ireland, which passed almost wholly under the control of the natives and the French. Nevertheless, the Irish Sea was rather a danger to the English—a weak point in their communications—than an advantage to the French. The latter did not venture their ships-of-the-line in its narrow waters, and expeditions intending to land were directed upon the ocean ports in the south and west. At the supreme moment the great French fleet was sent upon the south coast of England, where it decisively defeated the allies, and at the same time twenty-five frigates were sent to St. George's Channel, against the English communications. In the midst of a hostile people, the English army in Ireland was seriously imperilled, but was saved by the battle of the Boyne and the flight of James II. This movement against the enemy's communications was strictly strategic, and would be just as dangerous to England now as in 1690.

Spain, in the same century, afforded an impressive lesson of the weakness caused by such separation when the parts are not knit together by a strong sea power. She then still retained, as remnants of her past greatness, the Netherlands (now Belgium), Sicily, and other Italian possessions, not to speak of her vast colonies in the New World. Yet so low had the Spanish sea power fallen, that a well-informed and sober-minded Hollander of the day could claim that "in Spain all the coast is navigated by a few Dutch ships; and since the peace of 1648 their ships and seamen are so few that they have publicly begun to hire our ships to sail to the Indies, whereas they were formerly careful to exclude all foreigners from there. . . . It is manifest," he goes on, "that the West Indies, being as the stomach to Spain (for from it nearly all the revenue is drawn), must be joined to the Spanish head by a sea force; and that Naples and the Netherlands, being like two arms, they, cannot lay out their strength for Spain, nor receive anything thence but by shipping—all which may easily be done by our shipping in peace, and by it obstructed in war." Half a century before, Sully, the great minister of Henry IV, had characterized Spain "as one of those States whose legs and arms are strong and powerful, but the heart infinitely weak and feeble." Since his day the Spanish navy had suffered not only disaster, but annihilation; not only humiliation, but degradation. The consequences briefly were that shipping was destroyed; manufactures perished with it. The government depended for its support, not upon a widespread healthy commerce and industry that could survive many a staggering blow, but upon a narrow stream of silver trickling through a few treasure-ships from America, easily and frequently intercepted by an enemy's cruisers. The loss of half a dozen galleons more than once paralyzed its movements for a year. While the war in the Netherlands lasted, the Dutch control of the sea forced Spain to send her troops by a long and costly journey overland instead of by sea; and the same cause reduced her to such straits for necessaries that, by a mutual arrangement which seems very odd to modern ideas, her wants were supplied by Dutch ships, which thus maintained the enemies of their country, but received in return specie which was welcome in the Amsterdam exchange. In America, the Spanish protected themselves as best they might behind masonry, unaided from home; while in the Mediterranean they escaped insult and injury mainly through the indifference of the Dutch, for the French and English had not yet begun to contend for mastery there. In the course of history the Netherlands, Naples, Sicily, Minorca, Havana, Manila, and Jamaica were wrenched away, at one time or another, from this empire without a shipping. In short, while Spain's maritime impotence may have been primarily a symptom of her general decay, it became a marked factor in precipitating her into the abyss from which she has not yet wholly emerged.

Except Alaska, the United States has no outlying possession—no foot of ground inaccessible by land. Its contour is such as to present few points specially weak from their saliency, and all important parts of the frontiers can be readily attained— cheaply by water, rapidly by rail. The weakest frontier, the Pacific, is far removed from the most dangerous of possible enemies. The internal resources are boundless as compared with present needs; we can live off ourselves indefinitely in "our little corner," to use the expression of a French officer to the author. Yet should that little corner be invaded by a new commercial route through the Isthmus, the United States in her turn may have the rude awakening of those who have abandoned their share in the common birthright of all people, the sea.

III. *Extent of Territory*

The last of the conditions affecting the development of a nation as a sea power, and touching the country itself as distinguished from the people who dwell there, is Extent of Territory. This may be dismissed with comparatively few words.

As regards the development of sea power, it is not the total number of square miles which a country contains, but the length of its coast-line and the character of its harbors that are to be considered. As to these it is to be said that, the geographical and physical conditions being the same, extent of sea-coast is a source of strength or weakness according as the population is large or small. A country is in this like a fortress; the garrison must be proportioned to the *enceinte*. A recent familiar instance is found in the American War of Secession. Had the South had a people as numerous as it was warlike, and a navy commensurate to its other resources as a sea power, the great extent of its sea-coast and its numerous inlets would have been elements of great strength. The people of the United States and the Government of that day justly prided themselves on the effectiveness of the blockade of the whole Southern coast. It was a great feat, a very great feat; but it would have been an impossible feat had the Southerners been more numerous, and a nation of seamen. What was there shown was not, as has been said, how such a blockade can be maintained, but that such a blockade is possible in the face of a population not only unused to the sea, but also scanty in numbers. Those who recall how the blockade was maintained, and the class of ships that blockaded during great part of the war, know that the plan, correct under the circumstances, could not have been carried out in the face of a real navy. Scattered unsupported along the coast, the United States ships kept their places, singly or in small detachments, in face of an extensive network of inland water communications which favored secret concentration of the enemy. Behind the first line of water communications were long estuaries, and here and there strong fortresses, upon either of which the enemy's ships could always fall back to elude pursuit or to receive protection. Had there been a Southern navy to profit by such advantages, or by the scattered condition of the United States ships, the latter could not have been distributed as they were; and being forced to concentrate for mutual support, many small but useful approaches would have been left open to commerce. But as the Southern coast, from its extent and many inlets, might have been a source of strength, so, from those very characteristics, it became a fruitful source of injury. The great story of the opening of the Mississippi is but the most striking illustration of an action that was going on incessantly all over the South. At every breach of the sea frontier, war-ships were entering. The streams that had carried the wealth and supported the trade of the seceding States turned against them, and admitted their enemies to their hearts. Dismay, insecurity, paralysis, prevailed in regions that might, under happier auspices, have kept a nation alive through the most exhausting war. Never did sea power play a greater or a more decisive part than in the contest which determined that the course of the world's history would be modified by the existence of one great nation, instead of several rival States, in the North American continent. But while just pride is felt in the well-earned glory of those days, and the greatness of the results due to naval preponderance is admitted, Americans who understand the facts should never fail to remind the over-confidence of their countrymen that the South not only had no navy, not only was not a seafaring people, but that also its population was not proportioned to the extent of the sea-coast which it had to defend.

IV. *Number of Population*

After the consideration of the natural conditions of a country should follow an examination of the characteristics of its population as affecting the development of sea power; and first among these will be taken, because of its relations to the extent of the territory, which has just been discussed, the number of the people who live in it. It has been said that in respect of dimensions it is not merely the number of square miles, but the extent and character of the sea-coast that is to be considered with reference to sea power; and so, in point of population, it is not only the grand total, but the number following the sea, or at least readily available for employment on ship-board and for the creation of naval material, that must be counted.

For example, formerly and up to the end of the great wars following the French Revolution, the population of France was much greater than that of England; but in respect of sea power in general, peaceful commerce as well as military efficiency, France was much inferior to England. In the matter of military efficiency this fact is the more remarkable because at times, in point of military preparation at the outbreak of war, France had the advantage; but she was not able to keep it. Thus in 1778, when war broke out, France, through her maritime inscription, was able to man at once fifty ships-of-the-line. England, on the contrary, by reason of the dispersal over the globe of that very shipping on which her naval strength so securely rested, had much trouble in manning forty at home; but in 1782 she had one hundred and twenty in commission or ready for commission, while France had never been able to exceed seventy-one. Again, as late as 1840, when the two nations were on the verge of war in the Levant, a most accomplished French officer of the day, while extolling the high state of efficiency of the French fleet and the eminent qualities of its admiral, and expressing confidence in the results of an encounter with an equal enemy, goes on to say: "Behind the squadron of twenty-one ships-of-the-line which we could then assemble, there was no reserve; not another ship could have been commissioned within six months." And this was due not only to lack of ships and of proper equipments, though both were wanting. "Our maritime inscription," he continues, "was so exhausted by what we had done [in manning twenty-one ships], that the permanent levy established in all quarters did not supply reliefs for the men, who were already more than three years on cruise."

A contrast such as this shows a difference in what is called staying power, or reserve force, which is even greater than appears on the surface; for a great shipping afloat necessarily employs, besides the crews, a large number of people engaged in the various handicrafts which facilitate the making and repairing of naval material, or following other callings more or less closely connected with the water and with craft of all kinds. Such kindred callings give an undoubted aptitude for the sea from the outset. There is an anecdote showing curious insight into this matter on the part of one of England's distinguished seamen, Sir Edward Pellew. When the war broke out in 1793, the usual scarceness of seamen was met. Eager to get to sea and unable to fill his complement otherwise than with landsmen, he instructed his officers to seek for Cornish miners; reasoning from the conditions and dangers of their calling, of which he had personal knowledge, that they would quickly fit into the demands of sea life. The result showed his sagacity, for, thus escaping an otherwise unavoidable delay, he was fortunate enough to capture the first frigate taken in the war in single combat; and what is especially instructive is, that although but a few weeks in commission, while his opponent had been over a year, the losses, heavy on both sides, were nearly equal.

It may be urged that such reserve strength has now nearly lost the importance it once had, because modern ships and weapons take so long to make, and because modern States aim at developing the whole power of their armed force, on the outbreak of war, with such rapidity as to strike a disabling blow before the enemy can organize an equal effort. To use a familiar phrase, there will not be time for the whole resistance of the national fabric to come into play; the blow will fall on the organized military fleet, and if that yield, the solidity of the rest of the structure will avail nothing. To a certain extent this is true; but then it has always been true, though to a less extent formerly than now. Granted the meeting of two fleets which represent practically the whole present strength of their two nations, if one of them be destroyed, while the other remains fit for action, there will be much less hope now than formerly that the vanquished can restore his navy for that war; and the result will be disastrous just in proportion to the dependence of the nation upon her sea power. A Trafalgar would have been a much more fatal blow to England than it was to France, had the English fleet then represented, as the allied fleet did, the bulk of the nation's power. Trafalgar in such a case would have been to England what Austerlitz was to Austria, and Jena to Prussia; an empire would have been laid prostrate by the destruction or disorganization of its military forces, which, it is said, were the favorite objective of Napoleon.

But does the consideration of such exceptional disasters in the past justify the putting a low value upon that reserve strength, based upon the number of inhabitants fitted for a certain kind of military life, which is here being considered? The blows just mentioned were dealt by men of exceptional genius, at the head of armed bodies of exceptional training, *esprit-de-corps,* and prestige, and were, besides, inflicted upon opponents more or less demoralized by conscious inferiority and previous defeat. Austerlitz had been closely preceded by Ulm, where thirty thousand Austrians laid down their arms without a battle; and the history of the previous years had been one long record of Austrian reverse and French success. Trafalgar followed closely upon a cruise, justly called a campaign, of almost constant failure; and farther back, but still recent, were the memories of St. Vincent for the Spaniards, and of the Nile for the French, in the allied fleet. Except the case of Jena, these crushing overthrows were not single disasters, but final blows; and in the Jena campaign there was a disparity in numbers, equipment, and general preparation for war, which makes it less applicable in considering what may result from a single victory.

England is at the present time the greatest maritime nation in the world; in steam and iron she has kept the superiority she had in the days of sail and wood. France and England are the two powers that have the largest military navies; and it is so far an open question which of the two is the more powerful, that they may be regarded as practically of equal strength, in material for a sea war. In the case of a collision can there be assumed such a difference of *personnel,* or of preparation, as to make it probable that a decisive inequality will result from one battle or one campaign? If not, the reserve strength will begin to tell; organized reserve first, then reserve of seafaring population, reserve of mechanical skill, reserve of wealth. It seems to have been somewhat forgotten that England's leadership in mechanical arts gives her a reserve of mechanics, who can easily familiarize themselves with the

appliances of modern iron-clads; and as her commerce and industries feel the burden of the war, the surplus of seamen and
mechanics will go to the armed shipping.

The whole question of the value of a reserve, developed or
undeveloped, amounts now to this: Have modern conditions of
warfare made it probable that, of two nearly equal adversaries,
one will be so prostrated in a single campaign that a decisive
result will be reached in that time? Sea warfare has given no
answer. The crushing successes of Prussia against Austria, and of
Germany against France, appear to have been those of a stronger
over a much weaker nation, whether the weakness were due to
natural causes, or to official incompetency. How would a delay
like that of Plevna have affected the fortune of war, had Turkey
had any reserve of national power upon which to call?

If time be, as is everywhere admitted, a supreme factor in war,
it behooves countries whose genius is essentially not military,
whose people, like all free people, object to pay for large military
establishments, to see to it that they are at least strong enough to
gain the time necessary to turn the spirit and capacity of their
subjects into the new activities which war calls for. If the existing
force by land or sea is strong enough so to hold out, even though
at a disadvantage, the country may rely upon its natural resources
and strength coming into play for whatever they are worth—its
numbers, its wealth, its capacities of every kind. If, on the other
hand, what force it has can be overthrown and crushed quickly,
the most magnificent possibilities of natural power will not save it
from humiliating conditions, nor, if its foe be wise, from guaran-
tees which will postpone revenge to a distant future. The story is
constantly repeated on the smaller fields of war: "If so-and-so can
hold out a little longer, this can be saved or that can be done;" as
in sickness it is often said: "If the patient can only hold out so
long, the strength of his constitution may pull him through."

England to some extent is now such a country. Holland was
such a country; she would not pay, and if she escaped, it was but

by the skin of her teeth. "Never in time of peace and from fear of a rupture," wrote their great statesman, De Witt, "will they take resolutions strong enough to lead them to pecuniary sacrifices beforehand. The character of the Dutch is such that, unless danger stares them in the face, they are indisposed to lay out money for their own defence. I have to do with a people who, liberal to profusion where they ought to economize, are often sparing to avarice where they ought to spend."

That our own country is open to the same reproach, is patent to all the world. The United States has not that shield of defensive power behind which time can be gained to develop its reserve of strength. As for a seafaring population adequate to her possible needs, where is it? Such a resource, proportionate to her coast-line and population, is to be found only in a national merchant shipping and its related industries, which at present scarcely exist. It will matter little whether the crews of such ships are native or foreign born, provided they are attached to the flag, and her power at sea is sufficient to enable the most of them to get back in case of war. When foreigners by thousands are admitted to the ballot, it is of little moment that they are given fighting-room on board ship.

Though the treatment of the subject has been somewhat discursive, it may be admitted that a great population following callings related to the sea is, now as formerly, a great element of sea power; that the United States is deficient in that element; and that its foundations can be laid only in a large commerce under her own flag.

V. *National Character*

The effect of national character and aptitudes upon the development of sea power will next be considered.

If sea power be really based upon a peaceful and extensive commerce, aptitude for commercial pursuits must be a distinguishing feature of the nations that have at one time or another been great upon the sea. History almost without exception affirms that this is true. Save the Romans, there is no marked instance to the contrary.

All men seek gain and, more or less, love money; but the way in which gain is sought will have a marked effect upon the commercial fortunes and the history of the people inhabiting a country.

If history may be believed, the way in which the Spaniards and their kindred nation, the Portuguese, sought wealth, not only brought a blot upon the national character, but was also fatal to the growth of a healthy commerce and so to the industries upon which commerce lives, and ultimately to that national wealth which was sought by mistaken paths. The desire for gain rose in them to fierce avarice; so they sought in the new-found worlds which gave such an impetus to the commercial and maritime development of the countries of Europe, not new fields of industry, not even the healthy excitement of exploration and adventure, but gold and silver. They had many great qualities; they were bold, enterprising, temperate, patient of suffering, enthusiastic, and gifted with intense national feeling. When to these qualities are added the advantages of Spain's position and well-situated ports, the fact that she was first to occupy large and rich portions of the new worlds and long remained without a competitor, and that for a hundred years after the discovery of America she was the leading State in Europe, she might have been expected to take the foremost place among the sea powers. Exactly the contrary was the result, as all know. Since the battle of Lepanto in 1571, though engaged in many wars, no sea victory of any consequence shines on the pages of Spanish history; and the decay of her commerce sufficiently accounts for the painful and sometimes ludicrous inaptness shown on the decks of her ships of war. Doubtless such a result is not to be attributed to one cause only. Doubtless the government of Spain was in many ways such as to cramp and blight a free and healthy development of private enterprise; but the character of a great people breaks through or shapes the character of its government, and it can hardly be doubted that had the bent of the people been toward trade, the action of government would have been drawn into the same current. The great field of the colonies, also, was remote from the centre of that despotism which blighted the growth of old Spain. As it was, thousands of Spaniards, of the working as well as the upper classes, left Spain; and the occupations in which they engaged abroad sent home little but specie, or merchandise of small bulk, requiring but small tonnage. The mother-country herself produced little but wool, fruit, and iron; her manufactures were naught; her industries suffered; her population steadily decreased. Both she and her colonies depended upon the Dutch for so many of the necessaries of life, that the products of their scanty industries could not suffice to pay for them. "So that Holland merchants," writes a contemporary, "who carry money to most parts of the world to buy commodities, must out of this single country of Europe carry home money, which they receive in payment of their goods." Thus their eagerly sought emblem of wealth passed quickly from their hands. It has already been pointed out how weak, from a military point of view, Spain was from this decay of her shipping. Her wealth being in small bulk on a few ships, following more or less regular routes, was easily seized by an enemy, and the sinews of war paralyzed; whereas the wealth of England and Holland, scattered over thousands of ships in all parts of the world, received many bitter blows in many exhausting wars, without checking a growth which, though painful, was steady. The fortunes of Portugal, united to Spain during a most critical period of her history, followed the same downward path although foremost in the beginning of the race for development by sea, she fell utterly behind. "The mines of Brazil were the ruin of Portugal, as those of Mexico and Peru had been of Spain; all manufactures fell into insane contempt; ere long the English

supplied the Portuguese not only with clothes, but with all merchandise, all commodities, even to salt-fish and grain. After their
gold, the Portuguese abandoned their very soil; the vineyards of
Oporto were finally bought by the English with Brazilian gold,
which had only passed through Portugal to be spread throughout
England." We are assured that in fifty years, five hundred millions of dollars were extracted from "the mines of Brazil, and
that at the end of the time Portugal had but twenty-five millions
in specie,"—a striking example of the difference between real
and fictitious wealth.

The English and Dutch were no less desirous of gain than the
southern nations. Each in turn has been called "a nation of
shopkeepers;" but the jeer, in so far as it is just, is to the credit
of their wisdom and uprightness. They were no less bold, no less
enterprising, no less patient. Indeed, they were more patient, in
that they sought riches not by the sword but by labor, which is
the reproach meant to be implied by the epithet; for thus they
took the longest, instead of what seemed the shortest, road to
wealth. But these two peoples, radically of the same race, had
other qualities, no less important than those just named, which
combined with their surroundings to favor their development by
sea. They were by nature business-men, traders, producers,
negotiators. Therefore both in their native country and abroad,
whether settled in the ports of civilized nations, or of barbarous
eastern rulers, or in colonies of their own foundation, they
everywhere strove to draw out all the resources of the land, to
develop and increase them. The quick instinct of the born
trader, shopkeeper if you will, sought continually new articles to
exchange; and this search, combined with the industrious
character evolved through generations of labor, made them
necessarily producers. At home they became great as manufacturers; abroad, where they controlled, the land grew richer continually, products multiplied, and the necessary exchange
between home and the settlements called for more ships. Their

shipping therefore increased with these demands of trade, and nations with less aptitude for maritime enterprise, even France herself, great as she has been, called for their products and for the service of their ships. Thus in many ways they advanced to power at sea. This natural tendency and growth were indeed modified and seriously checked at times by the interference of other governments, jealous of a prosperity which their own people could invade only by the aid of artificial support,—a support which will be considered under the head of governmental action as affecting sea power.

The tendency to trade, involving of necessity the production of something to trade with, is the national characteristic most important to the development of sea power. Granting it and a good seaboard, it is not likely that the dangers of the sea, or any aversion to it, will deter a people from seeking wealth by the paths of ocean commerce. Where wealth is sought by other means, it may be found; but it will not necessarily lead to sea power. Take France. France has a fine country, an industrious people, an admirable position. The French navy has known periods of great glory, and in its lowest estate has never dishonored the military reputation so dear to the nation. Yet as a maritime State, securely resting upon a broad basis of sea commerce, France, as compared with other historical sea-peoples, has never held more than a respectable position. The chief reason for this, so far as national character goes, is the way in which wealth is sought. As Spain and Portugal sought it by digging gold out of the ground, the temper of the French people leads them to seek it by thrift, economy, hoarding. It is said to be harder to keep than to make a fortune. Possibly; but the adventurous temper, which risks what it has to gain more, has much in common with the adventurous spirit that conquers worlds for commerce. The tendency to save and put aside, to venture timidly and on a small scale, may lead to a general diffusion of wealth on a like small scale, but not to the risks and development of external trade and shipping interests. To illustrate—and the incident is given only for what it is worth—a French officer, speaking to the author about the Panama Canal, said: "I have two shares in it. In France we don't do as you, where a few people take a great many shares each. With us a large number of people take one share or a very few. When these were in the market my wife said to me, 'You take two shares, one for you and one for me.'" As regards the stability of a man's personal fortunes this kind of prudence is doubtless wise; but when excessive prudence or financial timidity becomes a national trait, it must tend to hamper the expansion of commerce and of the nation's shipping. The same caution in money matters, appearing in another relation of life, has checked the production of children, and keeps the population of France nearly stationary.

The noble classes of Europe inherited from the Middle Ages a supercilious contempt for peaceful trade, which has exercised a modifying influence upon its growth, according to the national character of different countries. The pride of the Spaniards fell easily in with this spirit of contempt, and cooperated with that disastrous unwillingness to work and wait for wealth which turned them away from commerce. In France, the vanity which is conceded even by Frenchmen to be a national trait led in the same direction. The numbers and brilliancy of the nobility, and the consideration enjoyed by them, set a seal of inferiority upon an occupation which they despised. Rich merchants and manufacturers sighed for the honors of nobility, and upon obtaining them, abandoned their lucrative professions. Therefore, while the industry of the people and the fruitfulness of the soil saved commerce from total decay, it was pursued under a sense of humiliation which caused its best representatives to escape from it as soon as they could. Louis XIV, under the influence of Colbert, put forth an ordinance "authorizing all noblemen to take an interest in merchant ships, goods and merchandise, without being considered as having derogated from nobility, provided they did not sell at retail;" and the reason given for this action was, "that it imports the good of our subjects and our own satisfaction, to efface the relic of a public opinion, universally prevalent, that maritime commerce is incompatible with nobility." But a prejudice involving conscious and open superiority is not readily effaced by ordinances, especially when vanity is a conspicuous trait in national character; and many years later Montesquieu taught that it is contrary to the spirit of monarchy that the nobility should engage in trade.

In Holland there was a nobility; but the State was republican in name, allowed large scope to personal freedom and enterprise, and the centres of power were in the great cities. The foundation of the national greatness was money—or rather wealth. Wealth, as a source of civic distinction, carried with it also power in the State; and with power there went social position and consideration. In England the same result obtained. The nobility were proud; but in a representative government the power of wealth could be neither put down nor overshadowed. It was patent to the eyes of all it was honored by all; and in England, as well as Holland, the occupations which were the source of wealth shared in the honor given to wealth itself. Thus, in all the countries named, social sentiment, the outcome of national characteristics, had a marked influence upon the national attitude toward trade.

In yet another way does the national genius affect the growth of sea power in its broadest sense; and that is in so far as it possesses the capacity for planting healthy colonies. Of colonization, as of all other growths, it is true that it is most healthy when it is most natural. Therefore colonies that spring from the felt wants and natural impulses of a whole people will have the most solid foundations; and their subsequent growth will be surest when they are least trammelled from home, if the people have the genius for independent action. Men of the past three centuries have keenly felt the value to the mother-country of colonies as outlets for the home products and as a nurser for commerce and shipping; but efforts at colonization have not had the same general origin, nor have different systems all had the same success. The efforts of statesmen, however far-seeing and careful, have not been able to supply the lack of strong natural impulse; nor can the most minute regulation from home produce as good results as a happier neglect, when the germ of self-development is found in the national character. There has been no greater display of wisdom in the national administration of successful colonies than in that of unsuccessful. Perhaps there has been even less. If elaborate system and supervision, careful adaptation of means to ends, diligent nursing, could avail for colonial growth, the genius of England has less of this systematizing faculty than the genius of France; but England, not France, has been the great colonizer of the world. Successful colonization, with its consequent effect upon commerce and sea power, depends essentially upon national character; because colonies grow best when they grow of themselves, naturally. The character of the colonist, not the care of the home government, is the principle of the colony's growth.

This truth stands out the clearer because the general attitude of all the home governments toward their colonies was entirely selfish. However founded, as soon as it was recognized to be of consequence, the colony became to the home country a cow to be milked; to be cared for, of course, but chiefly as a piece of property valued for the returns it gave. Legislation was directed toward a monopoly of its external trade; the places in its government afforded posts of value for occupants from the mother-country; and the colony was looked upon, as the sea still so often is, as a fit place for those who were ungovernable or useless at home. The military administration, however, so long as it remains a colony, is the proper and necessary attribute of the home government.

The fact of England's unique and wonderful success as a great colonizing nation is too evident to be dwelt upon; and the reason for it appears to lie chiefly in two traits of the national character. The English colonist naturally and readily settles down in his new country, identifies his interest with it, and though keeping an affectionate remembrance of the home from which he came, has no restless eagerness to return. In the second place, the Englishman at once and instinctively seeks to develop the resources of the new country in the broadest sense. In the former particular he differs from the French, who were ever longingly looking back to the delights of their pleasant land; in the latter, from the Spaniards, whose range of interest and ambition was too narrow for the full evolution of the possibilities of a new country.

The character and the necessities of the Dutch led them naturally to plant colonies; and by the year 1650 they had in the East Indies, in Africa, and in America a large number, only to name which would be tedious. They were then far ahead of England in this matter. But though the origin of these colonies, purely commercial in its character, was natural, there seems to have been lacking to them a principle of growth. "In planting them they never sought an extension of empire, but merely an acquisition of trade and commerce. They attempted conquest only when forced by the pressure of circumstances. Generally they were content to trade under the protection of the sovereign of the country." This placid satisfaction with gain alone, unaccompanied by political ambition, tended, like the despotism of France and Spain, to keep the colonies mere commercial dependencies upon the mother-country, and so killed the natural principle of growth.

Before quitting this head of the inquiry, it is well to ask how far the national character of Americans is fitted to develop a great sea power, should other circumstances become favorable.

It seems scarcely necessary, however, to do more than appeal to a not very distant past to prove that, if legislative hindrances be removed, and more remunerative fields of enterprise filled up, the sea power will not long delay its appearance. The instinct for commerce, bold enterprise in the pursuit of gain, and a keen scent for the trails that lead to it, all exist; and if there be in the future any fields calling for colonization, it cannot be doubted that Americans will carry to them all their inherited aptitude for self-government and independent growth.

VI. *Character of the Government*

In discussing the effects upon the development of a nation's sea power exerted by its government and institutions, it will be necessary to avoid a tendency to over-philosophizing, to confine attention to obvious and immediate causes and their plain results, without prying too far beneath the surface for remote and ultimate influences.

Nevertheless, it must be noted that particular forms of government with their accompanying institutions, and the character of rulers at one time or another, have exercised a very marked influence upon the development of sea power. The various traits of a country and its people which have so far been considered constitute the natural characteristics with which a nation, like a man, begins its career; the conduct of the government in turn corresponds to the exercise of the intelligent will-power, which, according as it is wise, energetic and persevering, or the reverse, causes success or failure in a man's life or a nation's history.

It would seem probable that a government in full accord with the natural bias of its people would most successfully advance its growth in every respect; and, in the matter of sea power, the most brilliant successes have followed where there has been intelligent direction by a government fully imbued with the spirit of the people and conscious of its true general bent. Such a government is most certainly secured when the will of the people, or of their best natural exponents, has some large share in making it; but such free governments have sometimes fallen short, while on the other hand despotic power, wielded with judgment and consistency, has created at times a great sea commerce and a brilliant navy with greater directness than can be reached by the slower processes of a free people. The difficulty in the latter case is to insure perseverance after the death of a particular despot.

England having undoubtedly reached the greatest height of sea power of any modern nation, the action of her government first claims attention. In general direction this action has been consistent, though often far from praiseworthy. It has aimed steadily at the control of the sea. One of its most arrogant expressions dates back as far as the reign of James I, when she had scarce any possessions outside her own islands; before Virginia or Massachusetts was settled. Here is Richelieu's account of it:—

> "The Duke of Sully, minister of Henry IV [one of the most chivalrous princes that ever lived], having embarked at Calais in a French ship wearing the French flag at the main, was no sooner in the Channel than, meeting an English despatch-boat which was there to receive him, the commander of the latter ordered the French ship to lower her flag. The Duke, considering that his quality freed him from such an affront, boldly refused; but this refusal was followed by three cannon-shot, which, piercing his ship, pierced the heart likewise of all good Frenchmen. Might forced him to yield what right forbade, and for all the complaints he made he could get no better reply

from the English captain than this: 'That just as his
duty obliged him to honor the ambassador's rank, it
also obliged him to exact the honor due to the flag of
his master as sovereign of the sea.' If the words of King
James himself were more polite, they nevertheless had
no other effect than to compel the Duke to take coun-
sel of his prudence, feigning to be satisfied, while his
wound was all the time smarting and incurable. Henry
the Great had to practise moderation on this occasion;
but with the resolve another time to sustain the rights
of his crown by the force that, with the aid of time, he
should be able to put upon the sea."

This act of unpardonable insolence, according to modern
ideas, was not so much out of accord with the spirit of nations in
that day. It is chiefly noteworthy as the most striking, as well as
one of the earliest indications of the purpose of England to assert
herself at all risks upon the sea; and the insult was offered under
one of her most timid kings to an ambassador immediately representing the bravest and ablest of French sovereigns. This empty
honor of the flag, a claim insignificant except as the outward
manifestation of the purpose of a government, was as rigidly
exacted under Cromwell as under the kings. It was one of the
conditions of peace yielded by the Dutch after their disastrous
war of 1654. Cromwell, a despot in everything but name, was
keenly alive to all that concerned England's honor and strength,
and did not stop at barren salutes to promote them. Hardly yet
possessed of power, the English navy sprang rapidly into a new
life and vigor under his stern rule. England's rights, or reparation
for her wrongs, were demanded by her fleets throughout the
world—in the Baltic, in the Mediterranean, against the Barbary
States, in the West Indies; and under him the conquest of
Jamaica began that extension of her empire, by force of arms,
which has gone on to our own days. Nor were equally strong

peaceful measures for the growth of English trade and shipping forgotten. Cromwell's celebrated Navigation Act declared that all imports into England or her colonies must be conveyed exclusively in vessels belonging to England herself, or to the country in which the products carried were grown or manufactured. This decree, aimed specially at the Dutch, the common carriers of Europe, was resented throughout the commercial world; but the benefit to England, in those days of national strife and animosity, was so apparent that it lasted long under the monarchy. A century and a quarter later we find Nelson, before his famous career had begun, showing his zeal for the welfare of England's shipping by enforcing this same act in the West Indies against American merchant-ships. When Cromwell was dead, and Charles II sat on the throne of his father, this king, false to the English people, was yet true to England's greatness and to the traditional policy of her government on the sea. In his treacherous intrigues with Louis XIV, by which he aimed to make himself independent of Parliament and people, he wrote to Louis: "There are two impediments to a perfect union. The first is the great care France is now taking to create a commerce and to be an imposing maritime power. This is so great a cause of suspicion with us, who can possess importance only by our commerce and our naval force, that every step which France takes in this direction will perpetuate the jealousy between the two nations." In the midst of the negotiations which preceded the detestable attack of the two kings upon the Dutch republic, a warm dispute arose as to who should command the united fleets of France and England. Charles was inflexible on this point. "It is the custom of the English," said he, "to command at sea;" and he told the French ambassador plainly that, were he to yield, his subjects would not obey him. In the projected partition of the United Provinces he reserved for England the maritime plunder in positions that controlled the mouths of the rivers Scheldt and Meuse. The navy under Charles preserved for some time the spirit and discipline impressed on it by Cromwell's iron rule; though it shared in the general decay of *morale* which marked late this evil reign. Monk, having by a great strategic blunder sent off a fourth of his fleet, found himself in 1666 in presence of a greatly superior Dutch force. Disregarding the odds, he attacked without hesitation, and for three days maintained the fight with honor, though with loss. Such conduct is not war; but in the single eye that looked to England's naval prestige and dictated his action, common as it was to England's people as well as to her government, has lain the secret of final success following many blunders through the centuries. Charles's successor, James II, was himself a seaman, and had commanded in two great sea-fights. When William III came to the throne, the governments of England and Holland were under one hand, and continued united in one purpose against Louis XIV until the Peace of Utrecht in 1713; that is, for a quarter of a century. The English government more and more steadily, and with conscious purpose, pushed on the extension of her sea dominion and fostered the growth of her sea power. While as an open enemy she struck at France upon the sea, so as an artful friend, many at least believed, she sapped the power of Holland afloat. The treaty between the two countries provided that of the sea forces Holland should furnish three eighths, England five eighths, or nearly double. Such a provision, coupled with a further one which made Holland keep up an army of 102,000 against England's 40,000, virtually threw the land war on one and the sea war on the other. The tendency, whether designed or not, is evident; and at the peace, while Holland received compensation by land, England obtained, besides commercial privileges in France, Spain, and the Spanish West Indies, the important maritime concessions of Gibraltar and Port Mahon in the Mediterranean; of Newfoundland, Nova Scotia, and Hudson's Bay in North America. The naval power of France and Spain had disappeared; that of Holland thenceforth steadily declined. Posted thus in America, the West Indies, and the Mediterranean, the English government thenceforth moved firmly forward on the path which made of the English kingdom the British Empire. For the twenty-five years following the Peace of Utrecht, peace was the chief aim of the ministers who directed the policy of the two great seaboard nations, France and England; but amid all the fluctuations of continental politics in a most unsettled period, abounding in petty wars and shifty treaties, the eye of England was steadily fixed on the maintenance of her sea power. In the Baltic, her fleets checked the attempts of Peter the Great upon Sweden, and so maintained a balance of power in that sea, from which she drew not only a great trade but the chief part of her naval stores, and which the Czar aimed to make a Russian lake. Denmark endeavored to establish an East India company aided by foreign capital; England and Holland not only forbade their subjects to join it, but threatened Denmark, and thus stopped an enterprise they thought adverse to their sea interests. In the Netherlands, which by the Utrecht Treaty had passed to Austria, a similar East India company, having Ostend for its port, was formed, with the emperor's sanction. This step, meant to restore to the Low Countries the trade lost to them through their natural outlet of the Scheldt, was opposed by the sea powers England and Holland; and their greediness for the monopoly of trade, helped in this instance by France, stifled this company also after a few years of struggling life. In the Mediterranean, the Utrecht settlement was disturbed by the emperor of Austria, England's natural ally in the then existing state of European politics. Backed by England, he, having already Naples, claimed also Sicily in exchange for Sardinia. Spain resisted; and her navy, just beginning to revive under a vigorous minister, Alberoni, was crushed and annihilated by the English fleet off Cape Passaro in 1718; while the following year a French army, at the bidding of England, crossed the Pyrenees and completed the work by destroying the Spanish dock-yards. Thus England, in addition to Gibraltar and Mahon in her own hands, saw Naples and Sicily in those of a friend, while an enemy was struck down. In Spanish America, the limited privileges to English trade, wrung from the necessities of Spain, were abused by an extensive and scarcely disguised smuggling system; and when the exasperated Spanish government gave way to excesses in the mode of suppression, both the minister who counselled peace and the opposition which urged war defended their opinions by alleging the effects of either upon England's sea power and honor. While England's policy thus steadily aimed at widening and strengthening the bases of her sway upon the ocean, the other governments of Europe seemed blind to the dangers to be feared from her sea growth. The miseries resulting from the overweening power of Spain in days long gone by seemed to be forgotten; forgotten also the more recent lesson of the bloody and costly wars provoked by the ambition and exaggerated power of Louis XIV. Under the eyes of the statesmen of Europe there was steadily and visibly being built up a third overwhelming power, destined to be used as selfishly, as aggressively, though not as cruelly, and much more successfully th n any that had preceded it. This was the power of the sea, whose workings, because more silent than the clash of arms, are less often noted, though lying clearly enough on the surface. It can scarcely be denied that England's uncontrolled dominion of the seas, during almost the whole period chosen for our subject, was by long odds the chief among the military factors that determined the final issue. So far, however, was this influence from being foreseen after Utrecht, that France for twelve years, moved by personal exigencies of her rulers, sided with England against Spain; and when Fleuri came into power in 1726, though this policy was reversed, the navy of France received no attention, and the only blow at England was the establishment of a Bourbon prince, a natural enemy to her, upon the throne of the two Sicilies in 1736. When war broke out with Spain in 1739, the navy of England was in numbers more than equal to the combined navies of Spain and France; and during the quarter of a century of nearly uninterrupted war that followed, this numerical disproportion increased. In these wars England, at first instinctively, afterward with conscious purpose under a government that recognized her opportunity and the possibilities of her great sea power, rapidly built up that mighty colonial empire whose foundations were already securely laid in the characteristics of her colonists and the strength of her fleets. In strictly European affairs her wealth, the outcome of her sea power, made her play a conspicuous part during the same period. The system of subsidies, which began half a century before in the wars of Marlborough and received its most extensive development half a century later in the Napoleonic wars, maintained the efforts of her allies, which would have been crippled, if not paralyzed, without them. Who can deny that the government which with one hand strengthened its fainting allies on the continent with the life-blood of money, and with the other drove its own enemies off the sea and out of their chief possessions, Canada, Martinique, Guadeloupe, Havana, Manila, gave to its country the foremost rôle in European politics; and who can fail to see that the power which dwelt in that government, with a land narrow in extent and poor in resources, sprang directly from the sea? The policy in which the English government carried on the war is shown by a speech of Pitt, the master-spirit during its course, though he lost office before bringing it to an end. Condemning the Peace of 1763, made by his political opponent, he said: "France is chiefly, if not exclusively, formidable to us as a maritime and commercial power. What we gain in this respect is valuable to us, above all, through the injury to her which results from it. You have left to France the possibility of reviving her navy." Yet England's gains were enormous; her rule in India was assured, and all North America east of the Mississippi in her hands. By this time the onward path of her government was clearly marked out, had assumed the force of a tradition, and was consistently followed. The war of the American Revolution was, it is true, a great mistake, looked at from the point of view of sea power; but the government was led into it insensibly by a series of natural blunders. Putting aside political and constitutional considerations, and looking at the question as purely military or naval, the case was this: The American colonies were large and growing communities at a great distance from England. So long as they remained attached to the mother-country, as they then were enthusiastically, they formed a solid base for her sea power in that part of the world; but their extent and population were too great, when coupled with the distance from England, to afford any hope of holding them by force, *if* any powerful nations were willing to help them. This "if," however, involved a notorious probability; the humiliation of France and Spain was so bitter and so recent that they were sure to seek revenge, and it was well known that France in particular had been carefully and rapidly building up her navy. Had the colonies been thirteen islands, the sea power of England would quickly have settled the question; but instead of such a physical barrier they were separated only by local jealousies which a common danger sufficiently overcame. To enter deliberately on such a contest, to try to hold by force so extensive a territory with a large hostile population, so far from home, was to renew the Seven Years' War with France and Spain, and with the Americans, against, instead of for, England. The Seven Years' War had been so heavy a burden that a wise government would have known that the added weight could not be borne, and have seen it was necessary to conciliate the colonists. The government of the day was not wise, and a large element of England's sea power was sacrificed; but by mistake, not wilfully; through arrogance, not through weakness.

This steady keeping to a general line of policy was doubtless made specially easy for successive English governments by the clear indications of the country's conditions. Singleness of purpose was to some extent imposed. The firm maintenance of her sea power, the haughty determination to make it felt, the wise state of preparation in which its military element was kept, were yet more due to that feature of her political institutions which practically gave the government during the period in question, into the hands of a class—a landed aristocracy. Such a class, whatever its defects other wise, readily takes up and carries on a sound political tradition, is naturally proud of its country's glory, and comparatively insensible to the sufferings of the community by which that glory is maintained. It readily lays on the pecuniary burden necessary for preparation and for endurance of war. Being as a body rich, it feels those burdens less. Not being commercial, the sources of its own wealth are not so immediately endangered, and it does not share that political timidity which characterizes those whose property is exposed and business threatened—the proverbial timidity of capital. Yet in England this class was not insensible to anything that touched her trade for good or ill. Both houses of Parliament vied in careful watchfulness over its extension and protection, and to the frequency of their inquiries a naval historian attributes the increased efficiency of the executive power in its management of the navy. Such a class also naturally imbibes and keeps up a spirit of military honor, which is of the first importance in ages when military institutions have not yet provided the sufficient substitute in what is called *esprit-de-corps*. But although full of class feeling and class prejudice, which made themselves felt in the navy as well as elsewhere, their practical sense left open the way of promotion to its highest honors to the more humbly born; and every age saw admirals who had sprung from the lowest of the people. In this the temper of the English upper class differed markedly from that of the French. As late as 1789, at the outbreak of the Revolution, the French Navy List still bore the name of an official whose duty was to verify the proofs of noble birth on the part of those intending to enter the naval school.

Since 1815, and especially in our own day, the government of England has passed very much more into the hands of the people at large. Whether her sea power will suffer therefrom remains to be seen. Its broad basis still remains in a great trade, large mechanical industries, and an extensive colonial system. Whether a democratic government will have the foresight, the keen sensitiveness to national position and credit, the willingness to insure its prosperity by adequate outpouring of money in times of peace, all which are necessary for military preparation, is yet an open question. Popular governments are not generally favorable to military expenditure, however necessary, and there are signs that England tends to drop behind.

It has already been seen that the Dutch Republic, even more than the English nation, drew its prosperity and its very life from the sea. The character and policy of its government were far less favorable to a consistent support of sea power. Composed of seven provinces, with the political name of the United Provinces, the actual distribution of power may be roughly described to Americans as an exaggerated example of States Rights. Each of the maritime provinces had its own fleet and its own admiralty, with consequent jealousies. This disorganizing tendency was partly counteracted by the great preponderance of the Province of Holland, which alone contributed five sixths of the fleet and fifty-eight per cent of the taxes, and consequently had a proportionate share in directing the national policy. Although intensely patriotic, and capable of making the last sacrifices for freedom, the commercial spirit of the people penetrated the government, which indeed might be called a commercial aristocracy, and made it averse to war, and to the expenditures which are necessary in preparing for war. As has before been said, it was not until danger stared them in the face that the burgomasters were willing to pay for their defences. While the republican government lasted, however, this economy was practised least of all upon the fleet; and until the death of John De Witt, in 1672, and the peace with

England in 1674, the Dutch navy was in point of numbers and equipment able to make a fair show against the combined navies of England and France. Its efficiency at this time undoubtedly saved the country from the destruction planned by the two kings. With De Witt's death the republic passed away, and was followed by the practically monarchical government of William of Orange. The life-long policy of this prince, then only eighteen, was resistance to Louis XIV and to the extension of French power. This resistance took shape upon the land rather than the sea—a tendency promoted by England's withdrawal from the war. As early as 1676, Admiral De Ruyter found the force given him unequal to cope with the French alone. With the eyes of the government fixed on the land frontier, the navy rapidly declined. In 1688, when William of Orange needed a fleet to convoy him to England, the burgomasters of Amsterdam objected that the navy was incalculably decreased in strength, as well as deprived of its ablest commanders. When king of England, William still kept his position as stadtholder, and with it his general European policy. He found in England the sea power he needed, and used the resources of Holland for the land war. This Dutch prince consented that in the allied fleets, in councils of war, the Dutch admirals should sit below the junior English captain; and Dutch interests at sea were sacrificed as readily as Dutch pride to the demands of England. When William died, his policy was still followed by the government which succeeded him. Its aims were wholly centred upon the land, and at the Peace of Utrecht, which closed a series of wars extending over forty years, Holland, having established no sea claim, gained nothing in the way of sea resources, of colonial extension, or of commerce.

Of the last of these wars an English historian says: "The economy of the Dutch greatly hurt their reputation and their trade. Their men-of-war in the Mediterranean were always victualled short, and their convoys were so weak and ill-provided that for one ship that we lost, they lost five, which begat a general notion that we were the safer carriers, which certainly had a good effect. Hence it was that our trade rather increased than diminished in this war."

From that time Holland ceased to have a great sea power, and rapidly lost the leading position among the nations which that power had built up. It is only just to say that no policy could have saved from decline this small, though determined, nation, in face of the persistent enmity of Louis XIV. The friendship of France, insuring peace on her landward frontier, would have enabled her, at least for a longer time, to dispute with England the dominion of the seas; and as allies the navies of the two continental States might have checked the growth of the enormous sea power which has just been considered. Sea peace between England and Holland was only possible by the virtual subjection of one or the other, for both aimed at the same object. Between France and Holland it was otherwise; and the fall of Holland proceeded, not necessarily from her inferior size and numbers, but from faulty policy on the part of the two governments. It does not concern us to decide which was the more to blame.

France, admirably situated for the possession of sea power, received a definite policy for the guidance of her government from two great rulers, Henry IV and Richelieu. With certain well-defined projects of extension eastward upon the land were combined a steady resistance to the House of Austria, which then ruled in both Austria and Spain, and an equal purpose of resistance to England upon the sea. To further this latter end, as well as for other reasons, Holland was to be courted as an ally. Commerce and fisheries as the basis of sea power were to be encouraged, and a military navy was to be built up. Richelieu left what he called his political will, in which he pointed out the opportunities of France for achieving sea power, based upon her position and resources; and French writers consider him the virtual founder of the navy, not merely because he equipped ships, but from the breadth of his views and his measures to insure sound institutions, and steady growth. After his death, Mazarin inherited his views and general policy, but not his lofty and martial spirit, and during his rule the newly formed navy disappeared. When Louis XIV took the government into his own hands, in 1661, there were but thirty ships of war, of which only three had as many as sixty guns. Then began a most astonishing manifestation of the work which can be done by absolute government ably and systematically wielded. That part of the administration which dealt with trade, manufactures, shipping, and colonies, was given to a man of great practical genius, Colbert, who had served with Richelieu and had drunk in fully his ideas and policy. He pursued his aims in a spirit thoroughly French. Everything was to be organized, the spring of everything was in the minister's cabinet. "To organize producers and merchants as a powerful army, subjected to an active and intelligent guidance, so as to secure an industrial victory for France by order and unity of efforts, and to obtain the best products by imposing on all workmen the processes recognized as best by competent men. . . . To organize seamen and distant commerce in large bodies like the manufactures and internal commerce, and to give as a support to the commercial power of France a navy established on a firm basis and of dimensions hitherto unknown,"—such, we are told, were the aims of Colbert as regards two of the three links in the chain of sea power. For the third, the colonies at the far end of the line, the same governmental direction and organization were evidently purposed; for the government began by buying back Canada, Newfoundland, Nova Scotia, and the French West India Islands from the parties who then owned them. Here, then, is seen pure, absolute, uncontrolled power gathering up into its hands all the reins for the guidance of a nation's course, and proposing so to direct it as to make, among other things, a great sea power.

To enter into the details of Colbert's action is beyond our purpose. It is enough to note the chief part played by the government in building up the sea power of the State, and that this very great man looked not to any one of the bases on which it rests to the exclusion of the others, but embraced them all in his wise and provident administration. Agriculture, which increases the products of the earth, and manufactures, which multiply the products of man's industry; internal trade routes and regulations, by which the exchange of products from the interior to the exterior is made easier; shipping and customs regulations tending to throw the carrying trade into French hands, and so to encourage the building of French shipping, by which the home and colonial products should be carried back and forth; colonial administration and development, by which a far-off market might be continually growing up to be monopolized by the home trade; treaties with foreign States favoring French trade, and imposts on foreign ships and products tending to break down that of rival nations—all these means, embracing countless details, were employed to build up for France (1) Production; (2) Shipping; (3) Colonies and Markets—in a word, sea power. The study of such a work is simpler and easier when thus done by one man, sketched out by a kind of logical process, than when slowly wrought by conflicting interests in a more complex government. In the few years of Colbert's administration is seen the whole theory of sea power put into practice in the systematic, centralizing French way; while the illustration of the same theory in English and Dutch history is spread over generations. Such growth, however, was forced, and depended upon the endurance of the absolute power which watched over it; and as Colbert was not king, his control lasted only till he lost the king's favor. It is, however, most interesting to note the results of his labors in the proper field for governmental action—in the navy. It has been said that in 1661, when he took office, there were but thirty armed ships, of which three only had over sixty guns. In 1666 there were seventy, of which fifty were ships of the line and twenty were fire-ships; in 1671, from seventy the number had increased to one hundred and ninety-six. In 1683 there were one hundred and seven ships of from twenty-four to one hundred and twenty guns, twelve of which carried over seventy-six guns, besides many smaller vessels. The order and system introduced into the dock-yards made them vastly more efficient than the English. An English captain, a prisoner in France while the effect of Colbert's work still lasted in the hands of his son, writes:—

"When I was first brought prisoner thither, I lay four months in a hospital at Brest for care of my wounds. While there I was astonished at the expedition used in manning and fitting out their ships, which till then I thought could be done nowhere sooner than in England, where we have ten times the shipping, and consequently ten times the seamen, they have in France; but there I saw twenty sail of ships, of about sixty guns each, got ready in twenty days' time; they were brought in and the men were discharged; and upon an order from Paris they were careened, keeled up, rigged, victualled, manned, and out again in the said time with the greatest ease imaginable. I likewise saw a ship of one hundred guns that had all her guns taken out in four or five hours' time; which I never saw done in England in twenty-four hours, and this with the greatest ease and less hazard than at home. This I saw under my hospital window."

A French naval historian cites certain performances which are simply incredible, such as that the keel of a galley was laid at four o'clock, and that at nine she left port, fully armed. These traditions may be accepted as pointing, with the more serious statements of the English officer, to a remarkable degree of system and order, and abundant facilities for work.

Yet all this wonderful growth, forced by the action of the government, withered away like Jonah's gourd when the government's favor was withdrawn. Time was not allowed for its roots to strike down deep into the life of the nation. Colbert's work was in the direct line of Richelieu's policy, and for a time it seemed there would continue the course of action which would make France great upon the sea as well as predominant upon the land. For reasons which it is not yet necessary to give, Louis came to have feelings of bitter enmity against Holland; and as these feelings were shared by Charles II, the two kings determined on the destruction of the United Provinces. This war, which broke out in 1672, though more contrary to natural feeling on the part of England, was less of a political mistake for her than for France, and especially as regards sea power. France was helping to destroy a probable, and certainly an indispensable, ally; England was assisting in the ruin of her greatest rival on the sea, at this time, indeed, still her commercial superior. France, staggering under debt and utter confusion in her finances when Louis mounted the throne, was just seeing her way clear in 1672, under Colbert's reforms and their happy results. The war, lasting six years, undid the greater part of his work. The agricultural classes, manufactures, commerce, and the colonies, all were smitten by it; the establishments of Colbert languished, and the order he had established in the finances was overthrown. Thus the action of Louis—and he alone was the directing government of France—struck at the roots of her sea power, and alienated her best sea ally. The territory and the military power of France were increased, but the springs of commerce and of a peaceful shipping had been exhausted in the process; and although the military navy was for some years kept up with splendor and efficiency, it soon began to dwindle, and by the end of the reign had practically disappeared. The same false policy, as regards the sea, marked the rest of this reign of fifty-four years. Louis steadily turned his back upon the sea interests of France, except the fighting-ships, and either could not or would not see that the latter were of little use and uncertain life, if the peaceful shipping and the industries, by which they were supported, perished. His policy, aiming at supreme power in Europe by military strength and territorial extension, forced England and Holland into an alliance, which, as has before been said, directly drove France off the sea, and indirectly swamped Holland's power thereon. Colbert's navy perished, and for the last ten years of Louis' life no great French fleet put to sea, though there was constant war. The simplicity of form in an absolute monarchy thus brought out strongly how great the influence of government can be upon both the growth and the decay of sea power.

The latter part of Louis' life thus witnessed that power failing by the weakening of its foundations, of commerce, and of the wealth that commerce brings. The government that followed, likewise absolute, of set purpose and at the demand of England, gave up all pretence of maintaining an effective navy. The reason for this was that the new king was a minor; and the regent, being bitterly at enmity with the king of Spain, to injure him and preserve his own power, entered into alliance with England. He aided her to establish Austria, the hereditary enemy of France, in Naples and Sicily to the detriment of Spain, and in union with her destroyed the Spanish navy and dock-yards. Here again found a personal ruler disregarding the sea interests of France, ruining a natural ally, and directly aiding, as Louis XIV indirectly and unintentionally aided, the growth of a mistress of the seas. This transient phase of policy passed away with the death of the regent in 1726; but from that time until 1760 the government of France continued to disregard her maritime interests. It is said, indeed, that owing to some wise modifications of her fiscal regulations, mainly in the direction of free trade (and due to Law, a minister of Scotch birth), commerce with the East and West Indies wonderfully increased, and that the islands of Guadeloupe and Martinique became very rich and thriving; but both commerce and colonies lay at the mercy of England when war came, for the navy fell into decay. In 1766, when things were no longer at their worst, France had but forty-five ships-of-the-line, England nearly one hundred and thirty; and when the forty-five were to be armed and equipped, there was found to be neither material nor rigging nor supplies; not even enough artillery. Nor was this all.

"Lack of system in the government," says a French writer, "brought about indifference, and opened the door to disorder and lack of discipline. Never had unjust promotions been so frequent; so also never had more universal discontent been seen. Money and intrigue took the place of all else, and brought in their train commands and power. Nobles and upstarts, with influence at the capital and self-sufficiency in the seaports, thought themselves dispensed with merit. Waste of the revenues of the State and of the dock-yards knew no bounds. Honor and modesty were turned into ridicule. As if the evils were not thus great enough, the ministry took pains to efface the heroic traditions of the past which had escaped the general wreck. To the energetic fights of the great reign succeeded, by order of the court, 'affairs of circumspection.' To preserve to the wasted material a few armed ships, increased opportunity was given to the enemy. From this unhappy principle we were bound to a defensive as advantageous to the enemy as it was foreign to the genius of our people. This circumspection before the enemy, laid down for us by orders, betrayed in the long run the national temper; and the abuse of the system led to acts of indiscipline and defection under fire, of which a single instance would vainly be sought in the previous century."

A false policy of continental extension swallowed up the resources of the country, and was doubly injurious because, by leaving defenceless its colonies and commerce, it exposed the greatest source of wealth to be cut off, as in fact happened. The small squadrons that got to sea were destroyed by vastly superior force; the merchant shipping was swept away, and the colonies, Canada, Martinique, Guadeloupe, India, fell into England's hands. If it did not take too much space, interesting extracts might be made, showing the woeful misery of France, the country that had abandoned the sea, and the growing wealth of England amid all her sacrifices and exertions. A contemporary writer has thus expressed his view of the policy of France at this period:—

> "France, by engaging so heartily as she has done in the German war, has drawn away so much of her attention and her revenue from her navy that it enabled us to give such a blow to her maritime strength as possibly she may never be able to recover. Her engagement in the German war has likewise drawn her from the defence of her colonies, by which means we have conquered some of the most considerable she possessed. It has withdrawn her from the protection of her trade, by which it is entirely destroyed, while that of England has never, in the profoundest peace, been in so flourishing a condition. So that, by embarking in this German war, France has suffered herself to be undone, so far as regards her particular and immediate quarrel with England."

In the Seven Years' War France lost thirty-seven ships-of-the-line and fifty-six frigates—a force three times as numerous as the whole navy of the United States at any time in the days of sailing-ships. "For the first time since the Middle Ages," says a

French historian, speaking of the same war, "England had conquered France single-handed, almost without allies, France having powerful auxiliaries. She had conquered solely by the
superiority of her government." Yes; but it was by the superiority
of her government using the tremendous weapon of her sea
power—the reward of a consistent policy perseveringly directed
to one aim.

The profound humiliation of France, which reached its depths
between 1760 and 1763, at which latter date she made peace, has
an instructive lesson for the United States in this our period of
commercial and naval decadence. We have been spared her
humiliation; let us hope to profit by her subsequent example.
Between the same years (1760 and 1763) the French people rose,
as afterward in 1793, and declared they would have a navy. "Popular feeling, skilfully directed by the government, took up the cry
from one end of France to the other, 'The navy must be
restored!' Gifts of ships were made by cities, by corporations, and
by private subscriptions. A prodigious activity sprang up in the
lately silent ports; everywhere ships were building or repairing."
This activity was sustained; the arsenals were replenished, the
material of every kind was put on a satisfactory footing, the
artillery reorganized, and ten thousand trained gunners drilled
and maintained.

The tone and action of the naval officers of the day instantly
felt the popular impulse, for which indeed some loftier spirits
among them had been not only waiting but working. At no time
was greater mental and professional activity found among
French naval officers than just then, when their ships had been
suffered to rot away by governmental inaction. Thus a prominent French officer of our own day writes:—

> "The sad condition of the navy in the reign of Louis
> XV, by closing to officers the brilliant career of bold
> enterprises and successful battles, forced them to fall

back upon themselves. They drew from study the knowledge they were to put to the proof some years later, thus putting into practice that fine saying of Montesquieu, 'Adversity is our mother, Prosperity our step-mother.' . . . By the year 1769 was seen in all its splendor that brilliant galaxy of officers whose activity stretched to the ends of the earth, and who embraced in their works and in their investigations all the branches of human knowledge. The Académie de Marine, founded in 1752, was reorganized."[1]

The Académie's first director, a post-captain named Bigot de Morogues, wrote an elaborate treatise on naval tactics, the first original work on the subject since Paul Hoste's, which it was designed to supersede. Morogues must have been studying and formulating his problems in tactics in days when France had no fleet, and was unable so much as to raise her head at sea under the blows of her enemy. At the same time England had no similar book; and an English lieutenant, in 1762, was just translating a part of Hoste's great work, omitting by far the larger part. It was not until nearly twenty years later that Clerk, a Scotch private gentleman, published an ingenious study of naval tactics, in which he pointed out to English admirals the system by which the French had thwarted their thoughtless and ill-combined attacks. "The researches of the Académie de Marine, and the energetic impulse which it gave to the labors of officers, were not, as we hope to show later, without influence upon the relatively prosperous condition in which the navy was at the beginning of the American war."

It has already been pointed out that the American War of Independence involved a departure from England's traditional

---

[1] Gougeard: La Marine de Guerre; Richelieu et Colbert.

and true policy, by committing her to a distant land war, while powerful enemies were waiting for an opportunity to attack her at sea. Like France in the then recent German wars, like Napoleon later in the Spanish war, England, through undue self-confidence, was about to turn a friend into an enemy, and so expose the real basis of her power to a rude proof. The French government, on the other hand, avoided the snare into which it had so often fallen. Turning her back on the European continent, having the probability of neutrality there, and the certainty of alliance with Spain by her side, France advanced to the contest with a fine navy and a brilliant, though perhaps relatively inexperienced, body of officers. On the other side of the Atlantic she had the support of a friendly people, and of her own or allied ports, both in the West Indies and on the continent. The wisdom of this policy, the happy influence of this action of the government upon her sea power, is evident; but the details of the war do not belong to this part of the subject. To Americans, the chief interest of that war is found upon the land; but to naval officers upon the sea, for it was essentially a sea war. The intelligent and systematic efforts of twenty years bore their due fruit; for though the warfare afloat ended with a great disaster, the combined efforts of the French and Spanish fleets undoubtedly bore down England's strength and robbed her of her colonies. In the various naval undertakings and battles the honor of France was upon the whole maintained; though it is difficult, upon consideration of the general subject, to avoid the conclusion that the inexperience of French seamen as compared with English, the narrow spirit of jealousy shown by the noble corps of officers toward those of different antecedents, and above all, the miserable traditions of three quarters of a century already alluded to, the miserable policy of a government which taught them first to save their ships, to economize the material, prevented French admirals from reaping, not the mere glory, but the positive advantages that more than once were within their grasp. When Monk said the nation that would rule upon the sea must always attack, he set the keynote to England's naval policy; and had the instructions of the French government consistently breathed the same spirit, the war of 1778 might have ended sooner and better than it did. It seems ungracious to criticise the conduct of a service to which, under God, our nation owes that its birth was not a miscarriage; but writers of its own country abundantly reflect the spirit of the remark. A French officer who served afloat during this war, in a work of calm and judicial tone, says:

> "What must the young officers have thought who were at Sandy Hook with D'Estaing, at St. Christopher with De Grasse, even those who arrived at Rhode Island with De Ternay, when they saw that these officers were not tried at their return?"[1]

Again, another French officer, of much later date, justifies the opinion expressed, when speaking of the war of the American Revolution in the following terms:

> "It was necessary to get rid of the unhappy prejudices of the days of the regency and of Louis XV; but the mishaps of which they were full were too recent to be forgotten by our ministers. Thanks to a wretched hesitation, fleets, which had rightly alarmed England, became reduced to ordinary proportions. Intrenching themselves in a false economy, the ministry claimed that, by reason of the excessive expenses necessary to maintain the fleet, the admirals must be ordered to maintain the '*greatest circumspection*,' as though in war half measures have not always led to disasters.

---

[1] La Serre: Essais Hist. et Crit. sur la Marine Française.

So, too, the orders given to our squadron chiefs were to keep the sea as long as possible, without engaging in actions which might cause the loss of vessels difficult to replace; so that more than once complete victories, which would have crowned the skill of our admirals and the courage of our captains, were changed into successes of little importance. A system which laid down as a principle that an admiral should not use the force in his hands, which sent him against the enemy with the fore-ordained purpose of receiving rather than making the attack, a system which sapped moral power to save material resources, must have unhappy results. . . . It is certain that this deplorable system was one of the causes of the lack of discipline and startling defections which marked the periods of Louis XVI, of the [first] Republic, and of the [first] Empire."[1]

Within ten years of the peace of 1783 came the French Revolution; but that great upheaval which shook the foundations of States, loosed the ties of social order, and drove out of the navy nearly all the trained officers of the monarchy who were attached to the old state of things, did not free the French navy from a false system. It was easier to overturn the form of government than to uproot a deep-seated tradition. Hear again a third French officer, of the highest rank and literary accomplishments, speaking of the inaction of Villeneuve, the admiral who commanded the French rear at the battle of the Nile, and who did not leave his anchors while the head of the column was being destroyed:—

---

[1] Lapeyrouse.Bonfils: Hist. de la Marine Française.

"A day was to come [Trafalgar] in which Villeneuve in his turn, like De Grasse before him, and like Duchayla, would complain of being abandoned by part of his fleet. We have come to suspect some secret reason for this fatal coincidence. It is not natural that among so many honorable men there should so often be found admirals and captains incurring such a reproach. If the name of some of them is to this very day sadly associated with the memory of our disasters, we may be sure the fault is not wholly their own. We must rather blame the nature of the operations in which they were engaged, and that system of defensive war prescribed by the French government, which Pitt, in the English Parliament, proclaimed to be the forerunner of certain ruin. That system, when we wished to renounce it, had already penetrated our habits; it had, so to say, weakened our arms and paralyzed our self-reliance. Too often did our squadrons leave port with a special mission to fulfil, and with the intention of avoiding the enemy; to fall in with him was at once a piece of bad luck. It was thus that our ships went into action; they submitted to it instead of forcing it. . . . Fortune would have hesitated longer between the two fleets, and not have borne in the end so heavily against ours, if Brueys, meeting Nelson half way, could have gone out to fight him. This fettered and timid war, which Villaret and Martin had carried on, had lasted long, thanks to the circumspection of some English admirals and the traditions of the old tactics. It was with these traditions that the battle of the Nile had broken; the hour for decisive action had come."[1]

---

[1] Jurien de la Gravière: Guerres Maritimes.

Some years later came Trafalgar, and again the government of France took up a new policy with the navy. The author last quoted speaks again:—

> "The emperor, whose eagle glance traced plans of campaign for his fleets as for his armies, was wearied by these unexpected reverses. He turned his eyes from the one field of battle in which fortune was faithless to him, and decided to pursue England elsewhere than upon the seas; he undertook to rebuild his navy, but without giving it any part in the struggle which became more furious than ever. . . . Nevertheless, far from slackening, the activity of our dockyards redoubled. Every year ships-of-the-line were either laid down or added to the fleet. Venice and Genoa, under his control, saw their old splendors rise again, and from the shores of the Elbe to the head of the Adriatic all the ports of the continent emulously seconded the creative thought of the emperor. Numerous squadrons were assembled in the Scheldt, in Brest Roads, and in Toulon. . . . But to the end the emperor refused to give this navy, full of ardor and self-reliance, an opportunity to measure its strength with the enemy. . . . Cast down by constant reverses, he had kept up our armed ships only to oblige our enemies to blockades whose enormous cost must end by exhausting their finances."

When the empire fell, France had one hundred and three ships-of-the-line and fifty-five frigates.

To turn now from the particular lessons drawn from the history of the past to the general question of the influence of government upon the sea career of its people, it is seen that that influence can work in two distinct but closely related ways.

First, in peace: The government by its policy can favor the natural growth of a people's industries and its tendencies to seek adventure and gain by way of the sea; or it can try to develop such industries and such sea-going bent, when they do not naturally exist; or, on the other hand, the government may by mistaken action check and fetter the progress which the people left to themselves would make. In any one of these ways the influence of the government will be felt, making or marring the sea power of the country in the matter of peaceful commerce; upon which alone, it cannot be too often insisted, a thoroughly strong navy can be based.

Secondly, for war: The influence of the government will be felt in its most legitimate manner in maintaining an armed navy, of a size commensurate with the growth of its shipping and the importance of the interests connected with it. More important even than the size of the navy is the question of its institutions, favoring a healthful spirit and activity, and providing for rapid development in time of war by an adequate reserve of men and of ships and by measures for drawing out that general reserve power which has before been pointed to, when considering the character and pursuits of the people. Undoubtedly under this second head of warlike preparation must come the maintenance of suitable naval stations, in those distant parts of the world to which the armed shipping must follow the peaceful vessels of commerce. The protection of such stations must depend either upon direct military force, as do Gibraltar and Malta, or upon a surrounding friendly population, such as the American colonists once were to England, and, it may be presumed, the Australian colonists now are. Such friendly surroundings and backing, joined to a reasonable military provision, are the best of defences, and when combined with decided preponderance at sea, make a scattered and extensive empire, like that of England, secure; for while it is true that an unexpected attack may cause disaster in some one quarter, the actual superiority of naval power prevents such disaster from being general or irremediable. History has sufficiently proved this. England's naval bases have been in all parts of the world; and her fleets have at once protected them, kept open the communications between them, and relied upon them for shelter.

Colonies attached to the mother-country afford, therefore, the surest means of supporting abroad the sea power of a country. In peace, the influence of the government should be felt in promoting by all means a warmth of attachment and a unity of interest which will make the welfare of one the welfare of all, and the quarrel of one the quarrel of all; and in war, or rather for war, by inducing such measures of organization and defence as shall be felt by all to be a fair distribution of a burden of which each reaps the benefit.

Such colonies the United States has not and is not likely to have. As regards purely military naval stations, the feeling of her people was probably accurately expressed by an historian of the English navy a hundred years ago, speaking then of Gibraltar and Port Mahon. "Military governments," said he, "agree so little with the industry of a trading people, and are in themselves so repugnant to the genius of the British people, that I do not wonder that men of good sense and of all parties have inclined to give up these, as Tangiers was given up." Having therefore no foreign establishments, either colonial or military, the ships of war of the United States, in war, will be like land birds, unable to fly far from their own shores. To provide resting-places for them, where they can coal and repair, would be one of the first duties of a government proposing to itself the development of the power of the nation at sea.

As the practical object of this inquiry is to draw from the lessons of history inferences applicable to one's own country and service, it is proper now to ask how far the conditions of the United States involve serious danger, and call for action on the part of the government, in order to build again her sea power. It will not be too much to say that the action of the government since the Civil War, and up to this day, has been effectively directed solely to what has been called the first link in the chain which makes sea power. Internal development, great production, with the accompanying aim and boast of self-sufficingness, such has been the object, such to some extent the result. In this the government has faithfully reflected the bent of the controlling elements of the country, though it is not always easy to feel that such controlling elements are truly representative, even in a free country. However that may be, there is no doubt that besides having no colonies, the intermediate link of a peaceful shipping, and the interests involved in it, are now likewise lacking. In short, the United States has only one link of the three.

The circumstances of naval war have changed so much within the last hundred years, that it may be doubted whether such disastrous effects on the one hand, or such brilliant prosperity on the other, as were seen in the wars between England and France, could now recur. In her secure and haughty sway of the seas England imposed a yoke on neutrals which will never again be borne; and the principle that the flag covers the goods is forever secured. The commerce of a belligerent can therefore now be safely carried on in neutral ships, except when contraband of war or to blockaded ports; and as regards the latter, it is also certain that there will be no more paper blockades. Putting aside therefore the question of defending her seaports from capture or contribution, as to which there is practical unanimity in theory and entire indifference in practice, what need has the United States of sea power? Her commerce is even now carried on by others; why should her people desire that which, if possessed, must be defended at great cost? So far as this question is economical, it is outside the scope of this work; but conditions which may entail suffering and loss on the country by war are directly pertinent to it. Granting therefore that the foreign trade of the United States, going and coming, is on board ships which an enemy cannot touch except when bound to a blockaded port,

what will constitute an efficient blockade? The present definition is, that it is such as to constitute a manifest danger to a vessel seeking to enter or leave the port. This is evidently very
elastic. Many can remember that during the Civil War, after a
night attack on the United States fleet off Charleston, the Con-
federates next morning sent out a steamer with some foreign
consuls on board, who so far satisfied themselves that no
blockading vessel was in sight that they issued a declaration to
that effect. On the strength of this declaration some Southern
authorities claimed that the blockade was technically broken,
and could not be technically re-established without a new notification. Is it necessary, to constitute a real danger to blockade-
runners, that the blockading fleet should be in sight? Half a
dozen fast steamers, cruising twenty miles off-shore between the
New Jersey and Long Island coast, would be a very real danger to
ships seeking to go in or out by the principal entrance to New
York; and similar positions might effectively blockade Boston, the
Delaware, and the Chesapeake. The main body of the blockading
fleet, prepared not only to capture merchant-ships but to resist
military attempts to break the blockade, need not be within sight,
nor in a position known to the shore. The bulk of Nelson's fleet
was fifty miles from Cadiz two days before Trafalgar, with a
small detachment watching close to the harbor. The allied fleet
began to get under way at 7 A.M., and Nelson, even under the
conditions of those days, knew it by 9:30. The English fleet at
that distance was a very real danger to its enemy. It seems possible, in these days of submarine telegraphs, that the blockading
forces in-shore and off-shore, and from one port to another,
might be in telegraphic communication with one another along
the whole coast of the United States, readily giving mutual support; and if, by some fortunate military combination, one detachment were attacked in force, it could warn the others and retreat
upon them. Granting that such a blockade off one port were broken on one day, by fairly driving away, the ships maintaining it,

the notification of its being re-established could be cabled all over the world the next. To avoid such blockades there must be a military force afloat that will at all times so endanger a blockading fleet that it can by no means keep its place. Then neutral ships, except those laden with contraband of war, can come and go freely, and maintain the commercial relations of the country with the world outside.

It may be urged that, with the extensive sea-coast of the United States, a blockade of the whole line cannot be effectively kept up. No one will more readily concede this than officers who remember how the blockade of the Southern coast alone was maintained. But in the present condition of the navy, and, it may be added, with any additions not exceeding those so far proposed by the government,[1] the attempt to blockade Boston, New York, the Delaware, the Chesapeake, and the Mississippi, in other words, the great centres of export and import, would not entail upon one of the large maritime nations efforts greater than have been made before. England has at the same time blockaded Brest, the Biscay coast, Toulon, and Cadiz, when there were powerful squadrons lying within the harbors. It is true that commerce in neutral ships can then enter other ports of the United States than those named; but what a dislocation of the carrying traffic of the country, what failure of supplies at times, what inadequate means of transport by rail or water, of dockage, of lighterage, of warehousing, will be involved in such an enforced change of the ports of entry! Will there be no money loss, no suffering, consequent upon this? And when with much pain and expense these evils have been partially remedied, the enemy may be led to stop the new inlets as he did the old. The people of the United States will certainly not starve, but they may suffer grievously.

---

[1] Since the above was written, the secretary of the navy, in his report for 1889, has recommended a fleet which would make such a blockade as here suggested very hazardous.

As for supplies which are contraband of war, is there not reason to fear that the United States is not now able to go alone if an emergency should arise?

The question is eminently one in which the influence of the government should make itself felt, to build up for the nation a navy which, if not capable of reaching distant countries, shall at least be able to keep clear the chief approaches to its own. The eyes of the country have for a quarter of a century been turned from the sea; the results of such a policy and of its opposite will be shown in the instance of France and of England. Without asserting a narrow parallelism between the case of the United States and either of these, it may safely be said that it is essential to the welfare of the whole country that the conditions of trade and commerce should remain, as far as possible, unaffected by an external war. In order to do this, the enemy must be kept not only out of our ports, but far away from our coasts.[1]

---

[1] The word "defence" in war involves two ideas, which for the sake of precision in thought should be kept separated in the mind. There is defence pure and simple, which strengthens itself and awaits attack. This may be called passive defence. On the other hand, there is a view of defence which asserts that safety for one's self, the real object of defensive preparation, is best secured by attacking the enemy. In the matter of sea-coast defence, the former method is exemplified by stationary fortifications, submarine mines, and generally all immobile works destined simply to stop an enemy if he tries to enter. The second method comprises all those means and weapons which do not wait for attack, but go to meet the enemy's fleet, whether it be but for a few miles, or whether to his own shores. Such a defence may seem to be really offensive war, but it is not; it becomes offensive only when its object of attack is changed from the enemy's fleet to the enemy's country. England defended her own coasts and colonies by stationing her fleets off the French ports, to fight the French fleet if it came out. The United States in the Civil War stationed her fleets off the Southern ports, not because she feared for her own, but to break down the Confederacy by isolation from the rest of the world, and ultimately by attacking the ports. The methods were the same; but the purpose in one case was defensive, in the other offensive.

The confusion of the two ideas leads to much unnecessary wrangling as to the proper sphere of army and navy in coast-defence. Passive defences belong to the army; everything that moves in the water to the navy, which has the prerogative of the offensive defence. If seamen are used to garrison forts, they become part of the land forces, as surely as troops, when embarked as part of the complement, become part of the sea forces.

Can this navy be had without restoring the merchant shipping? It is doubtful. History has proved that such a purely military sea power can be built up by a despot, as was done by Louis XIV; but though so fair seeming, experience showed that his navy was like a growth which having no root soon withers away. But in a representative government any military expenditure must have a strongly represented interest behind it, convinced of its necessity. Such an interest in sea power does not exist, cannot exist here without action by the government. How such a merchant shipping should be built up, whether by subsidies or by free trade, by constant administration of tonics or by free movement in the open air, is not a military but an economical question. Even had the United States a great national shipping, it may be doubted whether a sufficient navy would follow; the distance which separates her from other great powers, in one way a protection, is also a snare. The motive, if any there be, which will give the United States a navy, is probably now quickening in the Central American Isthmus. Let us hope it will not come to the birth too late.

Here concludes the general discussion of the principal elements which affect, favorably or unfavorably, the growth of sea power in nations. The aim has been, first to consider those elements in their natural tendency for or against, and then to illustrate by particular examples and by the experience of the past. Such discussions, while undoubtedly embracing a wider field, yet fall mainly within the province of strategy, as distinguished from tactics. The considerations and principles which enter into them belong to the unchangeable, or unchanging, order of things, remaining the same, in cause and effect, from age to age. They belong, as it were, to the Order of Nature, of whose stability so much is heard in our day; whereas tactics, using as its instruments the weapons made by man, shares in the change and progress of the race from generation to generation. From time to time the superstructure of tactics has to be altered or wholly torn down; but the old foundations of strategy so far remain, as though laid upon a rock. There will next be examined the general history of Europe and America, with particular reference to the effect exercised upon that history, and upon the welfare of the people, by sea power in its broad sense. From time to time, as occasion offers, the aim will be to recall and reinforce the general teaching, already elicited, by particular illustrations. The general tenor of the study will therefore be strategical, in that broad definition of naval strategy which has before been quoted and accepted: "Naval strategy has for its end to found, support, and increase, as well in peace as in war, the sea power of a country." In the matter of particular battles, while freely admitting that the change of details has made obsolete much of their teaching, the attempt will be made to point out where the application or neglect of true general principles has produced decisive effects; and, other things being equal, those actions will be preferred which, from their association with the names of the most distinguished officers, may be presumed to show how far just tactical ideas obtained in a particular age or a particular service. It will also be desirable, where analogies between ancient and modern weapons appear on the surface, to derive such probable lessons as they offer, without laying undue stress upon the points of resemblance. Finally, it must be remembered that, among all changes, the nature of man remains much the same; the personal equation, though uncertain in quantity and quality in the particular instance, is sure always to be found.

Sir Julian Corbett

SOME PRINCIPLES OF

MARITIME STRATEGY

BY

JULIAN S. CORBETT, LL.M.

1911

CONTENTS

151

EDITOR'S INTRODUCTION

This selection is from Julian Corbett's *Some Principles of Maritime Strategy,* a controversial book in its time. Corbett had never been able to surmount completely the naval service's distrust of civilian experts. And more than any other factor, his close connection to Lord John Fisher was resented by the "Syndicate of Discontent," as Fisher described the critics of his reforms. In addition, Corbett's 1910 study of Trafalgar, with its broad strategic analysis of the entire 1805 campaign and not just the single battle off Cape Trafalgar, appeared to denigrate that action's meaning and thus Nelson's image. Critics used the resultant controversy to vent their doubts concerning Corbett's philosophy and its possible effect on the War Course, even as he began work on *Some Principles.* The result was a special Admiralty Committee of inquiry formed to investigate the charges. Although the committee exonerated Corbett, the bizarre turn of events demonstrated the basic prejudices that would resurface the next year with the publication of Corbett's masterwork.[1]

There is no way to ascertain precisely the effects of these controversies on Corbett's approach to the writing of his new book. He did change the title of the book at that time from *The Principles* to *Some Principles of Maritime Strategy.* And certainly the introductory section concerning "The Theoretical Study of War" responsed to criticism and comments suggesting that many naval officers were resentful and mistrustful of any abstract approach to war. He began by downplaying any expectation that theory could produce scientific prescriptions for the conduct of war. "It does not pretend to give the power of conduct in the field," he wrote, "it claims no more than to increase the effective power of conduct."

> Its main practical value is that it can assist a capable man to acquire a broad outlook whereby he may be the surer his plan shall cover all the ground, and whereby he may with greater rapidity and certainty seize all the factors of a sudden situation.[2]

Moreover, theory could provide the basis for "mental solidarity" in the iterative consultation process that occurred between policy and strategy. "How often," Corbett asked, "have officers dumbly acquiesced in ill-advised operations simply for lack of the mental power and verbal apparatus to convince an impatient Minister where the error of his plan lay?"[3] It was essential, therefore, for a maritime power to understand a general war theory that both revealed a concept large enough to encompass naval and military strategy and allowed policy makers and strategists to understand the general character of a war before embarking on it.

> That the true nature of a war should be realised by contemporaries as clearly as it comes to be seen afterwards in the fuller light of history is seldom to be expected. At close range accidental factors will force themselves into undue prominence and tend to obscure the true horizon. Such error can scarcely ever be eliminated, but by theoretical study we can reduce it, nor by any other means can we hope to approach the clearness of vision with which posterity will read our mistakes. Theory is, in fact, a question of education and deliberation, and not of execution at all.[4]

The introductory chapter and the six chapters that form part I, "Theory of War," are reproduced in their entirety. Part I was the heart of Corbett's focus on "major strategy." He began the first chapter, "The Theory of War," with an overview of contemporary writing to make his case, based on British history, that maritime strategy was an extension of the "continental" or "German" school of strategy, not a competing alternative. In particular, he focused on the Clausewitzian dictum that war is a continuation of policy. "At first sight there seems little enough in it," he wrote. "It may seem perhaps that we have been watching a mountain in labour and nothing but a mouse has been produced."[5] But as Corbett convincingly demonstrated, that fundamental premise was the key to determining the nature of the war to be fought, the "primordial question" concerning the political objective of any conflict.[6] Like Clausewitz, he perceived that this rational control by policy could prevent wars from moving toward the "absolute" ideal, becoming total, or Napoleonic, in nature. For as Clausewitz had made clear, wars free from political control and thus shaped only by operational possibilities would probably move of their own accord toward the absolute form.

Clausewitz's political theory of war led Corbett to explore two classifications concerning the nature of war in his next two chapters. The first was that of "offensive"—"positive"—and "defensive"—"negative." Corbett did not find this classification useful, particularly the basic premise that offense and defense were mutually exclusive ideas, when for him they were mutually complementary. The essence of defense, in fact, was the counterattack. From this perspective, defense was "a condition of restrained activity—not a mere condition of rest"; and he warned against the "amateurish notion that defence is always stupid or pusillanimous, leading always to defeat, and that what is called the 'military spirit' means nothing but taking the offensive."[7] On the other hand, the second classification of "limited" versus "unlimited" wars was much more useful for the British theorists because it tied the commitment of force firmly to political objectives. In the case of the

Russo-Japanese War, he pointed out as an example, Russia's political objective was so limited "as to cause her to abandon it long before her whole force as an armed nation was exhausted or even put forth."[8]

Corbett linked the concept of limitations to Britain's maritime empire in the fourth chapter of part I. On land Clausewitz had established that for an objective to be limited, "it must be not merely limited in area, but of really limited political importance; and secondly, it must be so situated as to be strategically isolated or to be capable of being reduced to practical isolation by strategical isolation."[9] Corbett carried this one step further by arguing that maritime wars ranging from the Seven Years and the Crimean to the Spanish-American and Russo-Japanese had demonstrated the unique capabilities of maritime powers to meet those conditions. For the British theorist, it was nothing more than the "true meaning and highest military value" of command of the sea, "the secret of England's success against Powers so greatly superior to herself in military strength," which extended as far back in English history as the era he had addressed in his 1898 book, *Drake and the Tudor Navy.*[10] "We come, then, to this final proposition," he concluded,

> —that limited war is only permanently possible to island Powers or between Powers which are separated by sea, and then only when the Power desiring limited war is able to command the sea to such a degree as to be able not only to isolate the distant object, but also to render impossible the invasion of his home territory.[11]

With this capability, Corbett maintained in his next chapter, Britain had been able to conduct "Limited Interference in Unlimited War." From his perspective, limited war, or what Clausewitz called "War limited by contingent" in the continental form, "seldom or never" differed generically from unlimited war.[12] But control of the sea had allowed Britain to conduct what Corbett termed "combined operations" throughout history. The best examples of this type of "war with a disposal force," Corbett demonstrated, were Pitt's operations against Canada and particularly those of Wellington in Portugal and Spain during the peninsular campaign. "It was not till the Peninsular War developed," he concluded, "that we found a theatre for war limited by contingent in which all the conditions that make for success were present."

> The real secret of Wellington's success—apart from his own genius—was that in perfect conditions he was applying the limited form to an unlimited war. Our object was unlimited. It was nothing less than the overthrow of Napoleon. Complete success at sea had failed to do it, but that success had given us the power of applying the limited form, which was the most decisive form of offence within our means. Its substantial contribution to the final achievement of the object is now universally recognised.[13]

Corbett followed up these arguments in his last chapter on war theory, "Conditions of Strength in Limited War," by emphasizing that it was a form best suited for Britain's conditions and capabilities. To attribute all this, he cautioned, "as is sometimes the fashion, to an inherent lack of warlike spirit is sufficiently contradicted by the results it has achieved."[14] Such attribution was "only to be explained by the domination of the Napoleonic idea of war, against the universal application of which Clausewitz so solemnly protested. It is the work of men who have a natural difficulty in conceiving a war plan that does not culminate in a Jena or a Sedan."[15] Nevertheless, Corbett was not advocating a return to eighteenth-century maneuver warfare in which a battle had come to almost signify bad generalship. "With such parading limited war has nothing to do," he concluded, adding a more detailed warning:

The fact that the doctrine of limited war traverses the current belief that our primary object must always be the enemy's armed forces is liable to carry with it a false inference that it also rejects the corollary that war means the use of battles. Nothing is further from the conception. Whatever the form of war, there is no likelihood of our ever going back to the old fallacy of attempting to decide war by manœuvres. All forms alike demand the use of battles. By our fundamental theory war is always a "continuation of political intercourse, in which fighting is substituted for writing notes." However great the controlling influence of the political object, it must never obscure the fact that it is by fighting we have to gain our end.[16]

In parts II and III of *Some Principles* Corbett moved away from the general theory of war to what he called "minor" or naval strategy. In part II, "Theory of Naval War," the only selection is from his arguments in the first chapter, which reiterated his thinking on the command of the sea concept and the idea of common maritime communications as fundamental to the concept. From part III, "Conduct of Naval War," there is a short selection from Corbett's first chapter concerning differences between war on land and on sea. This is followed by a partial selection of the third chapter, "Methods of Disputing Command," containing Corbett's discussion on "Fleet in Being" doctrine, designed to show that defensive thinking was inherent in French and British naval practice since the seventeenth century. "At sea," he concluded, "the main conception is avoiding decisive action by strategical or tactical activity, so as to keep our fleet in being till the situation develops in our favour."[17]

There are two selections from the last chapter of the book, "Methods of Exercising Command." The reading from the penultimate section, "Attack and Defence of Trade," reflects Corbett's underestimation of the importance of convoys, which would be the source of so much criticism in the next war. At the same time, the reading also demonstrates Corbett's cautious approach in a time of great change to the subject of trade defense, a much neglected topic in the Victorian-Edwardian Navy. "Modern developments and changes in shipping and naval material," he observed, "have indeed so profoundly modified the whole conditions of commerce protection, that there is no part of strategy where historical deduction is more difficult or more liable to error."[18] Finally, the last selection from the section concerning support of military expeditions evinces a modern outlook in its operational examination of joint, or "conjunct operations" as they were known in the eighteenth century. Drawing on the historical experiences of such leaders as Drake and Wolfe and the successful joint arrangements in the Crimean War, Corbett demonstrated how combinations of transport and covering squadrons could provide protection for amphibious forces both in transit and on shore. It is in this "conception of the joint function of army and navy," Corbett's biographer concludes, "that his reputation ought chiefly to rest."[19]

The reviews on both sides of the Atlantic for *Some Principles* were generally enthusiastic. There were, of course, inevitable comparisons with Mahan, and one reviewer even dubbed the British theorist "Super Mahan."[20] At the same time, the controversy concerning his work on Trafalgar was reenergized by the new book, this time led by Henry Spenser Wilkinson, a leader in the Syndicate of Discontent. As a military correspondent for the conservative *Morning Post,* Wilkinson warned in early 1912 that Corbett's book would have "a disastrous effect upon the Navy," particularly in its de-emphasis of fleet actions as well as its emphasis on limited war.[21] But the most vitriolic attack was left to a "Captain R. N.," who believed that *Some Principles* was the "crowning mistake" of Corbett's career.

> For some years Mr. Corbett has, in the process of lecturing at the R. N. War College, permitted himself the indulgence of offering his audience his own views of the correctness or otherwise of the strategy adopted by naval officers in the past. His audience has usually

treated his amateur excursions in to the subject good naturedly; nevertheless his presumption has been resented, and he has apparently been deaf to the polite hints thrown out to him that his opinion on strategy was of no concern to his listeners because as a civilian he was obviously incompetent to assess at their proper value the *influences which purely naval considerations had on the problems* which he was gratuitously attempting to solve.[22]

Corbett's point, of course, was that there was no such thing as "purely naval considerations." In his 1907 study of the Seven Years War, he examined the complexity of the political-military connection in formulating policy and concluded that both military and policy elites had developed successfully a "wider vision" of naval strategy.[23] In that vision, as he demonstrated in *Some Principles,* naval strategy was not an autonomous concept. It was, instead, part of maritime strategy, that is, a broader approach to the use of naval force in conjunction with both other military components and other elements of national power to achieve political ends. This connection was Corbett's most important achievement. It was simply the idea that Britain's success as a great power involved the combined interplay and exploitation of naval resources as part of a comprehensive policy of military, economic, and diplomatic efforts. "In 1895," Donald Schurman points out concerning Corbett,

he came fresh to a subject that consisted of little more than a record of the glorious exploits of the broadside bashers and the impressive growth of a nation and Empire: the two were only vaguely linked. After upwards of twenty years' work, he left the two firmly connected through his illumination of the way statesmen and sailors had worked out a patter of seapower and built on it from generation to generation.[24]

SOME PRINCIPLES OF
MARITIME STRATEGY

INTRODUCTION

THE THEORETICAL STUDY OF WAR:
ITS USE AND LIMITATIONS

At first sight nothing can appear more unpractical, less promising of useful result, than to approach the study of war with a theory. There seems indeed to be something essentially antagonistic between the habit of mind that seeks theoretical guidance and that which makes for the successful conduct of war. The conduct of war is so much a question of personality, of character, of common-sense, of rapid decision upon complex and ever-shifting factors, and those factors themselves are so varied, so intangible, so dependent upon unstable moral and physical conditions, that it seems incapable of being reduced to anything like true scientific analysis. At the bare idea of a theory or "science" of war the mind recurs uneasily to well-known cases where highly "scientific" officers failed as leaders. Yet, on the other hand, no one will deny that since the great theorists of the early nineteenth century attempted to produce a reasoned theory of war, its planning and conduct have acquired a method, a precision, and a certainty of grasp which were unknown before. Still less will any one deny the value which the shrewdest and most successful leaders in war have placed upon the work of the classical strategical writers.

The truth is that the mistrust of theory arises from a misconception of what it is that theory claims to do. It does not pretend to give the power of conduct in the field; it claims no more than to increase the effective power of conduct. Its main practical value is that it can assist a capable man to acquire a broad outlook whereby he may be the surer his plan shall cover all the ground, and whereby he may with greater rapidity and certainty seize all the factors of a sudden situation. The greatest of the theorists himself puts the matter quite frankly. Of theoretical study he says, "It should educate the mind of the man who is to lead in war, or rather guide him to self-education, but it should not accompany him on the field of battle."

Its practical utility, however, is not by any means confined to its effects upon the powers of a leader. It is not enough that a leader should have the ability to decide rightly; his subordinates must seize at once the full meaning of his decision and be able to express it with certainty in well-adjusted action. For this every man concerned must have been trained to think in the same plane; the chief's order must awake in every brain the same process of thought; his words must have the same meaning for all. If a theory of tactics had existed in 1780, and if Captain Carkett had had a sound training in such a theory, he could not possibly have misunderstood Rodney's signal. As it was, the real intention of the signal was obscure, and Rodney's neglect to explain the tactical device it indicated robbed his country of a victory at an hour of the direst need. There had been no previous theoretical training to supply the omission, and Rodney's fine conception was unintelligible to anybody but himself.

Nor is it only for the sake of mental solidarity between a chief and his subordinates that theory is indispensable. It is of still higher value for producing a similar solidarity between him and his superiors at the Council table at home. How often have officers dumbly acquiesced in ill-advised operations simply for lack of the mental power and verbal apparatus to convince an impatient Minister where the errors of his plan lay? How often, moreover, have statesmen and officers, even in the most harmonious conference, been unable to decide on a coherent plan of war from inability to analyse scientifically the situation they had to face, and to recognise the general character of the struggle in which they were about to engage. That the true nature of a war should be realised by contemporaries as clearly as it comes to be seen after words in the fuller light of history is seldom to be expected. At close range accidental factors will force themselves into undue prominence and tend to obscure the true horizon. Such error can scarcely ever be eliminated, but by theoretical study we can reduce it, nor by any other means can we hope to approach the clearness of vision with which posterity will read our mistakes. Theory, is, in fact, a question of education and deliberation, and not of execution at all. That depends on the combination of intangible human qualities which we call executive ability.

This, then, is all the great authorities ever claimed for theory, but to this claim the chief of them at least, after years of active service on the Staff, attached the highest importance. "In actual operations," he wrote in one of his latest memoranda, "men are guided solely by their judgment, and it will hit the mark more or less accurately according as they possess more or less genius. This is the way all great generals have acted. . . . Thus it will always be in action, and so far judgment will suffice. But when it is a question not of taking action yourself, but of convincing others at the Council table, then everything depends on clear conceptions and the exposition of the inherent relations of things. So little progress has been made in this respect that most deliberations are merely verbal contentions which rest on no firm foundation, and end either in every one retaining his own opinion, or, in a compromise from considerations of mutual respect—a middle course of no actual value."[1]

---

[1] Clausewitz *On War*, p. ix.

The writer's experience of such discussions was rich and at first hand. Clear conceptions of the ideas and factors involved in a war problem, and a definite exposition of the relations between them, were in his eyes the remedy for loose and purposeless discussion; and such conceptions and expositions are all we mean by the theory or the science of war. It is a process by which we co-ordinate our ideas, define the meaning of the words we use, grasp the difference between essential and unessential factors, and fix and expose the fundamental data on which every one is agreed. In this way we prepare the apparatus of practical discussion; we secure the means of arranging the factors in manageable shape, and of deducing from them with precision and rapidity a practical course of action. Without such an apparatus no two men can even think on the same line; much less can they ever hope to detach the real point of difference that divides them and isolate it for quiet solution.

In our own case this view of the value of strategical theory has a special significance, and one far wider than its continental enunciators contemplated. For a world-wide maritime Empire the successful conduct of war will often turn not only on the decisions of the Council chamber at home, but on the outcome of conferences in all parts of the world between squadronal commanders and the local authorities, both civil and military, and even between commanders-in-chief of adjacent stations. In time of war or of preparation for war, in which the Empire is concerned, arrangements must always be based to an exceptional degree on the mutual relation of naval, military, and political considerations. The line of mean efficiency, though indicated from home, must be worked out locally, and worked out on factors of which no one service is master. Conference is always necessary, and for conference to succeed there must be a common vehicle of expression and a common plane of thought. It is for this essential preparation that theoretical study alone can provide; and herein lies its practical value for all who aspire to the higher responsibilities of the Imperial service.

So great indeed is the value of abstract strategical study from this point of view, that it is necessary to guard ourselves against over-valuation. So far from claiming for their so-called science more than the possibilities we have indicated, the classical strategists insist again and again on the danger of seeking from it what it cannot give. They even repudiate the very name of "Science." They prefer the older term "Art." They will permit no laws or rules. Such laws, they say, can only mislead in practice, for the friction to which they are subject from the incalculable human factors alone is such that the friction is stronger than the law. It is an old adage of lawyers that nothing is so misleading as a legal maxim, but a strategical maxim is undoubtedly and in every way less to be trusted in action.

What then, it will be asked, are the tangible results which we can hope to attain from theory? If all on which we have to build is so indeterminate, how are any practical conclusions to be reached? That the factors are infinitely varied and difficult to determine is true, but that, it must be remembered, is just what emphasises the necessity of reaching such firm standpoints as are attainable. The vaguer the problem to be solved, the more resolute must we be in seeking points of departure from which we can begin to lay a course, keeping always an eye open for the accidents that will beset us, and being always alive to their deflecting influences. And this is just what the theoretical study of strategy can do. It can at least determine the normal. By careful collation of past events it becomes clear that certain lines of conduct tend normally to produce certain effects; that wars tend to take certain forms each with a marked idiosyncrasy; that these forms are normally related to the object of the war and to its value to one or both belligerents; that a system of operations which suits one form may not be that best suited to another. We can even go further. By pursuing an historical and comparative method we can detect that even the human factor is not quite indeterminable. We can assert that certain situations will normally produce, whether in ourselves or in our adversaries, certain moral states on which we may calculate.

Having determined the normal, we are at once in a stronger position. Any proposal can be compared with it, and we can proceed to discuss clearly the weight of the factors which prompt us to depart from the normal. Every case must be judged on its merits, but without a normal to work from we cannot form any real judgment at all; we can only guess. Every case will assuredly depart from the normal to a greater or less extent, and it is equally certain that the greatest successes in war have been the boldest departures from the normal. But for the most part they have been departures made with open eyes by geniuses who could perceive in the accidents of the case a just reason for the departure.

Take an analogous example, and the province of strategical theory becomes clear at once. Navigation and the parts of seamanship that belong to it have to deal with phenomena as varied and unreliable as those of the conduct of war. Together they form an art which depends quite as much as generalship on the judgment of individuals. The law of storms and tides, of winds and currents, and the whole of meteorology are subject to infinite and incalculable deflections, and yet who will deny nowadays that by the theoretical study of such things the seaman's art has gained in coherence and strength? Such study will not by itself make a seaman or a navigator, but without it no seaman or navigator can nowadays pretend to the name. Because storms do not always behave in the same way, because currents are erratic, will the most practical seaman deny that the study of the normal conditions are useless to him in his practical decisions?

If, then, the theoretical study of strategy be approached in this way—if, that is, it be regarded not as a substitute for judgment and experience, but as a means of fertilising both, it can do no man harm. Individual thought and common-sense will remain the masters and remain the guides to point the general direction when the mass of facts begins to grow bewildering. Theory will warn us the moment we begin to leave the beaten track, and enable us to decide with open eyes whether the divergence is necessary or justifiable. Above all, when men assemble in Council it will hold discussion to the essential lines, and help to keep side issues in their place.

But beyond all this there lies in the theory of war yet another element of peculiar value to a maritime Empire. We are accustomed, partly for convenience and partly from lack of a scientific habit of thought, to speak of naval strategy and military strategy as though they were distinct branches of knowledge which had no common ground. It is the theory of war which brings out their intimate relation. It reveals that embracing them both is a larger strategy which regards the fleet and army as one weapon, which co-ordinates their action, and indicates the lines on which each must move to realise the full power of both. It will direct us to assign to each its proper function in a plan of war; it will enable each service to realise the better the limitations and the possibilities of the function with which it is charged, and how and when its own necessities must give way to a higher or more pressing need of the other. It discloses, in short, that naval strategy is not a thing by itself, that its problems can seldom or never be solved on naval considerations alone, but that it is only a part of maritime strategy—the higher learning which teaches us that for a maritime State to make successful war and to realise her special strength, army and navy must be used and thought of as instruments no less intimately connected than are the three arms ashore.

It is for these reasons that it is of little use to approach naval strategy except through the theory of war. Without such theory we can never really understand its scope or meaning, nor can we hope to grasp the forces which most profoundly affect its conclusions.

PART I

THEORY OF WAR

CHAPTER I

THE THEORY OF WAR

The last thing that an explorer arrives at is a complete map that will cover the whole ground he has travelled, but for those who come after him and would profit by and extend his knowledge his map is the first thing with which they will begin. So it is with strategy. Before we start upon its study we seek a chart which will show us at a glance what exactly is the ground we have to cover and what are the leading features which determine its form and general characteristics. Such a chart a "theory of war" alone can provide. It is for this reason that in the study of war we must get our theory clear before we can venture in search of practical conclusions. So great is the complexity of war that without such a guide we are sure to go astray amidst the bewildering multiplicity of tracks and obstacles that meet us at every step. If for continental strategy its value has been proved abundantly, then for maritime strategy, where the conditions are far more complex, the need of it is even greater.

By maritime strategy we mean the principles which govern a war in which the sea is a substantial factor. Naval strategy is but that part of it which determines the movements of the fleet when maritime strategy has determined what part the fleet must play in relation to the action of the land forces; for it scarcely needs saying that it is almost impossible that a war can be decided by naval action alone. Unaided, naval pressure can only work by a process of exhaustion. Its effects must always be slow, and so galling both to our own commercial community and to neutrals, that the tendency is always to accept terms of peace that are far from conclusive. For a firm decision a quicker and more drastic form of pressure is required. Since men live upon the land and not upon the sea, great issues between nations at war have always been decided—except in the rarest cases—either by what your army can do against your enemy's territory and national life or else by the fear of what the fleet makes it possible for your army to do.

The paramount concern, then, of maritime strategy is to determine the mutual relations of your army and navy in a plan of war. When this is done, and not till then, naval strategy can begin to work out the manner in which the fleet can best discharge the function assigned to it.

The problem of such co-ordination is one that is susceptible of widely varying solutions. It may be that the command of the sea is of so urgent an importance that the army will have to devote itself to assisting the fleet in its special task before it can act directly against the enemy's territory and land forces; on the other hand, it may be that the immediate duty of the fleet will be to forward military action ashore before it is free to devote itself whole-heartedly to the destruction of the enemy's fleets. The crude maxims as to primary objects which seem to have served well enough in continental warfare have never worked so clearly where the sea enters seriously into a war. In such cases it will not suffice to say the primary object of the army is to destroy the enemy's army, or that of the fleet to destroy the enemy's fleet. The delicate interactions of the land and sea factors produce conditions too intricate for such blunt solutions. Even the initial equations they present are too complex to be reduced by the simple application of rough-and-ready maxims. Their right handling depends upon the broadest and most fundamental principles of war, and it is as a standpoint from which to get a clear and unobstructed view of the factors in their true relations that a theory of war has perhaps its highest value.

The theory which now holds the field is that war in a fundamental sense is a continuation of policy by other means. The process by which the continental strategists arrived at it involved some hard philosophical reasoning. Practical and experienced veterans as they were, their method is not one that works easily with our own habit of thought. It will be well, therefore, to endeavour first to present their conclusions in a concrete form, which will make the pith of the matter intelligible at once. Take, now, the ordinary case of a naval or military Staff being asked to prepare a war plan against a certain State and to advise what means it will require. To any one who has considered such matters it is obvious the reply must be another question—What will the war be about? Without a definite answer or alternative answers to that question a Staff can scarcely do more than engage in making such forces as the country can afford as efficient as possible. Before they take any sure step further they must know many things. They must know whether they are expected to take something from the enemy, or to prevent his taking something either from us or from some other State. If from some other State, the measures to be taken will depend on its geographical situation and on its relative strength by land and sea. Even when the object is clear it will be necessary to know how much value the enemy attaches to it. Is it one for which he will be likely to fight to the death, or one which he will abandon in the face of comparatively slight resistance? If the former, we cannot hope to succeed without entirely overthrowing his powers of resistance. If the latter, it will suffice, as it often has sufficed, to aim at something less costly and hazardous and better within our means. All these are questions which lie in the lap of Ministers charged with the foreign policy of the country, and before the Staff can proceed with a war plan they must be answered by Ministers.

In short, the Staff must ask of them what is the policy which your diplomacy is pursuing, and where, and why, do you expect it to break down and force you to take up arms? The Staff has to carry on in fact when diplomacy has failed to achieve the object in view, and the method they will use will depend on the nature of that object. So we arrive crudely at our theory that war is a continuation of policy, a form of political intercourse in which we fight battles instead of writing notes.

It was this theory, simple and even meaningless as it appears at first sight, that gave the key to the practical work of framing a modern war plan and revolutionised the study of strategy. It was not till the beginning of the nineteenth century that such a theory was arrived at. For centuries men had written on the "Art of War," but for want of a working theory their labours as a whole had been unscientific, concerned for the most part with the discussion of passing fashions and the elaboration of platitudes. Much good work it is true was done on details, but no broad outlook had been obtained to enable us to determine their relation to the fundamental constants of the subject. No standpoint had been found from which we could readily detach such constants from what was readily accidental. The result was a tendency to argue too exclusively from the latest examples and to become entangled in erroneous thought by trying to apply the methods which had attained the last success to war as a whole. There was no means of determining how far the particular success was due to special conditions and how far it was due to factors common to all wars.

It was the Revolutionary and Napoleonic wars, coinciding as they did with a period of philosophic activity, that revealed the shallowness and empirical nature of all that had been done up to that time. Napoleon's methods appeared to his contemporaries to have produced so strenuous a revolution in the conduct of land warfare that it assumed a wholly new aspect, and it was obvious that those conceptions which had sufficed previously had become inadequate as a basis of sound study. War on land seemed to have changed from a calculated affair of thrust and parry between standing armies to a headlong rush of one nation in arms upon another, each thirsting for the other's life, and resolved to have it or perish in the attempt. Men felt themselves faced with a manifestation of human energy which had had no counterpart, at least in civilised times.

The assumption was not entirely true. For although the Continent had never before adopted the methods in question, our own country was no stranger to them either on sea or land. As we shall see, our own Revolution in the seventeenth century had produced strenuous methods of making war which were closely related to those which Napoleon took over from the French Revolutionary leaders. A more philosophic outlook might have suggested that the phenomenon was not really exceptional, but rather the natural outcome of popular energy inspired by a stirring political ideal. But the British precedent was forgotten, and so profound was the disturbance caused by the new French methods that its effects are with us still. We are in fact still dominated by the idea that since the Napoleonic era war has been essentially a different thing. Our teachers incline to insist that there is now only one way of making war, and that is Napoleon's way. Ignoring the fact that he failed in the end, they brand as heresy the bare suggestion that there may be other ways, and not content with assuming that his system will fit all land wars, however much their natures and objects may differ, they would force naval warfare into the same uniform under the impression apparently that they are thereby making it presentable and giving it some new force.

Seeing how cramping the Napoleonic idea has become, it will be convenient before going further to determine its special characteristics exactly, but that is no easy matter. The moment we approach it in a critical spirit, it begins to grow nebulous and very difficult to define. We can dimly make out four distinct ideas mingled in the current notion. First, there is the idea of making war not merely with a professional standing army, but with the whole armed nation—a conception which of course was not really Napoleon's. It was inherited by him from the Revolution, but was in fact far older. It was but a revival of the universal practice which obtained in the barbaric stages of social development, and which every civilisation in turn had abandoned as economically unsound and subversive of specialisation in citizenship. The results of the abandonment were sometimes good and sometimes bad, but the determining conditions have been studied as yet too imperfectly to justify any broad generalisation. Secondly, there is the idea of strenuous and persistent effort—not resting to secure each minor advantage, but pressing the enemy without pause or rest till he is utterly overthrown—an idea in which Cromwell had anticipated Napoleon by a century and a half. Scarcely distinguishable from this is a third idea—that of taking the offensive, in which there was really nothing new at all, since its advantages had always been understood, and Frederick the Great had pressed it to extremity with little less daring than Napoleon himself—nay even to culpable rashness, as the highest exponents of the Napoleonic idea admit. Finally, there is the notion of making the armed forces of the enemy and not his territory or any part of it your main objective. This perhaps is regarded as the strongest characteristic of Napoleon's methods, and yet even here we are confused by the fact that undoubtedly on some very important occasions—the Austerlitz campaign, for example—Napoleon made the hostile capital his objective as though he believed its occupation was the most effective step towards the overthrow of the enemy's power and will to resist. He certainly did not make the enemy's main army his primary objective—for their main army was not Mack's but that of the Archduke Charles.

On the whole then, when men speak of the Napoleonic system they seem to include two groups of ideas—one which comprises the conception of war made with the whole force of the nation; the other, a group which includes the Cromwellian idea of persistent effort, Frederick's preference for the offensive at almost any risk, and finally the idea of the enemy's armed forces as the main objective, which was also Cromwell's.

It is the combination of these by no means original or very distinct ideas that we are told has brought about so entire a change in the conduct of war that it has become altogether a different thing. It is unnecessary for our purpose to consider how far the facts seem to support such a conclusion, for in the inherent nature of things it must be radically unsound. Neither war nor anything else can change in its essentials. If it appears to do so, it is because we are still mistaking accidents for essentials, and this is exactly how it struck the acutest thinkers of Napoleonic times.

For a while it is true they were bewildered, but so soon as they had had time to clear their heads from the din of the struggle in which they had taken part, they began to see that the new phenomena were but accidents after all. They perceived that Napoleon's methods, which had taken the world by storm, had met with success in wars of a certain nature only, and that when he tried to extend those methods to other natures of war he had met with failure and even disaster. How was this to be explained? What theory, for instance, would cover Napoleon's successes in Germany and Italy, as well as his failures in Spain and Russia? If the whole conception of war had changed, how could you account for the success of England, who had not changed her methods? To us the answer to these questions is of living and infinite importance. Our standpoint remains still unchanged. Is there anything inherent in the conception of war that justifies that attitude in our case? Are we entitled to expect from it again the same success it met with in the past?

The first man to enunciate a theory which would explain the phenomena of the Napoleonic era and co-ordinate them with previous history was General Carl von Clausewitz, a man whose arduous service on the Staff and the actual work of higher instruction had taught the necessity of systematising the study of his profession. He was no mere professor, but a soldier bred in the severest school of war. The pupil and friend of Sharnborst and Gneisenau, he had served on the Staff of Blücher in 1813, he had been Chief of the Staff to Wallmoden in his campaign against Davoust on the Lower Elbe, and also to the Third Prussian Army Corps in the campaign of 1815. Thereafter for more than ten years he was Director of the General Academy of War at Berlin, and died in 1831 as Chief of the Staff to Marshal Gneisenau. For the fifty years that followed his death his theories and system were, as he expected they would be, attacked from all sides. Yet today his work is more firmly established than ever as the necessary basis of all strategical thought, and above all in the "blood and iron" school of Germany.

The process by which he reached his famous theory can be followed in his classical work *On War* and the *Notes* regarding it which he left behind him. In accordance with the philosophic fashion of his time he began by trying to formulate an abstract idea of war. The definition he started with was that "War is an act of violence to compel our opponent to do our will." But that act of violence was not merely "the shock of armies," as Montecuculi had defined it a century and a half before. If the abstract idea of war be followed to its logical conclusion, the act of violence must be performed with the whole of the means at our disposal and with the utmost exertion of our will. Consequently we get the conception of two armed nations flinging themselves one upon the other, and continuing the struggle with the utmost strength and energy they can command till one or other is no longer capable of resistance. This Clausewitz called "Absolute War." But his practical experience and ripe study of history told him at once that "Real War" was something radically different. It was true, as he said, that Napoleon's methods had approximated to the absolute and had given some colour to the use of the absolute idea as a working theory. "But shall we," he acutely asks, "rest satisfied with this idea and judge all wars by it however much they may differ from it—shall we deduce from it all the requirements of theory? We must decide the point, for we can say nothing trustworthy about a war plan until we have made up our minds whether war should only be of this kind or whether it may be of another kind." He saw at once that a theory formed upon the abstract or absolute idea of war would not cover the ground, and therefore failed to give what was required for practical purposes. It would exclude almost the whole of war from Alexander's time to Napoleon's. And what guarantee was there that the next war would conform to the Napoleonic type and accommodate itself to the abstract theory? "This theory," he says, "is still quite powerless against the force of circumstances." And so it proved, for the wars of the middle nineteenth century did in fact revert to the pre-Napoleonic type.

In short, Clausewitz's difficulty in adopting his abstract theory as a working rule was that his practical mind could not forget that war had not begun with the Revolutionary era, nor was it likely to end with it. If that era had changed the conduct of war, it must be presumed that war would change again with other times and other conditions. A theory of war which did not allow for this and did not cover all that had gone before was no theory at all. If a theory of war was to be of any use as a practical guide it must cover and explain not only the extreme manifestation of hostility which he himself had witnessed, but every manifestation that had occurred in the past or was likely to recur in the future.

It was in casting about for the underlying causes of the oscillations manifested in the energy and intensity of hostile relations that he found his solution. His experience on the Staff, and his study of the inner springs of war, told him it was never in fact a question of purely military endeavour aiming always at the extreme of what was possible or expedient from a purely military point of view. The energy exhibited would always be modified by political considerations and by the depth of the national interest in the object of the war. He saw that real war was in fact an international relation which differed from other international relations only in the method we adopted to achieve the object of our policy. So it was he arrived at his famous theory—"that war is a mere continuation of policy by other means."

At first sight there seems little enough in it. It may seem perhaps that we have been watching a mountain in labour and nothing but a mouse has been produced. But it is only upon some such simple, even obvious, formula that any scientific system can be constructed with safety. We have only to develop the meaning of this one to see how important and practical are the guiding lines which flow from it.

With the conception of war as a continuation of political intercourse before us, it is clear that everything which lies outside the political conception, everything, that is, which is strictly peculiar to military and naval operations, relates merely to the means which we use to achieve our policy. Consequently, the first desideratum of a war plan is that the means adopted must conflict as little as possible with the political conditions from which the war springs. In practice, of course, as in all human relations, there will be a compromise between the means and the end, between the political and the military exigencies. But Clausewitz held that policy must always be the master. The officer charged with the conduct of the war may of course demand that the tendencies and views of policy shall not be incompatible with the military means which are placed at his disposal; but however strongly this demand may react on policy in particular cases, military action must still be regarded only as a manifestation of policy. It must never supersede policy. The policy is always the object; war is only the means by which we obtain the object, and the means must always keep the end in view.

The practical importance of this conception will now become clear. It will be seen to afford the logical or theoretical exposition of what we began by stating in its purely concrete form. When a Chief of Staff is asked for a war plan he must not say we will make war in such and such a way because it was Napoleon's or Moltke's way. He will ask what is the political object of the war, what are the political conditions, and how much does the question at issue mean respectively to us and to our adversary. It is these considerations which determine the nature of the war. This primordial question settled, he will be in a position to say whether the war is of the same nature as those in which Napoleon's and Moltke's methods were successful, or whether it is of another nature in which those methods failed. He will then design and offer a war plan, not because it has the hall-mark of this or that great master of war, but because it is one that has been proved to fit the kind of war in hand. To assume that one method of conducting war will suit all kinds of war is to fall a victim to abstract theory, and not to be a prophet of reality, as the narrowest disciples of the Napoleonic school are inclined to see themselves.

Hence, says Clausewitz, the first, the greatest and most critical decision upon which the Statesman and the General have to exercise their judgment is to determine the nature of the war, to be sure they do not mistake it for something nor seek to make of it something which from its inherent conditions it can never be. "This," he declares, "is the first and the most far-reaching of all strategical questions."

The first value, then, of his theory of war is that it gives a clear line on which we may proceed to determine the nature of a war in which we are about to engage, and to ensure that we do not try to apply to one nature of war any particular course of operations simply because they have proved successful in another nature of war. It is only, he insists, by regarding war not as an independent thing but as a political instrument that we can read aright the lessons of history and understand for our practical guidance how wars must differ in character according to the nature of the motives and circumstances from which they proceed. This conception, he claims, is the first ray of light to guide us to a true theory of war and thereby enable us to classify wars and distinguish them one from another.

Jomini, his great contemporary and rival, though proceeding by a less philosophical but no less lucid method, entirely endorses this view. A Swiss soldier of fortune, his experience was much the same as that of Clausewitz. It was obtained mainly on the Staff of Marshal Ney and subsequently on the Russian headquarter Staff. He reached no definite theory of war, but his fundamental conclusions were the same. The first chapter of his final work, *Précis de l'art de la Guerre,* is devoted to "La Politique de la Guerre." In it he classifies wars into nine categories according to their political object, and he lays it down as a base proposition "That these different kinds of war will have more or less influence on the nature of the operations which will be demanded to attain the end in view, on the amount of energy that must be put forth, and on the extent of the undertakings in which we must engage." "There will," he adds, "be a great difference in the operations according to the risks we have to run."

Both men, therefore, though on details of means they were often widely opposed, are agreed that the fundamental conception of war is political. Both of course agree that if we isolate in our mind the forces engaged in any theatre of war the abstract conception reappears. So far as those forces are concerned, war is a question of fighting in which each belligerent should endeavour by all the means at his command and with all his energy to destroy the other. But even so they may find that certain means are barred to them for political reasons, and at any moment the fortune of war or a development of the political conditions with which it is entangled may throw them back upon the fundamental political theory.

That theory it will be unprofitable to labour further at this point. Let it suffice for the present to mark that it gives us a conception of war as an exertion of violence to secure a political end which we desire to attain, and that from this broad and simple formula we are able to deduce at once that wars will vary according to the nature of the end and the intensity of our desire to attain it. Here we may leave it to gather force and coherence as we examine the practical considerations which are its immediate outcome.

CHAPTER II

Natures of Wars—Offensive and Defensive

Having determined that wars must vary in character according to the nature and importance of their object, we are faced with the difficulty that the variations will be of infinite number and of all degrees of distinction. So complex indeed is the graduation presented that at first sight it appears scarcely possible to make it the basis of practical study. But on further examination it will be seen that by applying the usual analytical method the whole subject is susceptible of much simplification. We must in short attempt to reach some system of classification; that is, we must see if it is not possible to group the variations into some well-founded categories. With a subject so complex and intangible the grouping must of course be to some extent arbitrary, and in some places the lines of demarcation will be shadowy; but if classification has been found possible and helpful in Zoology or Botany, with the infinite and minute individual variations with which they have to deal, it should be no less possible and helpful in the study of war.

The political theory of war will at any rate give us two broad and well-marked classifications. The first is simple and well known, depending on whether the political object of the war is positive or negative. If it be positive—that is, if our aim is to wrest something from the enemy—then our war in its main lines will be offensive. If, on the other hand, our aim be negative, and we simply seek to prevent the enemy wresting some advantage to our detriment, then the war in its general direction will be defensive.

It is only as a broad conception that this classification has value. Though it fixes the general trend of our operations, it will not in itself affect their character. For a maritime Power at least it is obvious that this must be so. For in any circumstances it is impossible for such a Power either to establish its defence or develop fully its offence without securing a working control of the sea by aggressive action against the enemy's fleets. Furthermore, we have always found that however strictly our aim may be defensive, the most effective means of securing it has been by counter-attack over-sea, either to support an ally directly or to deprive our enemy of his colonial possessions. Neither category, then, excludes the use of offensive operations nor the idea of overthrowing our enemy so far as is necessary to gain our end. In neither case does the conception lead us eventually to any other objective than the enemy's armed forces, and particularly his naval forces. The only real difference is this—that if our object be positive our general plan must be offensive, and we should at least open with a true offensive movement; whereas if our object be negative our general plan will be preventive, and we may bide our time for our counter-attack. To this extent our action must always tend to the offensive. For counter-attack is the soul of defence. Defence is not a passive attitude, for that is the negation of war. Rightly conceived, it is an attitude of alert expectation. We wait for the moment when the enemy shall expose himself to a counter-stroke, the success of which will so far cripple him as to render us relatively strong enough to pass to the offensive ourselves.

From these considerations it will appear that, real and logical as the classification is, to give it the designation "offensive and defensive" is objectionable from every point of view. To begin with, it does not emphasise what the real and logical distinction is. It suggests that the basis of the classification is not so much a difference of object as a difference in the means employed to achieve the object. Consequently we find ourselves continually struggling with the false assumption that positive war means using attack, and negative war being content with defence.

That is confusing enough, but a second objection to the designation is far more serious and more fertile of error. For the classification "offensive and defensive" implies that offensive and defensive are mutually exclusive ideas, whereas the truth is, and it is a fundamental truth of war, that they are mutually complementary. All war and every form of it must be both offensive and defensive. No matter how clear our positive aim nor how high our offensive spirit, we cannot develop an aggressive line of strategy to the full without the support of the defensive on all but the main lines of operation. In tactics it is the same. The most convinced devotee of attack admits the spade as well as the rifle. And even when it comes to men and material, we know that without a certain amount of protection neither ships, guns, nor men can develop their utmost energy and endurance in striking power. There is never, in fact, a clean choice between attack and defence. In aggressive operations the question always is, how far must defence enter into the methods we employ in order to enable us to do the utmost within our resources to break or paralyse the strength of the enemy. So also with defence. Even in its most legitimate use, it must always be supplemented by attack. Even behind the walls of a fortress men know that sooner or later the place must fall unless by counter-attack on the enemy's siege works or communications they can cripple his power of attack.

It would seem, therefore, that it were better to lay aside the designation "offensive and defensive" altogether and substitute the terms "positive and negative." But here again we are confronted with a difficulty. There have been many wars in which positive methods have been used all through to secure a negative end, and such wars will not sit easily in either class. For instance, in the War of Spanish Succession our object was mainly to prevent the Mediterranean becoming a French lake by the union of the French and Spanish crowns, but the method by which we succeeded in achieving our end was to seize the naval positions of Gibraltar and Minorca, and so in practice our method was positive. Again, in the late Russo-Japanese War the main object of Japan was to prevent Korea being absorbed by Russia. That aim was preventive and negative. But the only effective way of securing her aim was to take Korea herself, and so for her the war was in practice positive.

On the other hand, we cannot shut our eyes to the fact that in the majority of wars the side with the positive object has acted generally on the offensive and the other generally on the defensive. Unpractical therefore as the distinction seems to be, it is impossible to dismiss it without inquiring why this was so, and it is in this inquiry that the practical results of the classification will be found to lie—that is, it forces us to analyse the comparative advantages of offence and defence. A clear apprehension of their relative possibilities is the corner stone of strategical study.

Now the advantages of the offensive are patent and admitted. It is only the offensive that can produce positive results, while the strength and energy which are born of the moral stimulation of attack are of a practical value that outweighs almost every other consideration. Every man of spirit would desire to use the offensive whether his object were positive or negative, and yet there are a number of cases in which some of the most energetic masters of war have chosen the defensive, and chosen with success. They have chosen it when they have found themselves inferior in physical force to their enemy, and when they believed that no amount of aggressive spirit could redress that inferiority.

Obviously, then, for all the inferiority of the defensive as a drastic form of war it must have some inherent advantage which the offensive does not enjoy. In war we adopt every method for which we have sufficient strength. If, then, we adopt the less desirable method of defence, it must be either that we have not sufficient strength for offence, or that the defence gives us some special strength for the attainment of our object.

What, then, are these elements of strength? It is very necessary to inquire, not only that we may know that if for a time we are forced back upon the defensive all is not lost, but also that we may judge with how much daring we should push our offensive to prevent the enemy securing the advantages of defence.

As a general principle we all know that possession is nine points of the law. It is easier to keep money in our pocket than to take it from another man's. If one man would rob another he must be the stronger or better armed unless he can do it by dexterity or stealth, and there lies one of the advantages of offence. The side which takes the initiative has usually the better chance of securing advantage by dexterity or stealth. But it is not always so. If either by land or sea we can take a defensive position so good that it cannot be turned and must be broken down before our enemy can reach his objective, then the advantage of dexterity and stealth passes to us. We choose our own ground for the trial of strength. We are hidden on familiar ground; he is exposed on ground that is less familiar. We can lay traps and prepare surprises by counter-attack, when he is most dangerously exposed. Hence the paradoxical doctrine that where defence is sound and well designed the advantage of surprise is against the attack.

It will be seen therefore that whatever advantages lie in defence they depend on the preservation of the offensive spirit. Its essence is the counter-attack—waiting deliberately for a chance to strike— not cowering in inactivity. Defence is a condition of restrained activity—not a mere condition of rest. Its real weakness is that if unduly prolonged it tends to deaden the spirit of offence. This is a truth so vital that some authorities in their eagerness to enforce it have travestied it into the misleading maxim, "That attack is the best defence." Hence again an amateurish notion that defence is always stupid or pusillanimous, leading always to defeat, and that what is called "the military spirit" means nothing but taking the offensive. Nothing is further from the teaching or the practice of the best masters. Like Wellington at Torres Vedras, they all at times used the defensive till the elements of strength inherent in that form of war, as opposed to the exhausting strain inherent in the form that they had fixed upon their opponents, lifted them to a position where they in their turn were relatively strong enough to use the more exhausting form.

The confusion of thought which has led to the misconceptions about defence as a method of war is due to several obvious causes. Counter-attacks from a general defensive attitude have been regarded as a true offensive, as, for instance, in Frederick the Great's best-known operations, or in Admiral Tegethoff's brilliant counterstroke at Lissa, or our own operations against the Spanish Armada. Again, the defensive has acquired an ill name by its being confused with a wrongly arrested offensive, where the superior Power with the positive object lacked the spirit to use his material superiority with sufficient activity and perseverance. Against such a Power an inferior enemy can always redress his inferiority by passing to a bold and quick offensive, thus acquiring a momentum both moral and physical which more than compensates his lack of weight. The defensive has also failed by the choice of a bad position which the enemy was able to turn or avoid. A defensive attitude is nothing at all, its elements of strength entirely disappear, unless it is such that the enemy must break it down by force before he can reach his ultimate objective. Even more often has it failed when the belligerent adopting it, finding he has no available defensive position which will bar the enemy's progress, attempts to guard every possible line of attack. The result is of course that by attenuating his force he only accentuates his inferiority.

Clear and well proven as these considerations are for land warfare, their application to the sea is not so obvious. It will be objected that at sea there is no defensive. This is generally true for tactics, but even so not universally true. Defensive tactical positions are possible at sea, as in defended anchorages. These were always a reality, and the mine has increased their possibilities. In the latest developments of naval warfare we have seen the Japanese at the Elliot Islands preparing a real defensive position to cover the landing of their Second Army in the Liao-tung Peninsula. Strategically the proposition is not true at all. A strategical defensive has been quite as common at sea as on land, and our own gravest problems have often been how to break down such an attitude when our enemy assumed it. It usually meant that the enemy remained in his own waters and near his own bases, where it was almost impossible for us to attack him with decisive result, and whence he always threatened us with counter-attack at moments of exhaustion, as the Dutch did at Sole Bay and in the Medway. The difficulty of dealing decisively with an enemy who adopted this course was realised by our service very early, and from first to last one of our chief preoccupations was to prevent the enemy availing himself of this device and to force him to fight in the open, or at least to get between him and his base and force an action there.

Probably the most remarkable manifestation of the advantages that may be derived in suitable conditions from a strategical defensive is also to be found in the late Russo-Japanese War. In the final crisis of the naval struggle the Japanese fleet was able to take advantage of a defensive attitude in its own waters which the Russian Baltic fleet would have to break down to attain its end, and the result was the most decisive naval victory ever recorded.

The deterrent power of active and dexterous operations from such a position was well known to our old tradition. The device was used several times, particularly in our home waters, to prevent a fleet, which for the time we were locally too weak to destroy, from carrying out the work assigned to it. A typical position of the kind was off Scilly, and it was proved again and again that even a superior fleet could not hope to effect anything in the Channel till the fleet off Scilly had been brought to decisive action. But the essence of the device was the preservation of the aggressive spirit in its most daring form. For success it depended on at least the will to seize every occasion for bold and harassing counter-attacks such as Drake and his colleagues struck at the Armada.

To submit to blockade in order to engage the attention of a superior enemy's fleet is another form of defensive, but one that is almost wholly evil. For a short time it may do good by permitting offensive operations elsewhere which otherwise would be impossible. But if prolonged, it will sooner or later destroy the spirit of your force and render it incapable of effective aggression.

The conclusion then is that although for the practical purpose of framing or appreciating plans of war the classification of wars into offensive and defensive is of little use, a clear apprehension of the inherent relative advantages of offence and defence is essential. We must realise that in certain cases, provided always we preserve the aggressive spirit, the defensive will enable an inferior force to achieve points when the offensive would probably lead to its destruction. But the elements of strength depend entirely on the will and insight to deal rapid blows in the enemy's unguarded moments. So soon as the defensive ceases to be regarded as a means of fostering power to strike and of reducing the enemy's power of attack it loses all its strength. It ceases to be even a suspended activity, and anything that is not activity is not war.

With these general indications of the relative advantages of offence and defence we may leave the subject for the present. It is possible of course to catalogue the advantages and disadvantages of each form, but any such bald statement—without concrete examples to explain the meaning—must always appear controversial and is apt to mislead. It is better to reserve their fuller consideration till we come to deal with strategical operations and are able to note their actual effect upon the conduct of war in its various forms. Leaving therefore our first classification of wars into offensive and defensive we will pass on to the second, which is the only one of real practical importance.

CHAPTER III

Natures of Wars—Limited and Unlimited

The second classification to which we are led by the political theory of war, is one which Clausewitz was the first to formulate and one to which he came to attach the highest importance. It becomes necessary therefore to examine his views in some detail—not because there is any need to regard a continental soldier, however distinguished, as an indispensable authority for a maritime nation. The reason is quite the reverse. It is because a careful examination of his doctrine on this point will lay open what are the radical and essential differences between the German or Continental School of Strategy and the British or Maritime School—that is, our own traditional School, which too many writers both at home and abroad quietly assume to have no existence. The evil tendency of that assumption cannot be too strongly emphasised, and the main purpose of this and the following chapters will be to show how and why even the greatest of the continental strategists fell short of realising fully the characteristic conception of the British tradition.

By the classification in question Clausewitz distinguished wars into those with a "Limited" object and those whose object was "Unlimited." Such a classification was entirely characteristic of him, for it rested not alone upon the material nature of the object, but on certain moral considerations to which he was the first to attach their real value in war. Other writers such as Jomini had attempted to classify wars by the special purpose for which they were fought, but Clausewitz's long course of study convinced him that such a distinction was unphilosophical and bore no just relation to any tenable theory of war. Whether, that is, a war was positive or negative mattered much, but its special purpose, whether, for instance, according to Jomini's system, it was a war "to assert rights" or to "assist an ally" or "to acquire territory," mattered not at all.

Whatever the object, the vital and paramount question was the intensity with which the spirit of the nation was absorbed in its attainment. The real point to determine in approaching any war plan was what did the object mean to the two belligerents, what sacrifices would they make for it, what risks were they prepared to run? It was thus he stated his view. "The smaller the sacrifice we demand from our opponent, the smaller presumably will be the means of resistance he will employ, and the smaller his means, the smaller will ours be required to be. Similarly the smaller our political object, the less value shall we set upon it and the more easily we shall be induced to abandon it." Thus the political object of the war, its original motive will not only determine for both belligerents reciprocally the aim of the force they use, but it will also be the standard of the intensity of the efforts they will make. So he concludes there may be wars of all degrees of importance and energy from a war of extermination down to the use of an army of observation. So also in the naval sphere there may be a life and death struggle for maritime supremacy or hostilities which never rise beyond a blockade.

Such a view of the subject was of course a wide departure from the theory of "Absolute War" on which Clausewitz had started working. Under that theory "Absolute War" was the ideal form to which all war ought to attain, and those which fell short of it were imperfect wars cramped by a lack of true military spirit. But so soon as he had seized the fact that in actual life the moral factor always must override the purely military factor, he saw that he had been working on too narrow a basis—a basis that was purely theoretical in that it ignored the human factor. He began to perceive that it was logically unsound to assume as the foundation of a strategical system that there was one pattern to which all wars ought to conform. In the light of his full and final apprehension of the value of the human factor he saw wars falling into two well-marked categories, each of which would legitimately be approached in a radically different manner, and not necessarily on the lines of "Absolute War."

He saw that there was one class of war where the political object was of so vital an importance to both belligerents that they would tend to fight to the utmost limit of their endurance to secure it. But there was another class where the object was of less importance, that is to say, where its value to one or both the belligerents was not so great as to be worth unlimited sacrifices of blood and treasure. It was these two kinds of war he designated provisionally "Unlimited" and "Limited," by which he meant not that you were not to exert the force employed with all the vigour you could develop, but that there might be a limit beyond which it would be bad policy to spend that vigour, a point at which, long before your force was exhausted or even fully developed, it would be wiser to abandon your object rather than to spend more upon it.

This distinction it is very necessary to grasp quite clearly, for it is often superficially confused with the distinction already referred to, which Clausewitz drew in the earlier part of his work—that is, the distinction between what he called the character of modern war and the character of the wars which preceded the Napoleonic era. It will be remembered he insisted that the wars of his own time had been wars between armed nations with a tendency to throw the whole weight of the nation into the fighting line, whereas in the seventeenth and eighteenth centuries wars were waged by standing armies and not by the whole nation in arms. The distinction of course is real and of far-reaching consequences, but it has no relation to the distinction between "Limited" and "Unlimited" war. War may be waged on the Napoleonic system either for a limited or an unlimited object.

A modern instance will serve to clear the field. The recent Russo-Japanese War was fought for a limited object—the assertion of certain claims over territory which formed no part of the possessions of either belligerent. Hostilities were conducted on entirely modern lines by two armed nations and not by standing armies alone. But in the case of one belligerent her interest in the object was so limited as to cause her to abandon it long before her whole force as an armed nation was exhausted or even put forth. The expense of life and treasure which the struggle was involving was beyond what the object was worth.

This second distinction—that is, between Limited and Unlimited wars—Clausewitz regarded as of greater importance than his previous one founded on the negative or positive nature of the object. He was long in reaching it. His great work *On War* as he left it proceeds almost entirely on the conception of offensive or defensive as applied to the Napoleonic ideal of absolute war. The new idea came to him towards the end in the full maturity of his prolonged study, and it came to him in endeavouring to apply his strategical speculations to the practical process of framing a war plan in anticipation of a threatened breach with France. It was only in his final section *On War Plans* that he began to deal with it. By that time he had grasped the first practical result to which his theory led. He saw that the distinction between Limited and Unlimited war connoted a cardinal distinction in the methods of waging it. When the object was unlimited, and would consequently call forth your enemy's whole war power, it was evident that no firm decision of the struggle could be reached till his war power was entirely crushed. Unless you had a reasonable hope of being able to do this it was bad policy to seek your end by force— that is, you ought not to go to war. In the case of a limited object, however, the complete destruction of the enemy's armed force was beyond what was necessary. Clearly you could achieve your end if you could seize the object, and by availing yourself of the elements of strength inherent in the defensive could set up such a situation that it would cost the enemy more to turn you out than the object was worth to him.

Here then was a wide difference in the fundamental postulate of your war plan. In the case of an unlimited war your main strategical offensive must be directed against the armed forces of the enemy; in the case of a limited war, even where its object was positive, it need not be. If conditions were favourable, it would suffice to make the object itself the objective of your main strategical offensive. Clearly, then, he had reached a theoretical distinction which modified his whole conception of strategy. No longer is there logically but one kind of war, the Absolute, and no longer is there but one legitimate objective, the enemy's armed forces. Being sound theory, it of course had an immediate practical value, for obviously it was a distinction from which the actual work of framing a war plan must take its departure.

A curious corroboration of the soundness of these views is that Jomini reached an almost identical standpoint independently and by an entirely different road. His method was severely concrete, based on the comparison of observed facts, but it brought him as surely as the abstract method of his rival to the conclusion that there were two distinct classes of object. "They are of two different kinds," he says, "one which may be called territorial or geographical . . . the other on the contrary consists exclusively in the destruction or disorganisation of the enemy's forces without concerning yourself with geographical points of any kind." It is under the first category of his first main classification "Of offensive wars to assert rights," that he deals with what Clausewitz would call "Limited Wars." Citing as an example Frederick the Great's war for the conquest of Silesia, he says, "In such a war . . . the offensive operations ought to be proportional to the end in view. The first move is naturally to occupy the provinces claimed" (not, be it noted, to direct your blow at the enemy's main force). "Afterwards," he proceeds, "you can push the offensive according to circumstances and your relative strength in order to obtain the desired cession by menacing the enemy at home." Here we have Clausewitz's whole doctrine of "Limited War"; firstly, the primary or territorial stage, in which you endeavour to occupy the geographical object, and then the secondary or coercive stage, in which you seek by exerting general pressure upon your enemy to force him to accept the adverse situation you have set up.

Such a method of making war obviously differs in a fundamental manner from that which Napoleon habitually adopted, and yet we have it presented by Jomini and Clausewitz, the two apostles of the Napoleonic method. The explanation is, of course, that both of them had seen too much not to know that Napoleon's method was only applicable when you could command a real physical or moral preponderance. Given such a preponderance, both were staunch for the use of extreme means in Napoleon's manner. It is not as something better than the higher road that they commend the lower one, but being veteran staff-officers and not mere theorists, they knew well that a belligerent must sometimes find the higher road beyond his strength, or beyond the effort which the spirit of the nation is prepared to make for the end in view, and like the practical men they were, they set themselves to study the potentialities of the lower road should hard necessity force them to travel it. They found that these potentialities in certain circumstances were great. As an example of a case where the lower form was more appropriate Jomini cites Napoleon's campaign against Russia in 1812. In his opinion it would have been better if Napoleon had been satisfied to begin on the lower method with a limited territorial object, and he attributes his failure to the abuse of a method which, however well suited to his wars in Germany, was incapable of achieving success in the conditions presented by a war with Russia.

Seeing how high was Napoleon's opinion of Jomini as a master of the science of war, it is curious how his views on the two natures of wars have been ignored in the present day. It is even more curious in the case of Clausewitz, since we know that in the plenitude of his powers he came to regard this classification as the master-key of the subject. The explanation is that the distinction is not very clearly formulated is his first seven books, which alone he left in anything like a finished condition. It was not till he came to write his eighth book *On War Plans* that he saw the vital importance of the distinction round which he had been hovering. In that book the distinction is clearly laid down, but the book unhappily was never completed. With his manuscript, however, he left a "Note" warning us against regarding his earlier books as a full presentation of his developed ideas. From the note it is also evident that he thought the classification on which he had lighted was of the utmost importance, that he believed it would clear up all the difficulties which he had encountered in his earlier books—difficulties which he had come to see arose from a too exclusive consideration of the Napoleonic method of conducting war. "I look upon the first six books," he wrote in 1827, "as only a mass of material which is still in a manner without form and which has still to be revised again. In this revision the two kinds of wars will be kept more distinctly in view all through, and thereby all ideas will gain in clearness, in precision, and in exactness of application." Evidently he had grown dissatisfied with the theory of Absolute War on which he had started. His new discovery had convinced him that that theory would not serve as a standard for all natures of wars. "Shall we," he asks in his final book, "shall we now rest satisfied with this idea and by it judge of all wars, however much they may differ?"[1] He answers his question in the negative. "You cannot

---

[1] *On War,* Book viii. Chap. ii.

determine the requirements of all wars from the Napoleonic type. Keep that type and its absolute method before you to use *when you can* or *when you must,* but keep equally before you that there are two main natures of war."

In his note written at this time, when the distinction first came to him, he defines these two natures of war as follows: "First, those in which the object is the *overthrow of the enemy,* whether it be we aim at his political destruction or merely at disarming him and forcing him to conclude peace on our terms; and secondly, those in which our object is *merely to make some conquests on the frontiers of his country,* either for the purpose of retaining them permanently or of turning them to account as a matter of exchange in settling terms of peace."[2] It was in his eighth book that he intended, had he lived, to have worked out the comprehensive idea he had conceived. Of that book he says, "The chief object will be to make good the two points of view above mentioned, by which everything will be simplified and at the same time be given the breath of life. I hope in this book to iron out many creases in the heads of strategists and statesmen, and at least to show the object of action and the real point to be considered in war."[3]

That hope was never realised, and that perhaps is why his penetrating analysis has been so much ignored. The eighth book as we have it is only a fragment. In the spring of 1830—an anxious moment, when it seemed that Prussia would require all her best for another struggle single-handed with France—he was called away to an active command. What he left of the book on "War Plans" he describes as "merely a track roughly cleared, as it were, through the mass, in order to ascertain the points of greatest moment." It was his intention, he says, to "carry the

[2] *Ibid.,* p. viii.
[3] *Ibid.,* Prefatory Notice, p. vii.

spirit of these ideas into his first six books"—to put the crown on his work, in fact, by elaborating and insisting upon his two great propositions, viz. that war was a form of policy, and that being so it might be Limited or Unlimited.

The extent to which he would have infused his new idea into the whole every one is at liberty to judge for himself; but this indisputable fact remains. In the winter in view of the threatening attitude of France in regard to Belgium he drew up a war plan, and it was designed not on the Napoleonic method of making the enemy's armed force the main strategical objective, but on seizing a limited territorial object and forcing a disadvantageous counter-offensive upon the French. The revolutionary movement throughout Europe had broken the Holy Alliance to pieces. Not only did Prussia find herself almost single-handed against France, but she herself was sapped by revolution. To adopt the higher form of war and seek to destroy the armed force of the enemy was beyond her power. But she could still use the lower form, and by seizing Belgium she could herself force so exhausting a task on France that success was well within her strength. It was exactly so we endeavoured to begin the Seven Years' War; and it was exactly so the Japanese successfully conducted their war with Russia; and what is more striking, it was on similar lines that in 1859 Moltke in similar circumstances drew up his first war plan against France. His idea at that time was on the lines which Jomini held should have been Napoleon's in 1812. It was not to strike directly at Paris or the French main army, but to occupy Alsace-Lorraine and hold that territory till altered conditions should give him the necessary preponderance for proceeding to the higher form or forcing a favourable peace.

In conclusion, then, we have to note that the matured fruit of the Napoleonic period was a theory of war based not on the single absolute idea, but on the dual distinction of Limited and Unlimited. Whatever practical importance we may attach to the distinction, so much must be admitted on the clear and emphatic pronouncements of Clausewitz and Jomini. The practical importance is another matter. It may fairly be argued that in continental warfare—in spite of the instances quoted by both the classical writers—it is not very great, for reasons that will appear directly. But it must be remembered that continental warfare is not the only form in which great international issues are decided. Standing at the final point which Clausewitz and Jomini reached, we are indeed only on the threshold of the subject. We have to begin where they left off and inquire what their ideas have to tell for the modern conditions of world-wide imperial States, where the sea becomes a direct and vital factor.

CHAPTER IV

LIMITED WAR AND MARITIME EMPIRES—DEVELOPMENT OF CLAUSEWITZ'S AND JOMINI'S THEORY OF A LIMITED TERRITORIAL OBJECT, AND ITS APPLICATION TO MODERN IMPERIAL CONDITIONS

The German war plans already cited, which were based respectively on the occupation of Belgium and Alsace-Lorraine, and Jomini's remarks on Napoleon's disastrous Russian campaign serve well to show the point to which continental strategists have advanced along the road which Clausewitz was the first to indicate clearly. We have now to consider its application to modern imperial conditions, and above all where the maritime element forcibly asserts itself. We shall then see how small that advance has been compared with its far-reaching effects for a maritime and above all an insular Power.

It is clear that Clausewitz himself never apprehended the full significance of his brilliant theory. His outlook was still purely continental, and the limitations of continental warfare tend to veil the fuller meaning of the principle he had framed. Had he lived, there is little doubt he would have worked it out to its logical conclusion, but his death condemned his theory of limited war to remain in the inchoate condition in which he had left it.

It will be observed, as was natural enough, that all through his work Clausewitz had in his mind war between two contiguous or at least adjacent continental States, and a moment's consideration will show that in that type of war the principle of the limited object can rarely if ever assert itself in perfect precision. Clausewitz himself put it quite clearly. Assuming a case where "the overthrow of the enemy"—that is, unlimited war—is beyond our strength, he points out that we need not therefore necessarily act on the defensive. Our action may still be positive and offensive, but the object can be nothing more than "the conquest of part of the enemy's country." Such a conquest he knew might so far weaken your enemy or strengthen your own position as to enable you to secure a satisfactory peace. The path of history is indeed strewn with such cases. But he was careful to point out that such a form of war was open to the gravest objections. Once you had occupied the territory you aimed at, your offensive action was, as a rule, arrested. A defensive attitude had to be assumed, and such an arrest of offensive action he had previously shown was inherently vicious, if only for moral reasons. Added to this you might find that in your effort to occupy the territorial object you had so irretrievably separated your striking force from your home-defence force as to be in no position to meet your enemy if he was able to retort by acting on unlimited lines with a stroke at your heart. A case in point was the Austerlitz campaign, where Austria's object was to wrest North Italy from Napoleon's empire. She sent her main army under the Archduke Charles to seize the territory she desired. Napoleon immediately struck at Vienna, destroyed her home army, and occupied the capital before the Archduke could turn to bar his way.

The argument is this: that, as all strategic attack tends to leave points of your own uncovered, it always involves greater or less provision for their defence. It is obvious, therefore, that if we are aiming at a limited territorial object the proportion of defence required will tend to be much greater than if we are directing our attack on the main forces of the enemy. In unlimited war our attack will itself tend to defend everything elsewhere by forcing the enemy to concentrate against our attack. Whether the limited form is justifiable or not therefore depends, as Clausewitz points out, on the geographical position of the object.

So far British experience is with him, but he then goes on to say the more closely the territory in question is an annex of our own the safer is this form of war, because then our offensive action will the more surely cover our home country. As a case in point he cites Frederick the Great's opening of the Seven Years' War with the occupation of Saxony—a piece of work which materially strengthened Prussian defence. Of the British opening in Canada he says nothing. His outlook was too exclusively continental for it to occur to him to test his doctrine with a conspicuously successful case in which the territory aimed at was distant from the home territory and in no way covered it. Had he done so he must have seen how much stronger an example of the strength of limited war was the case of Canada than the case of Saxony. Moreover, he would have seen that the difficulties, which in spite of his faith in his discovery accompanied his attempt to apply it, arose from the fact that the examples he selected were not really examples at all.

When he conceived the idea, the only kind of limited object he had in his mind was, to use his own words, "some conquests on the frontiers of the enemy's country," such as Silesia and Saxony for Frederick the Great, Belgium in his own war plan, and Alsace-Lorraine in that of Moltke. Now it is obvious that such objects are not truly limited, for two reasons. In the first place, such territory is usually an organic part of your enemy's country, or otherwise of so much importance to him that he will be willing to use unlimited effort to retain it. In the second place, there will be no strategical obstacle to his being able to use his whole force to that end. To satisfy the full conception of a limited object, one of two conditions is essential. Firstly, it must be not merely limited in area, but of really limited political importance; and secondly, it must be so situated as to be strategically isolated or to be capable of being reduced to practical isolation by strategical operations. Unless this condition exists, it is in the power of either belligerent, as Clausewitz himself saw, to pass to unlimited war if he so desires, and, ignoring the territorial objective, to strike at the heart of his enemy and force him to desist.

If, then, we only regard war between contiguous continental States, in which the object is the conquest of territory on either of their frontiers, we get no real generic difference between limited and unlimited war. The line between them is in any case too shadowy or unstable to give a classification of any solidity. It is a difference of degree rather than of kind. If, on the other hand, we extend our view to wars between worldwide empires, the distinction at once becomes organic. Possessions which lie oversea or at the extremities of vast areas of imperfectly settled territory are in an entirely different category from those limited objects which Clausewitz contemplated. History shows that they can never have the political importance of objects which are organically part of the European system, and it shows further that they can be isolated by naval action sufficiently to set up the conditions of true limited war.

Jomini approaches the point, but without clearly detaching it. In his chapter "On Great Invasions and Distant Expeditions," he points out how unsafe it is to take the conditions of war between contiguous States and apply them crudely to cases where the belligerents are separated by large areas of land or sea. He hovers round the sea factor, feeling how great a difference it makes, but without getting close to the real distinction. His conception of the inter-action of fleets and armies never rises above their actual co-operation in touch one with the other in a distant theatre. He has in mind the assistance which the British fleet afforded Wellington in the Peninsula, and Napoleon's dreams of Asiatic conquest, pronouncing such distant invasions as impossible in modern times except perhaps in combination with a powerful fleet that could provide the army of invasion with successive advanced bases. Of the paramount value of the fleet's isolating and preventive functions he gives no hint.

Even when he deals with oversea expeditions, as he does at some length, his grip of the point is no closer. It is indeed significant of how entirely continental thought had failed to penetrate the subject that in devoting over thirty pages to an enumeration of the principles of oversea expeditions, he, like Clausewitz, does not so much as mention the conquest of Canada; and yet it is the leading case of a weak military Power succeeding by the use of the limited form of war in forcing its will upon a strong one, and succeeding because it was able by naval action to secure its home defence and isolate the territorial object.

For our ideas of true limited objects, therefore, we must leave the continental theatres and turn to mixed or maritime wars. We have to look to such cases as Canada and Havana in the Seven Years' War, and Cuba in the Spanish-American War, cases in which complete isolation of the object by naval action was possible, or to such examples as the Crimea and Korea, where sufficient isolation was attainable by naval action owing to the length and difficulty of the enemy's land communications and to the strategical situation of the territory at stake.

These examples will also serve to illustrate and enforce the second essential of this kind of war. As has been already said, for a true limited object we must have not only the power of isolation, but also the power by a secure home defence of barring an unlimited counterstroke. In all the above cases this condition existed. In all of them the belligerents had no continuous frontiers and this point is vital. For it is obvious that if two belligerents have a common frontier, it is open to the superior of them, no matter how distant or how easy to isolate the limited object may be, to pass at will to unlimited war by invasion. This process is even possible when the belligerents are separated by a neutral State, since the territory of a weak neutral will be violated if the object be of sufficient importance, or if the neutral be too strong to coerce, there still remains the possibility that his alliance may be secured.

We come, then, to this final proposition—that limited war is only permanently possible to island Powers or between Powers which are separated by sea, and then only when the Power desiring limited war is able to command the sea to such a degree as to be able not only to isolate the distant object, but also to render impossible the invasion of his home territory.

Here, then, we reach the true meaning and highest military value of what we call the command of the sea, and here we touch the secret of England's success against Powers so greatly superior to herself in military strength. It is only fitting that such a secret should have been first penetrated by an Englishman. For so it was, though it must be said that except in the light of Clausewitz's doctrine the full meaning of Bacon's famous aphorism is not revealed. "This much is certain," said the great Elizabethan on the experience of our first imperial war; "he that commands the sea is at great liberty and may take as much or as little of the war as he will, whereas those that be strongest by land are many times nevertheless in great straits." It would be difficult to state more pithily the ultimate significance of Clausewitz's doctrine. Its cardinal truth is clearly indicated—that limited wars do not turn upon the armed strength of the belligerents, but upon the amount of that strength which they are able or willing to bring to bear at the decisive point.

It is much to be regretted that Clausewitz did not live to see with Bacon's eyes and to work out the full comprehensiveness of his doctrine. His ambition was to formulate a theory which would explain all wars. He believed he had done so, and yet it is clear he never knew how complete was his success, nor how wide was the field he had covered. To the end it would seem he was unaware that he had found an explanation of one of the most inscrutable problems in history—the expansion of

England—at least so far as it has been due to successful war. That a small country with a weak army should have been able to gather to herself the most desirable regions of the earth, and to gather them at the expense of the greatest military Powers, is a paradox to which such Powers find it hard to be reconciled. The phenomenon seemed always a matter of chance—an accident without any foundation in the essential constants of war. It remained for Clausewitz, unknown to himself, to discover that explanation, and he reveals it to us in the inherent strength of limited war when means and conditions are favourable for its use.

We find, then, if we take a wider view than was open to Clausewitz and submit his latest ideas to the test of present imperial conditions, so far from failing to cover the ground they gain a fuller meaning and a firmer basis. Apply them to maritime warfare and it becomes clear that his distinction between limited and unlimited war does not rest alone on the moral factor. A war may be limited not only because the importance of the object is too limited to call forth the whole national force, but also because the sea may be made to present an insuperable physical obstacle to the whole national force being brought to bear. That is to say, a war may be limited physically by the strategical isolation of the object, as well as morally by its comparative unimportance.

CHAPTER V

WARS OF INTERVENTION—LIMITED INTERFERENCE IN UNLIMITED WAR

Before leaving the general consideration of limited war, we have still to deal with a form of it that has not yet been mentioned. Clausewitz gave it provisionally the name of "War limited by contingent," and could find no place for it in his system. It appeared to him to differ essentially from war limited by its political object, or as Jomini put it, war with a territorial object. Yet it had to be taken into account and explained, if only for the part it had played in European history.

For us it calls for the most careful examination, not only because it baffled the great German strategist to reconcile it with his theory of war, but also because it is the form in which Great Britain most successfully demonstrated the potentiality for direct continental interference of a small army acting in conjunction with a dominant fleet.

The combined operations which were the normal expression of the British method of making war on the limited basis were of two main classes. Firstly, there were those designed purely for the conquest of the objects for which we went to war, which were usually colonial or distant oversea territory; and secondly, operations more or less upon the European seaboard designed not for permanent conquest, but as a method of disturbing our enemy's plans and strengthening the hands of our allies and our own position. Such operations might take the form of insignificant coastal diversions, or they might rise through all degrees of importance till, as in Wellington's operations in the Peninsula, they became indistinguishable in form from regular continental warfare.

It would seem, therefore, that these operations were distinguished not so much by the nature of the object as by the fact that we devoted to them, not the whole of our military strength, but only a certain part of it which was known as our "disposal force." Consequently, they appear to call for some such special classification, and to fall naturally into the category which Clausewitz called "War limited by contingent."

It was a nature of war well enough known in another form on the Continent. During the eighteenth century there had been a large number of cases of war actually limited by contingent—that is, cases where a country not having a vital interest in the object made war by furnishing the chief belligerent with an auxiliary force of a stipulated strength.

It was in the sixth chapter of his last book that Clausewitz intended to deal with this anomalous form of hostility. His untimely death, however, has left us with no more than a fragment, in which he confesses that such cases are "embarrassing to his theory." If, he adds, the auxiliary force were placed unreservedly at the disposal of the chief belligerent, the problem would be simple enough. It would then, in effect, be the same thing as unlimited war with the aid of a subsidised force. But in fact, as he observes, this seldom happened, for the contingent was always more or less controlled in accordance with the special political aims of the Government which furnished it. Consequently, the only conclusion he succeeded in reaching was that it was a form of war that had to be taken into account, and that it was a form of limited war that appeared to differ essentially from war limited by object. We are left, in fact, with an impression that there must be two kinds of limited war.

But if we pursue his historical method and examine the cases in which this nature of war was successful, and those in which it was unsuccessful, we shall find that wherever success is taken as an index of its legitimate employment, the practical distinction between the two kinds of limited war tends to disappear. The indications are that where the essential factors which justify the use of war limited by object are present in war limited by contingent, then that form of war tends to succeed, but not otherwise. We are brought, in fact, to this proposition, that the distinction "Limited by contingent" is not one that is inherent in war and is quite out of line with the theory in hand—that, in reality, it is not a *form* of war, but a *method* which may be employed either for limited or unlimited war. In other words, war limited by contingent, if it is to be regarded as a legitimate form of war at all, must take frankly the one shape or the other. Either the contingent must act as an organic unit of the force making unlimited war without any reservations whatever, or else it should be given a definite territorial object, with an independent organisation and an independent limited function.

Our own experience seems to indicate that war by contingent or war with "a disposal force" attains the highest success when it approaches most closely to true limited war—that is, as in the case of the Peninsula and the Crimea, where its object is to wrest or secure from the enemy a definite piece of territory that to a greater or less extent can be isolated by naval action. Its operative power, in fact, appears to bear some direct relation to the intimacy with which naval and military action can be combined to give the contingent a weight and mobility that are beyond its intrinsic power.

If, then, we would unravel the difficulties of war limited by contingent, it seems necessary to distinguish between the continental and the British form of it. The continental form, as we have seen, differs but little in conception from unlimited war. The contingent is furnished at least ostensibly with the idea that it is to be used by the chief belligerent to assist him in overthrowing the common enemy, and that its objective will be the enemy's organised forces or his capital. Or it may be that the contingent is to be used as an army of observation to prevent a counterstroke, so as to facilitate and secure the main offensive movement of the chief belligerent. In either case, however small may be our contribution to the allied force, we are using the unlimited form and aiming at an unlimited and not a mere territorial object.

If now we turn to British experience of war limited by contingent, we find that the continental form has frequently been used, but we also find it almost invariably accompanied by a popular repugnance, as though there were something in it antagonistic to the national instinct. A leading case is the assistance we sent to Frederick the Great in the Seven Years' War. At the opening of the war, so great was the popular repugnance that the measure was found impossible, and it was not till Frederick's dazzling resistance to the Catholic powers had clothed him with the glory of a Protestant hero, that Pitt could do what he wanted. The old religious fire was stirred. The most potent of all national instincts kindled the people to a generous warmth which overcame their inborn antipathy to continental operations, and it was possible to send a substantial contingent to Frederick's assistance. In the end the support fully achieved its purpose, but it must be noted that even in this case the operations were limited not only by contingent but also by object. It is true that Frederick was engaged in an unlimited way in which the continued existence of Prussia was at stake, and that the British force was an organic element in his war plan. Nevertheless, it formed part of a British subsidised army under Prince Ferdinand of Brunswick, who though nominated by Frederick was a British commander-in-chief. His army was in organisation entirely distinct from that of Frederick, and it was assigned the very definite and limited function of preventing the French occupying Hanover and so turning the Prussian right flank. Finally it must be noted that its ability to perform this function was due to the fact that the theatre of operations assigned to it was such that in no probable event could it lose touch with the sea, nor could the enemy cut its lines of supply and retreat.

These features of the enterprise should be noted. They differentiate it from our earlier use of war limited by contingent in the continental manner, of which Marlborough's campaigns were typical, and they exhibit the special form which Marlborough would have chosen had political exigencies permitted and which was to become characteristic of British effort from Pitt's time onward. In the method of our greatest War Minister we have not only the limit by contingent but also the limit of a definite and independent function, and finally we have touch with the sea. This is the really vital factor, and upon it, as will presently appear, depends the strength of the method.

In the earlier part of the Great War we employed the same form in our operations in North-Western Europe. There we had also the limited function of securing Holland and also complete touch with the sea, but our theatre of operations was not independent. Intimate concerted action with other forces was involved, and the result in every case was failure. Later on in Sicily, where absolute isolation was attainable, the strength of the method enabled us to achieve a lasting result with very slender means. But the result was purely defensive. It was not till the Peninsular War developed that we found a theatre for war limited by contingent in which all the conditions that make for success were present. Even there so long as our army was regarded as a contingent auxiliary to the Spanish army the usual failure ensued. Only in Portugal, the defence of which was a true limited object, and where we had a sea-girt theatre independent of extraneous allies, was success achieved from the first. So strong was the method here, and so exhausting the method which it forced on the enemy, that the local balance of force was eventually reversed and we were able to pass to a drastic offensive.

The real secret of Wellington's success—apart from his own genius—was that in perfect conditions he was applying the limited form to an unlimited war. Our object was unlimited. It was nothing less than the overthrow of Napoleon. Complete success at sea had failed to do it, but that success had given us the power of applying the limited form, which was the most decisive form of offence within our means. Its substantial contribution to the final achievement of the object is now universally recognised.

The general result, then, of these considerations is that war by contingent in the continental form seldom or never differs generically from unlimited war, for the conditions required by limited war are seldom or never present. But what may be called the British or maritime form is in fact the application of the limited method to the unlimited form, as ancillary to the larger operations of our allies—a method which has usually been open to us because the control of the sea has enabled us to select a theatre in effect truly limited.

But what if the conditions of the struggle in which we wish to intervene are such that no truly limited theatre is available? In that case we have to choose between placing a contingent frankly at the disposal of our ally, or confining ourselves to coastal diversion, as we did at Frederick the Great's request in the early campaigns of the Seven Years' War. Such operations can seldom be satisfactory to either party. The small positive results of our efforts to intervene in this way have indeed done more than anything to discredit this form of war, and to brand it as unworthy of a first-class Power. Yet the fact remains that all the great continental masters of war have feared or valued British intervention of this character even in the most unfavourable conditions. It was because they looked for its effects rather in the threat than in the performance. They did not reckon for positive results at all. So long as such intervention took an amphibious form they knew its disturbing effect upon a European situation was always out of all proportion to the intrinsic strength employed or the positive results it could give. Its operative action was that it threatened positive results unless it were strongly met. Its effect, in short, was negative. Its value lay in its power of containing force greater than its own. That is all that can be claimed for it, but it may be all that is required. It is not the most drastic method of intervention, but it has proved itself the most drastic for a Power whose forces are not adapted for the higher method. Frederick the Great was the first great soldier to recognise it, and Napoleon was the last. For years he shut his eyes to it, laughed at it, covered it with a contempt that grew ever more irritable. In 1805 he called Craig's expedition a "pygmy combination," yet the preparation of another combined force for an entirely different destination caused him to see the first as an advance guard of a movement he could not ignore, and he sacrificed his fleet in an impotent effort to deal with it.

It was not, however, till four years later that he was forced to place on record his recognition of the principle. Then, curiously enough, he was convinced by an expedition which we have come to regard as above all others condemnatory of amphibious operations against the Continent. The Walcheren expedition is now usually held as the leading case of fatuous war administration. Historians can find no words too bad for it. They ignore the fact that it was a step—the final and most difficult step—in our post-Trafalgar policy of using the army to perfect our command of the sea against a fleet acting stubbornly on the defensive. It began with Copenhagen in 1807. It failed at the Dardanelles because fleet and army were separated; it succeeded at Lisbon and at Cadiz by demonstration alone. Walcheren, long contemplated, had been put off till the last as the most formidable and the least pressing. Napoleon had been looking for the attempt ever since the idea was first broached in this country, but as time passed and the blow did not fall, the danger came to be more and more ignored. Finally, the moment came when he was heavily engaged in Austria and forced to call up the bulk of his strength to deal with the Archduke Charles. The risks were still great, but the British Government faced them boldly with open eyes. It was now or never. They were bent on developing their utmost military strength in the Peninsula, and so long as a potent and growing fleet remained in the North Sea it would always act as an increasing drag on such development. The prospective gain of success was in the eyes of the Government out of all proportion to the probable loss by failure. So when Napoleon least expected it they determined to act, and caught him napping. The defences of Antwerp had been left incomplete. There was no army to meet the blow—nothing but a polyglot rabble without staff or even officers. For a week at least success was in our hands. Napoleon's fleet only escaped by twenty-four hours, and yet the failure was not only complete but disastrous. Still so entirely were the causes of failure accidental, and so near had it come to success, that Napoleon received a thorough shock and looked for a quick repetition of the attempt. So seriously indeed did he regard his narrow escape that he found himself driven to reconsider his whole system of home defence. Not only did he deem it necessary to spend large sums in increasing the fixed defences of Antwerp and Toulon, but his Director of Conscription was called upon to work out a scheme for providing a permanent force of no less than 300,000 men from the National Guard to defend the French coasts. "With 30,000 men in transports at the Downs," the Emperor wrote, "the English can paralyse 300,000 of my army, and that will reduce us to the rank of a second-class Power."[1] The concentration of the British efforts in the Peninsula apparently rendered the realisation of this project unnecessary—that is, our line of operation was declared and the threat ceased. But none the less Napoleon's recognition of the principle remains on

---

[1] *Correspondance de Napoleon,* xix. 421, September 4.

record—not in one of his speeches made for some ulterior purpose, but in a staff order to the principal officer concerned.

It is generally held that modern developments in military organisation and transport will enable a great continental Power to ignore such threats. Napoleon ignored them in the past, but only to verify the truth that in war to ignore a threat is too often to create an opportunity. Such opportunities may occur late or early. As both Lord Ligonier and Wolfe laid it down for such operations, surprise is not necessarily to be looked for at the beginning. We have usually had to create or wait for our opportunity—too often because we were either not ready or not bold enough to seize the first that occurred.

The cases in which such intervention has been most potent have been of two classes. Firstly, there is the intrusion into a war plan which our enemy has designed without allowing for our intervention, and to which he is irrevocably committed by his opening movements. Secondly, there is intervention to deprive the enemy of the fruits of victory. This form finds its efficacy in the principle that unlimited wars are not always decided by the destruction of armies. There usually remains the difficult work of conquering the people afterwards with an exhausted army. The intrusion of a small fresh force from the sea in such cases may suffice to turn the scale, as it did in the Peninsula, and as, in the opinion of some high authorities, it might have done in France in 1871.

Such a suggestion will appear to be almost heretical as sinning against the principle which condemns a strategical reserve. We say that the whole available force should be developed for the vital period of the struggle. No one can be found to dispute it nowadays. It is too obviously true when it is a question of a conflict between organised forces, but in the absence of all proof we are entitled to doubt whether it is true for that exhausting and demoralising period which lies beyond the shock of armies.

CHAPTER VI

CONDITIONS OF STRENGTH IN LIMITED WAR

The elements of strength in limited war are closely analogous to those generally inherent in defence. That is to say, that as a correct use of defence will sometimes enable an inferior force to gain its end against a superior one, so are there instances in which the correct use of the limited form of war has enabled a weak military Power to attain success against a much stronger one, and these instances are too numerous to permit us to regard the results as accidental.

An obvious element of strength is that where the geographical conditions are favourable we are able by the use of our navy to restrict the amount of force our army will have to deal with. We can in fact bring up our fleet to redress the adverse balance of our land force. But apart from this very practical reason there is another, which is rooted in the first principles of strategy.

It is that limited war permits the use of the defensive without its usual drawbacks to a degree that is impossible in unlimited war. These drawbacks are chiefly that it tends to surrender the initiative to the enemy and that it deprives us of the moral exhilaration of the offensive. But in limited war, as we shall see, this need not be the case, and if without making these sacrifices we are able to act mainly on the defensive our position becomes exceedingly strong.

The proposition really admits of no doubt. For even if we be not in whole-hearted agreement with Clausewitz's doctrine of the strength of defence, still we may at least accept Moltke's modification of it. He held that the strongest form of war—that is, the form which economically makes for the highest development of strength in a given force—is strategic offensive combined with tactical defensive. Now these are in effect the conditions which limited war should give—that is, if the theatre and method be rightly chosen. Let it be remembered that the use of this form of war presupposes that we are able by superior readiness or mobility or by being more conveniently situated to establish ourselves in the territorial object before our opponent can gather strength to prevent us. This done, we have the initiative, and the enemy being unable by hypothesis to attack us at home, must conform to our opening by endeavouring to turn us out. We are in a position to meet his attack on ground of our own choice and to avail ourselves of such opportunities of counter-attack as his distant and therefore exhausting offensive movements are likely to offer. Assuming, as in our own case we always must assume, that the territorial object is sea-girt and our enemy is not able to command the sea, such opportunities are certain to present themselves, and even if they are not used will greatly embarrass the main attack—as was abundantly shown in the Russian nervousness during their advance into the Liaotung Peninsula, due to the fear of a counter-stroke from the Gulf of Pe-chi-li.

The actual situation which this method of procedure sets up is that our major strategy is offensive—that is, our main movement is positive, having for its aim the occupation of the territorial object. The minor strategy that follows should be in its general lines defensive, designed, so soon as the enemy sets about dislodging us, to develop the utmost energy of counter-attack which our force and opportunities justify.

Now if we consider that by universal agreement it is no longer possible in the present conditions of land warfare to draw a line between tactics and minor strategy, we have in our favour for all practical purposes the identical position which Moltke regarded as constituting the strongest form of war. That is to say, our major strategy is offensive and our minor strategy is defensive.

If, then, the limited form of war has this element of strength over and above the unlimited form, it must be correct to use it when we are not strong enough to use the more exhausting form and when the object is limited; just as much as it is correct to use the defensive when our object is negative and we are too weak for the offensive. The point is of the highest importance, for it is a direct negation of the current doctrine that in war there can be but one legitimate object, the overthrow of the enemy's means of resistance, and that the primary objective must always be his armed forces. It raises in fact the whole question as to whether it is not sometimes legitimate and even correct to aim directly at the ulterior object of the war.

An impression appears to prevail—in spite of all that Clausewitz and Jomini had to say on the point—that the question admits of only one answer. Von der Goltz, for instance, is particularly emphatic in asserting that the overthrow of the enemy must always be the object in modern war. He lays it down as "the first principle of modern warfare," that "the immediate objective against which all our efforts must be directed is the hostile main army." Similarly Prince Kraft has the maxim that "the first aim should be to overcome the enemy's army. Everything else, the occupation of the country, &c., only comes in the second line."

It will be observed that he here admits that the process of occupying the enemy's territory is an operation distinct from the overthrow of the enemy's force. Von der Goltz goes further, and protests against the common error of regarding the annihilation of the enemy's principal army as synonymous with the complete attainment of the object. He is careful to assert that the current doctrine only holds good "when the two belligerent states are of approximately the same nature." If, then, there are cases in which the occupation of territory must be undertaken as an operation distinct from defeating the enemy's forces, and if in such cases the conditions are such that we can occupy the territory with advantage without first defeating the enemy, it is surely mere pedantry to insist that we should put off till to-morrow what we can do better to-day. If the occupation of the enemy's whole territory is involved, or even a substantial part of it, the German principle of course holds good, but all wars are not of that character.

Insistence on the principle of "overthrow," and even its exaggeration, was of value, in its day, to prevent a recurrence to the old and discredited methods. But its work is done, and blind adherence to it without regard to the principles on which it rests tends to turn the art of war into mere bludgeon play.

Clausewitz, at any rate, as General Von Caemmerer has pointed out,[1] was far too practical a soldier to commit himself to so abstract a proposition in all its modern crudity. If it were true, it would never be possible for a weaker Power to make successful war against a stronger one in any cause whatever—a conclusion abundantly refuted by historical experience. That the higher form like the offensive is the more drastic is certain, if conditions are suitable for its use, but Clausewitz, it must be remembered, distinctly lays it down that such conditions presuppose in the belligerent employing the higher form a great physical or moral superiority or a great spirit of enterprise—an innate propensity for extreme hazards. Jomini did not go even so far as this. He certainly would have ruled out "an innate propensity to extreme hazards," for in his judgment it was this innate propensity which led Napoleon to abuse the higher form to his own undoing. So entirely indeed does history, no less than theory, fail to support the idea of the one answer, that it would seem that even in

---

[1] *Development of Strategical Science.*

Germany a reaction to Clausewitz's real teaching is beginning. In expounding it Von Caemmerer says, "Since the majority of the most prominent military authors of our time uphold the principle that in war our efforts must always be directed to their utmost limits and that a deliberate employment of lower means betrays more or less weakness, I feel bound to declare that the wideness of Clausewitz's views have inspired me with a high degree of admiration."

Now what Clausewitz held precisely was this—that when the conditions are not favourable for the use of the higher form, the seizure of a small part of the enemy's territory may be regarded as a correct alternative to destroying his armed forces. But he clearly regards this form of war only as a make-shift. His purely continental outlook prevented his considering that there might be cases where the object was actually so limited in character that the lower form of war would be at once the more effective and the more economical to use. In continental warfare, as we have seen, such cases can hardly occur, but they tend to declare themselves strongly when the maritime factor is introduced to any serious extent.

The tendency of British warfare to take the lower or limited form has always been as clearly marked as is the opposite tendency on the Continent. To attribute such a tendency, as is sometimes the fashion, to an inherent lack of warlike spirit is sufficiently contradicted by the results it has achieved. There is no reason indeed to put it down to anything but a sagacious instinct for the kind of war that best accords with the conditions of our existence. So strong has this instinct been that it has led us usually to apply the lower form not only where the object of the war was a well-defined territorial one, but to cases in which its correctness was less obvious. As has been explained in the last chapter, we have applied it, and applied it on the whole with success, when we have been acting in concert with continental allies for an unlimited object—where, that is, the common object has been the overthrow of the common enemy.

The choice between the two forms really depends upon the circumstances of each case. We have to consider whether the political object is in fact limited, whether if unlimited in the abstract it can be reduced to a concrete object that is limited, and finally whether the strategical conditions are such as lend themselves to the successful application of the limited form.

What we require now is to determine those conditions with greater exactness, and this will be best done by changing our method to the concrete and taking a leading case.

The one which presents them in their clearest and simplest form is without doubt the recent war between Russia and Japan. Here we have a particularly striking example of a small Power having forced her will upon a much greater Power without "overthrowing" her—that is, without having crushed her power of resistance. That was entirely beyond the strength of Japan. So manifest was the fact that everywhere upon the Continent, where the overthrow of your enemy was regarded as the only admissible form of war, the action of the Japanese in resorting to hostilities was regarded as madness. Only in England, with her tradition and instinct for what an island Power may achieve by the lower means, was Japan considered to have any reasonable chance of success.

The case is particularly striking; for every one felt that the real object of the war was in the abstract unlimited, that it was in fact to decide whether Russia or Japan was to be the predominant power in the Far East. Like the Franco-German War of 1870 it had all the aspect of what the Germans call "a trial of strength." Such a war is one which above all appears incapable of decision except by the complete overthrow of the one Power or the other. There was no complication of alliances nor any expectation of them. The Anglo-Japanese Treaty had isolated the struggle. If ever issue hung on the sheer fighting force of the two belligerents it would seem to have been this one. After the event we are inclined to attribute the result to the moral qualities and superior training and readiness of the victors. These qualities indeed played their part, and they must not be minimised; but who will contend that if Japan had tried to make her war with Russia, as Napoleon made his, she could have fared even as well as he did? She had no such preponderance as Clausewitz laid down as a condition precedent to attempting the overthrow of her enemy—the employment of unlimited war.

Fortunately for her the circumstances did not call for the employment of such extreme means. The political and geographical conditions were such that she was able to reduce the intangible object of asserting her prestige to the purely concrete form of a territorial objective. The penetration of Russia into Manchuria threatened the absorption of Korea into the Russian Empire, and this Japan regarded as fatal to her own position and future development. Her power to maintain Korean integrity would be the outward and visible sign of her ability to assert herself as a Pacific Power. Her abstract quarrel with Russia could therefore be crystallised into a concrete objective in the same way as the quarrel of the Western Powers with Russia in 1854 crystallised into the concrete objective of Sebastopol.

In the Japanese case the immediate political object was exceptionally well adapted for the use of limited war. Owing to the geographical position of Korea and to the vast and undeveloped territories which separate it from the centre of Russian power, it could be practically isolated by naval action. Further than this, it fulfilled the condition to which Clausewitz attached the greatest importance—that is to say, the seizure of the particular object so far from weakening the home defence of Japan would have the effect of greatly increasing the strength of her position. Though offensive in effect and intention it was also like Frederick's seizure of Saxony, a sound piece of defensive work. So far from exposing her heart, it served to cover it almost impregnably. The reason is plain. Owing to the wide separation of the two Russian arsenals at Port Arthur and Vladivostock, with a defile controlled by Japan interposed, the Russian naval position was very faulty.

The only way of correcting it was for Russia to secure a base in the Straits of Korea, and for this she had been striving by diplomatic means at Seoul for some time. Strategically the integrity of Korea was for Japan very much what the integrity of the Low Countries was for us, but in the case of the Low Countries, since they were incapable of isolation, our power of direct action was always comparatively weak. Portugal, with its unrivalled strategical harbour at Lisbon, was an analogous case in our old oceanic wars, and since it was capable of being in a measure isolated from the strength of our great rival by naval means we were there almost uniformly successful. On the whole it must be said that notwithstanding the success we achieved in our long series of wars waged on a limited basis, in none of them were the conditions so favourable for us as in this case they were for Japan. In none of them did our main offensive movement so completely secure our home defence. Canada was as eccentric as possible to our line of home defence, while in the Crimea so completely did our offensive uncover the British Islands, that we had to supplement our movement against the limited object by sending our main fighting fleet to hold the exit of the Baltic against the danger of an unlimited counter-stroke.[1]

Whether or not it was on this principle that the Japanese conceived the war from the outset matters little. The main considerations are that with so favourable a territorial object as Korea

---

[1] The strategical object with which the Baltic fleet was sent was certainly to prevent a counter-stroke—that is, its main function in our war plan was negative. Its positive function was minor and diversionary only. It also had a political object as a demonstration to further our efforts to form a Baltic coalition against Russia, which entirely failed. Public opinion mistaking the whole situation expected direct positive results from this fleet, even the capture of St. Petersburg. Such an operation would have converted the war from a limited to an unlimited one. It would have meant the "overthrow of the enemy," a task quite beyond the strength of the allies without the assistance of the Baltic Powers, and even so their assistance would not have justified changing the nature of the war, unless both Sweden and Prussia had been ready to make unlimited war, and nothing was further from their intention.

limited war was possible in its most formidable shape, that the war did in fact develop on limited lines, and that it was entirely successful. Without waiting to secure the command of the sea, Japan opened by a surprise seizure of Seoul, and then under cover of minor operations of the fleet proceeded to complete her occupation of Korea. As she faced the second stage, that of making good the defence of her conquest, the admirable nature of her geographical object was further displayed. The theoretical weakness of limited war at this point is the arrest of your offensive action. But in this case such arrest was neither necessary nor possible, and for these reasons. To render the conquest secure not only must the Korean frontier be made inviolable, but Korea must be permanently isolated by sea. This involved the destruction of the Russian fleet, and this in its turn entailed the reduction of Port Arthur by military means. Here, then, in the second stage Japan found herself committed to two lines of operation with two distinct objectives, Port Arthur and the Russian army that was slowly concentrating in Manchuria—a thoroughly vicious situation. So fortunate, however, was the geographical conformation of the theatre that by promptitude and the bold use of an uncommanded sea it could be reduced to something far more correct. By continuing the advance of the Korean army into Manchuria and landing another force between it and the Port Arthur army the three corps could be concentrated and the vicious separation of the lines of operations turned to good account. They could be combined in such a way as to threaten an enveloping counter-attack on Liao-yang before the Russian offensive concentration could be completed. Not only was Liao-yang the Russian point of concentration, but it also was a sound position both for defending Korea and covering the siege of Port Arthur. Once secured, it gave the Japanese all the advantages of defence and forced the Russians to exhaust themselves in offensive operations which were beyond their strength. Nor was it only ashore that this advantage was gained. The success of the system, which culminated in the fall of Port Arthur, went further still. Not only did it make Japan relatively superior at sea, but it enabled her to assume a naval defensive and so to force the final naval decision on Russia with every advantage of time, place, and strength in her own favour.

By the battle of Tsushima the territorial object was completely isolated by sea, and the position of Japan in Korea was rendered as impregnable as that of Wellington at Torres Vedras. All that remained was to proceed to the third stage and demonstrate to Russia that the acceptance of the situation that had been set up was more to her advantage than the further attempt to break it down. This the final advance to Mukden accomplished, and Japan obtained her end very far short of having overthrown her enemy. The offensive power of Russia had never been so strong, while that of Japan was almost if not quite exhausted.

Approached in this way, the Far Eastern struggle is seen to develop on the same lines as all our great maritime wars of the past, which continental strategists have so persistently excluded from their field of study. It presents the normal three phases— the initial offensive movement to seize the territorial object, the secondary phase, which forces an attenuated offensive on the enemy, and the final stage of pressure, in which there is a return to the offensive "according," as Jomini puts it, "to circumstances and your relative force in order to obtain the cession desired."

It must not of course be asked that these phases shall be always clearly defined. Strategical analysis can never give exact results. It aims only at approximations, at groupings which will serve to guide but will always leave much to the judgment. The three phases in the Russo-Japanese War, though unusually well defined, continually overlapped. It must be so; for in war the effect of an operation is never confined to the limits of its immediate or primary intention. Thus the occupation of Korea had the secondary defensive effect of covering the home country, while the initial blow which Admiral Togo delivered at Port Arthur to

cover the primary offensive movement proved, by the demoralisation it caused in the Russian fleet, to be a distinct step in the
secondary phase of isolating the conquest. In the later stages of
the war the line between what was essential to set up the second
phase of perfecting the isolation and the third phase of general
pressure seems to have grown very nebulous.

It was at this stage that the Japanese strategy has been most
severely criticised, and it was just here they seem to have lost
hold of the conception of a limited war, if in fact they had ever
securely grasped the conception as the elder Pitt understood it. It
has been argued that in their eagerness to deal a blow at the
enemy's main army they neglected to devote sufficient force to
reduce Port Arthur, an essential step to complete the second
phase. Whether or not the exigencies of the case rendered such
distribution of force inevitable or whether it was due to miscal-
culation of difficulties, the result was a most costly set-back. For
not only did it entail a vast loss of time and life at Port Arthur
itself, but when the sortie of the Russian fleet in June brought
home to them their error, the offensive movement on Liao-yang
had to be delayed, and the opportunity passed for a decisive
counter-stroke at the enemy's concentration ashore.

This misfortune, which was to cost the Japanese so dear, may
perhaps be attributed at least in part to the continental influences under which their army had been trained. We at least can
trace the unlimited outlook in the pages of the German Staff history. In dealing with the Japanese plan of operations it is
assumed that the occupation of Korea and the isolation of Port
Arthur were but preliminaries to a concentric advance on Liao-
yang, "which was kept in view as the first objective of the operations on land." But surely on every theory of the war the first
objective of the Japanese on land was Seoul, where they expected
to have to fight their first important action against troops
advancing from the Yalu; and surely their second was Port
Arthur, with its fleet and arsenal, which they expected to reduce

with little less difficulty than they had met with ten years before against the Chinese. Such at least was the actual progression of events, and a criticism which regards operations of such magnitude and ultimate importance as mere incidents of strategic deployment is only to be explained by the domination of the Napoleonic idea of war, against the universal application of which Clausewitz so solemnly protested. It is the work of men who have a natural difficulty in conceiving a war plan that does not culminate in a Jena or a Sedan. It is a view surely which is the child of theory, bearing no relation to the actuality of the war in question and affording no explanation of its ultimate success. The truth is, that so long as the Japanese acted on the principles of limited war, as laid down by Clausewitz and Jomini and plainly deducible from our own rich experience, they progressed beyond all their expectations, but so soon as they departed from them and suffered themselves to be confused with continental theories they were surprised by unaccountable failure.

The expression "Limited war" is no doubt not entirely happy. Yet no other has been found to condense the ideas of limited object and limited interest, which are its special characteristics. Still if the above example be kept in mind as a typical case, the meaning of the term will not be mistaken. It only remains to emphasise one important point. The fact that the doctrine of limited war traverses the current belief that our primary objective must always be the enemy's armed forces is liable to carry with it a false inference that it also rejects the corollary that war means the use of battles. Nothing is further from the conception. Whatever the form of war, there is no likelihood of our ever going back to the old fallacy of attempting to decide wars by manœuvres. All forms alike demand the use of battles. By our fundamental theory war is always "a continuation of political intercourse, in which fighting is substituted for writing notes." However great the controlling influence of the political object, it must never obscure the fact that it is by fighting we have to gain our end.

It is the more necessary to insist on this point, for the idea of making a piece of territory your object is liable to be confused with the older method of conducting war, in which armies were content to manœuvre for strategical positions, and a battle came almost to be regarded as a mark of bad generalship. With such parading limited war has nothing to do. Its conduct differs only from that of unlimited war in that instead of having to destroy our enemy's whole power of resistance, we need only overthrow so much of his active force as he is willing or able to bring to bear in order to prevent or terminate our occupation of the territorial object.

The first consideration, then, in entering on such a war is to endeavour to determine what that force will amount to. It will depend, firstly, on the importance the enemy attaches to the limited object, coupled with the nature and extent of his preoccupations elsewhere, and, secondly, it will depend upon the natural difficulties of his lines of communication and the extent to which we can increase those difficulties by our conduct of the initial operations. In favourable circumstances therefore (and here lies the great value of the limited form) we are able to control the amount of force we shall have to encounter. The most favourable circumstances and the only circumstances by which we ourselves can profit are such as permit the more or less complete isolation of the object by naval action, and such isolation can never be established until we have entirely overthrown the enemy's naval forces.

Here, then, we enter the field of naval strategy. We can now leave behind us the theory of war in general and, in order to pave the way to our final conclusions, devote our attention to the theory of naval warfare in particular.

PART II

THEORY OF NAVAL WAR

CHAPTER I

THEORY OF THE OBJECT—COMMAND OF THE SEA

The object of naval warfare must always be directly or indirectly either to secure the command of the sea or to prevent the enemy from securing it.

The second part of the proposition should be noted with special care in order to exclude a habit of thought, which is one of the commonest sources of error in naval speculation. That error is the very general assumption that if one belligerent loses the command of the sea it passes at once to the other belligerent. The most cursory study of naval history is enough to reveal the falseness of such an assumption. It tells us that the most common situation in naval war is that neither side has the command; that the normal position is not a commanded sea, but an uncommanded sea. The mere assertion, which no one denies, that the object of naval warfare is to get command of the sea actually connotes the proposition that the command is normally in dispute. It is this state of dispute with which naval strategy is most nearly concerned, for when the command is lost or won pure naval strategy comes to an end.

This truth is so obvious that it would scarcely be worth mentioning were it not for the constant recurrence of such phrases as: "If England were to lose command of the sea, it would be all over with her." The fallacy of the idea is that it ignores the power of the strategical defensive. It assumes that if in the face of some extraordinary hostile coalition or through some extraordinary mischance we found ourselves without sufficient strength to keep the command, we should therefore be too weak to prevent the enemy getting it—a negation of the whole theory of war, which at least requires further support than it ever receives.

And not only is this assumption a negation of theory; it is a negation both of practical experience and of the expressed opinion of our greatest masters. We ourselves have used the defensive at sea with success, as under William the Third and in the War of American Independence, while in our long wars with France she habitually used it in such a way that sometimes for years, though we had a substantial preponderance, we could not get command, and for years were unable to carry out our war plan without serious interruption from her fleet.

So far from the defensive being a negligible factor at sea, or even the mere pestilent heresy it is generally represented, it is of course inherent in all war, and, as we have seen, the paramount questions of strategy both at sea and on land turn on the relative possibilities of offensive and defensive, and upon the relative proportions in which each should enter into our plan of war. At sea the most powerful and aggressively-minded belligerent can no more avoid his alternating periods of defence, which result from inevitable arrests of offensive action, than they can be avoided on land. The defensive, then, has to be considered; but before we are in a position to do so with profit, we have to proceed with our analysis of the phrase, "Command of the Sea," and ascertain exactly what it is we mean by it in war.

In the first place, "Command of the Sea" is not identical in its strategical conditions with the conquest of territory. You cannot argue from the one to the other, as has been too commonly done. Such phrases as the "Conquest of water territory" and "Making the enemy's coast our frontier" had their use and meaning in the mouths of those who framed them, but they are really little but rhetorical expressions founded on false analogy, and false analogy is not a secure basis for a theory of war.

The analogy is false for two reasons, both of which enter materially into the conduct of naval war. You cannot conquer sea because it is not susceptible of ownership, at least outside territorial waters. You cannot, as lawyers say, "reduce it into possession," because you cannot exclude neutrals from it as you can from territory you conquer. In the second place, you cannot subsist your armed force upon it as you can upon enemy's territory. Clearly, then, to make deductions from an assumption that command of the sea is analogous to conquest of territory is unscientific, and certain to lead to error.

The only safe method is to inquire what it is we can secure for ourselves, and what it is we can deny the enemy by command of the sea. Now, if we exclude fishery rights, which are irrelevant to the present matter, the only right we or our enemy can have on the sea is the right of passage; in other words, the only positive value which the high seas have for national life is as a means of communication. For the active life of a nation such means may stand for much or it may stand for little, but to every maritime State it has some value. Consequently by denying an enemy this means of passage we check the movement of his national life at sea in the same kind of way that we check it on land by occupying his territory. So far the analogy holds good, but no further.

So much for the positive value which the sea has in national life. It has also a negative value. For not only is it a means of communication, but, unlike the means of communication ashore, it is also a barrier. By winning command of the sea we remove that barrier from our own path, thereby placing ourselves in position to exert direct military pressure upon the national life of our enemy ashore, while at the same time we solidify it against him and prevent his exerting direct military pressure upon ourselves.

Command of the sea, therefore, means nothing but the control of maritime communications, whether for commercial or military purposes. The object of naval warfare is the control of communications, and not, as in land warfare, the conquest of territory. The difference is fundamental. True, it is rightly said that strategy ashore is mainly a question of communications, but they are communications in another sense. The phrase refers to the communications of the army alone, and not to the wider communications which are part of the life of the nation.

But on land also there are communications of a kind which are essential to national life—the internal communications which connect the points of distribution. Here again we touch an analogy between the two kinds of war. Land warfare, as the most devoted adherents of the modern view admit, cannot attain its end by military victories alone. The destruction of your enemy's forces will not avail for certain unless you have in reserve sufficient force to complete the occupation of his inland communications and principal points of distribution. This power is the real fruit of victory, the power to strangle the whole national life. It is not until this is done that a high-spirited nation, whose whole heart is in the war, will consent to make peace and do your will. It is precisely in the same way that the command of the sea works towards peace, though of course in a far less coercive manner, against a continental State. By occupying her maritime communications and closing the points of distribution in which they terminate we destroy the national life afloat, and thereby check the vitality of that life ashore so far as the one is dependent on the other. Thus we see that so long as we retain the power and right to stop maritime communications, the analogy between command of the sea and the conquest of territory is in this aspect very close. And the analogy is of the utmost practical importance, for on it turns the most burning question of maritime war, which it will be well to deal with in this place.

It is obvious that if the object and end of naval warfare is the control of communications it must carry with it the right to forbid, if we can, the passage of both public and private property upon the sea. Now the only means we have of enforcing such control of commercial communications at sea is in the last resort the capture or destruction of sea-borne property. Such capture or destruction is the penalty which we impose upon our enemy for attempting to use the communications of which he does not hold the control. In the language of jurisprudence, it is the ultimate sanction of the interdict which we are seeking to enforce. The current term "Commerce destruction" is not in fact a logical expression of the strategical idea. To make the position clear we should say "Commerce prevention." . . .

To elucidate the point, it must be repeated that maritime communications, which are the root of the idea of command of the sea, are not analogous to military communications in the ordinary use of the term. Military communications refer solely to the army's lines of supply and retreat. Maritime communications have a wider meaning. Though in effect embracing the lines of fleet supply, they correspond in strategical values not to military lines of supply, but to those internal lines of communication by which the flow of national life is maintained ashore. Consequently maritime communications are on a wholly different footing from land communications. At sea the communications are, for the most part, common to both belligerents, whereas ashore each possesses his own in his own territory. The strategical effect is of far-reaching importance, for it means that at sea strategical offence and defence tend to merge in a way that is unknown ashore. Since maritime communications are common, we as a rule cannot attack those of the enemy without defending our own. In military operations the converse is the rule. Normally, an attack on our enemy's communications tends to expose our own. . . .

Thus it comes about that, whereas on land the process of economic pressure, at least in the modern conception of war, should only begin after decisive victory, at sea it starts automatically from the first. Indeed such pressure may be the only means of forcing the decision we seek, as will appear more clearly when we come to deal with the other fundamental difference between land and sea warfare.

Meanwhile we may note that at sea the use of economic pressure from the commencement is justified for two reasons. The first is, as we have seen, that it is an economy of means to use our defensive positions for attack when attack does not vitiate those positions, and it will not vitiate them if fleet cruisers operate with restraint. The second is, that interference with the enemy's trade has two aspects. It is not only a means of exerting the secondary economic pressure, it is also a primary means towards overthrowing the enemy's power of resistance. Wars are not decided exclusively by military and naval force. Finance is scarcely less important. When other things are equal, it is the longer purse that wins. It has even many times redressed an unfavourable balance of armed force and given victory to the physically weaker Power. Anything, therefore, which we are able to achieve towards crippling our enemy's finance is a direct step to his overthrow, and the most effective means we can employ to this end against a maritime State is to deny him the resources of sea-borne trade.

It will be seen, therefore, that in naval warfare, however closely we may concentrate our efforts on the destruction of our enemy's armed forces as the direct means to his overthrow, it would be folly to stay our hands when opportunities occur, as they will automatically, for undermining his financial position on which the continued vigour of those armed forces so largely depends. Thus the occupation of our enemy's sea communications and the confiscatory operations it connotes are in a sense primary operations, and not, as on land, secondary. . . .

If the object of the command of the sea is to control communications, it is obvious it may exist in various degrees. We may be able to control the whole of the common communications as the result either of great initial preponderance or of decisive victory. If we are not sufficiently strong to do this, we may still be able to control some of the communications; that is, our control may be general or local. Obvious as the point is, it needs emphasising, because of a maxim that has become current that "the sea is all one." Like other maxims of the kind, it conveys a truth with a trail of error in its wake. The truth it contains seems to be simply this, that as a rule local control can only avail us temporarily, for so long as the enemy has a sufficient fleet anywhere, it is theoretically in his power to overthrow our control of any special sea area.

It amounts indeed to little more than a rhetorical expression, used to emphasise the high mobility of fleets as contrasted with that of armies and the absence of physical obstacles to restrict that mobility. That this vital feature of naval warfare should be consecrated in a maxim is well, but when it is caricatured into a doctrine, as it sometimes is, that you cannot move a battalion oversea till you have entirely overthrown your enemy's fleet, it deserves gibbeting. It would be as wise to hold that in war you must never risk anything. . . .

For the purpose, then, of framing a plan of war or campaign, it must be taken that command may exist in various states or degrees, each of which has its special possibilities and limitations. It may be general or local, and it may be permanent or temporary. General command may be permanent or temporary, but mere local command, except in very favourable geographical conditions, should scarcely ever be regarded as more than temporary, since normally it is always liable to interruption from other theatres so long as the enemy possesses an effective naval force.

Finally, it has to be noted that even permanent general command can never in practice be absolute. No degree of naval superiority can ensure our communications against sporadic attack from detached cruisers, or even raiding squadrons if they be boldly led and are prepared to risk destruction. Even after Hawke's decisive victory at Quiberon had completed the overthrow of the enemy's sea forces, a British transport was captured between Cork and Portsmouth, and an Indiaman in sight of the Lizard, while Wellington's complaints in the Peninsula of the insecurity of his communications are well known. By general and permanent control we do not mean that the enemy can do nothing, but that he cannot interfere with our maritime trade and oversea operations so seriously as to affect the issue of the war, and that he cannot carry on his own trade and operations except at such risk and hazard as to remove them from the field of practical strategy. In other words, it means that the enemy can no longer attack our lines of passage and communication effectively, and that he cannot use or defend his own.

To complete our equipment for appreciating any situation for which operations have to be designed, it is necessary to remember that when the command is in dispute the general conditions may give a stable or an unstable equilibrium. It may be that the power of neither side preponderates to any appreciable extent. It may also be that the preponderance is with ourselves, or it may be that it lies with the enemy. Such preponderance of course will not depend entirely on actual relative strength, either physical or moral, but will be influenced by the inter-relation of naval positions and the comparative convenience of their situation in regard to the object of the war or campaign. By naval positions we mean, firstly, naval bases and, secondly, the terminals of the greater lines of communication or trade-routes and the focal areas where they tend to converge, as at Finisterre, Gibraltar, Suez, the Cape, Singapore, and many others.

Upon the degree and distribution of this preponderance will depend in a general way the extent to which our plans will be governed by the idea of defence or offence. Generally speaking, it will be to the advantage of the preponderating side to seek a decision as quickly as possible in order to terminate the state of dispute. Conversely, the weaker side will as a rule seek to avoid or postpone a decision in hope of being able by minor operations, the chances of war, or the development of fresh strength, to turn the balance in its favour. Such was the line which France adopted frequently in her wars with us, sometimes legitimately, but sometimes to such an excess as seriously to demoralise her fleet. Her experience has led to a hasty deduction that the defensive at sea for even a weaker Power is an unmixed evil. Such a conclusion is foreign to the fundamental principles of war. It is idle to exclude the use of an expectant attitude because in itself it cannot lead to final success, and because if used to excess it ends in demoralisation and the loss of will to attack. The misconception appears to have arisen from insistence on the drawbacks of defence by writers seeking to persuade their country to prepare in time of peace sufficient naval strength to justify offence from the outset. . . .

PART III

CONDUCT OF NAVAL WAR

CHAPTER I

INHERENT DIFFERENCES IN THE CONDITIONS OF WAR ON LAND AND ON SEA

Before attempting to apply the foregoing general principles in a definite manner to the conduct of naval war, it is necessary to clear the ground of certain obstacles to right judgment. The gradual elucidation of the theory of war, it must be remembered, has been almost entirely the work of soldiers, but so admirable is the work they have done, and so philosophical the method they have adopted, that a very natural tendency has arisen to assume that their broad-based conclusions are of universal application. That the leading lines which they have charted are in a certain sense those which must govern all strategy no one will deny. They are the real pioneers, and their methods must be in the main our methods, but what we have to remember is that the country we have to travel is radically different from that in which they acquired their skill.

A moment's consideration will reveal how far-reaching the differences are. Let us ask ourselves what are the main ideas around which all the military lore turns. It may be taken broadly that the general principles are three in number. Firstly, there is the idea of concentration of force, that is, the idea of overthrowing the enemy's main strength by bringing to bear upon it the utmost accumulation of weight and energy within your means; secondly, there is the idea that strategy is mainly a question of

definite lines of communication; and thirdly, there is the idea of
concentration of effort, which means keeping a single eye on the
force you wish to overthrow without regard to ulterior objects.
Now if we examine the conditions which give these principles so
firm a footing on land, we shall find that in all three cases they
differ at sea, and differ materially.

Take the first, which, in spite of all the deductions we have to
make from it in the case of limited wars, is the dominating one.
The pithy maxim which expresses its essence is that our primary
objective is the enemy's main force. In current naval literature
the maxim is applied to the sea in some such form as this: "The
primary object of our battle-fleet is to seek out and destroy that
of the enemy." On the surface nothing could look sounder, but
what are the conditions which underlie the one and the other?

The practical value of the military maxim is based upon the fact
that in land warfare it is always theoretically possible to strike at
your enemy's army, that is, if you have the strength and spirit to
overcome the obstacles and face the risks. But at sea this is not so.
In naval warfare we have a far-reaching fact which is entirely
unknown on land. It is simply this—that it is possible for your
enemy to remove his fleet from the board altogether. He may with-
draw it into a defended port, where it is absolutely out of your
reach without the assistance of an army. No amount of naval force,
and no amount of offensive spirit, can avail you. The result is that
in naval warfare an embarrassing dilemma tends to assert itself. If
you are in a superiority that justifies a vigorous offensive and
prompts you to seek out your enemy with a view to a decision, the
chances are you will find him in a position where you cannot
touch him. Your offence is arrested, and you find yourself in what,
at least theoretically, is the weakest general position known to war.

This was one of our earliest discoveries in strategy. It followed
indeed immediately and inevitably upon our discovery that the
most drastic way of making war was to concentrate every effort
on the enemy's armed forces. In dealing with the theory of war

in general a caveat has already been entered against the too common assumption that this method was an invention of Napoleon's or Frederick's, or that it was a foreign importation at all. In the view at least of our own military historians the idea was born in our Civil Wars with Cromwell and the New Model Army. It was the conspicuous feature that distinguished our Civil War from all previous wars of modern times. So astonishing was its success—as foreign observers remarked—that it was naturally applied by our soldier-admirals at sea so soon as war broke out with the Dutch. Whatever may be the claims of the Cromwellian soldiers to have invented for land warfare what is regarded abroad as the chief characteristic of the Napoleonic method, it is beyond doubt that they deserve the credit of it at sea. All three Dutch wars had a commercial object, and yet after the first campaign the general idea never was to make the enemy's commerce a primary objective. That place was occupied throughout by their battle-fleets, and under Monk and Rupert at least those objectives were pursued with a singleness of purpose and a persistent vehemence that was entirely Napoleonic.

But in the later stages of the struggle, when we began to gain a preponderance, it was found that the method ceased to work. The attempt to seek the enemy with a view to a decisive action was again and again frustrated by his retiring to his own coasts, where either we could not reach him or his facilities for retreat made a decisive result impossible. He assumed, in fact, a defensive attitude with which we were powerless to deal, and in the true spirit of defence he sprang out from time to time to deal us a counter-stroke as he saw his opportunity.

It was soon perceived that the only way of dealing with this attitude was to adopt some means of forcing the enemy to sea and compelling him to expose himself to the decision we sought. The most cogent means at hand was to threaten his commerce. Instead, therefore, of attempting to seek out his fleet directly, our own would sit upon the fairway of his homeward-bound trade, either on the Dogger Bank or elsewhere, thereby setting up a situation which it was hoped would cost him either his trade or his battle-fleet, or possibly both. Thus in spite of the fact that with our increasing preponderance our preoccupation with the idea of battle decision had become stronger than ever, we found ourselves forced to fall back upon subsidiary operations of an ulterior strategical character. It is a curious paradox, but it is one that seems inherent in the special feature of naval war, which permits the armed force to be removed from the board altogether.

The second distinguishing characteristic of naval warfare which relates to the communication idea is not so well marked, but it is scarcely less important. It will be recalled that this characteristic is concerned with lines of communication is so far as they tend to determine lines of operation. It is a simple question of roads and obstacles. In land warfare we can determine with some precision the limits and direction of our enemy's possible movements. We know that they must be determined mainly by roads and obstacles. But afloat neither roads nor obstacles exist. There is nothing of the kind on the face of the sea to assist us in locating him and determining his movements. True it is that in sailing days his movements were to some extent limited by prevailing winds and by the elimination of impossible courses, but with steam even these determinants have gone, and there is practically nothing to limit the freedom of his movement except the exigencies of fuel. Consequently in seeking to strike our enemy the liability to miss him is much greater at sea than on land, and the chances of being eluded by the enemy whom we are seeking to bring to battle become so serious a check upon our offensive action as to compel us to handle the maxim of "Seeking out the enemy's fleet" with caution.

The difficulty obtruded itself from the moment the idea was born. It may be traced back—so far at least as modern warfare is concerned—to Sir Francis Drake's famous appreciation in the year of the Armada. This memorable despatch was written when an acute difference of opinion had arisen as to whether it were better to hold our fleet back in home waters or to send it forward to the coast of Spain. The enemy's objective was very uncertain. We could not tell whether the blow was to fall in the Channel or Ireland or Scotland, and the situation was complicated by a Spanish army of invasion ready to cross from the Flemish coast, and the possibility of combined action by the Guises from France. Drake was for solving the problem by taking station off the Armada's port of departure, and fully aware of the risk such a move entailed, he fortified his purely strategical reasons with moral considerations of the highest moment. But the Government was unconvinced, not as is usually assumed out of sheer pusillanimity and lack of strategical insight, but because the chances of Drake's missing contact were too great if the Armada should sail before our own fleet could get into position.

Our third elementary principle is the idea of concentration of effort, and the third characteristic of naval warfare which clashes with it is that over and above the duty of winning battles, fleets are charged with the duty of protecting commerce. In land warfare, at least since laying waste an undefended part of your enemy's country ceased to be a recognised strategical operation, there is no corresponding deflection of purely military operations. It is idle for purists to tell us that the deflection of commerce protection should not be permitted to turn us from our main purpose. We have to do with the hard facts of war, and experience tells us that for economic reasons alone, apart from the pressure of public opinion, no one has ever found it possible to ignore the deflection entirely. So vital indeed is financial vigour in war, that more often than not the maintenance of the flow of trade has been felt as a paramount consideration. Even in the best days of our Dutch wars, when the whole plan was based on ignoring the enemy's commerce as an objective, we found ourselves at times forced to protect our own trade with seriously disturbing results.

Nor is it more profitable to declare that the only sound way to protect your commerce is to destroy the enemy's fleet. As an enunciation of a principle it is a truism—no one would dispute it. As a canon of practical strategy, it is untrue; for here our first deflection again asserts itself. What are you to do if the enemy refuses to permit you to destroy his fleets? You cannot leave your trade exposed to squadronal or cruiser raids while you await your opportunity, and the more you concentrate your force and efforts to secure the desired decision, the more you will expose your trade to sporadic attack. The result is that you are not always free to adopt the plan which is best calculated to bring your enemy to a decision. You may find yourself compelled to occupy, not the best positions, but those which will give a fair chance of getting contact in favourable conditions, and at the same time afford reasonable cover for your trade. Hence the maxim that the enemy's coast should be our frontier. It is not a purely military maxim like that for seeking out the enemy's fleet, though the two are often used as though they were interchangeable. Our usual positions on the enemy's coast were dictated quite as much by the exigencies of commerce protection as by primary strategical reasons. To maintain a rigorous watch close off the enemy's ports was never the likeliest way to bring him to decisive action—we have Nelson's well-known declaration on the point—but it was the best way, and often the only way, to keep the sea clear for the passage of our own trade and for the operations of our cruisers against that of the enemy.

For the present these all-important points need not be elaborated further. As we proceed to deal with the methods of naval warfare they will gather force and lucidity. Enough has been said to mark the shoals and warn us that, admirably constructed as is the craft which the military strategists have provided for our use, we must be careful with our navigation. . . .

CHAPTER III

METHODS OF DISPUTING COMMAND

DEFENSIVE FLEET OPERATIONS—
A FLEET IN BEING

In dealing with the theory of sea command, attention was called to the error of assuming that if we are unable to win the command we therefore lose it. It was pointed out that this proposition, which is too often implied in strategical discussion, denies in effect that there can be such a thing as strategical defensive at sea, and ignores the fact that the normal condition in war is for the command to be in dispute. Theory and history are at one on the point. Together they affirm that a Power too weak to win command by offensive operations may yet succeed in holding the command in dispute by assuming a general defensive attitude.

That such an attitude in itself cannot lead to any positive result at sea goes without saying, but nevertheless even over prolonged periods it can prevent an enemy securing positive results, and so give time for the other belligerent to dominate the situation by securing his ends ashore.

It is seldom that we have been forced even for a time to adopt such an attitude, but our enemies have done so frequently to our serious annoyance and loss. In the Seven Years' War, for instance, the French by avoiding offensive operations likely to lead to a decision, and confining themselves to active defence, were able for five campaigns to prevent our reducing Canada, which was the object of the war. Had they staked the issue on a great fleet action in the first campaign, and had the result been against them we could certainly have achieved our object in half the time. In the end, of course, they failed to prevent the conquest, but during all the time the catastrophe was postponed France had abundant opportunity of gaining offensively elsewhere territory which, as she at all events believed, would have compelled us to give up our conquest at the peace.

Again, in our last great naval war Napoleon by avoiding general actions was able to keep the command in dispute till by alliances and otherwise he had gathered force which he deemed sufficient to warrant a return to the offensive. Eventually that force proved unequal to the task, yet when it failed and the command passed to his enemy, he had had time to consolidate his power so far that the loss of his fleet seemed scarcely to affect it, and for nine years more he was able to continue the struggle.

Such examples—and there are many of them—serve to show how serious a matter is naval defence in the hands of a great military Power with other means of offence. They tell us how difficult it is to deal with, and how serious therefore for even the strongest naval Power is the need to give it careful study.

And not for this reason only, but also because the strongest naval Power, if faced with a coalition, may find it impossible to exert a drastic offensive anywhere without temporarily reducing its force in certain areas to a point relatively so low as to permit of nothing higher than the defensive. The leading case of such a state of affairs, which we must further consider presently, was our own position in the War of American Independence, when, as we have seen, in order to secure an adequate concentration for offence in the West Indies we were forced to reduce our home fleet to defensive level.

What, then, do we mean by naval defence? To arrive at a right answer we must first clear our mind of all confusing shadows cast by the accidents of land defence. Both on land and at sea defence means of course taking certain measures to defer a decision until military or political developments so far redress the balance of strength that we are able to pass to the offensive. In the operations of armies the most usual means employed are the holding of positions and forcing our superior enemy to exhaust his strength in attacking them. Consequently the idea of military defence is dominated by the conception of entrenched positions and fortresses.

In naval warfare this is not so. At sea the main conception is avoiding decisive action by strategical or tactical activity, so as to keep our fleet in being till the situation develops in our favour. In the golden age of our navy the keynote of naval defence was mobility, not rest. The idea was to dispute the control by harassing operations, to exercise control at any place or at any moment as we saw a chance, and to prevent the enemy exercising control in spite of his superiority by continually occupying his attention. The idea of mere resistance was hardly present at all. Everything was counter-attack, whether upon the enemy's force or his maritime communications. On land, of course, such methods of defence are also well known, but they belong much more to guerilla warfare than to regular operations. In regular warfare with standing armies, however brilliantly harassing operations and counter-attack are used, the fundamental conception is the defended or defensible position.

Similarly at sea, although the essence of defence is mobility and an untiring aggressive spirit rather than rest and resistance, yet there also defended and defensible positions are not excluded. But they are only used in the last resort. A fleet may retire temporarily into waters difficult of access, where it can only be attacked at great risk, or into a fortified base, where it is practically removed from the board and cannot be attacked at all by a fleet alone. But the occasions on which such expedients can be used at sea are far rarer than on land. Indeed except for the most temporary purposes they can scarcely be regarded as admissible at sea, however great their value on land. The reason is simple. A fleet withdrawing to such a position leaves open to the enemy the ulterior object, which is the control of sea communications, whereas on land an army in a good position may even for a prolonged period cover the ulterior object, which is usually territory. An army in position, moreover, is always doing something to exhaust its opponent and redress the unfavourable balance, but a fleet in inactivity is too often permitting the enemy to carry on operations which tend to exhaust the resources of its own country.

For a maritime Power, then, a naval defensive means nothing but keeping the fleet actively in being—not merely in existence, but in active and vigorous life. No phrase can better express the full significance of the idea than "A fleet in being," if it be rightly understood. Unfortunately it has come to be restricted, by a misunderstanding of the circumstances in which it was first invented, to one special class of defence. We speak of it as though it were essentially a method of defence against invasion, and so miss its fuller meaning. If, however, it be extended to express defence against any kind of maritime attack, whether against territory or sea communications, its broad truth will become apparent, and it will give us the true conception of the idea as held in the British service. . . .

CHAPTER IV

METHODS OF EXERCISING COMMAND

ATTACK AND DEFENCE OF TRADE

The base idea of the attack and defence of trade may be summed up in the old adage, "Where the carcase is, there will the eagles be gathered together." The most fertile areas always attracted the strongest attack, and therefore required the strongest defence; and between the fertile and the infertile areas it was possible to draw a line which for strategical purposes was definite and constant. The fertile areas were the terminals of departure and destination where trade tends to be crowded, and in a secondary degree the focal points where, owing to the conformation of the land, trade tends to converge. The infertile areas were the great routes which passed through the focal points and connected the terminal areas. Consequently attack on commerce tends to take one of two forms. It may be terminal or it may be pelagic, terminal attack being the more profitable, but demanding the greater force and risk, and pelagic attack being the more uncertain, but involving less force and risk.

These considerations lead us directly to the paradox which underlies the unbroken failure of our enemies to exercise decisive pressure upon us by operations against our trade. It is that where attack is most to be feared, there defence is easiest. A plan of war which has the destruction of trade for its primary object implies in the party using it an inferiority at sea. Had he superiority, his object would be to convert that superiority to a working command by battle or blockade. Except, therefore, in the rare cases where the opposed forces are equal, we must assume that the belligerent who makes commerce destruction his primary object will have to deal with a superior fleet. Now, it is true that the difficulty of defending trade lies mainly in the extent of sea it covers. But, on the other hand, the areas in which it tends to congregate and in which alone it is seriously vulnerable, are few and narrow, and can be easily occupied if we are in superior force. Beyond those areas effective occupation is impossible, but so also is effective attack. Hence the controlling fact of war on commerce, that facility of attack means facility of defence.

Beside this fundamental principle we must place another that is scarcely less important. Owing to the general common nature of sea communications, attack and defence of trade are so intimately connected that the one operation is almost indistinguishable from the other. Both ideas are satisfied by occupying the common communications. The strongest form of attack is the occupation of the enemy's terminals, and the establishment of a commercial blockade of the ports they contain. But as this operation usually requires the blockade of an adjacent naval port, it also constitutes, as a rule, a defensive disposition for our own trade, even when the enemy's terminal area does not overlap one of our own. In the occupation of focal areas the two ideas are even more inseparable, since most, if not all, such areas are on lines of communication that are common. It will suffice, therefore, to deal with the general aspect of the subject from the point of view of defence.

It was in conformity with the distinction between fertile and infertile areas that our old system of trade defence was developed. Broadly speaking, that system was to hold the terminals in strength and in important cases the focal points as well. By means of a battle-squadron with a full complement of cruisers they were constituted defended areas, or "tracts" as the old term was, and the trade was regarded as safe when it entered them. The intervening trade-routes were left as a rule undefended. . . .

The general theory of these defended terminal and focal areas, it will be seen, was to hold in force those waters which converging trade made most fertile, and which therefore furnished an adequate field for the operations of raiding squadrons. In spite of the elaborate defensive system, such squadrons might, and sometimes did, intrude by surprise or stealth, and were then able to set at defiance both convoy escorts and the cruiser outposts. But, as experience proved, the system of terminal defence by battle-squadrons made it impossible for such raiding squadrons to remain long enough on the ground to cause any serious interruption or to do serious harm. It was only by a regular fleet of superior strength that the system could be broken down. In other words, the defence could only fall when our means of local control was destroyed by battle.

So much for the defended areas. With regard to the great routes that connected them, it has been said they were left undefended. By this is meant that the security of ships passing along them was provided for, not by patrols but by escort. The convoy system was adopted, and the theory of that system is that while vessels are on the great routes they are normally liable only to sporadic attack, and they are consequently collected into fleets and furnished with an escort sufficient to repel sporadic attack. In theory, cruiser escort is sufficient, but in practice it was found convenient and economical to assign the duty in part to ships-of-the-line which were going out to join the distant terminal squadron or returning from it for a refit or some other reason; in other words, the system of foreign reliefs was made to work in with the supplementary escort system. Where no such ships were available and the convoys were of great value, or enemy's ships-of-the-line were known to be out, similar units were specially detailed for convoy duty to go and return, but this use of battle units was exceptional.

Such a method of dealing with the great routes is the corollary of the idea of defended areas. As those areas were fertile and likely to attract raiding squadrons, so the great routes were infertile, and no enemy could afford to spend squadrons upon them. It is obvious, however, that the system had its weak side, for the mere fact that a convoy was upon a great route tended to attract a squadron, and the comparative immunity of those routes was lost. The danger was provided for to a great extent by the fact that the enemy's ports from which a squadron could issue were all within defended areas and watched by our own squadrons. Still, the guard could not be made impenetrable. There was always the chance of a squadron escaping, and if it escaped towards a critical trade-route, it must be followed. Hence there were times when the convoy system seriously disturbed our dispositions, as, for instance, in the crisis of the Trafalgar campaign, when for a short time our chain of defended areas was broken down by the escape of the Toulon squadron. That escape eventually forced a close concentration on the Western Squadron, but other considerations apart, it was felt to be impossible to retain the mass for more than two days owing to the fact that the great East and West Indies convoys were approaching, and Villeneuve's return to Ferrol from Martinique exposed them to squadronal attack. It was, in fact, impossible to tell whether the mass had not been forced upon us with this special end in view.

In the liability to deflection of this kind lay the most serious strategical objection to the convoy system. It was sought to minimise it by giving the convoys a secret route when there was apprehension of squadronal interference. It was done in the case just cited, but the precaution seemed in no way to lessen the anxiety. It may have been because in those days of slow communication there could be no such certainty that the secret route had been received as there would be now.

Modern developments and changes in shipping and naval material have indeed so profoundly modified the whole conditions of commerce protection, that there is no part of strategy where historical deduction is more difficult or more liable to error. To avoid such error as far as possible, it is essential to keep those developments in mind at every step. The more important of them are three in number. Firstly, the abolition of privateering; secondly, the reduced range of action for all warships; and thirdly, the development of wireless telegraphy. There are others which must be dealt with in their place, but these three go to the root of the whole problem. . . .

By the abolition of privateering, then, it would seem that the most disturbing part of the problem has been eliminated. It is, of course, uncertain how far the Declaration of Paris will hold good in practice. It is still open even to the parties to it to evade its restrictions to a greater or less extent by taking up and commissioning merchantmen as regular ships of war. But it is unlikely that such methods will extend beyond the larger privately owned vessels. Any attempt to revive in this way the old *picaresque* methods could only amount to a virtual repudiation of statutory international law, which would bring its own retribution. Moreover, for home waters at least, the conditions which favoured this *picaresque* warfare no longer exist. In the old wars the bulk of our trade came into the Thames, and thence the greater part of it was distributed in small coasting vessels. It was against this coast-wise traffic that the small, short-range privateers found their opportunity and their richest harvest. But, now that so many other great centres of distribution have established themselves, and that the bulk of the distribution is done by internal lines of communication, the Channel is no longer the sole artery, and the old troublesome disturbance can be avoided without a vital dislocation of our commercial system.

The probability, then, is that in the future the whole problem will be found to be simplified, and that the work of commerce protection will lie much more within the scope of large strategical treatment than it ever did before, with the result that the change should be found to tell substantially in favour of defence and against attack. . . .

From these and similar considerations it is obvious that the possibilities of operations on the great trade-routes are much less extensive than they were formerly, while to speak of cruisers "infesting" those routes is sheer hyperbole. Under modern conditions it is scarcely more feasible than it would be to keep up a permanent blockade of the British Islands. It would require a flow of ships in such numbers as no country but our own can contemplate possessing, and such as could not be maintained without having first secured a very decided preponderance at sea. The loss of radius of action therefore, though it does not increase the power of defence, sensibly lessens that of attack by pelagic operations.

For the great increase in the powers of defence we must turn to the extraordinary development in the means of distant communication. Under former conditions it was possible for a cruising ship to remain for days upon a fertile spot and make a number of captures before her presence was known. But since most large merchantmen have been fitted with wireless installations, she cannot now attack a single one of them without fear of calling down upon her an adversary. Moreover, when she is once located, every ship within wireless reach can be warned of her presence and avoid her. She must widely and constantly shift her position, thereby still further reducing her staying power. On the whole, then, it would appear that in so far as modern developments affect the problem, they certainly render pelagic operations far more difficult and uncertain than they used to be. Upon the great routes the power of attack has been reduced and the means of evasion has increased to such an extent as to demand entire reconsideration of the defence of trade between terminal areas. The whole basis of the old system would seem to be involved. That basis was the convoy system, and it now becomes doubtful whether the additional security which convoys afforded is sufficient to outweigh their economical drawbacks and their liability to cause strategical disturbance. . . .

ATTACK, DEFENCE, AND SUPPORT OF
MILITARY EXPEDITIONS

The attack and defence of oversea expeditions are governed in a large measure by the principles of attack and defence of trade. In both cases it is a question of control of communications, and in a general way it may be said, if we control them for the one purpose, we control them for the other. But with combined expeditions freedom of passage is not the only consideration. The duties of the fleet do not end with the protection of the troops during transit, as in the case of convoys, unless indeed, as with convoys, the destination is a friendly country. In the normal case of a hostile destination, where resistance is to be expected from the commencement of the operations, the fleet is charged with further duties of a most exacting kind. They may be described generally as duties of support, and it is the intrusion of these duties which distinguish the naval arrangements for combined operations most sharply from those for the protection of trade. Except for this consideration there need be no difference in the method of defence. In each case the strength required would be measured by the dangers of interference in transit. But as it is, that standard will not serve for combined expeditions; for however small those risks, the protective arrangements must be sufficiently extensive to include arrangements for support.

. . . We may now turn to the larger and more complex question of the conduct of such expeditions. . . .

By the conduct, be it remembered, we mean not only their defence but also their support, and for this reason the starting-point of our inquiry is to be found, as above indicated, in the contrast of combined expeditions with convoys. A convoy consists of two elements—a fleet of merchantmen and an escort. But a combined expedition does not consist simply of an army and a squadron. It is an organism at once more complex and more homogeneous. Its constitution is fourfold. There is, firstly, the army; secondly, the transports and landing flotilla—that is, the flotilla of flat-boats and steamboats for towing them, all of which may be carried in the transports or accompany them; thirdly, the "Squadron in charge of transports," as it came to be called, which includes the escort proper and the supporting flotilla of lighter craft for inshore work; and lastly, the "Covering squadron."

Such at least is a combined expedition in logical analysis. But so essentially is it a single organism, that in practice these various elements can seldom be kept sharply distinct. They may be interwoven in the most intricate manner. Indeed to a greater or less extent each will always have to discharge some of the functions of the others. Thus the covering squadron may not only be indistinguishable from the escort and support, but it will often provide the greater part of the landing flotilla and even a portion of the landing force. Similarly, the escort may also serve as transport, and provide in part not only the supporting force, but also the landing flotilla. The fourfold constitution is therefore in a great measure theoretical. Still its use is not merely that it serves to define the varied functions which the fleet will have to discharge. As we proceed it will be seen to have a practical strategical value.

From a naval point of view it is the covering squadron which calls first for consideration, because of the emphasis with which its necessity marks not only the distinction between the conduct of combined expeditions and the conduct of commercial convoys, but also the fact that such expeditions are actually a combined force, and not merely an army escorted by a fleet.

In our system of commerce protection the covering squadron had no place. The battle-fleet, as we have seen, was employed in holding definite terminal areas, and had no organic connection with the convoys. The convoys had no further protection than their own escort and the reinforcements that met them as they approached the terminal areas. But where a convoy of transports forming part of a combined expedition was destined for an enemy's country and would have to overcome resistance by true combined operations, a covering battle-squadron was always provided. In the case of distant objectives it might be that the covering squadron was not attached till the whole expedition assembled in the theatre of operations; during transit to that theatre the transports might have commerce protection escort only. But once the operations began from the point of concentration, a covering squadron was always in touch. . . .

The length to which the supporting functions of the fleet may be carried will always be a delicate question. The suggestion that its strength must be affected by the need of the army for the men of the fleet or its boats, which imply its men as well, will appear heretical. A battle-squadron, we say, is intended to deal with the enemy's battle-squadron and its men to fight the ships, and the mind revolts at the idea of the strength of a squadron being fixed by any other standard. Theoretically nothing can seem more true, but it is an idea of peace and the study. The atmosphere of war engendered a wider and more practical view. The men of the old wars knew that when a squadron is attached to a combined expedition it is something different from a purely naval unit. They knew, moreover, that an army acting oversea against hostile territory is an incomplete organism incapable of striking its blow in the most effective manner without the assistance of the men of the fleet. It was the office, then, of the naval portion of the force not only to defend the striking part of the organism, but to complete its deficiencies and lend it the power to strike. Alone and unaided the army cannot depend on getting itself ashore, it cannot supply itself, it cannot secure its retreat, nor can it avail itself of the highest advantages of an amphibious force, the sudden shift of base or line of operation. These things the fleet must do for it, and it must do them with its men. . . .

It is obvious that the foregoing considerations, beyond the strategical reactions already noted, will have another of the first importance, in that they must influence the choice of a landing place. The interest of the army will always be to fix it as near to the objective as is compatible with an unopposed landing. The ideal was one night's march but this could rarely be attained except in the case of very small expeditions, which could be landed rapidly at the close of day and advance in the dark. In larger expeditions, the aim was to effect the landing far enough from the objective to prevent the garrison of the place or the enemy's local forces offering opposition before a footing was secured. The tendency of the navy will usually be in the opposite direction; for normally the further they can land the army away from the enemy's strength, the surer are they of being able to protect it against naval interference. Their ideal will be a place far enough away to be out of torpedo range, and to enable them to work the covering and the transport squadron in sound strategical independence.

To reduce these divergencies to a mean of efficiency some kind of joint Staff is necessary, and to ensure its smooth working it is no less desirable to ascertain, so far as possible, the principles and method on which it should proceed. In the best recent precedents the process has been for the Army Staff to present the limits of coast-line within which the landing must take place for the operation to have the desired effect, and to indicate the known practicable landing points in the order they would prefer them. It will then be for the Naval Staff to say how nearly in accordance with the views of the army they are prepared to act. Their decision will turn on the difficulties of protection and the essentials of a landing place from the point of view of weather, currents, beach and the like, and also in a secondary measure upon the extent to which the conformation of the coast will permit of tactical support by gun-fire and feints. If the Naval Staff are unwilling to agree to the point or points their colleagues most desire, a question of balance of risk is set up, which the higher Joint Staff must adjust. It will be the duty of the Naval Staff to set out frankly and clearly all the sea risks the proposal of the army entails, and if possible to suggest an alternative by which the risk of naval interference can be lessened without laying too heavy a burden on the army. Balancing these risks against those stated by the army, the superior Staff must decide which line is to be taken, and each service then will do its best to minimise the difficulties it has to face. Whether the superior Staff will incline to the naval or the military view will depend upon whether the greater danger likely to be incurred is from the sea or on land.

Where the naval conditions are fairly well known the line of operations can be fixed in this way with much precision. But if, as usually happens, the probable action of the enemy at sea cannot be divined with sufficient approximation, then assuming there is serious possibility of naval interference, the final choice within the limited area must be left to the admiral. The practice has been to give him instructions which define in order of merit the points the army desire, and direct him to select the one which in the circumstances, as he finds them, he considers within reasonable risk of war. Similarly, if the danger of naval interference be small and the local conditions ashore imperfectly known, the final choice will be with the general, subject only to the practicable possibilities of the landing place he would choose.

During the best period of our old wars there was seldom any difficulty in making things work smoothly on these lines. After the first inglorious failure at Rochefort in 1757 the practice was, where discretion of this kind had been allowed, for the two commanders-in-chief to make a joint coast-reconnaissance in the same boat and settle the matter amicably on the spot.

It was on these lines the conduct of our combined operations was always arranged thenceforth. Since the elder Pitt's time it has never been our practice to place combined expeditions under either a naval or a military commander-in-chief and allow him to decide between naval and military exigencies. The danger of possible friction between two commanders-in-chief came to be regarded as small compared with the danger of a single one making mistakes through unfamiliarity with the limitations of the service to which he does not belong. . . .

There remains a form of support which has not yet been considered, and that is diversionary movements or feints by the fleet to draw the enemy's attention away from the landing place. . . .

This power of disturbing the enemy with feints is of course inherent in the peculiar attributes of combined expeditions, in the facility with which their line of operation can be concealed or changed, and there seems no reason why in the future it should be less than in the past. Good railway connections in the theatre of the descent will of course diminish the effect of feints, but, on the other hand, the means of making them have increased. In mine-sweeping vessels, for instance, there is a new instrument which in the Russo-Japanese War proved capable of creating a very strong impression at small cost to the fleet. Should a flotilla of such craft appear at any practicable part of a threatened coast and make a show of clearing it, it will be almost a moral impossibility to ignore the demonstration.

On the whole then, assuming the old methods are followed, it would seem that with a reasonable naval preponderance the power of carrying out such operations over an uncommanded sea is not less than it has proved to be hitherto. The rapidity and precision of steam propulsion perhaps places that power higher than ever. It would at any rate be difficult to find in the past a parallel to the brilliant movement on Seoul with which the Japanese opened the war in 1904. It is true the Russians at the last moment decided for political reasons to permit the occupation to take place without opposition, but this was unknown to the Japanese, and their arrangements were made on the assumption that their enemy would use the formidable means at his disposal to obstruct the operation. The risk was accepted, skilfully measured, and adequately provided for on principles identical with those of the British tradition. But, on the other hand, there has been nothing to show that where the enemy has a working command of the sea the hazard of such enterprises has been reduced. Against an enemy controlling the line of passage in force, the well-tried methods of covering and protecting an oversea expedition will no more work to-day than they did in the past. Until his hold is broken by purely naval action, combined work remains beyond all legitimate risk of war.

Giulio Douhet

The Command
of The Air

━━━◆━━━

BY
GIULIO DOUHET

TRANSLATED BY
DINO FERRARI

1921 and 1927

CONTENTS

BOOK TWO:
The Probable Aspects of the War of the Future

EDITOR'S INTRODUCTION

This section contains selections from the 1942 English translation by Dino Ferrari of five of Giulio Douhet's works entitled *The Command of the Air*. The first selection is from Douhet's 1921 edition of *Command*, published as part I of Book One in the Ferrari translation. That edition represented in somewhat preliminary and limited form the basic theory, which Douhet had formulated in his early years, that strategic bombing would provide the antidote for a warfare that had become increasingly total and stagnated in form. The Great War simply provided more detail for his theory. War on land was truly stalemated; and societies were fragile organizations whose structure could disintegrate even as large armies continued to exist. Moreover, the few small attempts at strategic bombing appeared to have been disproportionately effective. All this was contained in the first edition published under the auspices of the War Department, an indication of the degree to which Douhet's name had been restored since his court-martial. Nevertheless, the combination of his wartime reputation and the primitive state of aviation virtually assured that the 1921 edition of *Command* was not taken seriously even by those involved in or generally sympathetic to aviation.[1]

Douhet spent the next six years, largely out of the public eye, reworking his concepts in an increasingly radical direction. The result was the second edition of *Command* in 1927, included here almost in its entirety as part II of Book One from the 1942 translation. The new edition, which provided a more comprehensive expression of Douhet's theories, included a more extreme position in terms of the criticality of strategic airpower at the expense of the auxiliary aviation for the army and the navy. At the same time, there was a much greater faith in the bomber's capability to penetrate without escorts into the enemy's airspace and destroy targets. It was this controversial edition that was soon translated into various European languages.

The other readings in the 1942 translation represent how Douhet reacted in the last three years of his life to the controversy engendered by the second edition of *Command.* By that time, each year had brought new increases in aircraft capabilities, and airpower under Benito Mussolini had assumed new importance. One result was heated debates by Douhet with military peers who saw his ideas as a threat to both sea and land power. Douhet's 1928 monograph, "The Probable Aspects of the War of the Future" was one type of response by the Italian theorist to his articles. It became part II of the 1942 Ferrari translation, a portion of which is included in this volume. Douhet also responsed to his critics with his polemic "Recapitulation," the third part of the 1942 translation—but not included in this volume. "Recapitulation" was simply a collection of letters by the Italian theorist to the editor of the aviation journal, *Rivista Aeronautica,* written from 1927 to 1930 in response to critical letters that were not included in the translation.[2]

The impact of these debates on Douhet's theories was mixed. At the very least, they caused him to tighten up definitions of terms like "command of the air"—"to explain repeatedly and at length what I meant by those words."[3] But the debates also increased Douhet's intransigence concerning airpower's dominance over surface warfare and tended to push his associated ideas in a more radical direction. Those tendencies culminated in "The War of ——," a monograph written in the last months of his life and published in *Rivista Aeronautica* shortly after his death. The monograph, which was added as the last part of the 1942 translation, but which is not included in this volume, was a compendium of all Douhet's more extreme views. To begin with, Douhet envisions a war between Germany and a Franco-Belgium coalition that is over in less than two days, leaving dozens of major cities in ruin. The victorious German strategic bombers suffer huge losses; but wave after wave of these battleplanes prove ultimately unstoppable. The belligerent land forces have barely begun to exercise their mobilization timetables, as the national will of the French and Belgian civilian populations collapses and the political leadership of both countries sues for peace. In contrast to the Great War, this vision of airpower in a rapid, violent, relatively bloodless future conflict was almost hopeful and utopian.[4]

It was a vision that was in keeping with an age of speculation about the airplane in which prophecy was normally well ahead of technology. Making errors was a natural concomitant of the process, and Douhet was no exception. But the Italian theorist also practiced the strict discipline of logical reasoning and prided himself on how he always had to *"submit to the tight rein of logic"* in his thinking.[5] Consequently, the errors in Douhet's strategic philosophy were not to be found in the deductions that he drew from the premises of that philosophy, but in the premises themselves.

The most fundamental premise was that victory based on superior airpower would be swift and complete. This, in turn, led to a series of other interlocking premises, beginning with the efficiency of aerial bombardment. To win and exploit command of the air required highly efficient and devastating physical and moral effects for each ton of bombs dropped. But Douhet hardly explored this premise in a serious manner, postulating absurdly uniform and effective aerial bombardment and disregarding the possibilities of duds, misses, overlap, and differences in target composition and construction. He always claimed that his methods were scientifically and mathematically valid. His "unit of bombardment," for instance, was a ten-plane force with each plane carrying two tons of bombs. When the twenty tons were dropped in a uniform pattern, he concluded without explanation, the result should be the destruction of targets "exactly the area of a circle 500 meters in diameter," known as a "unit of destruction."[6] But there was very little empirical evidence to support his assertions; and for a trained engineer, as Phillip Meilinger points out, "Douhet's mathematical and technical gaffes—as well as his sophomoric attempts to estimate bomb damage 'scientifically'—are baffling."[7]

There are similar problems in terms of the efficacy of aerial bombardment with Douhet's contention that key target systems must be attacked. He emphasized, "the selection of objectives . . . and determining the order in which they are to be destroyed is the most difficult and delicate task in aerial warfare, constituting what may be defined as aerial strategy."[8] And yet Douhet, like Mitchell, never went beyond the most basic stages of attempting to identify five "vital centers": industry, transportation infrastructure, communication nodes, government buildings, and the will of the people. "How could one who had so little idea of what it is necessary to hit," Bernard Brodie asked in exasperation, "be quite so sure of the tremendous results which would inevitably follow from the hitting?"[9]

One answer, of course, was that Douhet was convinced that the will of the people was so intrinsically decisive, that any elaboration on the other "vital centers" was unnecessary. In 1908 H. G. Wells had begun to examine the psychology of air warfare in his book, *The War in the Air*, in which stubborn, irrational patriotism had fueled a will to resist on the part of civilians exposed to strategic bombing.[10] But Douhet's fundamental premise in this regard was just the opposite—that in fact civilian morale would quickly disintegrate under aerial bombardment. This in turn led him into a somewhat superficial moral justification for airpower, which was primarily linked to the paradox that humanity would benefit if war could be sufficiently horrible. "[T]he decision will be quick in this kind of war," he conjectured," since the decisive blows will be directed at civilians, that element of the countries at war least able to sustain them. These future wars may yet prove to be more humane than wars in the past in spite of all, because they may in the long run shed less blood."[11]

This paradox caused in Douhet a peculiar ambivalence concerning the righteousness of airpower that he never resolved. In one case he dismissed the possibility of unacceptable damage that could be inflicted on civilians in his own country while Italian planes destroyed the enemy's moral resistance. *"We must therefore resign ourselves,"* he wrote in the first edition of *Command, "to the offensives the enemy inflicts upon us, while striking to put all our resources to work to inflict even heavier ones upon him."*[12] In his second edition, the Italian theorist was equally adamant, emphasizing that under no circumstances should aerial resources "be diverted to secondary purposes, such as auxiliary aviation, local air defense, and antiaircraft defenses."[13] A year later, responding in "Recapitulation" to objections that the Italian people might succumb to an aerial offense, Douhet acknowledged that "no population can steel itself enough to endure aerial offenses forever."[14] Nevertheless, he concluded in an assumption he was unwilling to grant to the enemy: If the possibility of certain and imminent victory were conveyed to a population, the problem of interim punishment would disappear. "A heroic people can endure the most frightful offensive as long as there is hope that they can come to an end. . . ."[15]

Douhet's premise concerning civilian populations was based on two other premises. The first was that the offensive was supreme in aerial combat, particularly as his plans for twenty thousand bombers in 1917 demonstrated, if combined with the idea of mass. For him, piecemeal attacks on the surface would be as counterproductive as they had been in the last war. Equally important was that speed and range were vital characteristics if aircraft in these mass strikes were to be flexible enough to simultaneously strike sufficient targets to bring about paralysis and collapse culminating in the disintegration of civilian morale.[16] Concomitant to this was the premise that air defense was useless. In the air, Douhet would not grant to defensive airpower the same flexibility, speed, and ability to mass that he granted to offensive aircraft and thus virtually ignored the counterforce air battle as a prerequisite for command of the air. And on the ground, the same applied to antiaircraft weapons despite the fact that allied gunners had shot down over one thousand German aircraft in World War I. "Nothing man can do on the surface of the earth," he concluded early in the first edition of *Command*, "can interfere with a plane in flight, moving freely in the third dimension."[17]

Douhet's statement also indicated the one-dimensional aspect of his thinking based on the last of his fundamental premises: Defense will dominate surface warfare, and land fronts therefore will be static. It was a premise on which he became progressively more radical. And because surface forces would not be decisive, Douhet gave very little thought to their future development, organization, or employment. Early in his career, he had written presciently about the potential of army mechanization. But in the 1920s, despite his lofty ideas for improvements in air technology, the Italian theorist could not conceive of any evolution in surface systems and weapons that could possibly keep ground warfare from a state of perpetual equilibrium. As a consequence, he ignored tank development and emerging armor doctrine as the decade came to an end, even in his last work, "The War of —." That monograph did describe a strong French tank contingent in the fictitious conflict. But Douhet was also at pains to point out that German airpower caused France to lose the war before the tanks could be used.[18]

THE COMMAND OF THE AIR

PREFACE

The First Edition of *The Command of The Air* was published in 1921 under the auspices of the Ministry of War. In the years since then many of the ideas incorporated in the present edition have been put into effect. In fact, the cardinal points of the program for national defense which I proposed have been accepted and incorporated into the organization of the armed forces of the nation; namely:

1. Co-ordination of army, navy, and air force under a unified command, a concept I propounded in the 1922 issue of *National Defense.*

2. The constitution of a Council, then of a Ministry, of Aeronautics.

3. A distinction between an Independent Air force and auxiliary aviation, thereby putting into effect a concept which I held to be of vital importance to national defense and in correspondence with the facts of the present situation.

It may seem that if my ideas have been accepted and put into practice, there is no need for a second edition of my book. But I think there is a need for it, and here are my reasons for reprinting what I wrote then and adding to it a second part:

When I wrote the first version in 1921, more than ten years had passed since I first voiced the ideas expressed there. During all those years I had been trying with all my might to drive home the realization of the importance of air power, but all my efforts met defeat at the hands of military authorities and government bureaucracies. Finally, in 1921, owing to a change in circumstances which need not be mentioned here, I succeeded in getting it published by the Ministry of War and distributed among the personnel of the army and navy. This was the first success won by my long and arduous labors. But at that time, in order to accomplish anything practical and useful for my country, I had to be careful not to oppose too strongly certain notions firmly held in high places. Therefore, I was forced to emasculate my thought, confining myself to indispensable fundamentals, and wait for more favorable circumstances before presenting my ideas in full. Fortunately, conditions are different today. Willing or unwilling, military authorities have had to modify their views on the air arm. The first step has been taken; and now it is fitting that I should round out my thoughts on the subject of air power. Part II of Book One should therefore be considered complementary to Part I.

The ideas expressed in this second part will seem daring, perhaps strange, but I am certain that they too will make their way and finally be accepted like the others. It is only a question of time.

Giulio Douhet
[*Second Edition*, 1927]

BOOK ONE

THE COMMAND
OF THE AIR

Originally published in book form in 1921.

PART I
CHAPTER I

THE NEW FORM OF WAR

THE TECHNICAL MEANS OF WARFARE

Aeronautics opened up to men a new field of action, the field of the air. In so doing it of necessity created a new battlefield; for wherever two men meet, conflict is inevitable. In actual fact, aeronautics was widely employed in warfare long before any civilian use was made of it.[1] Still in its infancy at the outbreak of the World War, this new science received then a powerful impetus to military development.

The practical use of the air arm was at first only vaguely understood. This new arm had sprung suddenly into the field of war; and its characteristics, radically different from those of any other arm employed up to that time, were still undefined. Very few possibilities of this new instrument of war were recognized when it first appeared. Many people took the extreme position that it was impossible to fight in the air; others admitted only that it might prove a useful auxiliary to already existing means of war.

At first the speed and freedom of action of the airplane—the air arm chiefly used in the beginning—caused it to be

---

[1] It was first employed by Italy in Libya during the Italo-Turkish War of 1911-12 for reconnaissance and liaison purposes.—Tr.

considered primarily an instrument of exploration and reconnaissance. Then gradually the idea of using it as a range-finder for the artillery grew up. Next, its obvious advantages over surface means led to its being used to attack the enemy on and behind his own lines, but no great importance was attached to this function because it was thought that the airplane was incapable of transporting any heavy load of offensive materiel. Then, as the need of counteracting enemy aerial operations was felt, antiaircraft guns and the so-called pursuit planes came into being.

Thus, in order to meet the demands of aerial warfare, it became necessary step by step to increase aerial power. But because the needs which had to be met manifested themselves during a war of large scope, the resulting increase was rapid and hectic, not sound and orderly. And so the illogical concept of utilizing the new aerial weapon solely as an auxiliary to the army and navy prevailed for almost the entire period of the World War. It was only toward the end of the war that the idea emerged, in some of the belligerent nations, that it might be not only feasible but wise to entrust the air force with independent offensive missions. None of the belligerents fully worked out this idea, however—perhaps because the war ended before the right means for actuating the idea became available.

Now, however, this idea has emerged again and seems to be impressing itself strongly on the national authorities most concerned with these matters. It is, in fact, the only logical answer to the imperative need of defense against these new weapons of warfare. Essentially man lives close to the earth's surface, and no doubt he began his battling there. We do not know whether, when he first began to navigate the seas, he regarded naval warfare as a mere auxiliary to land operations; but we do know that from time immemorial we have been fighting on the sea independently of, though in co-operation with, land forces. Today, however, the sky is of far greater interest to man, living on the surface of the earth, than is the sea; and nothing, therefore, can *a priori* prevent him from reaching the conclusion that the air constitutes a battlefield of equal importance.

Though an army is primarily a land force, it possesses navigable means of warfare which it can use to help integrate its land operations; and that fact does not preclude the navy's accomplishing, solely with its own naval means, war missions from which the army is completely excluded. Similarly, while a navy is primarily a sea force, it possesses land means of warfare which it may use to assist and integrate its naval operations; and that fact does not preclude the army's carrying out war missions solely with its own land means, entirely independent of any naval means. In like manner, both the army and navy may well possess aerial means to aid and integrate their respective military and naval operations; but that does not preclude the possibility, the practicability, even the necessity, of having an air force capable of accomplishing war missions solely with its own means, to the complete exclusion of both army and navy.

In such a case, an air force should logically be accorded equal importance with the army and navy and bear the same relation to them as they now bear to each other. Obviously, both the army and the navy, each in its own field, must operate toward the same objective—i.e., to win the war. They must act accordingly, but independently of each other. To make one dependent on the other would restrict the freedom of action of the one or the other, and thus diminish their total effectiveness. Similarly, an air force should at all times co-operate with the army and the navy; but it must be independent of them both.

At this point I should like to outline the general aspects of the problem which faces us today and to emphasize the great importance of it. Now that we are released from the pressure of the World War, with its trial-and-error methods, it behooves us to work toward the solution of this problem by an entirely different method, one calculated to obtain for us the maximum return with the minimum of effort.

The state must make such disposition of its defenses as will put it in the best possible condition to sustain any future war. But in order to be effective, these dispositions for defense must provide means of warfare suited to the character and form future wars may assume. In other words, the character and form assumed by the war of the future is the fundamental basis upon which depends what dispositions of the means of war will provide a really effective defense of the state.

The prevailing forms of social organization have given war a character of national totality—that is, the entire population and all the resources of a nation are sucked into the maw of war. And, since society is now definitely evolving along this line, it is within the power of human foresight to see now that future wars will be total in character and scope. Still confining ourselves to the narrow limits of human foresight, we can nevertheless state, with complete certainty, that probable future wars will be radically different in character from those of the past.

The form of any war—and it is the form which is of primary interest to men of war—depends upon the technical means of war available. It is well known, for instance, that the introduction of firearms was a powerful influence in changing the forms of war in the past. Yet firearms were only a gradual development, an improvement upon ancient engines of war—such as the bow and arrow, the ballista, the catapult, et cetera—utilizing the elasticity of solid materials. In our own lifetime we have seen how great an influence the introduction of small-caliber, rapid-fire guns—together with barbed wire—has had on land warfare, and how the submarine changed the nature of sea warfare. We have also assisted in the introduction of two new weapons, the air arm and poison gas. But they are still in their infancy, and are entirely different from all others in character; and we cannot yet estimate exactly their potential influence on the form of future wars. No doubt that influence will be great, and I have no hesitation in asserting that it will completely upset all forms of war so far known.

These two weapons complement each other. Chemistry, which has already provided us with the most powerful of explosives, will now furnish us with poison gases even more potent, and bacteriology may give us even more formidable ones. To get an idea of the nature of future wars, one need only imagine what power of destruction that nation would possess whose bacteriologists should discover the means of spreading epidemics in the enemy's country and at the same time immunize its own people. Air power makes it possible not only to make high-explosive bombing raids over any sector of the enemy's territory, but also to ravage his whole country by chemical and bacteriological warfare.

If, then, we pause to take stock of the potentialities of these new weapons—which will no doubt be improved and developed in the future—we must be convinced that the experience of the World War can serve only as a point of departure—a point already left far behind us. It cannot serve as a basis for the preparation of national defense, a preparation which must be undertaken with an eye to the necessities of the future.

We must also bear in mind this fact: we are faced today with conditions which favor intensive study and wide application of these new weapons, the potentialities of which are unknown; and these conditions are the very ones to which Germany has been relegated. The Allies compelled Germany to disarm and to scrap her standing army. Will she accept patiently this inferior status? Or will she, forced by necessity, look for new weapons to replace the old ones now forbidden to her, and with them wreak her revenge? The fact that Germany leads the world in both fields, chemico-bacteriological and mechanical, must not be lost sight of. Already we can see signs that she is thinking along those lines, that she will apply the intensity, the unswerving purpose which have always distinguished her people, to the development of those new weapons of war. She can do so in the secrecy of her laboratories, where all foreign disarmament control—if any such control was ever effective—is bound to be futile.

Quite apart from what Germany may or may not do, however, it is impossible to ignore the value of these new weapons or to deny their vital role in any preparation for national defense. But in order to make an accurate estimate of the importance of these weapons, we must know exactly what their value is, both in themselves and in relation to the army and navy. Such an estimate is the primary object of this study.

THE NEW POSSIBILITIES

As long as man remained tied to the surface of the earth, his activities had to be adapted to the conditions imposed by that surface. War being an activity which necessitates wide movements of forces, the terrain upon which it was fought determined its essential features. The uneven configuration of the land surface presents all kinds of obstacles which hinder movements of solid bodies over it. Hence man has had either to move along the lines of least resistance, or by long and arduous labor surmount the obstacles encountered in the more difficult zones. Thus the surface of the earth gradually became covered with lines of easy transit intersecting at various points, at others separated by zones less easy of access, sometimes impassable.

The sea, on the contrary, being everywhere uniform in character, is equally navigable over all parts of its surface. But because the sea is bound by coast lines, freedom of navigation is often precluded except between points of contact situated on the same coastline or along arbitrary routes under foreign control, to avoid which long journeys around the coasts themselves must be undertaken.

War is a conflict between two wills basically opposed one to the other. On one side is the party who wants to occupy a certain portion of the earth; over against him stands his adversary, the party who intends to oppose that occupation, if necessary by force of arms. The result is war.

The attacking force tries to advance along the lines of least resistance, or easiest accessibility, toward the region he intends to occupy. The defender naturally deploys his forces along the line of the enemy's advance in an effort to bar his way. The better to oppose the advance of the enemy, he tries to deploy his forces where the terrain is in his favor or along lines of obstacles most difficult to pass. Because these natural obstacles are permanent and unchanging, just as are the rich and fertile—hence most coveted—regions of the earth, certain portions of the earth's surface seem singled out by destiny to be humanity's battle grounds for all time.

Since war had to be fought on the surface of the earth, it could be waged only in movements and clashes of forces along lines drawn on its surface. Hence, to win, to gain control of the coveted area, one side had to break through the fortified defensive lines of the other and occupy the area. As making war increasingly required the entire resources of nations, in order to protect themselves from enemy invasion warring nations have been forced to spread out their forces along battle lines constantly extended as the fighting went on, to a point where, as in the last war, the lines extended over practically the whole battlefield, thus barring all troop passage either way.

Behind those lines, or beyond certain distances determined by the maximum range of surface weapons, the civilian populations of the warring nations did not directly feel the war. No enemy offensive could menace them beyond that predetermined distance, so civilian life could be carried on in safety and comparative tranquillity. The battlefield was strictly defined; the armed forces were in a category distinct from civilians, who in their turn were more or less organized to fill the needs of a nation at war. There was even a legal distinction made between combatants and noncombatants. And so, though the World War sharply affected whole nations, it is nonetheless true that only a minority of the peoples involved actually fought and died. The majority went on working in safety and comparative peace to furnish the minority with the sinews of war. This state of affairs arose from the fact that *it was impossible* to invade the enemy's territory without first breaking through his defensive lines.

But that situation is a thing of the past; for now *it is possible* to go far behind the fortified lines of defense without first breaking through them. It is air power which makes this possible.

The airplane has complete freedom of action and direction; it can fly to and from any point of the compass in the shortest time—in a straight line—by any route deemed expedient. Nothing man can do on the surface of the earth can interfere with a plane in flight, moving freely in the third dimension. All the influences which have conditioned and characterized warfare from the beginning are powerless to affect aerial action.

By virtue of this new weapon, the repercussions of war are no longer limited by the farthest artillery range of surface guns, but can be directly felt for hundreds and hundreds of miles over all the lands and seas of nations at war. No longer can areas exist in which life can be lived in safety and tranquillity, nor can the battlefield any longer be limited to actual combatants. On the contrary, the battlefield will be limited only by the boundaries of the nations at war, and all of their citizens will become combatants, since all of them will be exposed to the aerial offensives of the enemy. There will be no distinction any longer between soldiers and civilians. The defenses on land and sea will no longer serve to protect the country behind them; nor can victory on land or sea protect the people from enemy aerial attacks unless that victory insures the destruction, by actual occupation of the enemy's territory, of all that gives life to his aerial forces.

All of this must inevitably effect a profound change in the form of future wars, because the essential characteristics of those wars will be radically different from those of any previous ones. We may thus be able to understand intuitively how the continuing development of air power, whether in its technical or in its practical aspects, will conversely make for a relative decrease in the effectiveness of surface weapons, in the extent to which these weapons can defend one's country from the enemy.

The brutal but inescapable conclusion we must draw is this: in face of the technical development of aviation today, in case of war the strongest army we can deploy in the Alps and the strongest navy we can dispose on our seas will prove no effective defense against determined efforts of the enemy to bomb our cities.

THE UPHEAVAL

The World War was a long-drawn-out war which almost completely exhausted both victor and vanquished. This was owing to the technical aspects of the conflict more than to anything else— that is, to new developments in firearms which strongly favored the defensive over the offensive; and, to a lesser degree, to a psychology which could not grasp immediately the advantage conferred on the defensive by the improvement in firearms. Advocates of the offensive were in the saddle everywhere extolling the advantages of the offensive war, but at the same time forgetting that one must have the means to back it up in order to take the offensive successfully. Of the defensive attitude, on the other hand, there was hardly any talk at all, only occasional casual mentions, as though it were a painful subject not to be discussed. This attitude encouraged the belief, held quite generally by military men, that the increased power of firearms favored the offensive rather than the defensive. This belief proved to be an error; the truth was the exact opposite, and clear thinking could have foreseen it, as subsequent war experiences plainly showed.

The truth is that *every development or improvement in firearms favors the defensive.* Defensive action not only permits the conservation of one's weapons for a longer time, but also puts them in the best position to increase their efficacy. It is therefore understandable that, in the absolute sense, the more powerful the weapon, the more valuable will be those dispositions which contribute to its preservation and the increase of its efficacy. This is clearly demonstrated by the fact that never before had there been such a widespread and thorough use of systems of defense as in the World War, in which they assumed formidable proportions. And to prove the fact, we have only to consider what those formidable systems of defense, which for a long period during the war formed the main bulwark of the battle line, would have been worth if the infantry and artillery manning them had been armed like those in the time of Gustavus Adolphus. They would have been worth next to nothing.

But with the increased efficacy of firearms, the defensive had both absolute and relative advantages over the offensive. Let us imagine a soldier posted in a trench protected by barbed-wire entanglements and the attacking enemy exposed on open ground for one minute; and let us also suppose that both sides are armed with muzzle-loading muskets capable of firing one shot a minute. Then we have the mathematical certainty that for the attacker to reach the trench defended by the single soldier, only two men are necessary, because in the minute of time allowed, only one of the two can be hit and put out of action by the defender. But if both sides are armed with rifles which can fire thirty rounds a minute, to have the same mathematical certainty the trench must be stormed by thirty-one men. All the rounds these men might have fired before attacking would have no bearing on the case if the lone defender is effectively covered by his own barbed-wire trench.

In the first instance one man on the offensive is effectively checkmated by one man on the defensive; in the second instance thirty men are effectively checkmated by one man because the rifle used was thirty times more effective. With this increased power of firearms, the offensive must, in order to win, upset this equilibrium by a preponderance of forces.

In actual fact, during the World War the enormous increase in the power of small-caliber arms made it possible for the defensive to let waves of attacking infantry come close to its own prepared positions and then stop them dead in their tracks; or the defensive could force the offensive, if desperately bent on reaching its objective, to shift its infantry attacks on men in prepared positions and lay down costly artillery barrages of all calibers which literally churned up the very ground, burying its defenders along with it. So that never before were offensive operations so difficult and so costly as during the World War.

But to say that the increased power of new weapons favors the defensive is not to question the indisputable principle that wars can be won only by offensive action. It means simply that, by virtue of increased fire power, offensive operations demand a much larger force proportionately than defensive ones.

Unfortunately, this fact was not realized until late in the war. So during that long conflict attacks were launched without adequate means, attacks which completely failed or only partly succeeded at a great waste of time, money, and men. Because of the inevitable slowness entailed in the process of getting together the enormous quantity of men and matériel to carry them through, these ill-prepared attempts at offensive action succeeded only in wearing down the forces engaged and prolonging the war. And it is certain that if the armies engaged in that struggle had been armed only with muzzle-loading muskets, we should have seen neither reinforced concrete trenches nor barbed-wire entanglements; and the war would have been decided in a few months. Instead, what we saw was a prolonged duel of powerful weapons against even more powerful defense fortresses until, by dint of sheer repeated battering, the fortified defenses were finally crumbled and the heart of the enemy bared. This prolonging of the war saved the day for the Allies simply because it gave them time to procure new allies and fresh troops; but on the other hand it almost completely exhausted both victor and vanquished.

In their war preparations the Germans took into account the value the increased power of firearms might give the defensive. They conceived of war in its most offensive aspect, and so provided themselves with the most adequate means—the 305 and 420 mm. guns—with which to wage war and to clear the road of permanent fortifications as quickly as possible. Thus they began the struggle with decisive offensive action; but when circumstances on the French front forced them to adopt the defensive, they covered their position with a system of defense so thorough and so adequate that it surprised the Allies. It could not possibly have been improvised; it must have been thoroughly worked out and planned long in advance to meet just such eventualities.

Germany had also to consider in her preparations for war the possibility of being compelled to fight on more than one front, and to consider the advantage of a defensive under such circumstances—of holding one front with a minimum of effectives while she struck at the other with her maximum forces. No doubt, therefore, she thoroughly systematized some such plan, and no sooner had circumstances shown the necessity of it than she put it into action. This shows clearly how well aware Germany was of the value of the defensive both in itself and relative to the offensive, even though she held firmly to the principle that victory can be won only by offensive action.

Although the preponderance of forces necessary for the offensive to tip the scale made offensive operations more difficult than defensive ones, yet indirectly the situation worked to the advantage of the offensive by making it possible for the offensive to thin out its own defensive lines and mass the greatest possible force in the sector chosen for attack. All the strategic moves of the Germans can be reduced to this formula: to hold a part of the enemy's forces with a small force of her own along a well-systematized line of defense, at the same time attacking another part of the enemy's forces with the largest force she could thus make available. This strategy was often successful over a long period of time.

Caught by surprise, the Allies no sooner saw the German march into the heart of France halted, than they deluded themselves into believing—their lack of defensive preparations notwithstanding—that they could win the war with comparative ease; so, having failed to do at once what should have been done at the beginning of hostilities to insure victory, they were forced to do it in successive stages. In the purely military sense, the war was prolonged by failure to understand the exact nature and demands of modern war. This lack of comprehension produced a series of inconclusive offensives which used up matériel as fast as it was gathered to launch them, thus time and again frittering away that preponderance of forces necessary to upset the equilibrium between the opposing forces which alone could have ended the war sooner.

Though the destruction wrought by the World War was enormous, the nations were able to keep up the struggle for the very reason that the fighting was sporadic and drawn out over a long period of time, so that they could replace their successive material and moral losses and go on throwing all their resources into the struggle until they were exhausted. Never, at any time during the war, was a death-blow struck—a blow which leaves a deep gaping wound and the feeling of imminent death. Instead both sides struck innumerable blows and inflicted many wounds; but the wounds were light ones and always had time to heal. Such wounds, while leaving the body weaker and weaker, still left the patient with the hope of living and recovering strength enough to deal to an equally weakened enemy that last pinprick capable of drawing the last drop of blood. As a matter of fact, the final decision was reached through battles less bloody than earlier ones which had brought only relative results. There is no doubt now that half of the destruction wrought by the war would have been enough if it had been accomplished in three months instead of four years. A quarter of it would have been sufficient if it had been wrought in eight days.

The special character of the World War, then, was shaped by the development of firearms during the last few decades. Now, since the nature of development is dynamic, not static, if there were no new facts to be taken into consideration, the war of the future would have the same general characteristics as the last one, only those characteristics would be accentuated. In other words, in future wars it would be logical to rely upon the continually increasing advantages of the defensive over the offensive, and concomitantly on the still greater difficulty in tipping the scale between the two sides, a necessity if a war is to be won.

If this were the case, protected as we are by a solid frontier of mountains and having no lust for conquest, we should be in an excellent position to face any enemy. With a small force and limited means we could easily provide for the defense of our territory even against attack by greatly superior forces, and rely upon gaining enough time to meet any eventuality of the conflict. But this is not the case; for the new weapons—as we shall see later in this study—reverse this situation by magnifying the advantages of the offensive and at the same time minimizing, if not nullifying, the advantages of the defensive; and, moreover, depriving those who are not fully prepared and ready for instant action of time in which to prepare for defense. No fortifications can possibly offset these new weapons, which can strike mortal blows into the heart of the enemy with lightning speed.

Confronted as we are by this upheaval in the character of war, which encourages nations who lust for conquest and feel neither hesitation nor remorse, it is imperative that we stop and examine calmly, coolly, but searchingly into the question of what is the right path for us to follow in providing for an effective national defense.

THE OFFENSIVE ARM

Because of its independence of surface limitations and its superior speed—superior to any other known means of transportation—the airplane is the offensive weapon par excellence.

The greatest advantage of the offensive is having the initiative in planning operations—that is, being free to choose the point of attack and able to shift its maximum striking forces; whereas the enemy, on the defensive and not knowing the direction of the attack, is compelled to spread his forces thinly to cover all possible points of attack along his line of defense, relying upon being able to shift them in time to the sector actually attacked as soon as the intentions of the offensive are known. In that fact lies essentially the whole game of war tactics and strategy.

From this it is obvious that those nations which have the means to mass their forces rapidly and strike at whatever point they choose of the enemy's forces and supply lines are the nations which have the greatest potential offensive power. In the days when war was fought with small, light, fast-moving bodies of forces, it offered a wide field for tactical and strategic moves; but as the masses engaged grew larger, the playground diminished in size and the game became more restricted. During the World War the masses involved were enormous, and extremely slow and heavy; as a consequence their movements were reduced to a minimum and the war as a whole became a direct, brutal clash between opposite forces.

The airplane, in contrast, can fly in any direction with equal facility and faster than any other means of conveyance. A plane based at point A, for example, is a potential threat to all surface points within a circle having A for its center and a radius of hundreds of miles for its field of action. Planes based anywhere on the surface of this same circle can simultaneously converge in mass on point A. Therefore, an aerial force is a threat to all points within its radius of action, its units operating from their separate bases and converging in mass for the attack on the designated target faster than with any other means so far known. For this reason air power is a weapon superlatively adapted to offensive operations, because it strikes suddenly and gives the enemy no time to parry the blow by calling up reinforcements.

The striking power of the airplane is, in fact, so great that it results in a paradox: for its own protection it needs a greater striking force for defense than for attack. For example, let us suppose that the enemy has an air force with the offensive capacity of X. Even if its bases are scattered, such a force can easily concentrate its action, gradually or however it sees fit, on any number of objectives within its radius of action. To be exact, let us say that there are twenty of these objectives. In this case, in order to defend ourselves from *what force X can do,* we are obliged to station near each of these twenty objectives a defensive force corresponding to force X, in all twenty times as many planes as the enemy has. So that to defend ourselves we would need a minimum aerial force twenty times as large as the attacking force of the enemy—a solution of the problem which partakes of the absurd because the airplane is not adaptable to defense, being pre-eminently an offensive weapon.

The suddenness with which this weapon appeared during the last war made it impossible to study thoroughly the problems posed by its use as a combat weapon. Aerial offensives were instinctively and empirically met by anti-aerial defense alone, whether operating in the air or from the ground. Thus were born antiaircraft guns, and reconnaissance and pursuit planes. But subsequent experience demonstrated that all these means of defense were inadequate, despite the fact that aerial offensives in the last war were of minor importance, haphazardly planned and executed. Every time an aerial offensive was carried out resolutely, it accomplished its purpose. Venice was bombed repeatedly from beginning to end of the war; Treviso was almost razed under our very eyes; and Padua had to be abandoned by the Supreme Command. In other countries, both Allied and enemy, the same thing happened.

In spite of the most elaborate system of signals, if our pursuit squadrons were not already in the air when the enemy reached its objective—and obviously they could not remain in the air continuously—they could seldom take off in time to prevent the enemy from dropping his load of bombs on his chosen targets.

There was artillery fire, but it seldom hit the mark; when it did, it scored by chance, as a sparrow might be hit by chance with a rifle bullet. Antiaircraft guns, too, went into action, giving chase through the streets of towns and cities and through the open country in their effort to hit planes diving here, there, and everywhere at will. They behaved much like a man trying to catch a homing pigeon by following him on a bicycle! In the descending curve of its trajectory, artillery fire was metamorphosed into projectiles falling from above. And all of this defensive fire amounted to nothing but a useless dispersion of enormous quantities of our national resources, sometimes wasted on the notion of preventing, not an actual attack, but a possible one! How many guns lay waiting month after month, even years, mouths gaping to the sky, on the watch for an attack which never came! How many pursuit planes immobilized men and materials without ever getting a chance to defend anything! How many people, after staring long and vainly at the sky for the enemy to appear, went soundly and happily to sleep!

I do not know whether an account has ever been drawn up of the weapons and resources scattered over the countryside for aerial defense; but there is no doubt that the total must have been very large. And all that effort, all those resources, so prodigally wasted, could have been profitably used for other purposes.

This dispersion of means, contrary to the fundamental principles of war and to a sound economy of warfare, was caused, as I have already said, by the disorientation produced by the suddenness with which air power came into being, which made for a fallacious concept of defense against it. When a mad dog runs amok in a village, the villagers do not post themselves separately on their own doorsteps, each man armed with a club, waiting on the pleasure of the dog to make an appearance and be killed. That kind of behavior would interrupt their work, but would not prevent the animal from biting someone. No villagers would behave that way. They would gather in groups of three, four, or more of the bolder spirits and go after the dog, track it to its lair, and there kill it.

Similarly, there is no practical way to prevent the enemy from attacking us with his air force except to destroy his air power before he has a chance to strike at us. It is now axiomatic—and has long been so—that coastlines are defended from naval attacks, not by dispersing ships and guns along their whole extent, but by conquering the command of the seas; that is, by preventing the enemy from navigating. The surface of the earth is the coastline of the air. The conditions pertaining to both elements, the air and the sea, are analogous; so that the surface of the earth, both solid and liquid, should be defended from aerial attack, not by scattering guns and planes over its whole extent, but by preventing the enemy from flying. In other words, by "conquering the command of the air."

This is the logical and rational concept which should be recognized, even for simple defense—namely, to prevent the enemy from flying or from carrying out any aerial action at all.

Conquering the command of the air implies positive action— that is, offensive and not defensive action, the very action best suited to air power.

THE MAGNITUDE OF AERIAL OFFENSIVES

Some conception of the magnitude aerial offensives may reach in the future is essential to an evaluation of the command of the air, a conception which the World War can clarify for us in part.

Aerial bombs have only to fall on their target to accomplish their purpose; hence their construction does not require as much metal as is needed in artillery shells. If bombs containing high explosives require a large amount of metal in proportion to their internal charge in order to ensure an effective explosion, the proportion of metal in bombs containing incendiaries or poison gases may be reduced to a minimum. We may be not far off if we figure roughly the proportion of metal in them at 50 percent of their total weight. The construction of aerial bombs does not call for high-grade steel, other special metals, nor for precision work. What it does demand is that the active ingredients of the bombs—the explosives, incendiaries, and poison gases—have the maximum efficacy, and that research be directed to this end.

Aerial bombardment can certainly never hope to attain the accuracy of artillery fire; but this is an unimportant point because such accuracy is unnecessary. Except in unusual cases, the targets of artillery fire are designed to withstand just such fire; but the targets of aerial bombardment are ill-prepared to endure such onslaught. Bombing objectives should always be large; small targets are unimportant and do not merit our attention here.

The guiding principle of bombing actions should be this: *the objective must be destroyed completely in one attack, making further attack on the same target unnecessary.* Reaching an objective is an aerial operation which always involves a certain amount of risk and should be undertaken once only. The complete destruction of the objective has moral and material effects, the repercussions of which may be tremendous. To give us some idea of the extent of these repercussions, we need only envision what would go on among the civilian population of congested cities once the enemy announced that we would bomb such centers relentlessly, making no distinction between military and non-military objectives.

In general, aerial offensives will be directed against such targets as peacetime industrial and commercial establishments; important buildings, private and public; transportation arteries and centers; and certain designated areas of civilian population as well. To destroy these targets three kinds of bombs are needed—explosive, incendiary, and poison gas—apportioned as the situation may require. The explosives will demolish the target, the incendiaries set fire to it, and the poison-gas bombs prevent fire fighters from extinguishing the fires.

Gas attacks must be so planned as to leave the target permeated with gas which will last over a period of time, whole days, indeed, a result which can be attained either by the quality of the gases used or by using bombs with varying delayed-action fuses. It is easy to see how the use of this method, even with limited supplies of explosive and incendiary bombs, could completely wreck large areas of population and their transit lines during crucial periods of time when such action might prove strategically invaluable.

As an illustration of the magnitude of aerial power, let us assume that 100 kilograms of active material is capable of destroying the area of a circle 25 meters in radius. This supposition is consistent with present practice. Then, in order to extend the destructive action of this active material over a surface 500 meters in diameter, 100 times 100 kilograms, or 10 tons, will be required. Now, 10 tons of active material requires 10 tons of metal casing or shell. Today there are airplanes which can easily carry 2 tons of bombs in addition to their crews; so 10 such planes could carry all the bombs necessary to destroy everything within this circle of 500 meters diameter. To obtain this result it is necessary only to train the crews of ten airplanes to drop their bombs as uniformly as possible over that area.

This gives us the concept of the basic unit of power needed for effective bombing operations; namely, *the unit of bombardment must have the potentiality to destroy any target on a given surface.* In my opinion, the extent of this surface should be exactly the area of a circle 500 meters in diameter. Then, if the above assumptions are correct, this unit should be 10 planes, each capable of carrying 2 tons of bombs. The exact ratio, however, can well be left to experience.

As I said, bombing pilots should be trained to spread their loads over such surfaces as uniformly as possible, releasing their bombs from a medium altitude of, say, 3,000 meters. This dissemination can be accomplished by artificially extending—by variations of sighting data—the natural rose-shaped aim of the squadron formation. If a specified surface contains very vulnerable targets, the area can be extended beyond the 500-meter diameter simply by increasing the number of planes taking part. Conversely, surfaces containing targets more difficult to destroy can be contracted by reducing the number of planes.

But these details are of secondary importance. Of prime importance is the fact that the adoption of such tactics makes the bomber a definite and precise offensive power, no longer a vague, indeterminate one.

When, on the other hand, the surface of a specified objective is smaller, but nevertheless important for military reasons, it should be so designated on the map. It makes no difference if a few bombs go wide of the mark during the attack. But if an objective with a surface larger than 500 meters in diameter is marked for attack, the entire area should be so designated. If the aim is to destroy everything on a surface of, say, 1,000 meters, it is sufficient to divide the target into separate zones and attack with 4 separate but co-ordinated squadrons of planes, with 9 squadrons if the area is 1,500 meters, with 16 squadrons if 2,000 meters, and so forth. Such bombing expeditions, however, cannot be undertaken successfully unless they are directed against very large centers of civilian population. In fact, we have no difficulty in imagining what would happen when areas of 500 to 2,000 meters in diameter in the center of large cities such as London, Paris, or Rome were being unmercifully bombed. With 1,000 bombers of the type described—an actual type in use today, not a hypothetical type in some blueprint of the future—with their necessary maintenance and replacements for daily losses, 100 such operating squadrons can be constituted. Operating 50 of these daily, such an aerial force in the hands of those who know how to use it could destroy 50 such centers every day. This is an offensive power so far superior to any other offensive means known that the power of the latter is negligible in comparison.

As a matter of fact, this same offensive power, the possibility of which was not even dreamed of fifteen years ago, is increasing daily, precisely because the building and development of large, heavy planes goes on all the time. The same thing is true of new explosives, incendiaries, and especially poison gases. What could an army do faced with an offensive power like that, its lines of communication cut, its supply depots burned or blown up, its arsenals and auxiliaries destroyed? What could a navy do when it could no longer take refuge in its own ports, when its bases were burned or blown up, its arsenals and auxiliaries destroyed? How could a country go on living and working under this constant threat, oppressed by the nightmare of imminent destruction and death? How indeed! We should always keep in mind that aerial offensives can be directed not only against objectives of least physical resistance, but against those of least moral resistance as well. For instance, an infantry regiment in a shattered trench may still be capable of some resistance even after losing two-thirds of its effectives; but when the working personnel of a factory sees one of its machine shops destroyed, even with a minimum loss of life, it quickly breaks up and the plant ceases to function.

All this should be kept in mind when we wish to estimate the potential power of aerial offensives possible even today. To have command of the air means to be in a position to wield offensive power so great it defies human imagination. It means to be able to cut an enemy's army and navy off from their bases of operation and nullify their chances of winning the war. It means complete protection of one's own country, the efficient operation of one's army and navy, and peace of mind to live and work in safety. In short, it means to be in a position *to win. To be defeated* in the air, on the other hand, is finally to be defeated and to be at the mercy of the enemy, with no chance at all of defending oneself, compelled to accept whatever terms he sees fit to dictate.

This is the meaning of the "command of the air."

THE COMMAND OF THE AIR

To have command of the air means to be in a position to prevent the enemy from flying while retaining the ability to fly oneself. Planes capable of carrying moderately heavy loads of bombs already exist, and the construction of enough of them for national defense would not require exceptional resources. The active ingredients of bombs or projectiles, the explosives, the incendiaries, the poison gases, are already being produced. An aerial fleet capable of dumping hundreds of tons of such bombs can easily be organized; therefore, the striking force and magnitude of aerial offensives, considered from the standpoint of either material or moral significance, is far more effective than those of any other offensive yet known. A nation which has command of the air is in a position to protect its own territory from enemy aerial attack and even to put a halt to the enemy's auxiliary actions in support of his land and sea operations, leaving him powerless to do much of anything. Such offensive actions can not only cut off an opponent's army and navy from their bases of operations, but can also bomb the interior of the enemy's country so devastatingly that the physical and moral resistance of the people would also collapse.

All this is a present possibility, not one in the distant future. And the fact that this possibility exists, proclaims aloud for any one to understand that to have command of the air is to have *victory*. Without this command, one's portion is defeat and the acceptance of whatever terms the victor is pleased to impose. Reasoning from the facts along the lines of logic, this is the conclusion we have reached. But since this conclusion applies to matters of very great practical importance, and since it is sharply at variance with the accepted way of looking at things, it behooves us to stop and amplify our statement before going on.

When conclusions are reached by reasoning with strict adherence to logic from actual verifiable facts, those conclusions ought to be accepted as valid even if they seem strange and radical, in direct contradiction to conventional thought patterns or fixed habits of mind based upon other facts, equally positive and verifiable to be sure, but entirely different in nature. To come to any other conclusion would be to deny reason itself. It would be like the reasoning of a peasant who insists upon cultivating his land exactly as his father and grandfather did before him, despite the fact that by using chemical fertilizers and modern machinery he could double or treble his harvest. Such old-fashioned, die-hard perverseness gets him nothing except a handicap in the market place.

Twelve years ago, when the very first airplanes began to hedge-hop between field and air, hardly what we would call flying at all today, I began to preach the value of command of the air. From that day to this I have done my level best to call attention to this new weapon of warfare. I argued that the airplane should be the third brother of the army and navy. I argued that the day would come when thousands of military planes would ply the air under an independent Ministry of the Air. I argued that the dirigible and other lighter-than-air ships would give way before the superiority of the plane. And everything I argued for then has come true just as I predicted it in 1909.

I did not prophesy then, and I do not prophesy now. All I did then was to examine the new problem posed by the existence of the new arm and reason from verifiable data; but I did not hesitate to follow up the implications of the conclusions I reached, in spite of the fact that then, as now, they may have sounded paradoxical. I was convinced with mathematical certainty that the facts would prove me right.

When, by the exercise of cold logic and mathematical calculation, someone was able to find out the existence of an unknown planet and furnish an astronomer with all the data necessary for its discovery; when by mathematical reasoning the electro-magnetic waves were discovered, thus furnishing Hertz the means with which to carry on his experiments—then we too should have faith in the validity of human reasoning, at least to the extent that the astronomer and Hertz had faith in it. And how much more abstruse their reasonings were than the reasoning I am attempting here!

At this point I ask my readers to stop with me and consider what I have been saying—the arguments are worth while—so that each may come to his own conclusion about it. The problem does not admit of partial solution. It is right or it is not right.

What I have to say is this: In the preparations for national defense we have to follow an entirely new course because the character of future wars is going to be entirely different from the character of past wars.

I say: The World War was only a point on the graph curve showing the evolution of the character of war; at that point the graph curve makes a sharp swerve showing the influence of entirely new factors. For this reason clinging to the past will teach us nothing useful for the future, for that future will be radically different from anything that has gone before. The future must be approached from a new angle.

I say: If these facts are not given careful consideration, the country will have to make great sacrifices in an effort to bring its defense up to date; but even these sacrifices will be of little use, for the defenses could not possibly meet the demands of modern military requirements. This can be denied only by refuting my argument.

I ask again: Is it true or is it not true that the strongest army and navy we could muster would be powerless to prevent a determined, well-prepared enemy from cutting them off from their bases of operation and from spreading terror and havoc over the whole country?

We can answer, "No, it is not true," to this question only if we have no intention of providing ourselves with suitable means, in addition to those of the army and navy, with which to meet any such eventuality. But I, for one, have long been answering this question with a categorical "Yes, it is true"; and it is because I am convinced of the imminence of such an eventuality that I have deeply pondered the problem posed by the new forms and weapons of war.

THE EXTREME CONSEQUENCES

To conquer the command of the air means victory; to be beaten in the air means defeat and acceptance of whatever terms the enemy may be pleased to impose. The truth of this affirmation, which for me is an axiom in itself, will become increasingly apparent to readers who will take the trouble to follow this study, wherein I hope to make it completely clear.

From this axiom we come immediately to this first corollary: *In order to assure an adequate national defense, it is necessary—and sufficient—to be in a position in case of war to conquer the command of the air.* And from that we arrive at this second corollary: *All that a nation does to assure her own defense should have as its aim procuring for herself those means which, in case of war, are most effective for the conquest of the command of the air.*

Any effort, any action, or any resources diverted from this essential aim makes conquering the command of the air that much less probable; and it makes defeat in case of war that much more probable. Any diversion from this primary purpose is an error. In order to conquer the air, it is necessary to deprive the enemy of all means of flying, by striking at him in the air, at his bases of operation, or at his production centers—in short, wherever those means are to be found. This kind of destruction can be accomplished only in the air or in the interior of the enemy's country. It can therefore be accomplished only by aerial means, to the exclusion of army and navy weapons. Therefore, *the command of the air cannot be conquered except by an adequate aerial force.* From this affirmation and the above-mentioned first corollary, we may draw an inference of practical value; namely: *An adequate national defense cannot be assured except by an aerial force capable in case of war of conquering the command of the air.* To be sure, this statement is directly opposed to the prevailing conception of national defense, and it puts the air arm first in order of importance. Nevertheless, to deny this affirmation, we must also deny the value of command of the air. To break away from the past is disturbing; but so is man's conquest of space disturbing.

As I have pointed out, this conclusion means the superseding of traditional values by new ones not yet fully realized. Up to this time the army and navy have been the predominant forces, and no one questioned that supremacy. Space was closed to man. But there is no *a priori* reason why the air arm cannot become the predominant power in its relations with surface forces. In examining these relations, we come to the conclusion that the air force is destined to predominate over both land and sea forces; this because their radius of offensive action is limited in comparison to the vastly greater radius of the air force.

As I said, we find ourselves now at a particular point in the curve of the evolution of war. After this point the curve drops off abruptly in a new direction, breaking off all continuity with the past. Therefore, if we have a tendency to deviate as little as possible from the beaten path, we will find ourselves diverging from reality, and we will wind up far removed from the realities of our time. To catch up with things as they are, we must change our course sharply and follow reality itself. If reason, common sense, and the facts themselves tell us that the army and navy are declining in importance as compared with air power, we are doing a disservice to our own defense preparations when we insist upon crediting the army and navy with fictitious values which have no basis in actual fact.

Nature does not progress by leaps and bounds—still less does man. I do not imagine that between today and tomorrow the army and navy will be abolished and only the air force increased.

For the present I ask only that we give the air arm the importance it deserves—in Italy we are far from doing that—and that during the transition period we adopt the following modest program: *A progressive decrease of land and sea forces, accompanied by a corresponding increase of aerial forces until they are strong enough to conquer the command of the air.* This is a program which will approach nearer and nearer reality as we grow firmer in promoting it.

Victory smiles upon those who anticipate the changes in the character of war, not upon those who wait to adapt themselves after the changes occur. In this period of rapid transition from one form to another, those who daringly take to the new road first will enjoy the incalculable advantages of the new means of war over the old. This new character of war, emphasizing the advantages of the offensive, will surely make for swift, crushing decisions on the battlefield. Those nations who are caught unprepared for the coming war will find, when war breaks out, not only that it is too late for them to get ready for it, but that they cannot even get the drift of it. Those who are ready first not only will win quickly, but will win with the fewest sacrifices and the minimum expenditure of means. So that, when this change is completed, though decisions in the field will be swift, the actual war will be fought with increasingly formidable air forces. But during the period of transition a limited force will be adequate to checkmate any opponent's army and navy.

If we must wait to be convinced of this until someone else sets us an example, we will be left behind; and to be left behind during this period means to be defeated in case of war. And, as I have already pointed out, that, ironically enough, is just what is happening now. In an effort to safeguard themselves against Germany's possible thirst for revenge, the Allies forced her along the surest road toward accomplishing it. It is a fact that Germany, forced to disarm on land and sea, will be driven to arm in the air. As we shall see, an air force capable of conquering the command of the air, especially during this transition period, requires comparatively limited means, a small personnel, and modest resources; and all of this can be quietly disposed without awakening the attention of potential enemies. At the slightest chafing of the yoke imposed upon her by the Allies, the inner drive to be free will surely push Germany along the new road.

This new road is an economic road which makes it feasible for us to provide for national defense with a limited expenditure of energy and resources once the respective weapons of air, land, and sea are properly evaluated. We remember that in England there have been Admirals of the Fleet who questioned the value of battleships versus airplanes; and we remember, too, that in

America tests have been made which demonstrated that under certain conditions planes can sink armored ships.

Now we have reached the hour when we can no longer ignore this problem, which, in the interest of national defense, we should face squarely.

INDEPENDENT AIR FORCE AND
AUXILIARY AVIATION

Surveying the problem of national defense in outline, with particular reference to the aerial phase, we have emphasized aerial independence of surface forces and rapidity of movement; and we reached this conclusion: *An adequate national defense cannot be assured except by an aerial force capable in case of war of conquering the command of the air.* We have seen also that, in order to conquer the command of the air, all aerial means of the enemy must be destroyed whether in air combat, at their bases and airports, or in their production centers; in short, wherever they may be found or produced. And we have noted that neither the army nor the navy can help in any way in this work of destruction. The natural consequence of this situation is that an aerial force capable of conquering the command of the air is, by the very nature of things, organically self-sufficient and independent of land and sea forces in its operations. For the sake of simplicity, I shall hereafter refer to all those aerial means which, taken together, constitute an aerial force capable of conquering the command of the air, by the term, Independent Air Force. The foregoing conclusion may thus be stated: *National defense can be assured only by an Independent Air Force of adequate power.*

At present the only military use made of airplanes is to assist the operations of land and sea forces; and for this reason they are under the commands of the army and the navy. So far, an aerial force able to command the air does not exist anywhere in the world. If there were one, granting the uniformity of the air extending over land and sea alike, it could not depend for its being or for its operation on either the army or the navy, because such dependency would be an arbitrary one which, by forcing the Independent Air Force to divide its forces, would fail to fill the true needs of the situation. There are planes at present under the direct command of land and sea forces. An example is the observation plane, whose function is to direct artillery fire—a function, by the way, which is not essentially aerial; it would be performed by other means if aviation were not yet invented. Other examples are the bombing and pursuit specialties, which, while not operating directly under military and naval command, are nonetheless dependent upon them. The primary function of planes under direct army command is, naturally, the furthering of specifically army aims; of those under navy command, furthering specifically navy aims. In like manner, pursuit squadrons under army command have the specific duty of policing the sky above the land surface; those under navy command, of policing the sky over the sea surface.

In this situation we feel something which offends our sense of fitness. In face of this state of things, we can see clearly how easy a time a well-organized enemy bent on conquering the command of the air would have, and how helpless these auxiliary aerial means employed by the army and navy would be, confronted by an enemy Independent Air Force bent on conquest, inasmuch as no organized opposition would stand in his way. It is only natural that the army and navy should wish to be provided with aerial auxiliaries to assist their operations. But such aerial means, which integrate the separate operations of those two branches of the service, are nothing more than an extension of the army and navy. They cannot possibly be considered to constitute a real air force. Observation planes directing artillery fire are useful observers in aerial form, no more.

That fact is so self-evident that in our discussion of aerial warfare we have come to the inescapable conclusion that an Independent Air Force functioning completely independent of the army and the navy is of paramount importance.

When, a few years ago, we first encountered the term "flying service," it seemed a real triumph for the new instrument of war. But it only seemed so; for the term "flying service" expresses only a bond, inasmuch as a "service" is a mere part of a whole, which is the only entity which can be considered really independent. It is only when we arrive at the term "Independent Air Force" that we perceive an entity capable of fighting on the new battlefield, where neither army nor navy can take any part. Planes operating under command of the army or navy can be considered as no more than auxiliary weapons; so, for the sake of simplicity, I shall refer to them from now on as "auxiliary aviation of the army and navy."

Up to this point I have spoken of aerial means of warfare in general terms only, because I thought best to introduce the problem along general lines at the beginning of the book. But in fact aviation falls into two major categories, lighter-than-air and heavier-than-air ships, or dirigibles and airplanes. I should explain, for the sake of clarity, that from now on I shall confine myself to the heavier-than-air category, airplanes, as the only kind suitable for warfare.

CHAPTER II

THE INDEPENDENT AIR FORCE

STRUCTURE

We have defined an Independent Air Force as that complex total of aerial means which, taken as a whole, makes up an air force capable of conquering the command of the air; we have seen also that, in order to conquer the command of the air, it is necessary to destroy all the enemy's means of flying. Therefore, an Independent Air Force must be organized and employed with this destruction as the end in view.

But, if I may use a figure of speech, it is not enough to shoot down all birds in flight if you want to wipe out the species; there remain the eggs and the nests. The most effective method would be to destroy the eggs and the nests systematically, because, strictly speaking, no species of bird can remain continuously in flight without alighting. Similarly, destroying an enemy's airplanes by seeking them out in the air is, while not entirely useless, the least effective method. A much better way is to destroy his airports, supply bases, and centers of production. In the air his planes may escape; but, like the birds whose nests and eggs have been destroyed, those planes which were still out would have no bases at which to alight when they returned. Therefore, the best means of destroying such objectives is by aerial bombardment carried out by "units of bombardment."

Bombers, however, are by their very nature not intended for combat; so pursuit planes must clear the sky of enemy interference before the bombers can accomplish their mission. These pursuit squadrons I shall call "units of combat."

An Independent Air Force should be organically composed of bombing units and combat units, the first to direct offensive action against surface targets, the second to protect the bombers against possible enemy opposition. It follows, therefore, that the stronger the bombing units of an Independent Air Force, the greater its destructive capacity. The total strength of the combat units, on the other hand, should be only proportionately greater than the combat strength of the enemy; that is, they need be only strong enough to gain superiority over the enemy's combat forces. Once the Independent Air Force has conquered the command of the air, there will be no need of the combat units. The bombing units, on the contrary, once the Independent Air Force has won command of the air, now freed of aerial opposition, will be able to unleash without risk all their offensive power to cut off the enemy's army and navy from their bases of operation, spread terror and havoc in the interior of his country, and break down the moral and physical resistance of his people.

The following simple outline shows the skeleton upon which an Independent Air Force should be constituted:

1. Maximum bombing power
2. Combat power proportionate to the enemy's strength

UNIT OF BOMBARDMENT

The unit of bombardment must possess sufficient striking power to ensure really important results. I have already pointed out the fundamental principle which should govern offensive action from the air; namely, that a bombing attack must completely destroy the target at which it is directed, thus obviating the necessity of returning to make a second attack on the same target.

In my opinion the unit of bombardment should be capable of destroying everything on a specified surface of 500 meters in diameter. The area of that surface, then, should be the basis upon which to compute and establish the degree of power necessary to the bombing unit. Once the area of such a surface is determined by empirical criteria, or the number of targets on it, the next step is to determine the quantity of active material—explosives, incendiaries, and poison gases—necessary to demolish everything exposed on that surface. This quantity will be larger or smaller according to the efficacy of the active materials used in the actual bombs. If we stop to think that upon this necessary quantity of active material depends the number of bombers to a unit, other things being equal, we can easily see how great an advantage it would be to make use of the most efficient active materials.

Once the basic quantity of active materials is established and the ratio between it and the weight of the shell determined, it is a simple matter to calculate the total weight of the bomb load needed to destroy the surface under consideration. Once this weight is computed, we know the number of planes needed in a bombing unit. On the assumption that a quintal of active material is enough to destroy everything within a radius of 25 meters, and that on an average the active material in a bomb accounts for half its weight, we arrive at the conclusion that 20 tons of bombs are necessary to destroy a surface 500 meters in diameter. And further, allowing a carrying capacity of 2 tons of bombs to a plane, I conclude that the bombing unit should be a force of 10 planes. The assumptions upon which this computation is based are not pure speculation; they are derived from existing conditions. So that even if they are not absolutely exact, they furnish us with a reasonably accurate estimate which cannot be far from the truth. Only experience, of course, can establish the exact figures; and only experience can accurately determine the specific details of the organization of the bombing unit. But that is not of vital importance to us here. What interests us now is the principle of the matter and some realization of what should be the strength of a bombing unit capable of destroying a surface of, say, 500 meters diameter.

We may think from all this that a unit of bombardment established according to this principle represents a somewhat indefinite offensive power which might be capable of inflicting a certain amount of damage upon an opponent. That is not the case. Such a unit represents an exactly determined offensive power which possesses a definite known capacity for destruction over a given surface. When such a unit strikes against an enemy target within the specified surface, we have mathematical certainty that that target will be destroyed. The offensive power of an Independent Air Force as a whole, then, is computed from the number of bombing units composing it; and the number of these, in turn, from the number of given surfaces to be destroyed. This offensive—or better still, destructive—power can be launched against an enemy at whatever point it will prove most effective and most painful. Take, for example, an Independent Air Force of 500 planes, each carrying tons of bombs, and capable of destroying 50 surfaces, each 500 meters in diameter. Such an air force could destroy every day 50 enemy aviation nests—i.e. airports, supply depots, production plants, et cetera. At that rate, how long do you think it would take to ground the present air force of any of the great powers of Europe? What opposition, aerial or ground, could any of them offer against such attacks?

In discussing the unit of combat, let us first look into the possibility of aerial opposition, because it is the combat unit which will overcome the opposition. As for any opposition from ground forces, there can be none except antiaircraft guns; and I shall try to show how combat planes can counteract even the action of antiaircraft guns. But quite apart from this point, in actual fact the efficacy of antiaircraft guns can never be anything but very limited, both because of their inaccurate fire and because of the dispersion of means inherent in that kind of defense. Antiaircraft fire can certainly put out of action some planes in a bombing unit—a limited loss; but no one can hope to fight a war without taking some risks, especially when those risks can be reduced to a minimum. And that loss can easily be compensated for by simply keeping up the strength of the bombing units by a constant flow of replacement planes.

As to this question of replacement planes, an adequate supply of such planes should be kept on hand ready for instant action, and the quota of these planes should never be allowed to go below a certain limit. For example, taking the potentiality of the bombing unit as 20 tons of bombs, this amount of power can be developed by 10 machines, each carrying 2 tons; by 5 machines, each carrying 4 tons; or by a single machine—if such a machine existed—carrying the whole 20-ton load. From one point of view, it is better to have as few planes as possible to simplify the organization of the unit. But from another point of view, it is very unwise to make the number of planes in a unit too small, because the loss of even one plane would too greatly reduce the potentiality of the unit. For this reason I consider that the minimum number of planes per unit should never be less than 4; which, in the case under consideration, would mean planes carrying 5 tons each.

Now let us try to determine the general characteristics of planes suitable for bombing units. An airplane must have the characteristics of air-worthiness and usefulness. These are demanded of any flying machine in peace or war. It is the functional characteristics—the performance—of a plane we must determine here; and these include speed, radius of action, ceiling, armament, and useful-load capacity.

Speed: We have already noted that bombing units, which should carry out their mission in spite of enemy opposition, are supported by combat units. This means that they need not have the speed to outdistance enemy pursuit planes; a fact of utmost importance because it makes it unnecessary for bombing planes to enter a speed race, the outcome of which is bound to be uncertain. The nation which stakes its safety or its power simply on speed in the air, gambles on a very doubtful card—especially in view of the ever-increasing speed of airplanes. On the other hand, victory is never won by fleeing. Great speed in an airplane is always obtained at the expense of carrying capacity. So in planes of great carrying capacity we must be content with a moderate speed, which may actually prove to be best for practical purposes. The bombing plane, then, should be a plane of moderate speed, since, protected by combat planes, it need not flee or dodge the attacks of the enemy and thus sacrifice load to speed.

Radius of Action: The radius of action of a warplane is the greatest distance it can travel from its own airfield and return under its own power. A bombing plane's radius of action should therefore be the greatest possible; for the longer its radius of action, the deeper its penetration into enemy territory. The extent of the radius of action depends exclusively upon the fuel consumption of its motors and its carrying capacity. Therefore, the greater the carrying capacity, the longer its radius of action.

A bombing plane's carrying capacity, exclusive of the crew, should be proportionately divided between fuel load and bomb load. It is understood, of course, that, given the maximum total load of the plane—a predetermined fixed quantity—the radius of action can be increased simply by increasing the load of fuel and decreasing the bomb load, and vice versa. What we are concerned with here is determining the normal or average radius of action of the bombing plane; and that depends upon two factors: the disposition of enemy targets intended for attack during normal operations, and the choice of plane capable, within that normal radius of action, of carrying a load of bombs sufficient to destroy the target.

In my opinion, the normal radius of action of a bombing plane today should be between 200 and 300 kilometers. I said "normal radius of action"; in exceptional instances it can easily be modified. If the normal radius is 300 kilometers and an action is planned within 100 kilometers, it would be wasteful to carry a load of fuel sufficient for 300 kilometers instead of reducing the fuel load and using the weight thus saved to carry more bombs. Conversely, if the normal radius is 300 kilometers and an action at 400 kilometers is planned, the bomb load can be lightened by enough to correspond with the increase in fuel load. This elasticity in the radius of action of a plane can be secured by a few extra details of construction to allow for adjustment of the total load between fuel weight and bomb weight.

Ceiling: The higher the altitude, the less a warplane's vulnerability to antiaircraft fire. Since by their very nature bombing operations are characterized by dispersion rather than concentration of fire, bombing raids can be carried out effectively even at very high altitudes. The normal ceiling, therefore, should be between 3,000 and 4,000 meters. Considering the nature of our boundaries, made up for the most part of high mountain peaks, we need warplanes with ceilings high enough to surmount the entire Alpine range at any point without difficulty; which means ceilings between 6,000 and 7,000 meters.

Degree of Armament: Obviously, the first requisite, the chief purpose, of a bombing plane is to carry bombs and to be equipped with the proper mechanism for releasing them. But that is not all; something more is needed. For the sake of the crew's morale, some defensive armament is indispensable. Though a bombing plane cannot possibly be the ideal weapon for aerial combat, it would be poor judgment to leave its crew with a feeling of utter helplessness against possible attack by enemy pursuit planes. It is imperative, therefore, that the plane be supplied with small-caliber rapid-fire guns for its own defense, even though conscious of the fact that aerial combat should be left to combat units.

Useful Load: The maximum useful load of any type of plane is a predetermined fixed quantity equal to the sum of the weights of these three elements: crew, fuel, and armament. The crew, naturally, should be kept to an indispensable minimum, allowing for possible losses in personnel. The relationship between weight of fuel and weight of armament we have already discussed. Given, then, the amount of fuel and armament needed for normal operations, the total useful load of a bombing plane should be such as to allow a bomb weight substantial enough to avoid cumbersome bombing units of too many planes. In my opinion, the number of planes in a bombing unit should be between 4 and 12.

Such are the functional characteristics of a bomber—characteristics which, translated into specifications, should be required to be put into effect by plane designers and builders.

I have already called attention to the great importance of the efficacy of the active materials used in bombs. Doubling the efficacy of the active materials, in fact, automatically doubles the power of an Independent Air Force. It would be foolish indeed to be too economical in these matters or in any way stint appropriations for research into the nature and use of these materials.

Active materials fall into three major categories: explosives, incendiaries, and poison gases. Besides study and research into the efficacy of each of these, we should also investigate the potentialities of possible combinations of them in bombing operations. Even if we still have little knowledge of them, we can at least sense, and experience may confirm the impression, that high explosives will play a minor role in potential combinations, given a more extensive use of incendiaries and poison gases. This will be particularly true as regards civilian objectives such as warehouses, factories, stores, food supplies, and population centers, the destruction of which may be more easily accomplished by setting fires with incendiary bombs and paralyzing all human activity for a time with gas bombs. Only in exceptional cases will high-explosive bombs be useful, as in smashing runways and plowing up airfields with bomb bursts. But this matter of bombs is a particular detail to which I allude only in order to give you an idea of the scope of the whole problem of the formation of a bombing unit.

UNIT OF COMBAT

The essential function of the combat unit is to clear any possible aerial opposition out of the path of bombers while they carry out their mission. They should therefore be designed and equipped primarily for aerial combat.

In the days before the World War the opinion was current in military circles that combat in the air was an impossibility, and, except in rare instances, the first planes used in the war were provided with no armament suitable for combat. But aerial combat is a reality and is here to stay.

Any aerial action on the part of the foe is bound to be to his advantage, and our disadvantage, and we must contest it. During the World War it was considered poor policy to admit that our reconnaissance planes could do practically nothing to prevent enemy planes from carrying out their observations over our lines, and vice versa. But aerial combat developed spontaneously, in the natural course of events. Planes began to carry some armament, and pilots began to learn to attack and to defend themselves—the beginning of aerial maneuvers. And from these dog fights the fact emerged clearly that the faster planes had the advantage over slower ones; they could hit and run at will. Soon after, out of that experience came the pursuit plane, so named precisely because its purpose was to interfere with other planes and prevent them from fulfilling their missions. Speed and armament were the characteristics most stressed in the design of this type of plane; and as a consequence the pursuit plane immediately became master of the air and dominated all other types of plane in combat. Out of the necessity of protecting other types of plane from the pursuit plane, arose the need of another plane as fast or faster, a plane able, as it were, to give chase to the chaser.

Then the race was on to develop more and more speed in airplanes. More speed and greater maneuverability than the enemy, was the cry—for planes capable of performing aerial "acrobatics," by which, in case a pilot found his speed inferior, he could dodge the fight and flee to safety. Everything else was sacrificed to speed and maneuverability, the first requisite for gaining even temporary superiority over the enemy in the air. The crew was reduced to the minimum—a single pilot who also handled the machine gun. The radius of action was reduced to a minimum—an hour or a little more of flying time was all.

The function of pursuit planes, then, was to seek out other types of enemy plane and to protect their own planes from enemy pursuers. Since they were the fastest planes and designed for aerial acrobatics, hence the most difficult to handle, they were assigned to the most daring of the pilots. For two understandable reasons pilots preferred them to other types of plane.

In the first place, other types—reconnaissance, observation, and bomber planes—were sent out on definite missions, which put them at a disadvantage in encounters with enemy chasers. Pursuit planes, on the other hand, were given less definite missions and consequently had more freedom of action. They attacked enemy planes of other types, over which they had obvious advantages when it came to an encounter. Or, encountering enemy pursuit planes, they could engage them in dog fights, evade the encounter entirely, or, once engaged, cut the fight short in the middle and head for home. Their performance was thus more colorful, less restricted, less monotonous, and even, in a certain sense, less dangerous than the operations of other types of plane.

In the second place, pursuit planes usually operated near the headquarters of the High Commands, to whose protection, I may add, they directly contributed. In the war both sides kept trying to bomb Headquarters, and it was soon apparent that pursuit planes were the best defense against these attempts. With their quick take-off and fast climbing speed, these machines were more likely to succeed in intercepting the attacker before he could strike and, more often than not, in bringing down the slower enemy bombers. Policing the sky became the particular province of the pursuit planes, and they enjoyed the favor of the

High Commands, whose safety and peace of mind they could safeguard, at least during the day.

This favoritism produced a rapid growth of this flying specialty; but at the same time it obscured the problem of national defense and prevented a correct understanding of what the command of the air consists in. When the pursuit squadrons of one side in the war succeeded in bringing down more enemy ships than they lost of their own, that side would immediately claim command of the air. In reality all that had been gained was a temporary superiority which may have made aerial operations more difficult for the opponent for the time being. But it did not, and could not, preclude his engaging in aerial operations. Up to the very last days of the war, in fact, all belligerents carried out aerial operations against each other.

The fact of the matter is that, in spite of its claim to offensive characteristics, the pursuit plane was used almost entirely as a defensive means. It could not have been otherwise. With its very limited radius of action, the pursuit plane was forced to play a passive role instead of seeking out the enemy on his own grounds. The pursuit planes of those days could not have been differently employed. They were used primarily to shoot down enemy machines on observation patrol or directing artillery fire, and to defend important centers from bombardment. For the rest, their usefulness was as limited as their operations were scattered; and aerial combat became merely a series of duels in which the skill and courage of the individual aces were displayed in all their brilliance. Pursuit squadrons were a loose agglomeration of knights-errant of the air, rather than an effectively organized cavalry of the air.

We can see now that such a situation has something false in it, something that does not ring true; for war is no longer fought in a series of scattered individual encounters, no matter how brave or skillful the individuals may be. War today is fought by masses of men and machines. So this aerial knight-errantry ought to be supplanted by a real cavalry of the air—the Independent Air Force.

Earlier in these pages I remarked that to rely on speed alone in aerial combat is to stake one's all on a doubtful card. For instance, let a pursuit plane be chased by a faster one, and it ceases to be a pursuit plane. By its very nature the pursuit plane must be an exceptional machine, embodying at any given moment all the most recent technical developments, and manipulated by exceptional pilots. But war is fought with men and machines of average abilities and standards; and we must therefore change our present conception of aerial warfare—or go under.

What determines victory in aerial warfare is fire power. Speed serves only to come to grips with the foe or to flee from him, no more. A slower, heavily armed plane, able to clear its way with its own armament, can always get the best of the faster pursuit plane. A unit of combat composed of slower, heavily armed planes is in a position to stand up to the fire of enemy pursuit planes and carry out its mission successfully. As a matter of fact, it is not the business of a combat unit either to seek out an aerial foe or to flee from him. I have said, and I repeat it, that the primary function of a combat unit is to clear enemy aerial opposition out of the way of bombing units intent upon carrying out definite missions.

Let me use this simple example to illustrate what I mean: A bombing unit leaves point A to bomb point B. Combat units have no other purpose in this operation than to clear out of their path any enemy aerial obstacles attempting to bar the way of the bombing unit on the road from A to B. It is up to the enemy to prevent the bombardment of B if he can. He is the one who seeks battle, who makes the attack. If he does not, so much the better—the bombing of B can be performed with more safety. If he does attack, there are the combat units to fight off the attack. Therefore, combat units have no need of great speed in order to seek out the enemy and force him to give battle; all they need is enough to escort the bombing units and put up an adequate fight if the enemy attempts to interfere with their operations.

It is obvious, then, that the speed of combat units ought to be somewhat greater than that of bombing units. And, as a matter of fact, it goes without saying that the radius of action and ceiling of combat planes should be greater than those of bombing units, which they must escort and protect. In general the chief characteristics of combat planes should be speed, radius of action, and ceiling superior to those of bombing planes.

From this the conclusion may be drawn that there should, on the whole, be very little difference between one type of plane and the other, which implies that combat planes, like bombers, ought to be capable of carrying a substantial load in addition to an adequate supply of fuel. This increase in the carrying capacity of the combat unit should be made use of for increasing fire power and, if possible, armor protection. This is merely a matter of increasing the amount of the plane's armament and its ability to concentrate fire in any given direction. A certain amount of protection may be afforded by armor-plating the vital parts of the plane with light metal alloys. Certainly it would be absurd to expect complete armor protection against all possible hits; but it is not too much to expect that a very light armor-plating would deflect a great many bullets.

A plane designed and constructed along these lines would on the face of it be so superior in intensity of fire power as to outmatch any pursuit ship now existing. If a bombing plane capable of carrying two tons of bombs can be made, certainly it should be possible to construct one with slightly superior speed, radius of action, and ceiling, capable of carrying a one-ton load of bombs. Then if the carrying capacity thus saved were used for armament instead of bombs, we would have a plane equipped for combat with a much greater fire power than any pursuit plane now existing.

The organization of a combat unit must be such as to include a number of planes which can fight in formation; and the formation must be of a nature to concentrate maximum intensity of fire in any direction in order to ward off enemy aerial attack, or at least make it hazardous for the enemy to approach. Compared with such units—the purpose of which, I repeat, is not to attack, but to defend themselves against attack—pursuit planes, with all their superior speed and maneuverability, would have no advantage, but rather the disadvantage of light armament. Such a unit could be attacked with success only by a similar unit made up of a still larger number of planes, stronger, better armed, and better armored.

Only practical experience can furnish us with enough data to determine the proper organization of the combat unit in specific detail—i.e. number of planes, formation, and tactics. My purpose here is to present a schematic, but nonetheless concrete, idea of what the combat unit should be like.

STABILIZATION OF ARMAMENT

We have seen how an Independent Air Force should be organized, that it must include both bombing and combat units in order to be fully effective. It may include other types of plane in addition—fast planes for observation, dispatch bearing, and liaison duty between the various commands, for example. But its backbone must always be bombing and combat planes. In that lies stabilization of its armament.

One of the gravest problems confronting an air force is this question of stabilizing its armament. It is often said that military planes should be changed in design and construction every three months because of the constant and rapid technical progress being made in aviation. This is true in view of the concepts which today govern the organization of such forces. For instance, we have noted the importance accorded to pursuit planes at present. Since this branch of aviation derives its potential power from speed, and since new speed records are made and broken every day, pursuit aviation is clearly unstable; the plane which today is the last word in technical developments may be obsolete tomorrow.

This is true not only of pursuit planes. There are machines called "daylight bombers," in which a combination of great speed and bomb-carrying capacity is sought. In the prevailing concept of their purpose, these planes are called daylight bombers because they can carry out limited bombing operations—during daylight only—at the same time taking advantage of their greater speed to escape from enemy pursuit planes. These daylight bombers are considered to be the counterpart of the medium-speed bombers called "night bombers" because they are supposed to carry out their operations under cover of night. In both cases the same concept governs; namely, trying to carry out an operation *by fleeing!* This is a concept that cries aloud for revision. The idea is absurd inasmuch as war demands the power to carry out operations, whether on land, on the sea, or in the air, *in spite* of enemy opposition. But apart from that, these so-called daylight bombers must evidently remain unstabilized inasmuch as they rely upon speed alone for their effectiveness, a factor forever changing.

Very different indeed is my conception of the planes which should form the main body of an Independent Air Force. Whether bombers or combat planes, they need no more than a medium speed. No emphasis need be placed upon speed; it is of little importance that technical advances may soon produce bombing or combat planes which, while retaining other basic characteristics unaltered, will have a speed of 10 to 20 more miles per hour. To keep abreast of technical developments in armament, it will be enough to take into account the gradual improvement in armament itself. Theoretical perfection always demands the extreme; but our interest is in the middle road of practicality.

Therefore, it is the actual armament of an Independent Air Force which governs the stabilization of whatever armament is considered necessary for a really efficient air force. But there is more to it than that. If we examine carefully the functional characteristics of bombing and combat planes as I have tried to define them, we can readily see that they are in general almost identical with the functional characteristics of civil aviation. When all is said and done, the bombing plane is essentially a transport plane of medium speed and sufficient radius of action, especially equipped to carry bombs. In fact, to change its equipment is all that is necessary to transform it into a plane for civilian use. The same thing can be said of a combat plane of normal radius of action and medium speed (even if this is somewhat greater than the speed of a regular bomber), and of sufficient carrying capacity to carry out bombing operations (even if this is slightly less than the carrying capacity of the regular bomber). This also means—since the law of reciprocity works both ways—that, by mutual understanding between military and civil aviation, civilian planes could be turned into military planes in case of need. This in turn implies that, with the strides being made in civil aviation, an Independent Air Force can rely for many of its needs and much of its equipment upon civilian progress in addition to military progress. Based as it is upon planes of extreme characteristics, military aviation in its present state cannot boast of this advantage. As a result, military aviation today not only has failed to stabilize design and construction, but is also almost entirely dependent upon its own resources. I shall return to this argument, which is of the utmost importance, in my discussion of the relationship between military and civil aviation in later chapters.

CHAPTER III

Aerial Warfare

GENERAL PRINCIPLES

Before we can draw up an accurate estimate of the scope of an Independent Air Force, we must first consider the following point: An Independent Air Force is an offensive force which can strike with terrific speed against enemy targets on land or sea in any direction, and can force its way through any aerial opposition from the enemy. From this fact emerges this first principle governing its operation: *An Independent Air Force should always operate in mass.*

This is the same principle which governs warfare on land and sea; and therefore the material and moral effects of aerial offensives—as of any other kind of offensive—are greatest when the offensives are concentrated in time and space. In addition, keeping together in mass in its operations makes it possible for the Air Force to force its way through aerial opposition successfully.

The radius of action of an Independent Air Force obviously must depend upon the radius of action of the planes comprising its units. But because all its units cannot be located at a single base, the disposition of the various units in relation to one another and to the general theater of war have some influence upon the radius of action. Once the disposition of its units has been decided, the Air Force's field of mass operation against enemy targets can be shown on a military map simply by tracing the periphery which can be reached by *all* units. It is self-evident that any enemy target, on land or sea, within this line can be reached with equal facility by the entire Air Force in a few hours, at most in the time needed to cover the maximum distance between its bases of operation and any given point on that periphery. The attack may therefore be prepared in complete secrecy and launched without forewarning the enemy, with the offensive retaining the advantages of operational initiative. And, considering the suddenness of the attack, it is unlikely that the enemy would have time enough to parry the blow effectively either in the air or from the ground. Whatever he might be able to do, in general he could oppose the attack with no more than a fraction of his air forces.

Whatever the total strength of an Independent Air Force, provided it has at its disposal an adequate number of bombing units, the attack can be successfully directed not only against a single target, but against a number of them within the same zone. Since a bombing unit is potentially able to destroy any target on a specified surface, a fully activated Air Force is potentially capable of demolishing as many such targets, or surfaces, as there are bombing units. An Air Force of 50 bombing units, each capable of destroying a surface 500 meters in diameter, could in a single flight completely destroy 50 enemy objectives, such as supply depots, industrial plants, warehouses, railroad centers, population centers, et cetera.

In considering the objectives situated within striking distance of the Air Force, it would be advisable to subdivide the area into zones of 50 targets each. If we get 10 zones when the subdivision is mapped out, it means that the Air Force has the potential capacity to destroy all enemy objectives in that area of land or sea in ten days of operation, after which its striking power can be transferred to other zones designated for destruction.

All this sounds very simple; but as a matter of fact the selection of objectives, the grouping of zones, and determining the order in which they are to be destroyed is the most difficult and delicate task in aerial warfare, constituting what may be defined as aerial strategy. Objectives vary considerably in war, and the choice of them depends chiefly upon the aim sought, whether the command of the air paralyzing the enemy's army and navy, or shattering the morale of civilians behind the lines. This choice may therefore be guided by a great many considerations—military, political, social, and psychological, depending upon the conditions of the moment. For example, I have always maintained that the essential purpose of an Air Force is to conquer the command of the air by first wiping out the enemy's air forces. This, then, would seem to be always the first objective of an Independent Air Force. But this is not always the case. Take, for instance, a case when the enemy's aerial forces are so weak it would be a waste of time to devote men and materials to so unimportant an objective. It may be more profitable to subject the enemy to various other offensive actions instead, thereby doing him far more damage. Let us suppose—hypothetically, of course—that Germany had an Air Force of the strength described above, and decided to attack France, who was armed only with the aerial means now at her disposal. How long do you think it would take Germany to knock out not only the French flying forces, but the very heart of France?

The same thing is true of the grouping of enemy objectives into zones and in the disposition of the zones themselves, dependent as they are on diverse factors of vital consequence to the conduct of aerial operations as a whole. On this aspect of aerial warfare I do not believe it possible to lay down any specific rules. It will be enough to keep in mind the following basic principle, which is the same one which governs warfare on land and sea: *Inflict the greatest damage in the shortest possible time.*

In the light of this principle the value of the surprise attack is obvious. A really strong Independent Air Force such as the one described above would inflict upon an unprepared enemy such grave damage as to bring about a complete collapse of his forces in a very few days. To confirm the truth of this statement, I suggest that the reader solve for himself the following military problems:

Given a possible enemy armed with an Independent Air Force of enough bombing units, each capable of demolishing a surface 500 meters in diameter, and with an adequate radius of action—

1. How many bombing units would be needed to cut all rail communications between Piedmont and Liguria, and the rest of Italy, in a single day?

2. How many bombing units would be needed to cut Rome off from all rail, telegraph, telephone, and radio communication, and to plunge the city itself into terror and confusion by the destruction of governing bodies, banks, and other public services in a single day?

If the reader remembers that by a 500-meter surface we mean an area of that dimension upon which a variety of explosive, incendiary, and poison-gas bombs will be dropped, he needs must answer the questions with very small numbers indeed; and his conception of the power of this new weapon of warfare will be that much clearer and nearer the truth.

THE DEFENSE

The very magnitude of possible aerial offensives cries for an answer to the question, "How can we defend ourselves against them?" To this I have always answered, "By attacking."

More than once I have stressed the pre-eminently offensive character of the air arm. Like a cavalry corps (unless it is dismounted), whose best defense is always to attack, the air arm depends upon attack for its own best defense, to an even greater degree, in fact. But before we go on with the air arm, we should thoroughly understand what we mean by the term "to attack."

Let us suppose that Nation A is armed only with combat units and depends upon them in case of war to repel the attack of Nation B's Independent Air Force. What do you think would be their respective situations at the outbreak of hostilities? The probability is that the air force of Nation A would have to seek for B's Independent Air Force, find it, compel it to fight, and defeat it.

To find it is the crux of the matter. One may look—but where? The air is a uniform element everywhere; there are no signposts to show the road Independent Air Force B will follow in attacking Nation A. The word "seek" becomes an abstraction; and "to find" is a possibility, not a probability. For A's air force to compel B's Independent Air Force to engage in battle, A must have greater speed than B; to win, A must be stronger than B and have good luck besides. But while air force A's search for Independent Air Force B is going on unsuccessfully, B can strike at A's territory and do enormous damage, with A helpless to inflict any damage at all on Nation B. If, however, Nation B considers A's air force dangerous, her Independent Air Force will doubtless concentrate her attacks upon demolishing everything essential to the functioning of A's air force. A's wasted time looking for Independent Air Force B will then result not only in a futile joyride, but in a real if indirect defeat, since her air potential will have been wasted without her having had a chance to engage Independent Air Force B in combat.

If we also consider that the air force of Nation A must operate in mass in order to be in the best position to win, the question comes up of where and when to concentrate those forces, operating as they are from scattered airfields.

This kind of action is essentially defensive in spite of its offensive appearance, and it has all the disadvantages of the defensive. To attack on land means to attack, without the need of scouting for them, fixed targets immovable upon the surface, targets which are the very lifeblood of an opponent's air force. On the sea, conditions are different. Naval bases are as a rule so strongly fortified that it is practically impossible for hostile naval forces to destroy them. This fact increases the importance of naval battles fought to prevent or carry out subsequent possible action against land targets by one belligerent or the other. Things would be radically different, however, if naval bases could no longer be protected, and instead were subject to destruction in a few hours by naval forces. In such a case the destruction of naval bases would set the value of battle fleets at naught, because it would prove of incalculable help in crippling the operating efficiency of such fleets without wasting time and matériel trying to catch and sink them on the open seas.

For a nation to be equipped with an air force intended for aerial combat alone is not only to jeopardize the home front, but also to preclude any possibility of offensive action against enemy objectives—a condition of profound aerial inferiority.

The only really effective aerial defense cannot but be indirect; for it consists in reducing the offensive potentiality of the opponent's air forces by destroying the source of aerial power at its point of origin. The surest and most effective way of achieving this end is to destroy the enemy air force at its bases, which are found on the surface. This is the principle which governs the situation: it is easier and more effective to destroy the enemy's aerial power by destroying his nests and eggs on the ground than to hunt his flying birds in the air. And every time we ignore this principle we commit an error. Therefore, even if a nation has no other end in view than self-defense, it should be armed with an Independent Air Force capable of launching powerful offensives on land and sea.

It remains for us to take up the question of what I shall call local defense, meaning defense of singularly important points on one's land and sea territory. Theoretically there are two ways of making this defense effective: by preventing enemy bombardment of them and by immediate repair of the damage inflicted by bombardment. This last appears at once impossible to effect, since it would be impossible to bomb-shelter entire cities with their rail centers, port facilities, supply bases, factories, and so on. In a measure aerial enemies could be kept at a distance and prevented from bombing certain objectives either by antiaircraft fire or by defensive aerial operations. Since antiaircraft guns are limited in range and not effective enough, practically speaking, to be of any great value, large numbers of them would have to be used; and since any country has a great many vital centers to be defended, even partial protection of them would require an enormous number of antiaircraft guns.

Moreover, the fact must be taken into consideration that antiaircraft guns may be neutralized by the escorting combat units' drawing on themselves the fire of the guns. These operations are even safer at a low altitude than at a higher one, for the simple reason that the angular variation of the gunfire would have to be greater to keep the diving planes in sight. A plane flying at 100 meters is far more difficult to hit than one flying at 2,000 meters because the angular variation is about twenty times greater. If, therefore, the escorting combat planes should dive with machine guns wide open straight at the gun emplacements, it would be very unlikely that the gunners could stay at their posts and keep firing at the high-flying bombing units. In all probability, if they were not quite forced to drop the guns and take up the rifle, they would naturally shift their fire, trying to hit the immediate menace, hard as it might be to keep them in sight. For my part, I maintain—and war experience has already confirmed me in my opinion—that the use of antiaircraft guns is a mere waste of energy and resources.

As for the utilization of aerial units for purely defensive purposes, we have only to recall that if an enemy's Independent Air Force operates efficiently, as presumably it will, it will function in mass, so the defensive units must at least be equal to the combat units of the hostile Independent Air Force. To defend effectively all areas threatened by such an Air Force would require a defensive force equal to the total combat strength of the attacking Air Force, multiplied by as many times as there are defensive positions to be protected. To obtain even this negative result it would be necessary to spend an enormously greater amount of resources than the enemy had to spend to obtain a positive result. This clearly demonstrates that it is both cheaper and wiser to put these resources to work where they will do the most good, for offensive purposes.

In conclusion, no local defense can be very effective when confronted by an aerial offensive of this magnitude; therefore, the expenditure of men and resources for such a purpose goes against the principles of sound war economy.

Viewed in its true light, aerial warfare admits of no defense, only offense. *We must therefore resign ourselves to the offensives the enemy inflicts upon us, while striving to put all our resources to work to inflict even heavier ones upon him.* This is the basic principle which must govern the development of aerial warfare.

THE DEVELOPMENT OF AERIAL WARFARE

As long as aerial forces remain mere auxiliaries of the army and navy, there will be no real aerial warfare in case of conflict. True, there will be air battles of major and minor proportions, but always subject to land or sea operations. Before any real aerial warfare can take place, its basic elements, such as planes, personnel, and their organization into an autonomous fighting body, must first be created and forged into an efficient fighting organization.

Under the circumstances, the first nation to arm herself with a real Independent Air Force will be in a superior military position, at least until other nations follow her example; for she will be in possession of an offensive weapon of formidable power, while the others will be dependent upon mere aerial auxiliaries. No doubt the necessity of establishing military equilibrium among the nations will induce others to follow her lead.

To study the development of aerial warfare, let us consider two cases: (1) a war between Nation A, armed with an Independent Air Force, and Nation B, without one; and (2) a war between two nations, both armed with an Independent Air Force.

An Independent Air Force must be always ready for action; otherwise 90 per cent of its effectiveness is lost. Given the speed of its units, no matter how widely dispersed their bases of operation may be in time of peace, it should be able to concentrate its forces along its line of battle and be ready for action in a few hours. If civil aviation units, scattered over the country, are a part of the Air Force's organization, they must be located where their integration into the Air Force can be accomplished as quickly as possible. In short, the Independent Air Force must be organically and logistically organized so that it can go into action immediately upon the outbreak of hostilities.

Now let us examine the first case. Independent Air Force A begins its action to catch Nation B in the midst of mobilization. But let us assume that Nation B is found to have immediately mobilized all her military aviation. Only her pursuit and bombing specialties, however, could take part in the battle, because her other specialties are suitable only for integrating the action of her naval and land forces. It is clear, then, that Independent Air Force A will have freedom of action, for B's pursuit aviation certainly could not hinder it. On the contrary, assuming that Air Force A has an adequate number of combat units, it will be able to inflict losses on B's pursuit aviation. Thus Air Force A will rapidly gain command of the air by destroying the mobilization, maintenance, and production centers of Nation B's aviation.

Once the command of the air has been won, the combat units of A's Independent Air Force will naturally cease functioning solely to protect bombing units and will be used to neutralize the fire of antiaircraft batteries during bombing operations by the entire Air Force, and to bomb and machine-gun troop concentrations, supply trains, transport or marching columns, et cetera. Furthermore, if constructed to undergo the necessary conversion in equipment, these combat units can quickly be transformed into first-rate bombing planes. Therefore, with the command of the air an accomplished fact, Independent Air Force A will have won complete liberty of action to strike at will, with no risk to itself, over all the enemy's territory, and quickly bring him to his knees.

By bombing railroad junctions and depots, population centers at road junctions, military depots, and other vital objectives, Air Force A could handicap the mobilization of B's army. By bombing naval bases, arsenals, oil stores, battleships at anchor, and mercantile ports, it could prevent the efficient operation of B's navy. By bombing the most vital civilian centers it could spread terror through the nation and quickly break down B's material and moral resistance.

The reader who thinks this picture overdrawn has only to look at a map of Italy, and imagine himself the commander of an Independent Air Force belonging to any of the nations on our frontiers. Let him remember that his Air Force is capable of destroying 50 surfaces 500 meters in diameter every day; and then ask himself how many days of operation it would take to achieve the aim described above. He must also take into consideration the fact that, even in the present stage of aeronautical development, the daily operational strength of such an Independent Air Force would be, even if only half of it were used on alternate days, about a thousand machines, requiring only a few thousand men to man it. Then he may draw his own conclusions.

At this point I want to stress one aspect of the problem—namely, that the effect of such aerial offensives upon morale may well have more influence upon the conduct of the war than their material effects. For example, take the center of a large city and imagine what would happen among the civilian population during a single attack by a single bombing unit. For my part, I have no doubt that its impact upon the people would be terrible. Here is what would be likely to happen to the center of the city within a radius of about 250 meters: Within a few minutes some 20 tons of high-explosive, incendiary, and gas bombs would rain down. First would come explosions, then fires, then deadly gases floating on the surface and preventing any approach to the stricken area. As the hours passed and night advanced, the fires would spread while the poison gas paralyzed all life. By the following day the life of the city would be suspended; and if it happened to be a junction on some important artery of communication traffic would be suspended.

What could happen to a single city in a single day could also happen to ten, twenty, fifty cities. And, since news travels fast, even without telegraph, telephone, or radio, what, I ask you, would be the effect upon civilians of other cities, not yet stricken but equally subject to bombing attacks? What civil or military authority could keep order, public services functioning, and production going under such a threat? And even if a semblance of order was maintained and some work done, would not the sight of a single enemy plane be enough to stampede the population into panic? In short, normal life would be impossible in this constant nightmare of imminent death and destruction. And if on the second day another ten, twenty, or fifty cities were bombed, who could keep all those lost, panic-stricken people from fleeing to the open countryside to escape this terror from the air?

A complete breakdown of the social structure cannot but take place in a country subjected to this kind of merciless pounding from the air. The time would soon come when, to put an end to horror and suffering, the people themselves, driven by the instinct of self-preservation, would rise up and demand an end to the war—this before their army and navy had time to mobilize at all! The reader who thinks I have overcolored the picture has only to recall the panic created at Brescia when, during funeral services for the victims of an earlier bombing—a negligible one compared with the one I have pictured here—one of the mourners mistook a bird for an enemy plane.

Now to the second case, of two nations each armed with an Independent Air Force. It is easy to see that in this case, even more than in the first one, the nation who struck first would have the edge on the enemy; or, conversely, how imperative it would be to parry as well as possible the enemy's blow before it struck home. To simplify the situation, then, let us admit that both Independent Air Forces could begin operations simultaneously. We have already seen that the fundamental concept governing aerial warfare *is to be resigned to the damage the enemy may inflict upon us, while utilizing every means at our disposal to inflict even heavier damage upon him.* An Independent Air Force must therefore be completely free of any preoccupation with the actions of the enemy force. Its sole concern should be to do the enemy the greatest possible amount of surface damage in the shortest possible time, which depends upon the available air forces and the choice of enemy targets. Whatever resources, of men, money, and equipment, are diverted from the strength and essential purpose of an Independent Air Force will result in slowing down the conduct of the war and delaying its final outcome.

The choice of enemy targets, as I have already pointed out, is the most delicate operation of aerial warfare, especially when both sides are armed with Independent Air Forces. In such a case the final decision depends upon the disequilibrium between the damage suffered by the enemy and his powers of recuperating from a blow which must be struck as quickly as possible, lest the enemy strike at us first. Of course, it may still be possible for one side to use its Independent Air Force to conquer the command of the air, which would ultimately win the war. But there may not be time enough for this if the other side succeeds in striking first and throwing the country into complete confusion.

The truth of the matter is that no hard and fast rules can be laid down on this aspect of aerial warfare. It is impossible even to outline general standards, because the choice of enemy targets will depend upon a number of circumstances, material, moral, and psychological, the importance of which, though real, is not easily estimated. It is just here, in grasping these imponderables, in choosing enemy targets, that future commanders of Independent Air Forces will show their ability.

Once the choice of enemy objectives and the order of their destruction have been determined, the task of the Air Force becomes very simple—to get on with their destruction in the briefest possible time, with no other preoccupation. In the case we are considering, therefore, both Air Forces will, at least in theory, proceed simultaneously in mass from their points of concentration toward their chosen objectives, without seeking each other out on the way. Should they happen to meet in flight, an air battle is inevitable; but I repeat that their purpose is not to seek each other out and fight in the air.

I consider this phase of aerial warfare very important, and I should like to pause here to clarify it further. Let us suppose that one of the Air Forces does seek out the other; but meanwhile the latter, avoiding an encounter, goes straight to its chosen objectives. He who seeks may find; but he may also return empty-handed. If one Independent Air Force deviates from its essential purpose, wastes time and fritters away its own freedom of action by seeking out the enemy in the air, the chances are not only that it will fail to find the enemy Air Force in the air, but also that the latter is at that very moment carrying out unchallenged its operations against the home territory. The one will have accomplished its task successfully; the other will have missed its opportunity and failed. In this kind of war, in which time is a vital factor, such a failure may have grave consequences in the outcome of the war, and should at all costs be avoided.

Speaking of aerial actions, I have already mentioned the possibility of having units of an Independent Air Force operate on alternate days; but I meant it merely as an illustration of how an Air Force might achieve results of major importance even with only half her strength, or with a relatively small number of planes. But during actual operations it would be an error to employ the strength of the Air Force piecemeal; for the purpose of an Independent Air Force is to inflict upon the enemy the greatest possible damage in the shortest possible time. The potential strength of an Independent Air Force should always be used to its fullest, with no thought of economy, especially when confronted by another equally strong Air Force which could do equally heavy damage. To replace personnel and equipment with fresh reserves may be expedient; but the Air Force itself—that is, its full complement of planes—should always remain in the air battering at enemy targets. It is the total effect of these bombing operations which decides the outcome of the conflict in favor of that Air Force which succeeds in dumping the largest quantity of bombs in the shortest time.

In presenting these ideas of the general character of aerial warfare, I have attempted only to show that if aerial warfare in its broad outline looks like a simple matter, it nevertheless presents staggering problems, the solution of which is very complex. But even in this brief résumé we can catch a glimpse of the heights of atrocity to which aerial warfare may reach.

When we stop to think of the magnitude and power of aerial offensives, and realize that no really effective method of parrying them exists; and since it would be futile to divert aerial forces to defense, the phrase "to submit to whatever damage the enemy may inflict" becomes a phrase expressing actual circumstances of tragedy attending aerial warfare.

Tragic, too, to think that the decision in this kind of war must depend upon smashing the material and moral resources of a people caught up in a frightful cataclysm which haunts them everywhere without cease until the final collapse of all social organization.[1] Mercifully, the decision will be quick in this kind of war, since the decisive blows will be directed at civilians, that element of the countries at war least able to sustain them. These future wars may yet prove to be more humane than wars in the past in spite of all, because they may in the long run shed less blood. But there is no doubt that nations who find themselves unprepared to sustain them will be lost.

---

[1] Exactly what seems to have happened when the Germans bombed and broke the will to resist of Poland, Holland, Belgium, France, Greece, and Jugoslavia (and Norway to a lesser extent) in the aerial Blitzkrieg of 1940-41.—Tr.

PART II

(ADDED IN 1926)

1

When the first edition of *The Command of The Air* was published, I thought it wiser not to express all my thoughts on the problems of aeronautics because I did not want to upset too violently the prevailing ideas on the subject. My purpose then was simply to break ground for the acceptance and execution of a minimum program which would have constituted a point of departure for further progress.

In 1921 we had only an auxiliary air force—it could hardly be called even that—that is to say, some aerial means intended to facilitate and integrate land and sea operations. Notwithstanding the services rendered by the air arm during the war, it was really considered superfluous, especially in military circles. At that time if few paid attention to the needs of the army and navy, no one gave any attention to the needs of the air force. This being the case, it was a question at that time of bringing to notice the concept of the "command of the air," of giving a preliminary notion of its importance, of pleading for consideration of means better adapted to conquering the command of the air, of gaining acceptance or the idea of an air force independent of the army and navy. All this had to be done shortly after a major war during which the air force operated only as an auxiliary, and against the cherished convictions of all those—they were and are legion—who make ready for the future by looking at the past.

This was dangerous territory; and, notwithstanding the semi-official status given to *The Command of The Air* by its publication under the auspices of the Ministry of War, none of the high army and navy authorities deigned to concern themselves with the question, about which complete silence was preserved until the march on Rome. Then came a revolution which really provoked thought. Apparently the ideas expressed in Part I must have seemed doubtful, if not altogether insane, unless the indifference sprang from general congenital mental laziness. But had I not sacrificed much in permitting the retention of the auxiliary air force in order to propitiate the goddess of incomprehension? I had. In Part I I tried to make clear the essential importance of an independent aviation; but I made the admission that for the time being the auxiliary air force should be retained, though I was, and still am, convinced that one is incompatible with the other. This was a weakness on my part, I admit. But the things one must go through to make common sense prevail! For the rest, anyone who read Part I with attention must have understood perfectly that I considered auxiliary aviation *worthless, superfluous, harmful.*

In the section on "Independent Air Force and Auxiliary Aviation," after stating the conclusion: "An adequate national defense cannot be assured except by an aerial force capable, in case of war, of conquering the command of the air," I added: "We can see clearly how easy a time a well-organized enemy bent on conquering the command of the air would have, and how helpless these auxiliary aerial means employed by the army and navy would be, confronted by an enemy Independent Air Force bent on conquest." This means that an auxiliary air force is worth nothing if it does not succeed in conquering the command of the air. Now, in wartime an auxiliary air force is worthless; not only that, but harmful because its means could have been usefully employed in another way. In short, as I said in Chapter I, "Any effort, any action, any resources diverted from this essential aim (the command of the air) makes conquering the command of the air that much less probable; and it makes defeat in case of war that much more probable." Any diversion from this essential aim is an error.

I considered it an "error" to keep an auxiliary air force which was incapable of conquering the command of the air, but I admitted its right to existence so as not to upset too violently those whose minds found it too great a leap to abolish the auxiliary air force, the only air force allowed then, and create an independent aviation, an innovation which did not grow out of the war.

Even though I conceded it, I did not want to discuss it then, and in the section on "Auxiliary Aviation" I wrote: ". . . the responsibility for the organization of the army and navy auxiliary aviation rests with the army and navy. I shall not enter into a discussion of its merits here." Earlier in the same section I said that auxiliary aviation must be: "(1) included in the budgets of the army and navy respectively; and (2) placed absolutely under the direct command of the army or the navy, beginning with their organization and ending with their employment."

As long as I conceded the auxiliary aviation, that stand was perfectly logical; but in making the concession I had in mind a further aim. I thought that when a really worth-while auxiliary aviation had been organized and the army and navy compelled to pay for it out of their own budgets, and their authorities had been obliged seriously to study the organization and employment of it, they would automatically come to the conclusion that such auxiliary aviation was useless—and therefore not only superfluous, but contrary to the public interest.

These are the essential reasons why I did not then, as I do now, state that the only aerial organization whose existence is fully justified is the Independent Air Force.

2

By the term Independent Air Force—it seems to me I have made it clear since 1921—I do not mean any air force capable of carrying out any military action whatever, but *an air force fit to strive for conquest of the command of the air.* By the expression "command of the air" I do not mean supremacy in the air nor a preponderance of aerial means, but *that state of affairs in which we find ourselves able to fly in the face of an enemy who is unable to do likewise.* Given these definitions, the following affirmation is axiomatic: *The command of the air provides whoever possesses it with the advantages of protecting all his own land and sea territory from enemy aerial offensives and at the same time of subjecting the enemy's territory to his own offensives.*

In view of the carrying capacity and range of modern airplanes and the efficacy of present destructive materials, these advantages are such that a country *in possession of adequate air forces* can crush the material and moral resistance of the enemy; that is to say, that country can win *regardless of any other circumstances whatsoever.* This cannot be denied; for the material and moral resistance of the enemy is destroyed by means of the offensive, and offensives can be carried out by means of airplanes. The question will be one of delimiting *the quantity and quality* of the air offensive necessary to destroy the moral and material resistance of the enemy, but this need not concern us for the moment. With the proviso, "if adequate air forces are possessed," I intend merely to state that the air force must accord with the objective; that is, it must have the power to bring against the enemy that quantity and quality of offensives which will suffice to crush the enemy's material and moral resistance. Now, if the command of the air, controlled with an adequate air force, assures victory regardless of any other circumstances whatsoever, it logically follows as an immediate consequence that the air force adapted for the struggle for command of the air—*namely, an Independent Air Force—is the means suitable to assure victory regardless of other circumstances when it is capable of winning the command of the air with adequate forces.*

To deny this axiomatic truth, considering that it cannot be denied that airplanes fly and explosives destroy, it is to deny the possibility of the struggle for command of the air, or to deny the possibility of commanding the air in the sense in which I use the expression.

In order to conquer the command of the air—that is, to prevent the enemy from flying while keeping the power to fly oneself—the enemy must be deprived of the use of all his planes. For the present we need not investigate how this end may be achieved. It is enough to show the actual possibility of achieving it. This possibility does exist, because the enemy's planes can be destroyed, either in the air with airplanes or on the ground with air attacks directed against the places of maintenance, concentration, and production. These actions aimed at the destruction of the enemy's planes will, on the other hand, provoke retaliatory counteraction from the enemy to prevent the launching of such actions. Action and counteraction; hence, battle.

When I say that the Independent Air Force must be an air force capable of fighting for the command of the air, I mean that it must be *so fashioned* as to be able to crush the enemy's counteraction and destroy his airplanes. To prevent the enemy from flying does not, of course, mean to prevent even his flies from flying. In the absolute sense, it will certainly be hardly possible to destroy *all* the enemy's means of flying. The command of the air will be gained when the enemy's planes are reduced to a negligible number incapable of developing any aerial action of real importance in the war as a whole. A fleet can be said to have conquered the command of the sea even if the enemy still has a few boats; an Independent Air Force can be said to have conquered the command of the air even if the enemy still has a few flying machines. To say that having command of the air means to fly in the face of an enemy who has been prevented from doing likewise means *to have the ability to fly against an enemy so as to injure him, while he has been deprived of the power to do likewise.*

I must beg indulgence for dwelling so long on my definition of "the command of the air." I have done this because in general the expression is used ambiguously. "Command" of the air is often confused with "preponderance" or "supremacy" in the air. But these are two very different things. Whoever possesses preponderance or supremacy in the air will be able to conquer the command of the air more easily; but until he has conquered it he does not possess it and he cannot make use of it.

During the last phase of the war it was often said that we possessed the command of the air, when all we had was aerial preponderance and we even neglected to use this preponderance to conquer the command of the air—so much so that notwithstanding our preponderance in the air we did not have command of the air, and the enemy continued to make attacks up to the day of the Armistice. Some people, especially of late, have discovered the *relative command of the air,* namely, command of the air restricted to a particular zone of the sky, again, naturally, confusing preponderance with command. Considering the speed and range of action of the air arm, characteristics which prevent the cutting up of the sky into small slices, such a conception is faulty indeed. To be stronger in the air does not mean to command it, because to command means to be master of and excludes any suggestion of the comparative; and if we are content to be stronger, we are content with a potential condition which will not prevent a weaker opponent from injuring us.

Thus the Independent Air Force is shown to be the *best way to assure victory, regardless of any other circumstances whatever, when it has been organized in a way suitable to winning the struggle for the command of the air and to exploiting the command with adequate forces.*

To become the essential factor in victory, the Independent Air Force must therefore meet two conditions:

1. It must be capable of winning the struggle for the command of the air.

2. It must be capable of exploiting the command of the air, once it has been conquered, with forces capable of crushing the material and moral resistance of the enemy.

The first of these conditions is essential, the second is integral. An Air Force which meets the first condition only—that is, one which is capable of winning the struggle for the command of the air but is not able to exploit it with forces sufficient to crush the resistance of the enemy, will be in a position to: (1) prevent its own territory from being subjected to aerial offensives of the enemy; and (2) subject all the enemy's land and sea territory to aerial offensives—without, however, having enough offensive power to crush the material and moral resistance of the enemy. In other words, an Independent Air Force which meets only the first condition cannot decide the issue of the war, which will then depend upon other circumstances besides the aerial warfare. But an Independent Air Force which meets both conditions, essential and integral, decides the issue of the war without regard to any other circumstances whatever.

When an Independent Air Force meets only the first condition, the issue of the war will be decided by the struggle on land and sea. In what situation will this struggle put the one who conquers the command of the air? Plainly, a very advantageous situation if the Air Force retains the greater power after having conquered the command of the air, because (1) it will have blinded the army and navy of the enemy, while providing far-seeing eyes for its own army and navy; and (2) it will have retained the possibility of carrying out air offensives against the enemy—offensives which, if not completely successful in crushing his material and moral resistance, will seriously damage and weaken that resistance. Thus, an Independent Air Force which meets only the first condition will nonetheless be able to develop effective action for victory.

3

Auxiliary aviation is defined as that mass of air power which facilitates or integrates land and sea actions, or a mass of air power delegated to render designated services to the army or navy and strictly confined to that purpose; therefore not designed for the conquest of the command of the air. Consequently, *auxiliary aviation can in no way influence the issue of the struggle for command.* On the other hand, since to gain the command means to put the enemy in a position where he is no longer able to fly, the one defeated *will have been deprived even of the use of auxiliary aviation.* In other words, *the possibility of using auxiliary aviation is dependent upon the issue of the struggle for command of the air, an issue on which auxiliary aviation can have no influence at all.*

Consequently, *aerial means set aside for auxiliary aviation are means diverted from their essential purpose, and worthless if that purpose is not pursued.* Since diverting force from its essential purpose can bring about failure of that purpose, diversion of aerial means to auxiliary aviation can bring about defeat in the struggle to conquer the command of the air; consequently, auxiliary aviation is made useless.

Considering, then, that, if it seems worth while, there will be nothing to prevent detaching some of the planes from the Independent Air Force to use as auxiliaries after the command of the air has been conquered, we must logically conclude that auxiliary aviation is worthless, superfluous, harmful. *Worthless* because incapable of taking action if it does not have command of the air. *Superfluous* because a part of the Independent Air Force can be used as an auxiliary if the command of the air has been conquered. *Harmful* because it diverts power from its essential purpose, thus making it more difficult to achieve that purpose.

To make this assertion while auxiliary aviation is a dominant idea may seem bold; but it was even bolder to say in 1909:

. . . not less important than the command of the sea will be the command of the air. . . . Civilized nations will arm and prepare for the latest war; and, as has been the case for the army and navy, and still is, a headlong race checked only by economic limitations will begin in the field of air power. . . . Automatically, inevitably, air forces will make a dizzy ascent. . . . The conquest of the air will be bitterly contested. . . . Aeronautics will inevitably give rise to aerial warfare in its widest possible significance. . . . Henceforth we must accustom ourselves to the idea of aerial warfare. . . . From now on aerial means must be governed by a concept similar to that governing war means on land and sea, with aerial warfare in view. . . . Warplanes must essentially be capable of fighting in the air against other aerial weapons, and not merely of carrying out such special missions as observation, liaison duty, and so forth. . . . Besides the solution of the technical problem of aerial means, aerial warfare also involves the solution of a great many problems of preparation, organization, employment, et cetera, of aerial forces; and that calls for the creation, *ex novo,* of a third branch of the art of war, which branch may be accurately defined as the art of aerial warfare. . . . The army and navy must look upon airplanes not as auxiliaries to be put to use in certain circumstances only, but rather as a third brother, younger but no less important, in the great warrior family. . . . We shall have assisted and contributed toward the beginning of aerial warfare . . . and it would indeed be strange if we had never been aware of it!

Yet these bold assertions, offspring of iron-clad logic, an iron-clad logic based on facts, have now become mere common sense, even though their true inwardness has not yet been understood. So I may be permitted to hope that the things I say today may some day become common sense, since they rest on the same foundations.

Let us check this reasoning by the following: A and B are two nations which have the same amount of resources and the same standards of technical proficiency in their respective air forces. But, while Nation A uses all its resources to build an Independent Air Force capable of striving for conquest of the command of the air, Nation B divides its resources into two parts, one to create an Independent Air Force, the other to create an auxiliary aviation. Plainly, the Air Force of Nation A will be stronger than that of Nation B. Therefore, in case of war, all other things being equal, Nation A will win the command of the air, and Nation B will be unable to use its auxiliary aviation. In other words, Nation B will be defeated in aerial warfare simply because she diverted part of her resources from an Independent Air Force to establish auxiliary aviation, which became the cause of her defeat and from then on was worthless. However we look at it, the conclusion is the same: *auxiliary aviation is worthless, superfluous, harmful.*

In the World War airplanes were employed exclusively as auxiliaries, it is true. But what does this show? Simply that the value of the command of the air was not appreciated, hence was not sought, and no means designed to conquer it were prepared. The war broke out when aviation was still in its infancy. Few believed in it, and they were not in power. Indeed, they were regarded as enthusiasts, fanatics. The military authorities of the nations engaged in the war did not believe in aviation. Worse, the greater part of them knew nothing about it. Only in Germany was there some conception of aerial warfare; but fortunately Germany was led down the blind alley of the Zeppelin and put her faith in dirigibles instead of airplanes.

Aviation entered the war more from tolerance than from conviction, more in deference to public opinion—which was more clear-sighted than the military-technical authorities—than in the belief that it might be valuable. It was left to itself and treated as a secondary service—in Italy it was placed for a short time under the General Intendency![1] No one took any notice of it until bombs rained down on General Headquarters.

What use could this newest arm be put to under such conditions? Plainly, to an empirical use, for partial and particular objectives. In other words, it served as an auxiliary.

The credit for everything accomplished by aviation in the war belongs to the personnel, who displayed valor and initiative and accomplished things in spite of, sometimes in contradiction to, the actions of the army authorities. But the aviation personnel could not embrace the whole field of war in its entirety; it had to limit its vision to the narrow fields open to it. When someone like me—in 1915 I proposed the institution of a national Independent Air Force and in 1917, an Allied Independent Air Force—tried to bring to the attention of the high military authorities the importance of aerial means as a separate arm to be used in pursuing the general objectives of the war, the military authorities did not deign to take the matter under consideration.

Under such conditions a consistent, authentic aerial warfare could not, and did not, develop. Instead there could, and did, develop local aerial actions, chaotic and unorganized because directed by instinct rather than by reason.

Because it is easy to see well and to drop things from a high altitude, reconnaissance and bombardment are accepted; because defense against the damage inflicted by them is necessary, pursuit is accepted. Upon this simple fact rests all the action of aviation in warfare; it goes no further. Opposing air forces reconnoiter, bombard, and pursue throughout the war. The one

---

[1] A service analogous to our Quartermaster Corps.—Tr.

which gains preponderance in the air reconnoiters, bombards, and pursues more than the inferior one; and aviation, securely chained to the surface forces, does not leave them, but limits its action to the direct service of those forces in their own fields. It is not understood that this tie hampers the air arm, whose field of action is essentially different from the field of the surface arm; and the idea has not yet been born which can make aviation do all it can do once that chain is broken. Despite all this, circumstances forced the recognition of the great value of the air arm. What could this newest arm not have accomplished in the hands of someone who really understood it!

In view of this situation, what can the experience of the last war teach us? Nothing; in fact, less than nothing; for aviation was used with poor judgment, and it is easy to see that good sound judgment cannot grow out of the use of an arm which is not understood and is abandoned to its own devices. Just because in the last war aviation was used empirically, with no guiding principle, must we do likewise in a future war? In my judgment, to say this would be even bolder than not to say that auxiliary aviation is worthless, superfluous, harmful.

4

I have said that an Independent Air Force must meet two conditions: (1) the essential condition—namely, *to possess strength enough to conquer the command of the air;* (2) the integral condition—namely, *to keep up that strength after command of the air has been won and exploit it in such a way as to crush the material and moral resistance of the enemy.*

Also I have shown that if the command of the air means, as I define it, being in a position to fly in the face of an enemy who has been prevented from doing likewise, then (1) *an Independent Air Force which succeeds in conquering the command of the air, but does not keep up its strength and use it to crush the resistance of the enemy, will nevertheless be able to carry out actions very effective in the achievement of victory;* and (2) *an Independent Air Force which conquers the command of the air and keeps up enough strength to crush the resistance of the enemy will be able to achieve victory regardless of what happens on the surface.*

These two propositions are axiomatic. They cannot be refuted without altering the meaning of the expressions given here.

Now, to conquer the command of the air—that is, to put the enemy in a position where he is unable to fly, while preserving for oneself the ability to do so—it is necessary to deprive the enemy of all his means of flying; and this can only be done by destroying his means and still keeping at least a part of one's own means intact.

To exploit the command of the air in a manner calculated to crush the material and moral resistance of the enemy, it is necessary to have at one's disposal after command of the air has been won a sufficient number of aerial means to carry out offensives against the enemy strong enough to crush him.

These two propositions also are axiomatic and cannot be equivocated.

The enemy's flying forces can be found in the air or on the surface, in centers of maintenance, concentration, production, and so on; in either case they can only be destroyed by aerial offensives; and neither land nor sea forces can co-operate or collaborate in any way in such destruction. Air attacks which can be launched over the enemy's land and sea territory after command of the air has been won, obviously can be carried out only by air forces; and neither army nor navy can co-operate in any way in this purpose. Therefore, when considering the matter of the struggle for the command of the air and the launching of air offensives, one sees that the air forces assigned to accomplishing this—namely, the Independent Air Force—should not and cannot depend in any way upon the army and navy.

This is not in any sense to say that the Independent Air Force should not co-ordinate its actions with the actions of the army and navy in order to attain a common final objective. It is merely to say that such co-ordination should be planned by the authority which directs the use of all the armed forces of the nation. Neither does it mean that the Independent Air Force should never in any instance co-operate directly with the army and navy to give them assistance in special operations, just as the army and navy co-operate with each other. Plainly, there will be instances when the authority in charge of all the armed forces of the nation will consider it necessary—once the command of the air has been won—to put the Independent Air Force, or a designated part of it, temporarily in the service of a land or sea commander, thus depriving it of its independence.

To succeed in destroying enemy aerial means, one must be able to overcome the obstacles the enemy will put in his way to prevent that destruction. In this struggle we have authentic aerial warfare carried to its logical conclusion. In fact, whoever conquers the command of the air will find himself opposing an enemy who is unable to fly; and there can be no aerial warfare against an enemy deprived of his aerial means. All the actions an Independent Air Force can perform after conquering the command of the air must necessarily be directed against the surface. These actions will play a large, perhaps a decisive, part in deciding the issue of the war, but they can never be accurately classified as actions of aerial warfare. Therefore, the struggle for and conquest of the command of the air constitute the unique object of aerial warfare which the Independent Air Force should set up for itself.

To deprive the enemy of his means of flying, they must be destroyed wherever they are found, in the air or on the surface. Therefore, if an Independent Air Force is to be equal to the task of conquering the command of the air, it must be capable of carrying out destructive actions either in the air or on the surface. One air force cannot destroy another in the air except by aerial combat—that is, by subjecting the enemy to a more effective fire power than he can employ. In other words, destructive action in the air can be carried out only by means adapted to aerial combat, which for simplicity I have called "combat means." To destroy an air force on the surface, that surface must be attacked with destructive power, which, generally speaking, can be effected only by bombardment. It follows that the enemy's forces found on the surface can be destroyed only by means of *bombardments. Thus the Independent Air Force must possess both combat planes and bombers.* Thus, by a different route, I reach the same conclusions as I expressed in Part 1.

Can either of these two kinds of forces be spared in an Independent Air Force? My answer is, absolutely not, for these reasons:

1. An Independent Air Force made up of combat planes alone—that is, forces capable only of carrying out destructive actions against enemy aircraft in the air—might be put in the position of failing in its action whenever the enemy avoided an encounter—something he can do simply by descending to the surface, scarcely observed by the opposing Air Force. An Independent Air Force made up of combat planes alone, even if it had superiority in these means, would end by exhausting itself in futile actions directed at empty space. Whenever it was opposed to an Air Force inferior in combat planes but provided with bombers, it would have great difficulty in achieving even the negative objective of safeguarding its own territory from enemy air attacks, because the enemy, taking advantage of the rapidity with which air attacks can be carried out, might evade combat and try a surprise attack. Thus, an Independent Air Force made up of combat planes alone is not a true Independent Air Force, because it is unfit to strive for command of the air, and it is also unfit for the simple protection of its own territory from enemy attacks.

2. An Independent Air Force provided only with bombers could not operate except by evading air encounters and making surprise attacks, and it could offer no resistance to the will of the enemy.

The Independent Air Force in possession of both combat planes and bombers could travel with impunity to the enemy's sky and there launch offensives against the ground.

Lack of combat planes is therefore the lesser of the two evils; even though an air force provided only with bombers is not an Independent Air Force at all, merely the beginnings of one.

Consequently, there must be both combat planes and bombers in an Independent Air Force. In what proportion? For an Independent Air Force to maneuver freely and to be in a position to impose its will on the enemy, it must be able to travel to the designated points in the enemy's sky *in spite of the enemy's opposition.* That is, it should put itself in a position to overcome the enemy's opposition, an opposition manifested in the action of the adversary's combat means. To be in a position to win, all other things being equal, one must be stronger in the field of battle. Therefore, combat means should tend to be stronger than those of the enemy. As for bombers, it is obviously desirable to have the greatest possible number, because, whatever the circumstances, it is always opportune to launch major offensives. Therefore, there can be no set proportion of combat planes and bombers since both depend upon diverse independent circumstances.

For these reasons it can be said of the composition of an Independent Air Force only that (1) combat forces should aim to be stronger than like forces of the enemy; and (2) bombing means should strive to reach a maximum of power to produce the greatest effects, always remembering that an Independent Air Force cannot dispense with either type of plane and must at all costs prevent being left without one or the other.

In relation to what has been said, let us suppose that we have an Independent Air Force which disposes (1) a combat power superior to the enemy's and (2) a power of bombardment of limited capacity for the offensive. With such an Air Force we can fly anywhere in the enemy's sky, over any objective of our choice, traveling swiftly by the route most favorable for us, because (1) the enemy's Independent Air Force will not try to oppose us, so we have a free path, or (2) the enemy will try to offer resistance but will fail to contact us, so we have a free path, or (3) the enemy will offer resistance with an inferior combat force, thus putting us in a position to overcome it, so we have a free path.

Consequently, in the first and second cases we will be in a position to operate against the surface with impunity, inflicting damage upon the enemy in proportion to our bombing power. In the third case we will make the enemy suffer an aerial defeat, after which we will be in a position to inflict damage upon the surface in proportion to our bombing power.

If we have chosen as our objective the enemy's means of flying—centers of maintenance, concentration, production, and so forth—in any of the three cases we will have inflicted damage which will result in a diminution of his air potentiality. Therefore, *every time our Independent Air Force attacks the enemy's surface objectives directly, whatever else it may do, it will diminish his air potentiality.* The reduction of the enemy's air potentiality to zero, or conquering the command of the air, will be effected as rapidly as our Air Force can operate intensively, can possess the greater means of surface destruction, and can pick its objectives with care.

What action could the enemy's Independent Air Force bring against this action of ours? Will he try to oppose it directly? Obviously not, because he will either not succeed in contacting us and thus operate in empty space or succeed in contacting us and be defeated. Will he try to avoid combat and strike in turn against our territory? Plainly, that is what he must do, for only when he succeeds in avoiding combat can he strike against us in a way which can force a diminution of our air potentiality.

The battle for the command of the air between two Independent Air Forces of different combat powers will show these features:

1. The Air Force having the greater combat power, not being fettered by enemy action, hence in a position to impose its will,

will operate with full freedom of maneuver, choosing those objectives it considers most useful to its purpose.

2. The Air Force weaker in combat power will try to avoid combat and destroy those objectives it considers most useful to its purpose.

That is, the actions of the two Air Forces will be similar, but the struggle will be characterized by the preoccupation of the weaker Air Force with maintaining itself in action. Let us say that during such a struggle the weaker Air Force does succeed in keeping in action—that is, in avoiding battle. In this case every action of either Air Force will diminish the enemy's air potentiality, and that Air Force which first inflicts cumulative damage sufficient to wipe out the other's air potentiality will conquer the command of the air. Therefore, if the stronger Air Force must operate as intensively as possible, must employ the greatest possible destructive power against the surface, and must choose the objectives which will have the greatest effect in diminishing the enemy's air potentiality, all the more reason why the weaker should do likewise.

From this we can draw these conclusions of practical interest:

1. Immediately upon the opening of hostilities, aerial warfare should be conducted with the greatest possible intensity. The Independent Air Force should always be ready for action, and once the action is begun, it should be ready to carry on without let-up until the command of the air is conquered. Considering the magnitude of the offensives which the Independent Air Force can develop and the intensity with which they will be carried out, it is not possible to hope that new planes not yet ready at the opening of hostilities can carry any weight in aerial warfare—that is, in the conquest of the command of the air. In other words, the war will be decided by the air means ready to go into action at the opening of hostilities. Those prepared later will at best be used to exploit the command of the air after it has been conquered.

2. If the choice of objectives is of great importance for one side, the way those objectives are disposed in one's territory and how they present themselves to the enemy is of equal importance. That is to say, the location of a nation's potentiality should be so disposed as to make it difficult for the enemy to destroy them. It can readily be seen that if the planes, the life-blood of the Independent Air Force, are concentrated in a few centers along the frontier, the enemy will have an easy time of destroying them.

3. The issue of aerial warfare will of course depend upon the forces opposing each other, but in particular it will depend upon how the forces are employed—that is, upon the genius of the commanders, their prompt decisions and swift action, their exact knowledge of the air resources of the enemy.

In preceding paragraphs we concluded definitely that aerial warfare must be between two Independent Air Forces solely concerned with inflicting the greatest possible damage upon the enemy without giving heed to damage the enemy may inflict in turn. This conception of warfare, which has been explained in Part I, consists *in resigning oneself to submit to enemy attacks in order to use all possible means for launching the greatest offensives against the enemy.* It is difficult for this idea to penetrate the minds of people, because it departs from the conception of general warfare prevalent in the past. We are used to seeing the offensive and the defensive aspect in every battle, and we cannot grasp the idea of a battle which is all offensive, with no defensive aspect. Yet aerial warfare must be exactly this and nothing else, because the characteristics of the air arm are eminently offensive and completely unsuited for the defensive. The fact is this: with the air arm it is easy to strike but not to parry.

Let us take now the most favorable case, that of a nation whose Independent Air Force is much stronger in combat planes than the enemy's. Can this Air Force defend the nation from the enemy's Air Force? Two methods of defense offer themselves. One is to go in search of the enemy; the other is to wait and strike at him when he appears. Can an Independent Air Force go in search of the enemy's? Of course it can; but it may not find it, or if it does, may not be able to give battle and so will find no opportunity to attack it, especially if it is deliberately avoiding battle. Now, whenever an Air Force goes in search of an enemy force and finds no opportunity to attack it, that Air Force is thrusting at empty space, is exhausting itself to no end, and inflicts no damage on the enemy; but the enemy's Air Force, which has succeeded in evading the attack, can inflict indirect damage. So this first method of defense is illusory; it is nothing but sport for the enemy.

It can be said that nothing prevents the Air Force which sets out in search of the enemy's from inflicting some damage with its bombers. That is true. But in this case the Air Force does not have free choice of objectives, for these are secondary to its main purpose and contingent upon being located in the particular spot happened upon in the search for the enemy Air Force.

Can an Air Force lie in wait for the enemy and strike at him as he comes along? Certainly it can. But what are the chances of its gaining its objective? If the enemy Air Force comes in mass, as it must to have any chance of winning, the first Air Force must necessarily first concentrate in mass. Can any Independent Air Force, particularly if it thinks it is the stronger, passively await the enemy's convenience, submit to his initiative, with no assurance of ever contacting him and with the probability of being forced to endure his attack without being able to retaliate? Certainly not. So this second method of defense is illusory, is nothing but sport for the enemy.

Hence we must conclude that there is only one attitude to adopt in aerial warfare—namely, an intense and violent offensive, even at the risk of enduring the same thing from the enemy. The one effective method of defending one's own territory from an offensive by air is to destroy the enemy's air power with the greatest possible speed.

Any means of defense against an enemy aerial action will fail, and therefore benefits the enemy. This statement applies generally as well as to the specific Air Force action already examined. The intention is to oppose aerial offensives with aerial defenses made up of groups of airplanes, and with antiaircraft defenses employing surface arms. To be effective, the aerial defense of a center must crush the enemy's action, since its purpose is to hinder an offensive against that center. That means the aerial defense of a center must confront the enemy with a combat force at least equal to his own. Now, if the enemy operates by the sound rules of warfare, he will operate in mass. To be effective, the aerial defense of a center must have at its disposal a number of combat planes equal to the number of the enemy's combat planes in mass. Otherwise the aerial defense will be overcome and the center destroyed.

But since the air arm has a long range of action, potentially an Independent Air Force can threaten other centers. And since air offensives are carried out very rapidly, in order successfully to defend all centers potentially threatened, it would be necessary to station air forces in various parts of the territory attacked, and each of these forces would have to be equal in combat power to the mass combat power of the enemy. Besides that, it would be necessary to set up a complicated network of communications and keep all the air forces in constant readiness for action.

I repeat, the air arm is so essentially offensive in character that to use it defensively dooms it to the absurdity of being stronger than the attacker and yet being obliged to keep this preponderant air force completely inactive, because unable to pursue any positive objective, and thus at the mercy of the enemy's initiative.

Even admitting that defensive air forces could always arrive in time to be of some use would it be wise to use air forces in this manner? Plainly not, because this would mean an extremely dangerous dispersion of forces. Undoubtedly, one should instead use all possible resources to strengthen to the utmost one's own

Independent Air Force, because the stronger the Air Force, the more easily and rapidly it will be in a position to conquer the command of the air, the only effective way of protecting one's own territory from enemy air offensives.

To be effective, an antiaircraft defense of a center must be able to prevent the execution of an air offensive against the center. The range of action of the antiaircraft arm is very limited, hence there would have to be an adequate supply of antiaircraft guns for the protection of each center. Hence, to be of any use, antiaircraft defense would require an enormous quantity of equipment spread over the entire surface.

On the other hand, antiaircraft guns can easily be neutralized by air action, by attacks at low altitudes or wrapping in clouds of smoke, and so forth, so that effective retort could not be made. Certainly if the resources used for antiaircraft defense were employed to strengthen the Independent Air Force to the same extent, the rewards would be much greater, for the only valid method of defending one's territory is by conquering the command of the air. Therefore, there should be no air defense and no antiaircraft defense. The surface is defended from the air just as coasts are defended from the sea—by gaining command. No one would think of scattering ships and cannon along the coast in order to defend it from bombardment. The coast cities are left open and their defense entrusted indirectly to the fleet.

Therefore, all possible resources must be used to strengthen the Independent Air Force so that it can operate and defend itself in the air solely by means of intensive and violent offensives. I urge my readers to think about this statement, which is fundamental and admits no exceptions, implications, or reservations, because it must be made the basis for the formation and use of our aerial power.

To reach this conclusion it has been sufficient to consider aerial warfare in its general characteristics, or in the essential characteristics of the airplane itself—wide radius of action, great speed, ability to fight in the air, power to carry out an offensive against the surface—without going into technical details. Therefore, the conclusion itself is general in nature and does not depend upon technical details which can alter the essential characteristics of the planes at one's disposal, the future perfecting of which cannot but add weight to the conclusion drawn here. Proof of this conclusion can easily be obtained—simply contrast any other conception of air power with an Independent Air Force conceived and operating according to my ideas.

Let us imagine an encounter between such an Independent Air Force and an air force organized according to prevalent ideas, the resources for constructing them being equal in both cases.

It is clear that the Independent Air Force, having utilized all the resources at its disposal for building combat and bombing planes, will be able to employ a combat force superior to that of the other air force, because the latter will have subdivided its resources to provide a variety of planes designed for special uses, generally excluding combat. For the same reason the Independent Air Force will be superior in bombers.

In these circumstances the Independent Air Force will immediately take the initiative and pursue its aim intensely and without interruption, by means of a succession of offensives against the surface executed with the mass of its forces, paying no heed to contacting the enemy and so neither searching for nor evading him. Against this action the other air force could not retaliate directly except by confronting the Independent Air Force with its pursuit planes which, if they come to grips, will be beaten; and indirectly by using its bombers which, inferior to those of the Independent Air Force in offensive power, will conduct their operations in a way calculated to avoid combat. Not being adapted for combat and bombing operations, all this mass of auxiliaries cannot effectively influence the issue of the struggle for command of the air. They will have to remain almost entirely inactive, seeking to avoid destruction, especially on the surface.

Therefore, other things being equal, command of the air will certainly be conquered by the Independent Air Force. Nothing could oppose an Independent Air Force constituted according to my ideas except just such another Independent Air Force. Any other form of air force, any other standard of action, will result in an improper use of the air arm. I challenge anyone to prove the contrary.

5

All the conclusions I have stated have been made simply to establish that (1) combat forces must be suited to combat in the air and (2) bombers must be suited for offensives against the surface. Now we can go on to more concrete ideas of what should be the characteristics for combat or bombardment which the aerial means of an Independent Air Force must possess.

MEANS OF COMBAT

An aerial battle is fought by fire action between warplanes. The fitness of a plane for aerial battle is determined by its power of attack and defense. In aerial battle a warplane may be attacked by enemy fire from any direction. It must therefore be capable of returning this fire; and, all things being equal, the advantage lies with the plane which is more heavily armed and has greater fire power than its adversary. To best withstand enemy fire, the greatest measure of self-protection is needed. Therefore, other things being equal, the advantage lies with the plane which is more heavily armored.

Obviously, in an air battle it is an advantage to have greater speed and maneuverability than the adversary, which permits one to engage or refuse battle at one's discretion; or, once engaged, to cut the battle short. Again, other things being equal, the advantage lies with the faster and more maneuverable plane.

In fine, other things being equal, the plane with the greater radius of action will have the advantage because it can carry the action deeper into the enemy's territory.

Therefore, a warplane should possess to the maximum degree compatible with technical exigencies, the following four characteristics: *armament, armor protection, speed*, and *radius of action*.

These characteristics are reducible to terms of physical weight, the sum total being determined by the aerodynamic structure of the plane, subdivided to harmonize with these four characteristics. The problem here is analogous to the problem presented by warships. Nor could it be otherwise, considering the similarity of purpose. There are, however, other considerations to be taken into account in this case.

Armament: The combat planes of an Independent Air Force are not designed to fight alone, but in formation. They must therefore be grouped in units of combat capable of fighting together; and in this lies the basis of their tactics. Hence the maximum intensity of fire is wanted, not so much in the single plane, but essentially in the combat unit as a whole, the formation of which may be modified according to the direction of the attack by the enemy or the direction of the intended attack against the enemy. Hence the armament problem concerns both the individual plane and the formation of the unit, whether emphasis on the plane or emphasis on the formation as a whole is the deciding factor.

In fire power, likewise, it is not the individual plane that matters so much, but the unit of combat, a unit which must be considered indivisible. Here, too, the emphasis must lie on the formation, rather than on the individual plane, which must integrate in the best possible way the fire power of the individual planes. But in any case we can see that, though it is desirable for each plane to have a potential fire power above the bare minimum, we must not exaggerate the importance of such fire power, because it would seem that, as between two combat units of equal fire power, the unit which gets its power by the possession of more planes is in a better condition to effect a more enveloping action. Only experience can decide this for practical purposes, however.

Armor Protection: The purpose of armor protection is to conserve the power of the weapon by reducing its vulnerability. Obviously, as between two planes with equal armament, the one with the best armor protection has twice the offensive capacity of the other, because it can keep up its offensive power twice as long in the same action, or double its power for the same period of action. This characteristic of protection has not only a material but a moral value, and therefore it is erroneous to think that the weight used for armor protection is always a waste of power and material, even though it may exist at the expense of armament itself. The problem of armor protection has to do with the individual plane, not with the formation as a whole. Nevertheless, it is obvious that the total physical weight of armor protection grows relatively less as the number of planes is reduced, even though the formation as a whole keeps its total offensive capacity unaltered.

Speed: Though superior speed is indisputably an advantage in battle, the fact remains, as I have fully demonstrated, that an Independent Air Force should neither seek an encounter nor force a battle. Superior speed has therefore only a relative importance for a weaker Independent Air Force in avoiding an aerial battle. So it is not advisable to exalt speed at the expense of the other three characteristics.

Radius of Action: Possible offensive actions against enemy territory more or less depend upon the radius of action of the planes. Therefore, there is a radius of action, depending upon the operational distance necessary to reach enemy objectives, below which an Independent Air Force loses its value. Naturally, the radius of action should be the maximum whenever possible.

MEANS OF BOMBARDMENT

The function of bombing planes is integral with the action of combat planes, which are entrusted with clearing the air of enemy obstacles. Therefore, their characteristics should meet the following conditions:

Radius of Action: Equal to that of combat planes.

Speed: Equal to that of combat planes.

Armor Protection: If armor protection is considered necessary for a combat plane, there is no reason why it should not be equally necessary for bombers. Therefore, armor protection equal to that of combat planes.

Armament: Essentially the armament of a bomber should consist of bombs with which to attack the surface. But for the sake of the crew's morale, no warplane, which may be attacked in the air, should be completely unarmed. All characteristics except armament shall be the same for both combat and bombing planes. The difference between the two types of plane lies in the difference in distribution of weight for armament in the combat plane and for bomb-load in the bomber.

BATTLEPLANE

From this fact emerges the conception of a plane suitable for both combat and bombing which for simplicity I shall call "battleplane." This type of plane should have the radius of action, speed, and armor protection as described; but should have armament sufficient both for aerial combat and for offensives against the surface. If, after satisfying the other three characteristics, we denote by the letter W the rest of the weight at our disposal for armament—consisting of firearms, munitions, and crew—and if an Independent Air Force consists of combat planes, C, and bombing planes, B, its combat strength will be CW and its bombing strength B(W-w), w being the weight taken up by defensive armament in the bombing planes. But if the Independent Air Force consists entirely of battleplanes, the number of planes will be C + B, and the weight allowed for combat armament will be W (C + B), or CW + BW. Now, if the two types of arms—for aerial combat and for surface attack—are proportionately distributed in each plane, the total value of the armament which can be used against the surface is BW. In other words, this Independent Air Force would be identical with the other in combat power; but in offensive action against the surface it would be slightly superior owing to lack of defensive armament.

In this respect we should make another observation. If the total number of planes in an Independent Air Force is divided between combat and bombing planes, in case of an encounter with an enemy the action will be not simultaneous, but at different times. First will come an aerial battle to overcome the enemy opposition, then afterward the bombing action against surface objectives. Thus, only combat planes can take part in the first phase of the action and only bombers in the second. Similarly, only machine-gunners will be able to operate in the first phase, and only bombardiers in the second.

But if, instead, the Independent Air Force consists entirely of battleplanes, the same personnel could employ all the armament of the planes in aerial battle in the first phase of action, then strike against surface targets in the second phase. This means that the same crew can function both as machine-gunners and bombardiers, thus utilizing the weight saved in personnel to increase the fire power of the Independent Air Force as a whole.

Moreover, an Independent Air Force made up of bombing and combat planes will have to fight, in case of an encounter with the enemy, with only an aliquot part of its planes and without freedom of action, because this number will have to devote itself to protecting the bombing planes during the engagement. If the Air Force were made up entirely of battleplanes, all the planes could take part in the engagement, with full freedom of action. Therefore, from all points of view it is best that the bulk of an Independent Air Force be made up entirely of battleplanes designed for aerial combat and for bombing offensives against the surface.[1]

---

[1] If this interpretation of Douhet's thought is correct, the plane he is describing resembles our modern Flying Fortresses but is much more powerful.—Tr.

We can go even further in this respect. As a matter of fact, it would be better if these characteristics, or at least some of them, were *elastic.* For instance, since radius of action, armor protection, and armament can be translated into carrying capacity, and since the sum total of the weight of these in a given plane is constant, the weight of any of them may be increased at the expense of any or all of the others. Now, it may be expedient to do so because of the intended use. Consequently, it would be very useful to have these details in the construction of battleplanes allow of easy alteration of these characteristics.

If an Independent Air Force undertook an operation within a short radius of action, obviously it would be more useful to decrease the weight of the fuel load and increase the armament a corresponding amount. Conversely, if the action is far from the bases, it would be more useful to decrease the armor protection and perhaps even the armament. Once the command of the air had been conquered, there would of course no longer be any need for an Independent Air Force to engage in aerial battle—so there would no longer be any need of heavy armor protection and defensive aerial armament. The construction of a battleplane should therefore be such as to allow the ready adjustment or substitution of these two weight characteristics to increase the plane's radius of action or its striking power against surface targets. Everything being equal, it is better for a battleplane to be elastic in its characteristics.

We have determined all the basic characteristics of the battleplane which should make up the mass of our Independent Air Force. The problem left for technicians and builders is to produce the plane which will best meet the conditions desired within the limits of practicability. Such a plane must certainly be a heavy type, multimotored, and of medium speed if it is to fill all the requirements. Since the Independent Air Force will have to operate in mass over land and sea, the battleplane ought to be an amphibian. If it is impossible to realize this kind of plane at present, the Independent Air Force will have to be made up partly of hydroplanes and partly of land planes, both to have identical characteristics. The present state of technical development permits the realization of a plane which will meet these requirements to a certain degree, and surely further progress will tend to make the battleplane ever more efficient.

We have been able to determine through deduction the characteristics a battleplane should have—the *only* type of plane which should make up the operating mass of an Independent Air Force—the *only* organism necessary, because sufficient in itself, to wage aerial warfare.

But an Independent Air Force must maintain an efficient information service to keep from being surprised by the enemy, so it must be provided with reconnaissance means. Before we go on any further we must define "reconnaissance," a term which lends itself easily to ambiguity. Reconnaissance is obviously a war operation undertaken for one's own advantage and against the enemy's interests; and therefore, like all war operations, is subject to enemy counteraction. To accomplish this kind of operation successfully, it is first necessary to be in a position to defeat or circumvent the enemy's counteraction. That holds true on land or sea or in the air. For instance, cavalry may reconnoiter against the enemy either by employing large masses of cavalry troops capable of breaking through the enemy's lines to see what goes on behind them, or by using small, well-mounted patrols who can avoid contact with the enemy and slip behind his rear, then return with the needed information. In the air the situation is the same. If a reconnaissance in force to overcome enemy resistance is wanted, it is up to the Independent Air Force, or at least a part of it, to perform the task. If a small scouting operation is planned to report enemy moves in order to use the information to avoid contact with the enemy in subsequent operations, a type of plane entirely different from the combat plane is needed. We shall call this type of plane a *reconnaissance plane.*

To get behind the enemy aerial defense and at the same time avoid aerial combat, *superior speed* and more skillful flying than the enemy can oppose to it are necessary. To carry out successful reconnaissance, an active Independent Air Force needs special observation planes with a greater radius of action than that of the mass of the Air Force if it is to be of any use during the time the Air Force is operating in the air. In short, the essence of successful reconnaissance is to *see, understand,* and *report.* Therefore, a reconnaissance plane needs two eyes, an alert brain, and suitable means of communicating with the Independent Air Force.

RECONNAISSANCE PLANES

The characteristics of this plane should be as follows:

Speed: The maximum possible compatible with the actual state of technical aeronautical developments.

Radius of Action: At least equal to that of the Independent Air Force. If the Air Force has a range of six hours of flight, for example, the reconnaissance plane should have at least an equal range.

Armament and Armor Protection: It is useless to arm a plane intended to avoid combat. It is better to use the weight thus saved to increase speed and radius of action.

Means of Communication: The most perfect.

Crew: The absolutely indispensable minimum, possibly one person only.

To avoid combat, reconnaissance should be undertaken by individual planes operating singly, or by small groups, to allow for any possible loss during operations. An Independent Air Force operating in mass, preceded and surrounded at a convenient distance by a covey of such reconnaissance planes, will be protected from any surprise attack. At the same time it can use these reconnaissance planes to discover ground targets for eventual attack.

6

The characteristics of battle and reconnaissance planes defined so far are valid for any Independent Air Force. But we are essentially interested here in *our own* Independent Air Force, so we must take into account two other conditions particularly applicable to us. Our eventual enemies will be found either beyond the Alps or beyond the narrow sea surrounding us. Therefore, if we want to be in a position to strike at them, we must have an Independent Air Force capable of crossing the Alps and the narrow seas surrounding us. The first of these conditions determines the minimum ceiling the planes of our Air Force must have; the second the minimum radius of action of the whole Air Force. If we do not meet these two conditions, the value of the whole Independent Air Force will be nullified.

In this connection we should be careful not to confuse the radius of action of the individual plane with that of the Independent Air Force itself. The latter may be much less than the former. An Independent Air Force intending to act in mass must first of all assemble its forces, then operate, and finally disperse, each unit re-entering its proper base. The radius of action of an Independent Air Force is equal to the radius of action of the planes constituting it, minus twice the distance from the point of concentration to the base farthest from it.

From this consideration derives the importance of the disposition of air bases, or the home bases of the various units composing the Independent Air Force. The closer these bases are to the point of concentration, the more efficient the Air Force will be. But the points of concentration may vary with the enemy in question, and sometimes also with the operation intended against the chosen enemy. From this springs the necessity for numerous air bases more or less grouped to make the best use of the radius of action of each individual plane, so as to effect the maximum radius of action for the entire Independent Air Force.

That is part of aerial logistics, which must determine the best conditions for utilizing the greatest operating efficiency an Air Force is capable of. But I do not intend to speak of that now. For the present I merely want to point out the necessity of these numerous air bases to be used simply as landing fields. Wartime bases cannot be provided with hangars, because it would be practically impossible to dispose such a large number of them, and because the bases would be too easily identified by the enemy. The planes should therefore be made of metal resistant to all kinds of weather. Large peacetime air bases, at least those of no practical value, should be abandoned immediately upon declaration of war and the planes dispersed to substitute airfields.

An Independent Air Force should disappear from the surface immediately upon landing, and should never be left exposed to enemy attack on the open field. An able and daring enemy force, even if inferior, can make good use of this critical moment. When an Air Force is on the ground, it should be widely dispersed and camouflaged as much as possible. And, as we have seen, an Independent Air Force should dispose different groups of bases so as to have freedom of maneuver and to facilitate its dispersal. Aerial forces should be able to function at will, independent of the ground.

It is necessary, therefore, to create a logistical aerial unit, which will have to be provided with all the needs of life, movement, and combat, which must in turn be supplied by its own aerial organization. To fulfill its purpose, an Independent Air Force must be a completely self-sufficient organization able to move in the air and to change its location on the surface autonomously. That proves that an Independent Air Force worthy of the name is something very different from what is generally thought.

7

The type of battleplane suitable for our Independent Air Force— that is, a plane with a wide radius of action, a high enough ceiling to navigate the Alps, sufficient speed, and a carrying capacity large enough to allow a safe margin of armament and armor protection—is similar to a commercial transport plane utilized by civil aviation, once an equal weight of armament and armor were substituted for passengers, cargo, and mail. This shows the possibility of converting a civil machine into a battleplane by means of appropriate technical arrangements. I believe we should hasten and bend all our energies to this end: *to organize a civil aviation capable of being converted into a powerful military air force in case of national need.* During times of peace, which is to say normally, a military plane has only a potential function in what it may be able to do when war breaks out. All kinds of resources needed to maintain Such a military plane in power during all the time when the life of the nation flows normally are consumed in view of that potential action. On the other hand, a civilian plane capable of conversion immediately on the opening of hostilities has a potential value identical with that of the military plane. But it also represents a real value in peacetime in that it can perform useful civilian services.

It is understandable, therefore, how in choosing between two masses, one made up of military planes and the other of civilian ones capable of immediate conversion to military ones, there are moral and material advantages in choosing the second. No matter how limited the returns of a civil air service, materially speaking, the returns will always be a plus value. Therefore, a mass of civilian planes capable of being converted into military ones will always cost less than an equal number of military ones. By using convertible civilian planes we obtain from the same expenditure greater military power and at the same time the possibility of actively maintaining a very comprehensive civilian air service. This is so great an advantage that I have no hesitation in saying that the end we must work for is *to organize a powerful civil aviation capable of immediate conversion, in case of need, into a powerful military aviation, reducing the latter during peacetime to a skeleton force for instruction and command.*

I have already shown that the possibility for this unit exists as far as the mass of planes constituting an Independent Air Force according to the idea expressed here is concerned. The aeronautical world in general denies such a possibility. Considering the prevalent conception of air power—a conception which demands a great variety of specialized types of planes and sometimes even of extreme characteristics—is this denial altogether wrong? It may not be possible now to make civilian planes capable of immediate conversion into battleplanes, since these require, besides suitable armament for aerial combat and for surface offensives, installations for suitable armor protection. But it is certainly possible even now to make civilian planes capable of immediate conversion into bombing planes, because to do this we need only substitute bombs for the weight of passengers, cargo, and mail.

So from now on it will be possible to increase the bombing power of an Independent Air Force by using civil aviation to complement it. Depending upon circumstances, such complements could be used to increase the bombing power of an Independent Air Force during the struggle for command of the air or after the command has been conquered. Therefore, there is nothing to stop us from aiming at this goal.

I have said, and proved, that only those who have learned how to conquer the command of the air will be in a position to employ aerial means as auxiliary services with the army and navy, and that the only aerial force a nation must create for itself is the Independent Air Force. Conversely, an Independent Air Force which has conquered the command of the air can lend part of its complements to the army and navy for auxiliary services.

But are such complements adapted to such services? Most certainly they are. First of all we must note that when an independent Air Force confronts an enemy made incapable of flying, any aerial action, auxiliary or not, undertaken against him is accomplished with great ease and important results because the enemy is powerless to retaliate.

Once it has conquered the command of the air, an Independent Air Force may lend the army and navy, for auxiliary service, battle units (or units of combat and units of bombardment) and also observation units. These units can carry out with great facility, because in complete safety, all the auxiliary tasks of exploration, reconnaissance, and observation which the army and navy may require of them. The combat units, powerfully armed and capable of maximum intensity of fire in all directions, can serve best to attack marching troops, supply trains, rail movements, and so forth; while the bombing units can serve to destroy objectives bearing directly on surface operations. Therefore, there will be no need of pursuit planes once the command of the air has been conquered. And therefore the constitution of an Independent Air Force according to my ideas will make it able to render all imaginable auxiliary aerial services after it has conquered the command of the air.

8

In all the foregoing my purpose has been to demonstrate that an Independent Air Force, once it has conquered the command of the air, can also meet the needs of all auxiliary services required by the exigencies of war. I have made my demonstrations in abundance because I am convinced that, even after conquering the command of the air, an Independent Air Force should operate independently and not waste its time and disperse its means in actions of secondary importance. Once the command of the air is conquered, the Air Force should attempt to carry out offensives of such magnitude as to crush the material and moral resistance of the enemy. Even if this aim cannot be achieved in entirety, it is still necessary to weaken the enemy's resistance as much as possible, because that, better than any other means, facilitates the operations of the army and navy. But to achieve such an end, we must avoid dispersing our means and make the most possible use of them.

The maximum returns from aerial offensives must be sought beyond the field of battle. They must be sought in places where effective counteraction is negligible and where the most vital and vulnerable targets are to be found—targets which are, even though indirectly, much more relevant to the action and outcome on the field of battle. In terms of military results, it is much more important to destroy a railroad station, a bakery, a war plant, or to machine-gun a supply column, moving trains, or any other behind-the-lines objective, than to strafe or bomb a trench. The results are immeasurably greater in breaking morale, in disorganizing badly disciplined organizations, in spreading terror and panic, than in dashing against more solid resistance. There is no end to what a powerful Independent Air Force in command of the air could do to the enemy!

It seems paradoxical to some people that the final decision in future wars may be brought about by blows to the morale of the civilian population. But that is what the last war proved, and it will be verified in future wars with even more evidence. The outcome of the last war was only apparently brought about by military operations. In actual fact, it was decided by the breakdown of morale among the defeated peoples—a moral collapse caused by the long attrition of the people involved in the struggle. The air arm makes it possible to reach the civilian population behind the line of battle, and thus to attack their moral resistance directly. And there is nothing to prevent our thinking that some day this direct action may be on a scale to break the moral resistance of the people even while leaving intact their respective armies and navies. Was not the German Army still able to go on fighting at the time when it laid down its arms? Was not the German fleet turned over intact to the enemy when the German people felt their power of resistance weakening?

We must keep in mind, not what aviation *is* today, but what it *could be* today. Certainly if we said that the actual air powers of the various nations could decide the outcome of a war, we would be uttering not only paradox, but downright absurdity. But that means nothing, because we do not say that the actual aviations of today are what they should be in effectiveness. We should think, for example, what would happen if an enemy were to conquer the command of our sky with his Independent Air Force, enabling him to rove at will over Piedmont, Lombardy, and Liguria, dumping great quantities of explosive, incendiary, and poison-gas bombs on the most vital centers of these three northern provinces. If we think of that, we must conclude that the resistance of our surface forces would soon be broken by the disruption of everyday life in those three provinces—a disruption directly brought about by air power.

Even assuming—although I by no means concede it—that today it would be impossible to launch aerial offensives of the necessary magnitude, still the constant improvement of aerial weapons and increase in the efficiency of destructive materials show that the necessary magnitude will be possible in the not too distant future.

In any case, by common consent the fact remains that aerial offensives have already attained such material and moral efficacy as to compel surface armies to undertake arduous, time-consuming defensive measures—secret night movements of troops and supplies, et cetera—which tie up the movement of surface aerial defenses and antiaircraft guns which might be more useful elsewhere, thus causing a serious dispersion of means. This is true whenever we give credit to aviation for what it is, and for what it may and should be.

We must not rely on the fact that other nations organize and employ their air forces much as we do. One fine day one of our eventual enemies may decide to organize and employ his air forces as I would do myself, for example. And in that case, I ask anyone disposed to give me an honest answer, whether, taking into account the concepts of aerial organization and employment which prevail in our country and the location of our aerial resources on the surface, this potential enemy would not be in a position rapidly to conquer the command of the air over our sky; and whether, having conquered it, he could not perhaps inflict irreparable damage upon us. If anyone can conscientiously give me an unequivocable "no," I will lay down my arms and admit that I am wrong. But until I hear this unequivocable "no," for which someone is ready to assume full responsibility, I shall not cease to point out this grave danger and fight with everything in my power, thus fulfilling my solemn duty.

Following is a recapitulation of my ideas on the constitution of our air power:

1. The purpose of aerial warfare is the conquest of the command of the air. Having the command of the air, aerial forces should direct their offensives against surface objectives with the intention of crushing the material and moral resistance of the enemy.

2. We should seek no other purposes except the two described above if we want to avoid playing the enemy's game.

3. The only effective instrument for carrying out these purposes is an Independent Air Force made up of a mass of battle units and an aliquot part of reconnaissance units.

4. The Independent Air Force should embody the greatest power compatible with the resources at our disposal; therefore no aerial resources should under any circumstances be diverted to secondary purposes, such as auxiliary aviation, local air defense, and antiaircraft defenses.

5. The efficacy of destructive materials should be increased as much as possible, because, other things being equal, the offensive power of an Independent Air Force is in direct proportion to the efficacy of the destructive materials at its disposal.

6. Civil aviation should be so organized as to be utilized as a complement to military aviation in case of war. That organization should be in the direction of a powerful fleet of transports capable of immediate conversion into a powerful military air force. The latter should be reduced, in time of peace, to a simple organization for instruction and command.

7. Aerial warfare admits of no defensive attitude, only the offensive. Of two Independent Air Forces, the one stronger in

combat units should neither seek nor avoid aerial combat; the weaker should try to avoid it. But both stronger and weaker should always be in readiness to act even before hostilities break out; and once action has begun, both should keep in action incessantly and with the utmost violence, trying to hit the enemy's most vital targets—that is, targets more likely to cause repercussions on his air power and moral resistance.

8. Once an Independent Air Force has conquered the command of the air, it should keep up violent, uninterrupted action against surface objectives, to the end that it may crush the material and moral resistance of the enemy.

9. An Independent Air Force should be so organized as to move as quickly as possible over its own territory with its own means, in order to be of the greatest use against any potential enemy.

10. Aerial warfare will be fought and decided solely by aerial forces which are ready to act at the instant hostilities break out, because, owing to the great violence with which it will be fought, if the adversaries are fairly well matched in strength, it will be conducted and decided very rapidly.

11. An Independent Air Force formed with all the resources a nation has at its disposal for its aerial forces, made up of a mass of battleplanes and an aliquot part of reconnaissance planes, acting decisively and exclusively on the offensive, will soon wrest command of the air from an enemy air force constituted, organized, and performing in a different way.

In spite of the close reasoning by which I have arrived at these affirmations, I am sure they will seem extravagant to many. That does not affect me in the least. I am used to hearing my ideas, which often contrast with those of many people, who have clung fanatically to the same old ideas, called extravagant and worse. On the other hand, this will not prevent my ideas, even the most radical ones, from little by little being accepted by general opinion. Such stubbornness leaves me absolutely unaffected, because I have the mathematical certainty that the time will come when air forces of nations everywhere will conform exactly to the concepts described above. . . .

CONCLUSION

I feel sure there cannot be anyone today who can honestly maintain that the problem of air power is of only secondary importance. More and more every day the air arm is being consolidated, its radius of action widened, and its carrying capacity increased; and the efficacy of destructive materials is constantly being raised. With our geographical and political situation, all of our land and sea territory is exposed to eventual enemy offensives of imposing dimensions operating from land bases. The Alpine arc embraces our richest and most industrious provinces, *all* of which can be reached by enemy aerial offensives operating from the opposite slopes; and the narrow seas surrounding us offer little protection from aerial attacks launched from enemy shores.

Our extremely concentrated industries, with large centers of population exposed, the ease with which our main communication lines can be broken, and the degree to which we employ hydraulic resources, all put us in a position to fear aerial offensives more than any other nation. If on the one hand the Alpine barrier gives us the power to bar the door of our house, on the other hand, because of the difficult terrain and scarce roadways, it favors an enemy effectively armed in the air and bent upon cutting off from their bases our land forces operating in the mountains.

If we consider all this seriously, we cannot but agree that the command of its own sky is an indispensable condition of Italy's safety. Nevertheless, even today anyone who tries to point out the importance of air power in future wars is called a visionary. It is admitted that the enemy can compel us to evacuate entire cities by using aerial offensives; but it is denied that this can weigh heavily in the outcome of the war—as though an army deployed in the Alps would not be affected by the evacuation of Milan, Turin, and Genoa; or as though the evacuation of a city could be compared to moving out of an apartment house. Even though it is admitted that aerial offensives can stop industrial production, it is maintained that this small inconvenience can be obviated by transferring the factories farther inland, as though all industrial plants were not compelled to intensify their production during wartime. The idea that a war could be decided by the collapse of the nation's morale is considered paradoxical, and this in spite of the fact that the World War was decided by the collapse of the moral resistance of the defeated peoples.

The armies involved in that war were only the means by which the nations of each side tried to undermine the resistance of the other; so much so that, though the defeated side was the one whose armies won the most and greatest battles, when the morale of the civilian population began to weaken, these very armies either disbanded or surrendered, and an entire fleet was turned over intact to the enemy. This disintegration of nations in the last war was indirectly brought about by the actions of the armies in the field. In the future it will be accomplished directly by the actions of aerial forces. In that lies the difference between past and future wars.

An aerial bombardment which compels the evacuation of a city of some hundreds of thousands of inhabitants will certainly have more influence on the realization of victory than a battle of the kind often fought during the last war without appreciable results. A nation which once loses the command of the air and finds itself subjected to incessant aerial attacks aimed directly at its most vital centers and without the possibility of effective retaliation, this nation, whatever its surface forces may be able to do, must arrive at the conviction that all is useless, that all hope is dead. This conviction spells defeat.

Even admitting—I by no means concede it—that the command of the air exercised with adequate forces could not defeat the enemy without regard to other circumstances, it is nevertheless indisputable that the command of the air can bring serious material and moral damage to the enemy, thereby contributing effectively to his defeat. Therefore, apart from the value that may be attributed to the command of the air, it is of paramount importance that we should dominate our sky. The primary concern of the army and navy should be to see that their own aviation conquers the command of the air; otherwise all their actions will be put in jeopardy by an enemy in command of the air.

Though military and naval forces are not yet fully aware of the value of the air arm, they do feel the necessity of protecting themselves against aerial operations. The mere fact that it is possible to fly, and by flying to accomplish war operations, must be the determining factor in modifying the methods of combat on land and sea. A single example will suffice: It is no longer possible to imagine fuel deposits in the open sky. We must therefore consider seriously the new aerial factor in itself and its influence upon military and naval forces no less than upon the total civilian resources of the country. But if we are in a position to dominate our own sky, we will automatically be in a position to dominate the Mediterranean sky as well—that is, to control the sea which must be ours if we wish to create for ourselves an imperial destiny. The Independent Air Force must become Italy's impregnable shield and the sharp sword with which to carve out her future.

At present such ideas are in the embryonic stage, but it is certain that the nation which first learns to use them in the right way will have an advantage over all others. With time and experience, the Independent Air Forces of all nations will take on a similar form, as long ago their armies and navies did. Today ingenuity may still be useful; tomorrow quality alone will count. Thanks to the native aptitude of her people, though poorer than other nations, Italy may still forge for herself an Independent Air Force capable of commanding respect from others.

I have been harping on this theme for years, and I intend to keep on harping on it, confident of doing my duty as a citizen and a soldier, and at the same time of doing a work of sound collaboration in a period when the national government intends to lead Italy toward its bright future. We possess all the necessary elements for creating a superb air power: daring pilots, resourceful technicians, large guilds of skilled artisans and craftsmen, a unique geographical situation, and a strong government which knows what it wants and how to get it done. All we need do is unite in silent, intense labor, with the firm determination to get to the top and stay there.

Aviation has already shed its primitive, or I should say sporting, character, and has now entered upon a period of serious industrial production. At the beginning its aim was simply to fly; now its purpose is to accomplish something worth while through flying—to shorten great distances in peacetime, to fight in wartime. We must enter this second period with the determination to try to do something in the air, something better than the rest of the world.

BOOK TWO

THE PROBABLE ASPECTS
OF THE WAR
OF THE FUTURE

Originally published as a monograph in April 1928.

INTRODUCTION

The study of war, particularly the war of the future, presents some very interesting features. First is the vastness of the phenomenon which makes whole peoples hurl themselves against one another, forgetting for a time that they all wear the aspect of human beings, that they belong to the same family of humanity striving toward the same goal of ideal perfection; to become wolves and throw themselves into torment and a bloody work of destruction, as though possessed by blind folly. Next comes the impressive scale of war, which demands the assembling, ordering, and directing toward the single goal, victory, all the formidable material and moral forces of whole nations—the destructive forces to hurl against the enemy, the productive forces to turn out more destructive ones. This is an immense and varied undertaking which must still be done with foresight before the crisis, and must be integrated with fervor during the crisis, but always scientifically, so that it may yield the maximum results from the national resources poured into it. And, finally, there is what might be called the mysterious aspect of war, which, no matter how hard an individual may try to think of it as something improbable and far away, presses upon everyone, and is shrouded by a heavy veil of mystery in that it bears within it, vaguely descried, an eventuality of the future.

To prepare for war is to prepare to face this vaguely felt eventuality of the future. The preparation for war demands, then, exercise of the imagination; we are compelled to make a mental excursion into the future. A man who wants to make a good instrument must first have a precise understanding of what the instrument is to be used for; and he who intends to build a good instrument of war must first ask himself what the next war will be like. And he must try to find an answer which approximates most closely the reality of the future war, for the closer that approximation, the more suitable for dealing with the future reality will be his instrument. Research into the war of the future is not, therefore, an idle pastime. It is, rather, an ever-present practical necessity. And when we consider that such research proposes to discover the nature of the cataclysm which may come upon humanity, and that analysis of it cannot be accomplished except by exercise of the imagination within the confines of rigid logic, it becomes a fascinating study.

Defining with a larger measure of probability what the forms and characteristics of future wars will be like is not, as some lazy minds affirm, the province of the fortuneteller or the idle speculator. It is, rather, a serious problem, the solution to which must be worked out by logical progression from cause to effect.

There is a simple method of foretelling the future, simply asking of the present what it is preparing for the future, asking of the cause what its effect will be. Tomorrow is only the outgrowth of today; and the man who foretells it is like the farmer who knows what he will reap from what he sows, or the astronomer who can tell the precise instant at which the conjunction of Venus and Mars will occur.

In the period of history through which we are passing, war is undergoing a profound and radical change in character and forms, as I shall show; so that the war of the future will be very different from all wars of the past. That makes the problem even more interesting, because the war of the future will be a new and different thing. I shall try to accompany you on this excursion into the future. Our itinerary will be simple: we shall start from the past, look over the present, and from there jump into the future. We shall glance at the war of the past long enough to retrace its essential features; we shall ask of the present what it is preparing for the future; and, finally, we shall try to decide what modifications will be made in the character of war by the causes at work today in order to point out their inevitable consequences. You will find the road easy and even. I shall not try to tell you, for I do not know how, about matters abstruse or transcendental. War is simple, like good sense. Perhaps I shall tell you things quite different from what is commonly said, but even these things will be the modest offspring of common sense. . . .

CHAPTER IV

THE PROBLEM OF THE FUTURE

I come now to the most interesting problem, the problem of the future. This may seem difficult to the reader, but that is appearance rather than reality. We have already well established our starting point—we have seen the events which have been maturing. Now all we have to do is to deduce from them the effects which must follow. Human reasoning has this divining power which brings man closer to God. Using abstract calculus as a basis, Maxwell discovered and defined electromagnetic waves, which we cannot perceive with our senses. On the same basis Hertz built the instrument which revealed them; and Marconi in his turn put them to use and gave them to mankind. In the matter we are examining, we are confronted with facts which our senses can see and perceive, and therefore we should easily be able to define the consequences which must inevitably ensue from them, provided we free our minds from the set traditions of the past.

In a book of mine in 1921 I asked the following question: Is it not true that the strongest army deployed on the Alps and the strongest navy sailing our seas, could do nothing practical against an enemy adequately armed in the air who was determined to invade our territory and destroy from the air our communication, production, and industrial centers, and sow death, destruction, and terror in our population centers in order to break our material and moral resistance? The only possible answer then was: "It is true"; today the answer is the same, and tomorrow it must still be the same, unless one denies that airplanes fly and poison gases kill, which would be absurd. As I have said about the last war, the armies then functioned as organs of *indirect* attrition of national resistance, and the navies as organs to *accelerate or retard* this attrition.

While the armies and navies tend *indirectly* to break the enemy's resistance, the air arm, having the capacity to act upon the very source of resources, tends to break it *directly*—namely, with more speed and efficacy. Once one had to be content with destroying a battery with shells; today it is possible to destroy the factory where the guns for the batteries are being built. During the last war tons of explosives and whole mines of iron were fired at regions covered with barbed-wire entanglements in order to destroy them; the air arm can ignore that kind of objective and use its shells, explosives, and poison gases to much better advantage. An army can reach the enemy's capital only after facing the enemy army, defeating it, and pushing it back by a long, painful, onerous series of operations; the air arm instead may try for the destruction of the enemy's capital even before war is declared.

There is no comparison between the efficacy of direct and indirect destructive action against the vital resistance of a nation. In the days when a nation could shield itself behind the stout armor of an army and navy, blows from the enemy were barely felt by the nation itself, sometimes not at all. The blows were taken by institutions such as the army and navy, well organized and disciplined, materially and morally able to resist, and able to act and counteract. The air arm, on the contrary, will strike against entities less well-organized and disciplined, less able to resist, and helpless to act or counteract. It is fated, therefore, that the moral and material collapse will come about more quickly and easily. A body of troops will stand fast under intensive bombings, even after losing half or two-thirds of its men; but the workers in shop, factory, or harbor will melt away after the first losses.

The direct attack against the moral and material resistance of the enemy will hasten the decision of the conflict, and so will shorten the war. Fokker, the famous airplane builder, who understands the mentalities of all his international clients, said:

> Do not believe that tomorrow the enemy will make any distinction between military forces and the civilian population. He will use his most powerful and terrifying means, such as poison gas and other things, against the civilian population, even though in peacetime he may have professed the best intentions and subscribed to the strictest limitation of them. Squadrons of airplanes will be sent to destroy the principal cities. The future war, of which we now have only a vague idea will be frightful.

Fokker is right. We dare not wait for the enemy to begin using the so-called inhuman weapons banned by treaties before we feel justified in doing the same. This justification, useless anyhow, would be too costly since it would leave the initiative to the enemy. Owing to extreme necessity, all contenders must use all means without hesitation, whether or not they are forbidden by treaties, which after all are nothing but scraps of paper compared to the tragedy which would follow.

This is a dark and bloody picture I am drawing for you; but it is bound to happen and there is no use in burying one's head in the sand. And the picture grows still darker when one realizes that defense against aerial attacks as it is commonly envisaged is *illusory,* owing again to the essential characteristics of the air arm. An airplane taking off from the center of the island of

Corsica, with a 500-kilometer radius of action, could attack, besides all of Sardinia, every place else on the peninsula, from Trent and Venice in the east to Termoli and Salerno in the south. To defend all the centers exposed to the potential threat of this one airplane, we would have to distribute defense planes and antiaircraft artillery to each of these centers.

How many defense planes and how many antiaircraft guns would be needed to make sure of repelling that one plane? What look-out service should be organized on the ground so as not to be surprised by it? How long should the look-out service, the defense planes, and the antiaircraft guns be on the alert for it to put in an appearance, and all this without any certainty of being able to prevent its offensive if it should come? Anyhow, how many resources and how much energy would be immobilized for such a defense? And all for one lone airplane, which could accomplish the immobilization of all these resources and energies merely by its potential existence, without needing to take off and fly at all.

If that lone airplane is multiplied by a hundred or by a thousand—in other words, if we consider the size of the air forces we would have to contend with in case of war—we will realize immediately that defensive action would compel us to immobilize for a purely negative purpose a much larger amount of resources than those which would attack us—perhaps so much larger that we could not afford it. Would it not be better to renounce this passive and expensive attitude and send out against that threat, which could become a nightmare, an offensive aerial force of our own which would go in search of the enemy and destroy him in his nest, thus putting an end to the nightmare and the threat? Wouldn't this be the best way out, the way which would accomplish the most with the least?

The air arm is eminently offensive, but completely unsuitable for defensive action. In fact, one who used it defensively would be in the absurd situation of needing a defensive aerial force much larger than the enemy's offensive one. Although there were no exact rules for large-scale aerial offensives in the last war, those which were carried out with determination were successful. We bombed Pola every time it suited us, and the Austrians kept on bombing our Treviso right up to Armistice Day, although our aviation was in preponderance during the last months.

In England a few months ago an experiment was made in the aerial defense of London. The defense had at its disposal as many airplanes as the offensive side, besides the antiaircraft batteries and organization. Furthermore, it knew the days during which the offensive would be attempted. The offensive side, equal in strength to the defensive, had its objective limited in time and space. All the conditions were in favor of the defense; but the experiment proved that London would have been bombed.

Aerial defense should therefore be limited to the organization of all those means which would lessen the effects of aerial offensives, such as decentralization of vital organs, preparation of bomb shelters, protective measures against poison gas, and similar means. Only a center of exceptional importance should be defended by antiaircraft artillery, because it would be physically impossible to have as much as it would take to defend the whole national territory efficaciously. I have heard that 300 antiaircraft batteries would be necessary to defend Milan with some measure of efficacy. How many would be needed to insure the safety of all the important centers of Italy? The situation is the same for aerial offensives as for naval ones. Since it would be impossible to defend the whole coastline, or even the more important coastal points, from a naval offensive, defense is limited to the most important points from a military point of view—fortified naval bases—leaving all other points undefended, even the great maritime cities, their protection being entrusted to the fleet. Similarly, the protection of the national territory from aerial offensives should be entrusted to the aerial arm, which will be capable of repelling, defeating, and destroying the enemy's aerial force.

There is only one valid way to defend oneself from aerial offensives: namely, *to conquer the command of the air,* that is *to prevent the enemy from flying, while assuring this freedom for oneself.* To prevent the enemy from flying, one must destroy his means of flying. His means may be found in the air, on the ground in airfields, in hangars, in factories. To destroy the enemy's means of flying, one must have an aerial force capable of destroying them wherever they may be found or are being manufactured. In line with this concept, I have been preaching for years the necessity of an Independent Air Force, a mass of aerial means adequate to fight an aerial war to conquer the command of the air.

During the last war this concept was unknown. Aviation was used then as auxiliary means intended to facilitate and integrate land and sea actions. There was no true aerial warfare; there were aerial struggles and clashes, but only partial, limited, isolated, often individual ones. Aerial victory was not sought, only aerial preponderance. Until Armistice Day there were auxillary aerial actions carried on by both sides in proportion to the available forces. Today things are quite different; the magnitude of possible aerial forces leads to real aerial war, the struggle between masses of means.

Without going into details, which would be out of place here, we can easily understand that an Independent Air Force capable of aerial combat and of bombing the surface can aim at the conquest of the command of the air, because it can destroy enemy aerial means in the air or on the ground, wherever they are found or manufactured. Through its aerial offensive, therefore, an Independent Air Force can reduce the enemy's aerial means to a minimum, insignificant in relation to the economy of war in general. When it gets such a result it has won, inasmuch as it has conquered the command of the air.

The command of the air carries with it the following advantages:

1. It shields one's own territory and seas from enemy aerial offensives, because the enemy has been made powerless to carry out offensives. It protects, therefore, the material and moral resistance of the nation from direct and terrifying attacks by the enemy.

2. It exposes the enemy's territory to one's own aerial offensives, which can be carried on with the utmost ease, because the enemy has been made powerless to act in the air. It therefore facilitates a direct and terrifying attack on the enemy's resistance.

3. It completely protects the bases and communication lines of one's own army and navy, and threatens those of the enemy.

4. It prevents the enemy from helping his army and navy from the air, and at the same time insures aerial help for one's own army and navy.

To all these advantages must be added the fact that the one who has command of the air can prevent the enemy from rebuilding his aerial force, because he can destroy the sources of materials and the places of manufacture. This is equivalent to saying that the conquest of the air is final.

In consideration of the advantages which ensue from the command of the air, it must be admitted that the command of the air will have a decisive influence on the outcome of the war.

I have said that the command of the air is final, inasmuch as the one who conquers it can prevent the enemy from rebuilding his aerial forces. But there is more than that—the one who has command of the air can increase his own aerial forces to his liking. The nation dominated in the air must suffer without possibility of effective counteraction the aerial offensives carried by the enemy to its territory—offensives which will increase as the enemy increases his offensive aerial forces. Its army and navy will be powerless against these offensives. Quite apart from material damage, how great must be the moral effects both on the nation enduring this nightmare and on its armed forces, who would be conscious of their impotence to help?

In their turn the army and navy will see their lines of communication cut and their bases destroyed; the forwarding of supplies from the nation to its armed forces would be cut off completely or made irregular and dangerous. By simply destroying facilities in enemy mercantile ports, the dominant Independent Air Force can cut off maritime traffic even if the enemy nation is able to protect its seaways. Then is it not logical to assume that a nation placed in such a position of inferiority would begin to despair of a favorable outcome of the war? And would not that be the beginning of the end?

If you think about it you will realize how true it is. Dominated from the air, England would be lost. Her magnificent fleet, her naval predominance, would be of no avail. Even if her merchant marine could bring supplies to her ports, they could not be unloaded and forwarded. Hunger, desolation, and terror would stalk the country. These are some of the probabilities of the war to come. Do they not revolutionize all past ideas on the subject?

The conquest of the command of the air will be a necessary condition of future wars, even if it will not insure victory by itself. It will always be necessary; it will be sufficient if and when the Independent Air Force is left with enough offensive strength to crush the material and moral resistance of the enemy. If the Air Force is not left with enough strength, the conflict will be decided by the land and sea forces, whose task will be greatly facilitated by having the command of the air on their side.

Considering the decisive importance of the conquest of the command of the air, it is imperative to put oneself in condition to reach toward this aim. It is essential to have an Independent Air Force able to fight an aerial battle, the most powerful possible within one's resources; and to have this it is necessary to make use of *all* the *available resources* of the nation. This is the inflexible principle I advocate, allowing no exceptions; for any resources diverted from that essential end, or only partly used, or not at all, would reduce our chances of conquering the command of the air.

I have shown how aerial defense would demand immobilization of a larger quantity of means than the offense needs, since the defensive value of the aerial arm is much less than the offensive. One hundred airplanes offensively employed by an Independent Air Force would be worth more than 500 or 1,000 used defensively. If the enemy should conquer the command of the air, our army and navy auxiliary aviations would be destroyed without even having a chance to go into action; but if we conquer, our victorious Independent Air Force would be able to give substantial help to the army and navy. Therefore, auxiliary aviation will be useless in the first case, superfluous in the second.

Consequently, I say: No aerial defense, because it is practically useless. No auxiliary aviation, because it is practically useless or superfluous. Instead, a single Independent Air Force, to include all the aerial resources available to the nation, none excepted. This is my thesis. Some people call it extremist; but really it is just a thesis which differs from the average thesis. The latter is always a poor solution, and in wartime the worst of all. Supporting this thesis brings me into conflict with valorous opponents who hold a different opinion; but I am confident that I shall win this battle too.[1]

Since the only way to defend oneself from aerial offensives is to attack and destroy the enemy aerial forces, and since every resource diverted from this fundamental aim might jeopardize one's chances of conquering the command of the air, the fundamental principle of aerial warfare is this: *to resign oneself to endure enemy aerial offensives in order to inflict the greatest possible offensives on the enemy.*

At first this principle seems atrocious, especially when one thinks of the suffering and horror which would be caused by aerial offensives. But that is the principle upon which all war

---

[1] The "battles" to which Douhet refers were his battles for a unified command, an Air Ministry, and the creation of an Independent Air Force distinct from the auxiliary air force.—Tr.

actions are based. An army commander resigns himself to the probable loss of a hundred thousand men if he can inflict a larger loss on the enemy—a loss which, disregarding the number of men involved, might bring victory. A commander of a fleet resigns himself to the loss of some of his units in order to sink more of the enemy's. In like manner a nation must resign itself to endure the enemy's aerial offensives in order to inflict heavier ones on him, because victory comes only through inflicting more damage than one suffers.

When this general principle of war is applied to aerial warfare, it seems inhuman to us because of a traditional notion which must be changed. Everyone says, and is convinced of it, that war is no longer a clash between armies, but is a clash between nations, between whole populations. During the last war this clash took the form of a long process of attrition between armies, and that seemed natural and logical. Because of its direct action, the air arm pits populations directly against populations, nations directly against nations, and does away with the intervening armor which has kept them apart during past wars. Now it is actually populations and nations which come to blows and seize each other's throats.

This fact sharpens that peculiar traditional notion which makes people weep to hear of a few women and children killed in an air raid, and leaves them unmoved to hear of thousands of soldiers killed in action. All human lives are equally valuable; but because tradition holds that the soldier is fated to die in battle, his death does not upset them much, despite the fact that a soldier, a robust young man, should be considered to have the maximum individual value in the general economy of humanity.

In employing submarines the Germans had an end in view which . . . they came close to reaching. We were justified in stigmatizing the submarine warfare as atrocious in order to play upon the sensibilities of world public opinion. It was to our interest, and we had a right to do it. But the real reason we were worried about it was not that it was inhuman, simply that it was dangerous to us. Compared with the carnage wrought by means recognized as humane and civilized, which amounted to millions of dead and millions of mutilated, the approximately 17,000 victims of the submarine are insignificant. If the last war had been wholly a submarine war, it would have been decided with much less blood. War has to be regarded unemotionally as a science, regardless of how terrible a science.

A great furor was raised about submarines' leaving shipwrecked men to their fate without giving them any help. But the submarines were only doing as the English did when, after one of their ships was torpedoed in the act of picking up the survivors of another ship, the commander gave orders that shipwrecked men must be left to their fate to prevent the torpedoing of rescuers; and in this case the men in question were fellow Englishmen, not enemies. War is war. Either one wages war or one doesn't; but when one does, one must do it without gloves and without frills on either side. The French Jeune École advocated ideas on this subject very like the Germans'. Anyone who likes to pretend that war is something different from what it is, puts himself at a disadvantage because of that thinking.

Any distinction between belligerents and nonbelligerents is no longer admissible today either in fact or theory. Not in theory because when nations are at war, everyone takes a part in it: the soldier carrying his gun, the woman loading shells in a factory, the farmer growing wheat, the scientist experimenting in his laboratory. Not in fact because nowadays the offensive may reach anyone; and it begins to look now as though the safest place may be the trenches.

War is won by crushing the resistance of the enemy; and this can be done more easily, faster, more economically, and with less bloodshed by directly attacking that resistance at its weakest point. The more rapid and terrifying the arms are, the faster they will reach vital centers and the more deeply they will affect moral resistance. Hence the more civilized war will become, because damages will be corresponding to the number of people involved. The better arms are able to attack citizens in general, the more private interests are directly hurt, the fewer wars will be, for people will not be able to say any more: "Let us all arm for war, but you go and do the fighting."

A belief generally held nowadays is that wars will begin in the air, and that large-scale aerial actions will be carried out even before the declaration of war, because everyone will be trying to get the advantage of surprise. Aerial warfare will be intense and violent to a superlative degree; for each side will realize the necessity of inflicting upon the enemy the largest possible losses in the shortest possible time, and of ridding the air of enemy aerial means so as to prevent any possible retaliation from him. Independent Air Forces will hurl themselves against their enemies and try to repeat their offensives as quickly as possible in order to compress the effort into as short a space of time as possible. Therefore, the war in the air will be decided by *those aerial forces which are in being and ready when hostilities break out.* No reliance can be placed on forces to be activated during the war. One who is defeated will not be able to create another aerial force. All available forces must be thrown into the fray at once; every means reserved for some other use will be that much less weight on the scale of destiny. The principle of mass must be implicitly followed.

In land warfare it is possible to rely on the defensive to offset a disparity in strength and gain time to dig trenches, throw up barbed-wire entanglements, and occupy strong positions; but in the air nothing of the kind is possible. The air is uniform everywhere, and there is no chance to stop anywhere and make a stand to gain time. In the air, fighting forces are as naked as swords.

The intense, violent, naked, immediate action, the impossibility of gaining time and creating new forces, the rapidity and efficacy of aerial actions—all lead to the conclusion that the aerial conflict will come to a quick decision. The length of the last war, as I have shown, was caused by the great value acquired by the defensive. In the air the defensive has no value at all. He who is unprepared is lost. The aerial war will be short; one of the two sides will rapidly gain a preponderance which will mean the command of the air, a command which, once gained, will be permanent.

Undoubtedly a decision will come in the air sooner than on land and sea. Consequently, the army and navy will have to be prepared to fight on even if dominated from the air, because such an eventuality, no matter what we may think of it, will have to be taken into consideration, even if only for a short while.

In what situation would an army and navy find themselves if they were dominated from the air? Up to the present, war on land and sea has been chiefly dependent on the safety of bases and communication lines. Occupying the enemy's bases or cutting off his lines of communication was a brilliant tactical and strategical success, because it put the enemy in difficulty and danger. If an army and navy were dominated from the air, this very fact would expose their bases and communication lines, not only to enemy offensives, but to offensives they could not effectively counteract; which means that an army and navy dominated from the air would be permanently virtually cut off. Therefore—and please note well this inevitable consequence—if an army and navy want to keep their potentiality of action even when dominated from the air, they must arrange their forms and methods of action to make them as independent as possible of their bases and lines of communication.

The problem with which the air arm confronts the army and navy is a formidable one; but it is imperative that it be solved, even if radical and far-reaching changes have to be made. If it is not solved, the efficiency of an army and navy would be nullified almost automatically by the enemy's conquest of the command of the air. Because of their heavy equipment and large consumption, the huge modern armies have to be backed up by a large regular supply service by rail and road. If this service is disrupted, made irregular, or cut off, it means the debilitation of the army which relies upon it and the weakening of its striking power. It might also deprive the army of its strength, perhaps even immobilize it and make it impotent. An army dominated from the air may be the more easily put in a precarious situation, the more intense, regular, and continuous a supply service it needs. To visualize such a situation, we need only imagine our army deployed on the western Alps, and only four of our railroad centers destroyed—Ceva, Nizza Marrittima, Asti, and Chivasso. As a result no supplies could reach the army from the provinces of Lombardy and Liguria—that is, from its own country. Now, these four railroad centers are about a half-hour's flying distance from the border, and no one can doubt the ability of an enemy in command of the air, given the present potentiality of aerial offensives, to destroy them and keep them destroyed. In my opinion, therefore, it is imperative for modern armies to be less ponderous, and as much as possible autonomous and independent of their bases.

Similarly, a navy which means to keep on operating even under domination from the air must free itself from the bonds which at present tie navies to their bases. The large military ports, with their arsenals, warehouses, supply depots, and equipment of all kinds, are good targets for aerial offensives, whether they harbor a fleet or not. They may be defended by antiaircraft artillery, but their safety will always be doubtful, and certainly they will never be as invulnerable as they have been heretofore. It is imperative that navies think over the changed situation and do something about it.

Besides, an enemy in command of the air can easily cut off our maritime traffic regardless of his naval strength, simply by putting our commercial ports out of service. A Swiss Independent Air Force could cut off our maritime traffic if it succeeded in commanding the air. It does seem absurd; but it is nevertheless one of the possibilities of modern war.

These short summaries of the influence of the air arm on the forms of war on land and sea, an influence which should lead armies and navies to reorganize on a new basis, should suffice to make people realize the magnitude of the revolution and the seriousness of the problems which face the armies and navies. The necessary changes apply not only to exterior forms; they deeply affect the essence of these two organizations, and the new problems cannot be solved merely by adding an auxiliary aviation of one sort or another.

Another characteristic of the air arm is that it, shall we say, facilitates the waging of war. An Independent Air Force is comparatively much easier to prepare than an army or navy. A thousand 6,000-horsepower planes may cost approximately as much as ten battleships, will need only 20,000 tons of material—about the weight of one average battleship—and will need only 20,000 to 30,000 men, only 4,000 to 5,000 of them pilots. But an Independent Air Force a thousand planes strong can drop on an enemy nation, and every locality in it, from 4,000 to 6,000 tons of bombs on each flight, besides carrying 16,000 to 24,000 machine guns and 2,000 small-caliber cannon for combat in the air. In other words, an offensive capacity the like of which has never before been imagined, and one which only another similar Independent Air Force would be able to oppose and fight.

A thousand airplanes of this kind can be built very quickly by a nation with an adequate industrial organization, and ammunition for it can easily be supplied by a well-organized chemical organization. Instructing and training pilots is no difficult task in a country in which aerial transportation is well developed. Furthermore, a passenger plane can be converted into a military plane in a few hours' time, and its crew can be militarized in no time by simply changing their uniforms.

Thus the hope of revenge can be more easily nourished; for it would no longer imply the destruction of huge armies and formidable navies. Perhaps it has been a mistake to forbid the losers to recreate their army and navy, because that forced them to look toward the sky.

In order to get a better idea of the importance of the action of an Independent Air Force, we can compare the airplane to a special gun capable of firing shells a distance equal to its flying range, and with a special observer to guide the shells to their targets. Then we can compare the Independent Air Force to a large battery of guns which, though stationed over a wide area, can at will concentrate its fire on various objectives within its flying range.

Let us suppose, for instance, that we have in the Padua Valley an Independent Air Force with a range of 1,000 kilometers. The fire of this gun battery could be concentrated at will upon any objective in France, Germany, Austria, Yugoslavia, even on London. Let us think for the moment, not of our Independent Air Force, but of its equivalent, the large gun battery. Our eventual enemy, no matter who he is, will have a similar large gun battery capable of striking us almost anywhere in our territory. What would be the best way for us to ward off these special enemy shells? Certainly we could not put an armored umbrella over the whole country. Obviously, the easiest and most practical way would be to silence the battery by destroying it. And that would be the struggle for the command of the air.

After we had destroyed the enemy gun battery, we would be free to choose targets at our own convenience, because our country would be safe from enemy attacks. Which targets would we choose? Those which best suited our convenience under the circumstances. They might be targets directly affecting the resistance of the enemy, such as his capital cities, industrial and population centers, and so on, in which case we would be choosing to hammer the nation itself to make it give in. Or we could choose the bases and communication lines of the enemy's army in order to weaken its resistance to our army. Or we could attack the enemy's naval bases if the navy was annoying us too much; or destroy the enemy's mercantile ports if the nation was dependent on sea-borne supplies. The selection of targets for our powerful gun battery should be the province of the Supreme Commander of the war, because he would be the only one in possession of all the facts for intelligent selection. But in any and all cases, the battery would have to function in all its mass to get the maximum results from concentration of effort in time and space.

The advantage of having such a large gun battery with which to face an enemy deprived of a similar battery constitutes the value of the command of the air; but as the conquest of it implies the destruction of a similar battery belonging to the enemy, it is evident that not a single gun should be taken from our battery before it has accomplished its purpose. Therefore, aerial defense and auxiliary aviation should be ruled out, because they would be useless anyway if our own battery is destroyed, and superfluous if our battery succeeds in silencing the enemy's.

One more remark: The offensive strength of an Independent Air Force against the surface is determined by the quantity of destructive materials—explosive, incendiary, and poison-gas bombs—it can carry and drop on the enemy. But these materials may be of different efficacies; and therefore it is clear that the destructive power of the Independent Air Force is in direct proportion to the efficacy of the materials employed. Doubling the efficacy of the materials employed is enough to double the offensive power of the Independent Air Force if nothing else is altered. This gives us an idea of the importance of the task of improving the quality of destructive materials or, in other words, the importance of cooperation with war efforts on the part of the chemical industry. The air arm is built and strengthened not only in the aviation training fields, but in the factories where the wonderful air machines are built and in the laboratories where the chemist leans over his test tubes in quest of ever more powerful compounds.

I think I have made clear the importance of the air arm and victory in the air in a future conflict, and the revolutionary changes being made by the air arm on the forms and characteristics of war in its general aspect, including all forms of land and sea conflicts. Logically and rationally our imagination enables us then to visualize the war of the future.

Whatever its aims, the side which decides to go to war will unleash all its aerial forces in mass against the enemy nation the instant the decision is taken, without waiting to declare war formally, trying in this way to exploit to the utmost the factor of surprise by direct attack and by use of the chemical arm. Balanced against the advantages of surprise and prevention of counteraction, the time-honored diplomatic niceties will be discarded. Some morning at dawn capital cities, large centers, and important aviation fields may be struck and shaken as though by an earthquake. For instance, the Germans might decide to destroy Paris instead of fifty French aviation centers, preferring to destroy the heart of France instead of her aviation. Of course, counteraction from enemy aerial forces would not be long in coming; and then, while the aerial struggle rose to the climax of violence, the armies would mobilize and the navies begin their hostile actions, hampered in greater or less degree by aerial offensives. As the aerial struggle neared a decision, aerial offensives from one side against enemy nation, army, and navy would weaken, while similar offensives from the other side would grow stronger and more intense. Then the side which won the command of the air would insure its own territory from any aerial offensives, and the losing side would be helpless against them.

At that moment the most tragic phase of the war would begin. The side dominated from the air would have to fight an unequal fight and resign itself to endure implacable offensives. Its army and navy would have to function with bases and communication lines insecure, exposed to constant threat, against an army and navy with secure bases and lines of communication.

Its sea traffic would be cut off at the ports. All the most vital and vulnerable points in its territory would be subject to cruelly terrifying offensives.

Under these conditions, can a long, slow land war—which needs enormous quantities of supplies, means, labor, and matériel—give the air-dominated side any chance of a favorable decision? That is a question open to grave doubt. In all probability, unless there is a great disproportion of means and resources, a collapse in morale of the air-dominated nation will come before the outcome of war on land and sea could be decided.

Therefore I say, above all else, let us dominate our sky.

CONCLUSION

The picture I have drawn is naturally an imaginative one. Since it is an attempt to visualize the future, it could not be otherwise. But because I have painted with the colors of present realities and drawn according to logical reasoning, I think the future will be very much like my picture. At any rate, I think we can now answer along general lines the question: "What will a war of the near future be like?" with the following positive assertions:

1. It will be a struggle of nations grappling with each other, which will directly affect the lives and property of all citizens.

2. It will be a struggle in which the one who succeeds in conquering the command of the air will have secured a decisive advantage.

3. It will be a very violent struggle, terrifying in its nature, waged in order to strike at the moral resistance of the foe; a struggle which will be decided quickly, and therefore will not be very expensive economically.

4. It will be a struggle in which the side which finds itself unprepared will have no time to get ready; and therefore it will be decided by the forces ready at hand when hostilities begin.

In consequence of the foregoing, an adequate preparation for war at the present time requires:

1. The constitution of an Independent Air Force capable of conquering the command of the air, and the strongest possible to achieve within the limits of our national aerial resources.

2. The readiness of the Independent Air Force at all times, because it has to go into action instantly, even without a declaration of war, and cannot rely on reinforcements before the decision of the aerial struggle is reached.

3. A change in the organization of the army and navy and their methods of war, so as to make them as much as possible independent of bases and lines of communication in order that they may go on functioning even after the enemy has secured command of the air.

4. A study of the problem of co-operation between the armed forces, beginning with the premise that a new set of facts have given rise to different circumstances, showing the various functions each of the forces can perform.

5. A study of all provisions, of various kinds which will put the nation in a position to withstand aerial offensives with the least possible damage. Since the offensives will be aimed mainly at the morale of civilians, national pride and a sense of discipline must be strengthened as much as possible in the masses.

These general characteristics of the war of the future, and the new requirements which ensue from them, show how formidable are the problems concerning national defense which confront us today. I do not intend that my words, meant to show the importance of the air arm's role in future wars, should be construed as minimizing the value of land and sea forces. More than anyone else, I have always asserted that the three armed forces constitute an indivisible whole, a single three-pronged instrument of war. All men and means used to defend their country have the same value—they are all necessary, whether they function on land, on the sea, under the sea, or in the air. In all these fields there are equally important duties to perform, equally important functions to carry on, equal honors to be earned. But that does not mean that, in the interest of the Fatherland, which considers all its sons equals, we should not build a new instrument, more adequate to its defense, by changing when necessary the size, form, and function of any one of its three prongs in order to make it better fitted to bite deeply into the resistance of an eventual enemy.

I think our glance into the future has not been unprofitable, especially if it has been successful in convincing people of two simple truths.

1. All citizens must be interested in the aspects of the war of the future, because all of them will have to fight in it. As I said in the beginning, war is essentially based on common sense, especially in its broad outlines; but because it demands all the material and moral resources of a nation, it cannot be limited to a certain section of the nation, nor to a special class or number of its citizens. All forces and materials, tangible and intangible, have to be marshaled for the prosecution of war; and all citizens must become deeply interested in it, discussing and understanding it, in order to prepare themselves for the ordeal if it should come. If I may be forgiven the heresy, I have often wondered why, in the universities and colleges, where all subjects under the sun are taught, even to Sanskrit, no place has yet been found for the science of war.

2. We must look toward the future with anxious, wide-open eyes to steel ourselves for what may come, so that the reality may not take us by surprise. This is all the more necessary in the revolutionary period we are living through—so much so that he who is not ready will have no time to get ready or to correct the errors of the past. So we must not let ourselves be led astray by the magic of the past. It is always dangerous to keep looking backward when marching forward, and still more so now when the path is full of sharp detours.

Students of war are induced to rely on the experience of the past for their preparation for the future conflict by the fact that theories of war can't be proved except in a real war. This was the reason why the nations who went to war in 1914 entered the conflict with their minds on the War of 1870. But they soon found out their mistake and had to adapt themselves to the exigencies of the 1914 situation. They could do this with comparative ease, in spite of the serious difficulties and tremendous expense they endured in the process, because the intervening time between the two wars was a period of evolution only. But woe to him who tries to fight the war of the future with the theories and systems of 1914!

I do not mean to imply that the experience of past wars should be discarded as useless; I want only to say that it should be taken with a grain of salt—in fact, with a great deal of salt—because the future is closer to the present than to the past. Experience, the teacher of life, can teach a great deal to the man who knows how to interpret experience; but many people misinterpret it. Napoleon was a great captain; but we should not ask Napoleon about what he did, rather about what he would do if he were in our shoes, in our circumstances, in our time. It is likely that Napoleon could give us some valuable advice; but we should not forget that when the Corsican closed his eyes, the world was not yet girdled by ribbons of steel, guns were not yet breech-loading, machine guns were unknown, words were not transmitted over wires or ether waves, the automobile and the airplane were unknown. I think it is a good thing he cannot rise from his splendid tomb. Who knows what words would come from his disdainful lips in scorn of those who too often misuse his name and reputation?

This is the end of my analysis; but before closing it I want to point out an intimate characteristic of the air arm. The colossal armies and navies of today, although they cannot do without the human element, the soul of every machine, cost enormously; and so only the richest nations can afford them and enjoy their advantages. In comparison to these and in proportion to its offensive capacity, the air arm is much less expensive. Moreover, it is still very young and in a state of rapid and constant change. Everything in it, from its organization to its employment, is in the process of creation. The art of aerial warfare is not yet standardized, like the art of land and sea warfare, and there is still room for ingenuity. The war in the air is the true war of movement, in which swift intuition, swifter decision, and still swifter execution are needed. It is the kind of warfare in which the outcome will be largely dependent upon the genius of the commanders. In short, the air arm is the arm of high courage and bold deeds, material and spiritual, physical and intellectual.

The air arm is the arm not of a rich people, but of a young people, ardent, bold, inventive, who love space and height. It is therefore an arm eminently suited to us Italians. The importance it has attained and its influence on the general character of war are favorable to us; it is the arm best suited to the genius of our race; and surely the solid organization and strong discipline which bind the Italian people in unity is the most adequate force to give us courage to face the terrible effects which would come from an aerial war, even if victorious. Our geographical position, which serves us as a bridge across the Mediterranean, makes the air arm still more vital to us. Visualize Rome as the center of a zone with a radius of 1,000 kilometers, normal range for a plane today, and you will find within the circumference the whole of the ancient Roman Empire.

To dominate our own sky will mean to dominate the Mediterranean sky. Let us therefore look to the future with hope and confidence and give thanks to all those whose daring and ingenuity have made this arm powerful.

General William Mitchell

WINGED DEFENSE

The Development and Possibilities of
Modern Air Power—Economic
and Military

―――⟫●⟪―――

BY

WILLIAM MITCHELL

Former Assistant Chief of the Air Force, U.S.A.

1925

CONTENTS

EDITOR'S INTRODUCTION

This selection contains excerpts from Billy Mitchell's *Winged Defense,* a somewhat repetitious and, in his own words, "hastily compiled collection" in August 1925 of articles that had appeared in the *Saturday Evening Post* the previous winter as well as some of his more recent statements before Congress.[1] This reading demonstrates that Mitchell's strong point was not systematic or rigorous thinking. On the one hand, for instance, he offered his geopolitical appreciation that "the vulnerability of the whole country to aircraft" meant that the "former isolation of the United States is a thing of the past."[2] On the other, he concluded that "America could entirely dispense with her sea-going trade if she had to, and continue to exist and defend herself."[3] And of course there were the exaggerations tailored for the popular press that were so much of his exuberant style: Air "transportation is the essence of civilization."[4] But his arguments were sound for the use of civil and commercial aviation and for making institutional and budgetary adjustments in order to take advantage of the airplane's revolutionary potential.

In some respects, the book represented major changes in Mitchell's thinking since the war. At the end of that conflict, he stressed that it was important for an air force not only to support both of the other services, but to use airpower to attack hostile forces directly. The airplane, in other words, could make the task of defeating armies and navies much easier and less costly. In his first book published in 1921, Mitchell recommended an air force that allotted 60 percent of its resources to pursuit and 20 percent each to strategic bombardment and attack.[5] By the time *Winged Defense* was published in 1925, however, the emphasis was clearly on strategic bombardment. To begin with, Mitchell realized that auxiliary airpower provided no justification for an autonomous air force. In addition, he came to believe that auxiliary airpower offered very little hope against the technology of land warfare that he had observed in World War I. In contrast, independently applied airpower in the form of strategic bombers could paralyze an enemy's "vital centers," thus obviating the need to confront enemy surface forces or to even advance through enemy territory on the ground. "The influence of air power on the ability of one nation to impress its will on another in an armed conflict will be decisive," he concluded in *Winged Defense*.[6]

But in an era of isolationism, the linkage of such a conclusion to the offensive power of strategic bombardment could only be made in the most circumspect manner. In the deliberately titled *Winged Defense,* Mitchell wrote of "strings of island bases" that could be used to send U.S. air forces abroad to combat a major enemy.[7] And even these "strategic points" would be unnecessary in the northern hemisphere, where "there is no stretch of water greater than the present cruising range of airplanes that has to be crossed in going from America to Europe or from America to Asia."[8] At the same time, there was more than a hint of Douhet's tendency toward preemption based on the bomber's offensive power. "[I]n the future," Mitchell concluded, "the country that is ready with its air force and jumps on its opponent at once will bring about a speedy and lasting victory. Once an air force has been destroyed it is almost impossible to build it up after hostilities commence."[9]

In other respects, Mitchell's mixed approach to Douhet's concept of offensive decisiveness led to inconsistencies and contradictions. At one point, he argued that strategic bombing would ensure the democratization of future war while diminishing casualties by confining the fighting to specialists skilled in war similar to medieval knights. Mitchell was not clear how airpower would bring this "distinct benefit to civilization"—squaring the circle by asserting that "air forces will attack centers of production . . . not so much the people themselves."[10] But without an assault on populations, the argument for quick, decisive, and thus more humane combat could not be fully realized. This was also true for Mitchell's assertion that in the "future the mere threat of bombing a town . . . will cause it to be evacuated."[11] Equally important was Mitchell's contention throughout the book that air defenses could be effective, and in fact were the only effective defense against hostile air attack. It was an argument in keeping with his personal focus in the book on the defense of the United States. But it was also another qualification to the offensive decisiveness of the bomber that was fundamental to Douhet's theories.[12]

None of this represented any disagreement by Mitchell with Douhet's premise that the airplane was completely unique and potent as an instrument of war. And in fact, Mitchell tied this premise to the notion of air force autonomy by demonstrating how independent air operations, free of control by surface commanders and led by aviation officers with special expertise, could achieve decisive results without supporting land and sea forces. "[T]he one thing that has been definitely proved in all flying services," he testified in 1925, "is that a man must be an airman to handle air power."[13] For Mitchell, only "a community of airmen," his so-called "air-going people" who thought and acted differently from earthbound counterparts, could wage the unique new warfare of the air. It was a romantic vision of "a special class" of chivalrous aerial knights supported by the population—as incongruous as it was appealing in the wake of the attritive horrors of the Great War.[14]

Mitchell's perception of air force uniqueness colored his approach to the navy, particularly after the war when that service was attempting to deal with the adverse public reaction to the expense of navalism. Mitchell compounded those problems with his demonstration bombing against a series of ever larger ships, culminating by the summer of 1921 in the sinking of the dreadnought, *Ostfriesland,* off the Virginia coast. It was a spectacular success that undoubtedly proved that gravity bombs could destroy naval vessels. But that was far too modest a conclusion for Mitchell. The sinking of the great ship was nothing more than proof that the more economical and effective airplane had replaced the battleship as the primary instrument of national power. A battleship cost approximately $45 million to build and equip, he contended, while the price of a bomber was only $20 thousand. This translated into a choice between building one battleship or two thousand bombers, each of which could destroy a battleship.[15]

Such an alternative also translated into naval aviation under Admiral William A. Moffett. "I guess maybe the Navy will get its airplane carrier now," one general conjectured prophetically at the time of the *Ostfriesland* sinking.[16] Mitchell initially favored this development, viewing aircraft carriers as a means to win command of the air over the fleet and then to attack enemy ships. Such climactic air battles, he speculated in 1921, would occur as much as two hundred miles from the carriers, "where hostile gun fire would play no part whatsoever, and where [our] own navy would run no risk."[17] These views survived encounters with the equally strong personality of Admiral Moffett when both men served on a subcommittee during the Washington Naval Conference, which began that year. "When Mitchell breezed in with a secretary, all ready to take the chair," Moffett recalled, "I inquired by what authority he pretended to assume the chairmanship. He mumbled something about rank. 'Since when,' I demanded, 'does a one-star brigadier rate a two-star admiral?' That stopped him."[18]

In a few years, however, Mitchell's enthusiasm for the aircraft carrier began to wane. A major reason was his growing realization that big carriers would allow the Navy to become self-sufficient in airpower and would thus pose a threat to unification of an independent air force. In 1928 he characterized the carriers, then cautiously being adopted by the Navy, as "useless instruments of war because they are the most vulnerable of all ships under air attack."[19] It was a paradoxical connection to the demonstration sinking of the *Ostfriesland* that had given such initial impetus to naval aviation, and one that he had made as early as 1925. "The demonstration was absolutely conclusive," he wrote that year in a magazine article that would become a chapter in *Winged Defense.*

> Sea power as expressed in battleships is almost a thing of the past. . . . As a preliminary step in developing the whole theory of the limitation of armaments, it is believed at this time that it is practical to do away entirely with the surface battleship, the airplane carrier, certain naval bases and dock yards, and many useless and expensive organizations of ground coast defenses.[20]

In the same series of articles, Mitchell also began to attack his own service in addition to the navy as "psychologically unfit to develop this new arm to the fullest extent practicable with the methods and means at hand."[21] As Mitchell's public outbursts became more strident, many army leaders, in General Hap Arnold's description, "seemed to set their mouths tighter, draw more into their shell, and, if anything, take even a narrower point of view of aviation as an offensive power in warfare."[22] In March 1925, the Secretary of War relieved Mitchell as the Assistant Chief of the Air Service, citing his actions as "lawless," "lacking in reasonable teamwork," and "indicative of a personal desire for publicity at the expense of everyone with whom he associated. . . ."[23] The publication of the offending articles in *Winged Defense* the following August only added to the controversy. "Neither armies nor navies can exist unless the air is controlled over them," Mitchell wrote in the preface, adding that "officers in the Air Service with the rank of major, captain and even lieutenant, are charged with responsibilities even greater than those of generals in the Army or Admirals in the Navy."[24] In addition, the cover sheets for the book contained a collection of editorial cartoons from various newspapers that supported Mitchell's cause. This was done by the publisher, ostensibly without Mitchell's knowledge. In any event, it only added to the book's polemical nature.[25]

In early September 1925, even as government officials were examining *Winged Defense,* two naval aviation disasters occurred in quick succession. In response, Mitchell issued a nine-page indictment of "the incompetency, criminal negligence, and almost treasonable administration of the National Defense by the Navy and War Departments."[26] After two weeks of investigation, the War Department decided to court-martial Mitchell, and President Calvin Coolidge himself elected to prefer the charges. At the same time, the president appointed a board under the leadership of banker Dwight Morrow to investigate the status of aviation and to produce a report by the end of November. In his testimony before the Morrow Board, Mitchell was disadvantaged by the limitations imposed by isolationist sentiment as he attempted to focus only on possible attacks on the United States. The lack of any such credible threat undercut his attempts to make his theories tangible. Nor did he help his cause by spending his first four hours in the witness stand reading entire chapters of *Winged Defense* into the official record. "Come on Billy," General Arnold recalled that he wanted to shout, "put down that damned book! Answer their questions and step down, that'll show them!"[27]

The Morrow Board finished its public hearings before the court-martial began on 28 October 1925. The court focused on the conduct of the air theorist. Mitchell, instead, introduced evidence to support his theories, and the trial dragged on. The press, as usual, responded to Mitchell's lead and transformed the case into one of the sensations of the 1920s. Nevertheless, the ultimate result was foreshadowed by the editorial position of most newspapers that Mitchell had gone too far. He was found guilty on 17

December 1925 and was sentenced to five years' suspension from active duty without pay or allowances—later commuted by President Coolidge to five years' suspension at half pay. In one sense, the commutation was a moot action, since Mitchell resigned from the Army on 1 February 1928. But by not dismissing him, the administration had accomplished its objective of forcing Mitchell out without creating a martyr.[28]

Winged Defense did poorly, with only forty-five hundred copies sold in the last five months of 1925, the peak period of court-martial sensationalism. By that time, however, Mitchell had begun to realize that the concept of strategic bombardment rendered in dramatically stark terms stoked the era's publicity process. A five-week trip to Europe in 1927 confirmed him in this belief. But he never fully accepted such Douhetian concepts as the all-purpose "battle-plane" and the emphasis on unrestrained air offense at the expense of any defensive measures. He always kept open the possibility of pursuit aviation development and maintained that an exclusive focus on the air offensive would not be approved by an American public that demanded a defensive effort. By 1930, however, he no longer wavered concerning all-out attacks on populations, the fragility of which he now linked to "the betterment of civilization, because wars will be decided quickly and not drawn on for years."[29] The humanitarian motive notwithstanding, it was still a horrific picture that Mitchell described for his mass audience.

> Picture what the dropping of a gas bomb will mean. . . . This great concentration of gas surges along, entering the lower stories of buildings. Men, women and children come rushing out and fall dead in the streets. Gradually it reaches the upper stories and suffocates those who have stayed inside. . . . The news spreads everywhere of what has happened and just as this comes home to the people a second bomb of the same size or larger hits in another place, then another and

another. There is a wild and disorderly exodus from
the city. . . . The people are helpless. There is only one
alternative and that is surrender. It is a quick way of
deciding a war and really more humane than the present methods of blowing people to bits by cannon projectiles or butchering them with bayonets.[30]

In all this, given Mitchell's antipathy towards the navy, there was
more than a little irony in the similarities between his emerging concept of airpower and Mahan's concerning sea power. At the operational level, both theorists called for aggressive use of force to gain
command of their medium. In Mahan's case, there were the climactic battles between surface ships that would permit control of commerce and access to resources. In Mitchell's case, it was a matter of
either an air battle or the destruction of the enemy airpower on the
ground, whether at airfields or in factories. At the grand strategic
level, the naval theorist saw the basis for American sea power in such
interlocking fundamentals as favorable geography, a strong technological base, and support from both the public and the government.
For Mitchell, the underpinnings of airpower included the vast size
and global involvement of the United States, the creative genius of
the country's people as exemplified by the Wright brothers, and the
need for the public to become "air-minded" and for the government
to provide financial support to aviation. At the same time, there was
a striking parallel between Mahan's linkage of economic growth and
national vigor to Mitchell's call for creating a symbiotic triangular
relationship among military aviation, civilian aviation, and American industries.[31]

WINGED DEFENSE

FOREWORD

This book is dedicated to those officers and men of the air service who have given up their lives in the development of our
national air power.

Few people outside of the air fraternity itself know or understand the dangers that these men face, the lives that they lead and
how they actually act when in the air, how they find their way
across the continent with unerring exactness—over mountains,
forests, rivers and deserts; what they actually do in improving the
science and art of flying and how they feel when engaged in combat with enemy aircraft. No one can explain these things except
the airmen themselves. The number of these who have had experience and who are capable of expressing themselves, is rapidly
growing fewer. Every opportunity should be taken by those that
remain to enlighten their fellows on this subject.

The interest in the development of our national air power was
manifested by the people of the United States during the past
winter, and this interest is growing. The history of the development of air power has been very similar in all countries—it has
had to struggle hard to get on its feet. Air power has brought
with it a new doctrine of war which has caused a complete
rearrangement of the existing systems of national defense, and a

new doctrine of peace which eventually will change the relations of nations with each other due to the universal application and rapidity of aerial transport.

This little book has been thrown together hastily. It is compiled from evidence that has been given before the Congress of the United States, articles that have appeared in the public journals and from personal experiences. Its value lies in the ideas and theories that are advanced which it is necessary for our people to consider very seriously in the development of our whole national system. The great countries of Europe have already acted along the lines indicated in this book. We are still backward.

The book is intended to serve several purposes. First, that of putting down in words what the air men think about the organization of an air force and what our national defense should be. Next, to give to the people in general a book which will set before them facts about aeronautical development. And third, a book to which our people in the services, in the executive departments and in Congress can refer for data on aviation which is modern and which is the result of actual experience. So many erroneous doctrines have been enunciated about aviation by the older services that see in the development of air power the curtailment of their ancient prerogatives, privileges and authority, that we consider it time to challenge these proceedings and to make our own views known.

Aeronautics is such a new and rapidly developing science in the world that those concerned in it have not the age, rank or authority which, in the eyes of the older services, entitles them to speak. Most of the data that Congress gets on the subject of aviation comes from officers or agents who are not actual aeronautical officers and who have not come up through the mill of aeronautical experience, both in war and in peace. The airmen have gained their knowledge by actual experience, not by being members of an old well-established service that has gone on in the same rut of existence for decades.

As transportation is the essence of civilization, aviation furnishes the quickest and most expeditious means of communication that the world has ever known. Heretofore, we have been confined to either the earth or the water as the medium of transportation. Now, we can utilize the air which covers both the earth and the water, and the north and south poles, as the medium through which to travel.

With us air people, the future of our nation is indissolubly bound up in the development of air power. Not only will it insure peace and contentment throughout the nation because, in case of national emergency, air power, properly developed, can hold off any hostile air force which may seek to fly over and attack our country, but it can also hold off any hostile shipping which seeks to cross the oceans and menace our shores. At the same time, our national air power can be used in time of peace for some useful purpose. In this it differs very greatly from the old standing armies and navies which, in time of peace, have to be kept up, trained and administered for war only and are therefore a source of expenditure from which little return is forthcoming until an emergency arises.

The time has come when aviation must be developed for aviation's sake and not as an auxiliary to other existing branches. Unless the progressive elements that enter into our makeup are availed of, we will fall behind in the world's development.

Air power has rudely upset the traditions of the older services. It has been with the greatest difficulty that this new and dominating element has gone forward in the way it has. In the future, no nation can call itself great unless its air power is properly organized and provided for, because air power, both from a military and an economic standpoint, will not only dominate the land but the sea as well. Air power in the future will be a determining factor in international competitions, both military and civil. American characteristics and temperament are particularly suitable to its development.

W.M.

PREFACE

The former isolation of the United States is a thing of the past.

The revolutionary war made us an independent nation; our civil war, the greatest in history, knitted our people and our political fabric closely together. From that time until our Spanish war we were busy organizing our own economical development, establishing means of communication through the country, and consolidating our governmental system. The Spanish war broke down the barriers of our isolation and made us step into the arena of the world powers. The war in itself was no very great affair, but its influence on our own state and on the world was tremendous. We were over-producing commercially and we sought markets for our goods beyond the seas. With our great richness in raw materials, in the development of labor-saving machines, and in the enterprise and energy of the citizenry, we could cope with any other nation in any field of human endeavor that was required.

The World War in Europe, so far as we were concerned, gave us financial pre-eminence. The warring nations had to come to us to get materials to continue their struggle, and we sent them large consignments and in return received financial understandings. Again this was no strain on the United States: comparatively little of our physical force was used. The European countries, however, had to use all their physical powers and reserves at their command.

They emerged from the war with substantially changed military systems. Their national defense services were renovated from top to bottom. Methods in keeping with the times due to their geographical position and their financial ability were adopted. This is not the case in the United States where the old system which is substantially the same system as that used since the civil war, was re-established as firmly as ever. No very great change was brought about in our military methods, either over the land or over the sea, on account of the advent of air power.

Air power may be defined as the ability to do something in the air. It consists of transporting all sorts of things by aircraft from one place to another, and as air covers the whole world there is no place that is immune from influence by aircraft. Starting out as a mere auxiliary in observing for armies and navies, within the four years of the war, air power fought great battles against opposing air power, threw bombs down on hostile industrial centers, cities, railroads and ports, and showed decisively that, should any power in the future be deprived of its air forces, it could in no way hope to cope with an antagonist provided with an adequate air force.

In the United States our people have been slow to realize the changed conditions. Isolated as we have been from possible enemies, the people could see little chance for aggression by others. Separated as we are from Europe by the Atlantic, and from Asia by the Pacific which form most certain and tremendously strong defensive barriers, we seemed to be protected by the design of the Almighty. The coming of aircraft has greatly modified this isolation on account of the great range and speed which these agents of communications are developing. Air ships—that is, lighter-than-air crafts, also called dirigibles—have been designed which will go round the world on one charge of fuel. Airplanes have actually flown for 2,500 miles without landing. This fact, added to the development of chemical warfare and the proof that submarines can cover any part of the seas, have diminished the importance of surface seacraft. The vulnerability of the whole country to aircraft as distinguished from the old conditions that obtained when the frontiers or the coast had to be penetrated before an invasion of the country could be made, has greatly interested the people of the nation.

There never has been any lack of interest by the people in aviation in the United States. What has hindered its development has been the extreme conservatism of the executive departments of the government. The pressure of the people on Congress has resulted in the beginning of decisive congressional action.

For the first time in our history, a committee of Congress, during the winter 1924-1925, conducted hearings on every phase of our national defense as affected by air power, while another committee conducted hearings on a specific provision for the creation of a United Air Force, which could be discussed paragraph by paragraph. The evidence taken showed conclusively that the advent of air power has completely changed all former systems of national defense. Air power not only has decisive military advantages, but most of it can be used in time of peace for some useful purpose.

The hearings before these committees were reported in the public press throughout the country, and for the first time, it was brought home to our citizens what air power means. The frontiers in the old sense—the coast lines or borders—are no longer applicable to the air because aircraft can fly anywhere that there is air. Interior cities are now as subject to attack as those along the coast. Nothing can stop the attack of aircraft except other aircraft.

The evidence shows plainly that the United States has adopted no modern plan of organization for meeting the general world movement in the organization of its air power. It still adheres to the methods and systems of many years ago. This has resulted in a very much retarded development of our aeronautical resources entirely out of proportion with the aeronautical capabilities of our country. We lead the world in undeveloped aeronautical material, our men make the best flyers and mechanics, our factories are capable of turning out the best airplanes, and we have all the raw materials that are necessary.

From a military standpoint, no specific mission is assigned to our national aeronautics. It is regarded as an auxiliary to the Army and Navy. Actually there is no air force in the United States. The system of creating one is so complicated and so difficult to put in motion that an air force could only be brought to a state of efficiency after years of trial, hundreds of mistakes, and the wasting of many lives and millions of dollars in money. In other words, relatively we are little better off than we were at the beginning, of the World War.

Rapidity of modern means of communication, the sureness of various means of transportation, and the accessibility of all parts of the world to aircraft, which have been developed in an incredibly short space of time, make it absolutely necessary that we organize to meet modern conditions. Our various means of national defense must be accurately coördinated because the next contest will increase the swiftness with which decisions are reached and the nation that hangs its destiny on a false preparation will find itself hopelessly outclassed from the beginning.

Neither armies nor navies can exist unless the air is controlled over them. Air forces, on the other hand, are the only independent fighting units of the day, because neither armies nor navies can ascend and fight twenty thousand feet above the earth's surface.

The missions of armies and navies are very greatly changed from what they were. No longer will the tedious and expensive processes of wearing down the enemy's land forces by continuous attacks be resorted to. The air forces will strike immediately at the enemy's manufacturing and food centers, railways, bridges, canals and harbors. The saving of lives, man power and expenditures will be tremendous to the winning side. The losing side will have to accept without question the dominating conditions of its adversary, as he will stop entirely the manufacture of aircraft by the vanquished.

Surface navies have entirely lost their mission of defending a coast because aircraft can destroy or sink any seacraft coming within their radius of operation. In fact, aircraft today are the only effective means of coast protection. Consequently, navies have been pushed out on the high seas. The menace of submarines from below and aircraft from above constitutes such a condition that the surface ship as an element of war is disappearing. Today, the principal weapon in the sea is the submarine with its mine layers, gun fighters and torpedo craft.

In the future, campaigns across the seas will be carried on from land base to land base under the protection of aircraft. Expeditions across the sea such as occurred in the World War will be an impossibility. Water spaces between land bases in the northern hemisphere are very short. The space from America to Asia is only fifty-two miles across the Bering Straits and across the Atlantic it is scarcely more than four hundred.

Air power can hold and organize small islands in a manner which has been entirely impossible heretofore. These can be supplied by other aircraft, or by submarines, with everything that is necessary.

Should it be required to use surface ships, merchantmen may be taken and equipped with flying-off decks for use as airplane transports whenever the necessity arises. Consequently, the power of navies as a keystone in the arch of national defense has been relegated to a secondary position.

Each nation in the world is fully or partially recognizing these principles and is organizing its national defense system accordingly. What is necessary in this country is that the people find out the exact conditions concerning air power and the exact truth about what it can accomplish in time of peace as well as in time of war.

Every man who has had experience in the air is able to aid in this work. It is the biggest constructive program that we have before us. A reasonable solution of this problem clearly indicates that we should have a single Department of National Defense and under it a Department of Aeronautics, Department of the Army, and Department of the Navy. The views of the air must be heard in the national councils on an equal basis with those of the Army and Navy.

The mission of a Department of Aeronautics should be to provide for the complete aeronautical defense and aeronautical development of the country; that of the Army, for the protection of the land areas; that of the Navy, for naval operations out on the high seas and not along the coasts nor on the land.

A United Air Force would provide an aeronautical striking force designed to obtain control of the air and demolish whatever hostile land or water targets might be necessary, according to the military situation.

The personnel situation is very serious in all the Air Services. The air-going people actually form a separate class. They are more different from landsmen than are landsmen from seamen. At the present time, the air-going people in the national services are not accorded the position nor the rank to which the importance of their duties entitles them. Many officers in the Air Service with the rank of major, captain and even lieutenant, are charged with responsibilities even greater than those of generals in the Army or Admirals in the Navy.

Their position on the promotion list is hopeless. Some of our lieutenants can never rise above the rank of major or even captain. They see no future before them and consequently are not in the state of mind in which officers in so rapidly developing a service should be. Without satisfied, energetic, capable personnel, no air service can be developed.

Changes in military systems come about only through the pressure of public opinion or disaster in war. The Army and Navy have regularly organized publicity bureaus which can disseminate information about these services, but there is no medium through which essentially aeronautical information can be disseminated. The result is that the public and Congress are slow to get all the aeronautical facts.

The evidence before both Congressional Committees plainly showed that:

1. There should be a Department of Aeronautics charged with the complete aeronautical defense and the aeronautical development of the country.

2. There should be an aeronautical personnel entirely apart from the Army and Navy.

3. There should be a Department of National Defense with sub-heads for the Air, Army and Navy.

It remains for Congress to translate these principles into law.

I

The Aeronautical Era

The world stands on the threshold of the "aeronautical era." During this epoch the destinies of all people will be controlled through the air.

Our ancestors passed through the "continental era" when they consolidated their power on land and developed their means of communication and intercourse over the land or close to it on the seacoast. Then came the "era of the great navigators," and the competition for the great sea lanes of power, commerce, and communication, which were hitched up and harnessed to the land powers created in the continental era. Now the competition will be for the possession of the unhampered right to traverse and control the most vast, the most important, and the farthest reaching element of the earth, the air, the atmosphere that surrounds us all, that we breathe, live by, and which permeates everything.

Air power has come to stay. But what, it may be asked, is air power? Air power is the ability to do something in or through the air, and as the air covers the whole world, aircraft are able to go anywhere on the planet. They are not dependent on the water as a means of sustentation, nor on the land, to keep them up. Mountains, deserts, oceans, rivers, and forests, offer no obstacles. In a trice, aircraft have set aside all ideas of frontiers. The whole country now becomes the frontier and, in case of war, one place is just as exposed to attack as another place.

Aircraft move hundreds of miles in an incredibly short space of time, so that even if they are reported as coming into a country, across its frontiers, there is no telling where they are going to go to strike. Wherever an object can be seen from the air, aircraft are able to hit it with their guns, bombs, and other weapons. Cities and towns, railway lines and canals cannot be hidden. Not only is this the case on land, it is even more the case on the water, because on the water no object can be concealed unless it dives beneath the surface. Surface seacraft cannot hide, there are no forests, mountains, nor valleys to conceal them. They must stand boldly out on the top of the water.

Aircraft possess the most powerful weapons ever devised by man. They carry not only guns and cannon but heavy missiles that utilize the force of gravity for their propulsion and which can cause more destruction than any other weapon. One of these great bombs hitting a battleship will completely destroy it. Consider what this means to the future systems of national defense. As battleships are relatively difficult to destroy, imagine how much easier it is to sink all other vessels and merchant craft. Aerial siege may be laid against a country so as to prevent any communications with it, ingress or egress, on the surface of the water or even along railways or roads. In case of an insular power which is entirely dependent on its sea lanes of commerce for existence, an air siege of this kind would starve it into submission in a short time.

On the other hand, an attempt to transport large bodies of troops, munitions, and supplies across a great stretch of ocean, by seacraft, as was done during the World War from the United States to Europe, would be an impossibility. At that time aircraft were onl⌐ ᵇˡᵉ to go a hundred miles before replenishing their
f⌐   housand miles and carry weapons which
⌐   ' in the World War. For attacking cities
t⌐   t quantities of war munitions that are

necessary for the maintenance of an enemy army and country in case of war, the air force offers an entirely new method of subduing them. Heretofore, to reach the heart of a country and gain victory in war, the land armies always had to be defeated in the field and a long process of successive military advances made against it. Broken railroad lines, blown up bridges, and destroyed roads, necessitated months of hardships, the loss of thousands of lives, and untold wealth to accomplish. Now an attack from an air force using explosive bombs and gas may cause the complete evacuation of and cessation of industry in these places. This would deprive armies, air forces, and navies even, of their means of maintenance. More than that, aerial torpedoes which are really airplanes kept on their course by gyroscopic instruments and wireless telegraphy, with no pilots on board, can be directed for over a hundred miles in a sufficiently accurate way to hit great cities. So that in future the mere threat of bombing a town by an air force will cause it to be evacuated, and all work in munitions and supply factories to be stopped.

A new set of rules for the conduct of war will have to be devised and a whole new set of ideas of strategy learned by those charged with the conduct of war. No longer is the making of war gauged merely by land and naval forces. Both of these old, well understood factors in conducting war are affected by air power which operates over both of them. Already, we have an entirely new class of people that we may call "the air-going people" as distinguished from the "land-going people" and the "sea-going people." The air-going people have a spirit, language, and customs of their own. These are just as different from those on the ground as those of seamen are from those of land men. In fact, they are much more so because our sea-going and land-going communities have been with us from the inception of time and everybody knows something about them, whereas the air-going people form such a new class that only those engaged in its actual development and the younger generation appreciate what it means.

The airmen fly over the country in all directions constantly, winter and summer they go, as well as by night and by day. The average dweller on the earth never knows that above him aircraft in the United States are speeding between the Atlantic and Pacific and from the northern frontier to the southern frontier, on regular scheduled trips. The pilots of these planes, from vantage points on high, see more of the country, know more about it, and appreciate more what the country means to them than any other class of persons.

Take, for instance, a trip from the east coast out to the Middle States, accomplished in four or five hours. One starts in the morning from the Atlantic. Looking out across it for miles along the coast, the shipping coming from Europe can be plainly seen entering the harbors. Back from the coast itself stretch the industrial cities with their great factories, pushing out to the West; numberless steel lines of railways searching for the gaps in the mountains to take them through to the Middle States; the strip of cities with their heavy populations is passed, then the small farms straggling into the Alleghany Mountains; with the white roads growing fewer and fewer as the Blue Ridge Mountains are approached. Once into the Alleghanies, the utter lack of development makes itself evident at once; as far as the eye can reach there is scarcely a habitation, a road, or a clearing. The inhabitants, deprived of the means of communication, are probably our least educated citizens, although largely the purest-blooded Americans in the country. Across the Alleghanies we reach the rich lands of the Middle States. The great farms seem to crowd themselves against each other in order to produce the largest crops. The country is traversed by well-made roads, railroads, electric power, telegraph, and telephone lines. Bright, clean cities are dotted with splendid schools, fine public works, parks, and hospitals. The development of the animal industry is tremendous; cattle, pigs and sheep are in abundance. While interspersed in this great agricultural country, we still find great cities with high chimneys belching black smoke, indicating the presence of great industries.

A few hours more and the airplane traverses the whole country to the Pacific Coast. Certainly no other class of men appreciate their country or know so much about it as the "air-going fraternity."

The absorbing interest in this new development is so great that the youth of the country everywhere is being inspired to make this their specialty. Bold spirits that before wanted to "go down to the sea in ships," now want to go "up in the air in planes."

The air force has ceased to remain a mere auxiliary service for the purpose of assisting an army or navy in the execution of its task. The air force rises into the air in great masses of airplanes. Future contests will see hundreds of them in one formation. They fight in line, they have their own weapons and their own way of using them, special means of communications, signalling, and of attacking.

Armies on the ground or ships on the water have always fought on one surface because they could not get off it. The air force fights in three dimensions—on the level, from up above, and from underneath. Every air attack on other aircraft is based on the theory of surrounding the enemy in the middle of a sphere with all our own airplanes around the whole periphery shooting at it. If we attack a city or locality, we send airplanes over it at various altitudes from two or three hundred feet up to thirty thousand, all attacking at once so that if any means of defense were devised which could hit airplanes or cause them to be destroyed from the ground, the efforts would be completely nullified, because they could neither see, hear, nor feel all of them. No missile-throwing weapons or any other devices have yet been created or thought of which can actually stop an air attack, so that the only defense against aircraft are other aircraft which will contest the supremacy of the air by air battles. Great contests for control of the air will be the rule in the future. Once supremacy of the air has been established, airplanes can fly over a hostile country at will.

How can a hostile air force be forced to fight, it may be asked, if they do not desire to leave the ground? The air strategist answers: "By finding a location of such importance to the enemy that he must defend it against a bombardment attack by airplanes."

Such a place as New York, for instance, would have to be defended if attacked by hostile bombers, and, as no anti-aircraft guns or other efforts, from the ground alone, would be of any particular avail, aircraft would have to be concentrated for its defense and a succession of great air battles would result. Putting an opponent on the defensive in the air is much more valuable comparatively than putting him on the defensive on the ground. Armies may dig trenches, live in them, or sit around in them waiting for an enemy to attack them. This cannot be done in the air for airplanes have to return to the ground periodically for refueling. If they are not in the air when the hostile air force appears, they will have no effect on it, because they cannot arise to a great altitude and catch it. Consequently, not more than about one-third of an air force can be kept constantly in the air, so that in the future, the country that is ready with its air force and jumps on its opponent at once will bring about a speedy and lasting victory. Once an air force has been destroyed it is almost impossible to build it up after hostilities commence, because the places capable of building aircraft will be bombed and the big air stations that train pilots and flyers will be destroyed. Even if the country on the defensive is able to create small parcels of aviation, they will be destroyed in detail, one after the other, by the victorious air force which not only has control of the air but is protecting its own interior cities that manufacture and turn out their equipment, airplanes, and supplies.

From an aeronautical standpoint, there are three different classes of countries: First, those which are composed of islands subject to air attack from the coast of a continent. In this case the insular country must completely dominate the air if it wishes to use an army against its neighbors so as to be able to transport and land it on the shores of the Continent. If its opponents on the Continent control the air, they can cut off all the insular country's supplies that come over the seas, they can bomb its ports and its interior cities, and, with their air force alone, bring the war to a close.

The second class of country is the one that has a land frontier directly facing and joining its opponent and which is partially self-sustaining and partially dependent on food and supplies from outside, either by railways, by sea, or by air. In this case, there is a possibility that armies might come into hostile contact if the air forces did not act quickly enough. Even then if the air forces of one or the other were ready at the start of the war, all the important cities would be laid waste, the railroads and bridges destroyed, roadways constantly bombed and torn up so as to prevent automobile transportation, and all seaports demolished. Again the air force might bring victory unaided to the side which was able to control the air.

The third class of country is one which is entirely self-sustaining but is out of the ordinary aircraft range. The United States comes under this category. No armed force of an European or Asiatic nation can come against the United States except through the air or over the water. An efficient air force in this instance would be able to protect the country from invasion and would insure its independence but would not be able to subject a hostile country to invasion, or to defeat it without leaving the country itself.

Consequently, an entirely new method of conducting war at a distance will come into being. We have seen that a superior air power will dominate all sea areas when they act from land bases and that no seacraft, whether carrying aircraft or not, is able to contest their aerial supremacy.

Strings of island bases will be seized by the strong powers as strategic points so that their aircraft may fly successively from one to the other and as aircraft themselves can hold these islands against seacraft, comparatively small detachments of troops on the ground will be required for their maintenance. An island, instead of being easily starved out, taken or destroyed by navies as was the case in the past, becomes tremendously strong because it cannot be gotten at by any land forces and, while supremacy of the air is maintained, cannot be taken by sea forces.

In the northern hemisphere there is no stretch of water greater than the present cruising range of airplanes that has to be crossed in going from America to Europe or from America to Asia. The farther north we go the narrower the intervals of water between the continents. The Behring Straits are only fifty-two miles wide, while in their center are two islands that make the widest stretch twenty-one miles, scarcely more distance than across the English Channel. The greatest straight line distance over the narrowest stretch of water between America and Europe is about four hundred miles, or four hours flight.

Cold is no impediment to the action of aircraft. In fact, the colder the weather, the clearer the sky and the better the flying conditions. The sun's rays are what make most of the trouble for the aviator. In the first place, they cause heat, which makes the air hold more water. When the air cools it causes fogs, clouds and haze, because the moisture congeals as the air can no longer hold it. The heat from the sun causes ascending currents of air and the air around rushes in to take the place of the ascending currents. This makes storms of all kinds—causes what we used to call holes in the air, which are merely up and down currents, and introduces much the same difficulties that storms at sea cause to ships.

Light also interferes with our radio or wireless telegraph and telephone communication. Radio waves are really elongated light undulations, and whenever there is light in the air, we hear some of the overtones and undertones from it. That is why the best time for radio telegraphy is at two or three o'clock in the morning when all the light has gone out of the air and before more light has come. That is also the best time for flying because on account of the coldness of the night, the moisture has been deposited on the earth, the absence of light and heat has ceased to make up and down currents in the air and there are no heavy winds. This is the reason why all migratory birds, knowing this, fly at night in their migrations from north to south. It really is easier for the airman to fly at night instead of in the daytime, and in the future much of our traffic, especially for all heavy planes, will be conducted at night. Ice and snow cause the little holes, furrows, and ridges in the ground to be filled with a soft substance that makes natural airdromes everywhere and the sheets of water are turned into ice which can be utilized for landing.

Our aerial routes between the continents will not follow the old land and water ways parallel to the equator which have been used heretofore, because our old means of transportation used to be confined to land and water in warm parts of the earth. The new routes will follow the meridians, straight over the top of the earth, which cut off hundreds of miles, save weeks of time, untold effort, dangers and expense.

What will this new element in warfare result in? Unquestionably, the amelioration and bettering of conditions in war because it will bring quick and lasting results. It will require much less expense as compared with that of the great naval and land armies which have heretofore been the rule and it will cause a whole people to take an increasing interest as to whether a country shall go to war or not, because they are all exposed to attack by aircraft, no matter if they live in the remotest interior of the country.

Now, much of a country's population thinks because it does not live near a seacoast or a land frontier, that its homes will be safe from attack and destruction. The worst that can happen to them, in case of defeat in war, would be higher taxes to pay, and war debts, because navies cannot reach them and armies only with the greatest difficulty. Let us look back and see what warfare used to be and how it evolved.

Primitive man fought his neighbor with his teeth, his hands, and feet. His adversary was killed in the struggle. Great individual fighters developed who were stronger than their fellows. Next, the man obtained a club with which to hold his enemy off at a distance. Then came the thrown missile, such as a stone. Then, getting others to assist him, which in time resulted in what we call "armies" today. Good steel weapons were invented. Great armies were created using steel. This brought them body to body in their contests. Those who were vanquished, were entirely destroyed; their cities looted and burned, and the whole country, laid waste. At that time an entire country went to war. The men fought the enemy while the women and children supplied their wants, manufactured their clothing, and accompanied them on their marches. Gradually, the method of working steel became so excellent that armor could be made which would resist the attack of all known weapons, but, as armor cost a great deal and was hard to get, it developed into a few armed men doing all the fighting for their people. Instead of the armies being universal service institutions in which every man had to take part, as was formerly the case, only a few did the fighting while the others worked at their civil occupations. The advent of gunpowder changed all of this. The knight could no longer resist the peasant armed with a musket and, gradually, all the fighting nations were organized again so that all of their man power could be called to the colors or into the workshops when war was declared. This is the condition that exists today in all countries. The armies themselves, their operations, their strategy, and even their tactics are little different from what they were in the days of the Romans.

As weapons have been improved and made more terrible, such as the long range cannon, the machine gun, and toxic gas, just so much have the total casualties and losses been reduced, because the enemy and those engaged in combat are held further apart. Victories are sharp and decisive because it can be seen what the results will be, long ahead of time, and the defeated side can get away with its men as they are far off from their opponents and not body to body as they were in the days of the Romans.

The Great War in Europe, barely finished at the present time, was not as severe a contest for the fighters as our own Civil War in America was sixty years ago. The casualties at that time were much heavier in proportion to the numbers engaged. The proportion of the population serving under the colors of the armies was also much greater, and the utter destruction of the vanquished states in the South was ten times worse than anything that happened in Europe. This was because in 1914-1918 weapons of greater range were used—the machine gun gave greater defensive strength, and the men fighting were held farther apart.

As air power can hit at a distance, after it controls the air and vanquishes the opposing air power, it will be able to fly anywhere over the hostile country. The menace will be so great that either a state will hesitate to go to war, or, having engaged in war, will make the contest much sharper, more decisive, and more quickly finished. This will result in a diminished loss of life and treasure and will thus be a distinct benefit to civilization. Air forces will attack centers of production of all kinds, means of transportation, agricultural areas, ports and shipping; not so much the people themselves. They will destroy the means of making war because now we cannot cut a limb from a tree, pick a stone from a hill and make it our principal weapon. Today to make war we must have great metal and chemical factories that have to stay in one place, take months to build, and, if destroyed, cannot be replaced in the usual length of a modern war.

Navies, it is interesting to note, came into being as organized units as parts of armies to be used merely as the vehicle of transportation of the soldier so that he could get at close grips with the enemy and determine the possession of the sea areas. As long as the boats were propelled by oars and could go where the army officers told them, with certainty, they remained under the control of the army. Only within the last couple of centuries have the navies become independent of the armies. This came when navies used sails for propulsion and they could not tell with certainty whether they could go where they were ordered or not. Now that steam and the internal combustion engines have come for propelling seacraft, both surface and subsurface, and their power in war has been so tremendously curtailed by the advent of aircraft, it is probable that they will again revert to being an auxiliary of armies and air forces.

A comparatively small part of a population ever serves in navies, and, compared to armies, they, alone, practically never bring a war to an end. They have acted as auxiliaries to an army in clearing the sea of enemy ships, so as to be able to transport an army or to assist it in getting close to its enemy.

In considering the relations between armies, navies and air forces, we may say that the armies have reached an epoch of arrested development in which the controlling factors, as they have always been, are a man's physical strength, his power to march, and his power to see. The use of his weapons entirely depends on these attributes. Their augmentation by mechanical transportation and raised platforms for observation does not alter this general condition. Of course, everything begins and ends on the ground. A person cannot permanently live out on the sea nor can a person live up in the air, so that any decision in war is based on what takes place ultimately on the ground.

The rôle of armies and their way of making war will remain much the same in the future as it has in the past, if air power does not entirely prevent them from operating.

Navies, however, are able to control only the areas of water outside of the cruising radius of aircraft. These areas are constantly diminishing with the increasing flying powers of aircraft. It will be impossible for them to bombard or blockade a coast as they used to, or ascend the rivers, bays, or estuaries of a country adequately provided with air power.

The surface ship, as a means of making war, will gradually disappear, to be replaced by submarines that will act as transports for air forces and destroyers of commerce.

The advent of air power holds out the probability of decreasing the effort and expense required for naval armaments, not only in the craft themselves, but in the great bases, dry docks, and industrial organization that are necessary to maintain them. Differing from land armies, which are in a stage of arrested development, navies are in a period of decline and change. The air force is the great developing power in the world today. It offers not only the hope of increased security at home, but, also, on account of its speed of locomotion, of the greatest civilizing element in the future, because the essence of civilization is rapid transportation. It is probable that future wars again will be conducted by a special class, the air force, as it was by the armored knights in the Middle Ages. Again the whole population will not have to be called out in the event of a national emergency, but only enough of it to man the machines that are the most potent in national defense.

Each year the leading countries of the world are recognizing the value of air power more and more. All of the great nations, except the United States, have adopted a definite air doctrine as distinguished from their sea doctrine and their land doctrine. To develop anything, the underlying thought and reason must govern and then the organization must be built up to meet it. The doctrine of aviation of all of these great countries is that they must have sufficient air power to protect themselves in case they are threatened with war. Each one solves the matter in a way particularly adapted to its own needs.

All of them started out by having the aviation distributed under many different heads—the army having its part, the navy having its part, the civil and commercial aviation their parts, airplane constructors having another part, the weather or meteorological service and wireless communications still another. All of these services considered aviation as auxiliary or subsidiary to some other activity whose principal application was not aviation. Just as the navy always thinks first of the battleships and makes aviation secondary to that, the army thinks of the infantry and also makes aviation a secondary matter.

The armed services of a nation are the most conservative elements in its whole makeup. To begin with, they antedate the governments themselves, because all governments have been brought into being by great popular upheavals which have found expression in military forces. The traditions among all the armed services are much older than any government, more conservative than any department of government, and more sure to build on a foundation that they are certain of rather than to take any chances of making a mistake. As they have changed so little in their methods and ways of conducting war for so many centuries, they always look back to find a precedent for everything that is done.

Hindenburg looked back to Hannibal's battle of Cannæ, and made his dispositions to fight the Russians at Tannenberg. Napoleon studied the campaigns of Alexander the Great and Genghis Khan, the Mongol. The navies drew their inspiration from the battle of Actium in the time of the Romans and the sea fight of Trafalgar.

In the development of air power, one has to look ahead and not backward and figure out what is going to happen, not too much what has happened. That is why the older services have been psychologically unfit to develop this new arm to the fullest extent practicable with the methods and means at hand.

The trend in all nations has been to centralize their aeronautical efforts with a view of developing aviation for aviation's sake first; next, to cut out all the duplication and expense incident to having several agencies do the same thing. . . .

Not every nation is capable of developing an efficient air force. To create one, two things are necessary. First, a strong national morale, a patriotism and love of country which will impel its pilots to withstand tremendously high losses in case of war. Only a few nations have this power. China, for instance, is organized on the basis of family, commercial relations, and a biological supremacy, rather than on a pedestal of national defense by armed forces to keep foreign nations from disturbing her. She cannot create an efficient military aviation at this time because there is no central Government upholding the basic principles or maintaining the ideals which the intelligent people are willing to give up their lives and their all for. On the other hand, the American aviation at the battle of Château Thierry, with seventy-five per cent of its strength killed, wounded, and missing in little over two weeks, kept right on fighting with as great a morale as if these losses had not occurred. Suitable pilots can be drawn only from certain classes, such as the young men who go to our colleges and not only are proficient in their studies, but in athletics such as football, baseball, tennis, polo, and other equestrian exercises which make the body and mind act together quickly. The United States has the greatest reservoir of this kind of personnel of any nation in the world.

The second important element in the creation of an air force is the industrial condition of a country and its supply of raw materials that go into the creation of aeronautical equipment, engines, and airplanes. Seventy-eight different trades are represented in the building of a single plane. From the time it is devised until the time it is turned out in production, it takes as long as it does to build a battleship. Everything in the airplane revolves around the engine. Again we find very few countries capable of manufacturing suitable aeronautical engines. Think what is involved in this—the mining of all metals, their conversion into the toughest and lightest alloys that are known to science, then the designing, building and testing of these engines that weigh scarcely over a pound to the horse power and that are capable of pulling an airplane through the air once they are in flight, with hardly the use of any wings. Again using China as an example we find that no aeronautical engines are made in that country, nor any internal combustion engines for that matter, as her industries have never been organized along those lines. The United States, on the other hand, has the greatest motor industry on the earth, in the form of automobile manufacturers. These are conversant with all phases of the internal combustion, gasoline engine. For this reason we lead the world in the excellence of our aeronautical engines at the present time. At the same time the United States has within its own borders all the raw materials, fuels, and expert laborers that are necessary in the production of aeronautical equipment.

If a nation ambitious for universal conquest gets off to a "flying start" in a war of the future, it may be able to control the whole world more easily than a nation has controlled a continent in the past. The advent of air power has made every country and the world smaller. We do not measure distances by the unit of miles, but by the unit of hours. Communications all over the world today are instantaneous, either by the submarine telegraph, by the land line, or by radio telegraphy. Airplanes can be talked to while in flight anywhere. The airship or Zeppelin can cross any ocean. Should a nation, therefore, attain complete control of the air, it could more nearly master the earth than has ever been the case in the past.

Just as power can be exerted through the air, so can good be done, because there is no place on the earth's surface that air power cannot reach and carry with it the elements of civilization and good that comes from rapid communications.

II

Leadership in Aeronautics Goes to the United States

"There is no royal road to learning." This old saying holds more true in aviation than in any other calling.

In the old and well established branches of learning there is something to go on that has been developed before, that one can model on and study. In aviation, particularly in its application and use, there is almost nothing to go on. The air man has to "learn" himself, for the most part. Every new development, no matter what it is, requires the greatest preparation beforehand to insure its success and with us in aviation it has been essential that we be successful or we might not be allowed to carry on our experiments to the point where they would be of the utmost value to the country. We have constantly before us the example of Langley, who was on the verge of flying his heavier-than-air machine when the ridicule of some caused Congress to withhold funds, and to stop one of the most important single accomplishments that has occurred in the world's history. Fortunately Congress has been pretty good to aviation. Whenever it could see the why and the wherefore, and understood that was actually needed in aviation, it has provided the necessary funds. Furthermore, Congress has a good deal of vision, that is, seeing what might happen and being willing to gamble a little on the result.

A great sum of money was appropriated for aviation during the war and Congress expected immediate results, which, of course, were not forthcoming. At the end of the war it was beginning to be understood that money could not buy knowledge of aviation; that this was a matter of development that required time; that the fault had been not so much in the spending of the appropriation, but in not laying a sound foundation for the spending of the money before the European war started.

Practically nothing had been done by the Government to start a real air service. There were only about fourteen actual flyers when the war in Europe commenced. The prodigious effort put forth by the United States to create an aviation during the war had barely time to show results in the year and nine months of the contest. There was created though, an actual flying personnel; fifteen thousand of our citizens had received instruction in flying. These men were the finest pilot material in the world. Great numbers of factories were making aircraft, and no matter what may have been the reasons for the kinds of aircraft that they were building, they were making the types given them to construct better and more cheaply than any in Europe. Only a few of the flying men and a relatively small part of the material had gotten to Europe when the war ceased. We were still using foreign equipment because there had not been sufficient time to create our own.

It had been conclusively shown that aviation was a dominant element in the making of war even in the comparatively small way in which it was used by the armies in Europe. If either one of the opposing forces had been deprived of their aviation and the routes of the air had been perfectly clear to the other side, the side having the aviation would have been victorious within a couple of weeks.

The European War was only the kindergarten of aviation. It had machines that were just invented, the possibilities of their use were just beginning to be understood by the aviators themselves, while others looked on them as strange creations that were defying all known laws of science, of custom and of war.

During the year 1918, the American aviation received its baptism of fire in a terrific manner. Hurled in the midst of the Château Thierry struggle, with the Allies shot out of the air, we had to evolve our own system and salvation as best we could. Untired by three long years of war, our men thought out many new ways of applying and handling air forces, so that when the armistice came we had a fighting staff entirely conversant with the last minute ways of making air power felt, and pilots that had fought the hardest of air battles, that knew every kink of the air fighting game, and that knew they could defeat in single or Combined combat any aviators of the world.

In addition, we had handled the greatest combined force of aviation ever brought under one command during our St. Mihiel and Argonne operations. When the question was agitated of consolidating the command of water, land, and air under one direction on the Western Front for the campaign of 1919, it is probable that all sea forces would have been commanded by the British, all land forces by the French, and all air forces by the Americans. The power of aeronautical accomplishment was passing to the United States and without a doubt it would have had the utmost influence in settling the war had it lasted another year.

During the spring of 1919, our war-trained men came back from Europe. Most of them were discharged, many could see no future under the conditions under which aviation was being handled in this country, and others wished to return to private life. Enough remained in service, however, to lay the foundation of our future aviation. These men, mixed with the aviation officers that remained in the United States, who had been engaged in training pilots and testing equipment to send to Europe, formed the combination that was capable of thinking out what our air organization should be, more than any other class of men. They knew the actual conditions that existed and had sufficient vision to see what aviation could do in the future.

To the air officer, the conditions of a future war would be entirely and wholly different from anything that occurred in Europe. The armies in Europe at the commencement had no aviation. As each side developed its aviation, it maintained equality in the air, more or less, until within three or four months of the Armistice, when we were gaining a tremendous advantage; sufficient advantage, certainly, to determine the outcome of the war in 1919. On the other hand, any campaign in the United States would involve first a defense of our coast against foreign air or sea forces coming from Europe or Asia. In this, the ground army would have very little part and a properly organized air force could protect the country, not only the frontiers and seaports, but the smallest hamlet in the highest mountains, because all are exposed to air attack. If it became necessary to impose our will on an enemy, the campaign would have to be carried to him through the air because an effective air force on his part would prohibit the transportation across the water of armaments that has been possible in the past. Consequently, our development must be based on the grand hypothesis that future contests will depend primarily on the amount of air power that a nation could produce and apply.

Our own mission in aviation, as Air Officers of the United States, was to demonstrate its practicability, dependability, and efficiency.

The elements of air power are very numerous and complicated. To begin with, the personnel: officers, mechanics, designers, manufacturers, engineers, and inspectors, all have to be created especially for aviation work. This requires a long period of time. It must be based on the proper system of training, while the training, itself, must be based on how air power is to be used. The work of an air force depends on the men that fly the planes, not primarily on those that remain on the ground. The avenues along which military, civil and commercial air power is to be developed must be selected. What we call airways must be organized just as roads had to be laid down for automobiles and refueling stations installed; or, as lines for steamships had to be established with ports where fuel, coal, and oil could be obtained. Just so do our airways have to be made for air power. These airways can be used for both commercial and military planes. In the future we will see the merchant aeronautics alongside the military aeronautics, one being a direct assistance to the other, both using the same airways, the same navigating instruments, and the same methods of flying as the other.

In Europe, during the war, there were no airways because the front was so short that a flight of about two and one-half hours would carry an airplane, even a slow one of that time, from the Atlantic Ocean to the Swiss frontier. The United States had to be ready to organize our airways from the Atlantic to the Pacific, a distance of three thousand miles; and from the northern frontier to the southern frontier, a distance of two thousand miles. The airways had to be connected up by radio communications because we had found that the telephone and telegraph were too slow. We had to put in a weather service so that we could tell thirty-six hours ahead of time what the weather would be and then notify the pilots of the planes in sufficient time that they might be forewarned of fogs, storms or hurricanes. We had to show that we could distribute gasoline and oil, mechanics, and spare parts, to the places selected for landing and we had to show that the whole airway could be controlled from one point, so that in case an air force were stationed in the central part of the country it could move with great rapidity to either coast. More than anything else we had to show that it was practicable for airplanes in considerable numbers even to make a trip from one coast to the other. Most people were still of the opinion that planes could only go a short distance, then would have to stop, be repaired and overhauled. They thought they could fly only in clear weather and that storms, rains, and fogs would stop them. The successful demonstration of the movement of an air force would enable us to control the air along our frontiers and coasts without doubt.

But, even if we were successful in flying across the country, it remained to be demonstrated that we could sink battleships, because, in Europe, the war had been won on land. The Allies held the sea to a greater extent than any nation ever has in the past. Aircraft, therefore, had not been used to any appreciable extent against shipping. It had to be demonstrated that we could fly over the water as easily as we could fly over the land, and that we could work at night as well as by day. We had to perfect weapons and sights for hitting objects on the ground and water and methods of flying in all kinds of weather, in all climates, and under all conditions.

To put these things into effect we had almost no precedent to follow. We had to think them out for ourselves and then proceed to put our ideas and theories to the test. Many of the appliances and the equipment had to be made for the first time and a great deal of the equipment we possessed had to be used in a manner for which it was not designed because all of the aeronautical equipment had been made for service on the western front in Europe. Fortunately, we had the Liberty engine which had been perfected and had become the most reliable aeronautical engine in the world. We had a great accumulation of aviation material: guns, bombs, and instruments, which had never been sent to Europe and which, if not used within a short time, would deteriorate so that it would be useless.

The greatest of all of our assets, however, were the wonderful pilots and air officers which this country had created. They were filled with enthusiasm, with the full knowledge that air power was the dominating factor in the world's development, and with a perfect willingness on their part to give up their lives to demonstrating its usefulness and to bringing this great, new development to the point that would make America the world's leader in aviation. In 1919 we laid out a plan of development, which, although delayed at times, has been and is being followed at the present time.

The theory is to show that aeronautics can establish airways anywhere in the world and be able to operate from them; that wherever air power can operate, it can dominate sea areas against navies, and land areas against armies; that aircraft can establish the most rapid communication ever known between all of the great centers of population of the world and to the most remote and inaccessible points. This would give to all people, no matter how far removed from civilization, the benefits of rapid communication and the services that go with it. It was and still is a hard problem but the strides towards its solution by the American Air Service since 1919 have been tremendous.

Our first practical trial of these ideas came in the summer of 1919. We organized a definite airway across the continent of the United States, from New York to San Francisco. This had airdromes every two hundred miles, with intermediate landing fields every fifty miles, all of them connected by telegraph, telephone, and some by radio. We had a weather service installed and had gasoline, oil, mechanics, and spare parts distributed to all airdromes. After we actually began work, it took us only two weeks to put in this airway. The arrangements were as complete as was necessary for any operation, even with what we know now, with the exception of night lighting for the airway, which had not been developed at that time. Our airplanes, also, were not suitable for night work. . . .

The continental speed tests of 1919 really marked the beginning of the leadership of America in the application of air power, that is, in demonstrating how air power could actually be used, which has continued up to the present time. Our accomplishments have borne a great deal of fruit. They have been watched by the foreign nations even more carefully than they have been by our own Government, and the lessons from them have been carefully digested and methods adopted to use the advantageous features. In this way we have paid, to a very great extent, for the pioneering and experimentation, while others and the whole world have derived benefit.

During all of this time we were working on our bombs and equipment for sinking battleships. Try as we might, we could not get battleship targets from either the War or Navy Department in either the year 1919 or 1920. We gave intensive training, however, to our pilots in bombing and worked hard on our bomb sights, methods of navigation and tactics for this purpose.

Having demonstrated that we could go across the United States, we wanted to demonstrate that we could establish an airway to Alaska and Asia. The chance came in 1920, when, with the assistance of the Canadian authorities, we established an airway from New York through Canada to Alaska and Nome. Captain Streett took four airplanes from New York to Nome in the flying time of fifty-four hours, and returned in approximately the same time, without the loss of an airplane or a man. The airway again worked perfectly. At Nome, Captain Streett's men stood on the threshold of Asia and could have crossed to Siberia in an hour and a half's time. The reason that they did not was that we had no diplomatic relations with Russia and our State Department did not wish us to land in Russian territory. At that time, even, we could have made the circuit of the globe had we been allowed to prepare for it.

There was now no doubt that airways could be established anywhere desired in the world, and that not only military but also civil and commercial aviation could be used along them. The only question that remained was, to find out what it would be economical to use civil aviation for; in other words, what the relative cost between transportation by air, transportation on the ground and on the water would be and what articles could be transported with profit. In a military way, as to what actually could be accomplished from these airways in the attack of land and water establishments. . . .

We saw that our armament was rapidly becoming sufficiently perfected to destroy the greatest battleships. The sinking of ordinary merchant vessels, torpedo boats, or destroyers and cruisers, is comparatively easy, but to destroy the great battleships is a different matter. These war vessels have been developed consistently from the days of the old galleys: First, they were heavily armored against attack from missile-throwing weapons and cannon against their sides; next, the decks were armored for protection from plunging fire falling from great heights against them; then, after the advent of the torpedo, their sides were honeycombed so that any wound against them under the water line would be localized and would not affect the whole ship and cause her to sink.

It had always been held as a principle that the vessel had to be hit directly by a thrown missile in order to affect it. In studying the battleship, we found that its bottom was its most vulnerable place. It contained no armor and had sticking out of it the open water pipe connecting with the condenser system. The use of the water hammer, or water impelled with great force by an explosion under the bottom of the vessel would certainly cave in the bottom, spring the seams, and cause the vessel to sink. Most of us remember how, when boys, we knocked two stones together when diving under water and what an effect this had on our ears. It is this force that we utilize in attacking ships in the water. Explosions deep in the water at a distance from the ship would break the condenser system, which would stop the vessel from steaming. In fact, one of the most vulnerable points in a battleship is the condenser system. The propellers and their shafts could be bent, the rudder damaged, and the whole under water integrity of the vessel would be deranged. So we determined the best depths in the water at which bombs should explode to get these effects and made our fuses accordingly. These tremendous missiles, containing upwards of one thousand pounds of TNT, could not be tested in any ordinary way. We had to try them in water of various depths, taking note where they exploded merely by looking at them, because any instruments, nets, or wires designed to tell at what depth detonations took place, would be blown entirely to pieces and show nothing. We carried out the experiments in the water in the upper part of Chesapeake Bay near Aberdeen, Maryland. These terrible detonations killed thousands of fish, tore up the bottom, and stopped traffic in the vicinity while the experiments went on. The fuses of these great bombs were also arranged so that if they actually hit a vessel on its deck, they would cause an explosion which would dish or crack the deck, smash up the superstructure, tear down the masts, kill all exposed personnel by the detonation and others by the concussion, put out of commission the telephones, electric light systems, and speaking tubes, and would probably blow up the magazines and the boilers. One very serious difficulty in a modern battleship is its weight, due to its armor, which makes it quite top-heavy and easily unbalanced and sunk by the explosion of a bomb close to it under the water line.

Our experiments had gone forward so far in the fall of 1920 that I was able to announce definitely to Congress that we could destroy, put out of commission, and sink any battleship in existence or any that could be built. This resulted in an interesting controversy that merely showed how any innovation, particularly in methods of warfare, is kept down by the more conservative elements. It is an amusing fact that the Secretary of the Navy at that time announced that these things could not be done and that he was willing to stand on the bridge of the ship while we bombed it. Congress, however, took another view and Mr. Anthony in the House of Representatives, and Senator New in the Senate, introduced resolutions authorizing the President of the United States to designate warships to be used as targets for our experiments. Fortunately, the German prizes of war were about to be turned over to the United States, and, under the conditions, they had to be destroyed within a certain time, the idea being to let the various allied countries learn all the lessons they could from them, then sink them so as not to add them to their naval strength.

Forced to action by the joint resolutions of Congress, the Navy Department began drawing up conditions under which these vessels should be destroyed. There were several classes of ships: Submarines, destroyers, a beautiful cruiser, the Frankfurt, and the dreadnaught Ostfriesland. This splendid ship was designed under the German Admiral Von Tirpitz' orders especially for use in the North Sea against England, where many mines and torpedo attacks could be expected. Her under water construction was the best known and remains a good pattern to this day. Her water-tight compartments were many and each one had solid bulkheads or partitions not even pierced by doors, so that there would be no chances of there being openings in them in case one or more were flooded. She had three skins to her bottom and, of course, was very heavily armored. She was called the "unsinkable ship." She had participated in the battle of Jutland, had been hit by many projectiles, among them some of large caliber, and in addition two mines had hit her below the water line. In spite of this, she had made harbor under her own steam and had been thoroughly repaired. She was indeed a hard nut for us to crack on our initial attempt at something that had never been tried before. We had meetings between naval officers and air officers to arrange a program of bombing so that the maximum amount of knowledge could be gained from the experiments. The navy insisted on anchoring these target ships on what is known as the one hundred fathom curve which lies about seventy-five miles out to sea from the mouth of Chesapeake Bay. . . .

The reason that the ships were anchored in one hundred fathoms was because it was required that they be sunk in deep water by the terms of the international agreement, and, next, our bombs would not have so great an effect as they would if the water were shallow. In shallow water, if we can burst the bombs against the bottom, they explode up and against the bottoms of the vessels with very much greater force than where the water is deeper, in which case there is no "tamp" upward against shipping.

It was up to us, however, to show that what we advocated could be done, so we had to accept the conditions as they were offered. These made us operate under conditions that were about as hard as could be drawn up for the accomplishment of the difficult experiment.

Meanwhile, orders had been issued all over the United States for the concentration of our pilots and airplanes at Langley Field, Virginia. This airdrome lies only a short way from Hampton, which is one of the oldest, continuously inhabited, towns in America. It lies not far from where General McClellan's army, equipped with the first military aircraft in the form of Professor Lowe's balloons, invested Yorktown in 1862; where Cornwallis surrendered to General Washington and Lafayette; and only a few miles from Jamestown where John Smith planted his colony; and from where the Monitor and Merrimac had their great struggle. The results of the bombing might hold more far reaching consequences than even those events. Our pilots, observers, and mechanics had their imaginations fired with these events in our history, and were determined that the maximum results should be accomplished by our little air force.

The airplanes started coming in from the West, from the North and from the South. Three heavy bombers—one Handley-Page and two Capronis—made the flight from Texas. It was the first time that a continuous flight had been made by these large ships for such a distance. With them came their veteran crews of the Border Patrol.

What had remained of our air force had been deployed along the Mexican Border in 1919 and 1920, so as to protect our frontier in case of trouble. Our Martin bombers, large two-engined airplanes, had never been tried out in service for they were just being finished in the Martin airplane factory at Cleveland, Ohio. Our experience in flying large bombers from Italy to the western front in Europe had been quite disastrous, as nearly all crashed in transit across the Alps, and great fears were entertained that many accidents would happen to these great ships on their long journey. The planes were so well built, however, the crews so expert, that not one of the thirty transported was destroyed en route.

As each airplane came in it was assigned to its particular organization. The staff was organized along the same lines that we had found to be the best in Europe and regular plans were drawn up for the whole organization and for every operation. The air force was known as the First Provisional Air Brigade and it had every element necessary for the operation of a large air force. A pursuit aviation under Captain Baucom, who had so greatly distinguished himself in Europe, was organized to act as protection to the great bombers in case they were attacked by hostile pursuit aircraft. The light weight bombers, for which we used the old De Haviland airplanes, were designed to attack torpedo craft, transports, and light vessels, and, in case the anti-aircraft artillery from the warships amounted to anything serious, they could attack the big ships with their light bombs and machine guns at close quarters so as to nullify any effect against the heavy bombers from this source.

The heavy Martin bombers with their cruising ability of five hundred and fifty miles and their power to lift from two to three thousand pounds of bombs, were the most powerful airplanes that we had ever had. At first our men were unaccustomed to them and were a little nervous when flying them with their full loads, but they soon found how very airworthy they were and gained the utmost confidence in them.

The crews were first trained carefully over the land and then began working over the water. Both still and moving targets were used and, in some cases, automobiles were run along the roads to indicate the maximum speed at which seacraft might be able to go on water. Corners were turned and all changes of course in dodging on the part of the war vessels were simulated. Each class of seacraft was carefully studied and all of the personnel made familiar not only with their appearance, but with their structure and the sizes of bombs that were necessary to destroy each class of boat.

We were allowed to use only one weapon in the first maneuvers against the ships anchored off the Virginia capes. These were our high explosive bombs. Air forces, of course, can use contact mines, gas and smoke screens of various kinds, phosphorus bombs, thermite to cause great heat, water torpedoes, air torpedoes, and gliding bombs. The use of these weapons was explained and taught to our officers. . . .

Within a couple of months before the coming of the warships the organization of the Brigade at Langley Field was complete. Practice was begun over the water. First, we drew out a silhouette of a battleship on a marshy point near the mouth of the Back River, marking the exact points where the bombs should hit. It was practiced on every day. Then we obtained a tug and towed a target representing a battleship out into the Chesapeake. The bombing became so accurate that the crew of the tug had no fear in using a line only about three hundred feet long. Every day direct hits were made on these structures with our one hundred pound, sand loaded bombs, so that it was hard to keep sufficient targets on hand. Next, we bombed the wrecks of the old battleships, Texas and Indiana, close to Tangier Island, about fifty-four miles away from the airdrome. On these we used live bombs of heavy weight.

There, in the haze of the morning and evening, we ran into quite unusual conditions. As we were about eight miles away from the nearest land, it was often invisible and we found ourselves with no horizon or point of reference by which to level our planes, because everything was the same color—air, sky, and water. It was very much as if we were in the inside of a sphere all painted the same hue. Many who had had experience in overwater flying had held that it was impossible to level an airplane so that good bombing could be done for this reason, but we soon found by the aid of a gyroscope brought to us by Lawrence Sperry of the Sperry Aircraft Company, that we had no difficulty in maintaining direction or flying the planes on a level keel. One learns these things only by actual air work and experience. With the comparatively crude bomb sights that we had, this was a most important consideration. By that time our bombing, on all sorts of targets, was becoming so accurate that even the most doubting of our officers knew that whether hostile seacraft were at rest or moving, no matter how fast, there would be no difficulty in hitting them.

We then practiced at night. The airplanes left in formations at night, went through their regular bombing practice in the same way they did in the daytime, searched for their targets out over the water, signalled to each other and made their attacks. Each one of the Martin bombers was provided with radio telephones so that one plane could talk to the other. Flights were now made up and down the coast and every one was made familiar with the distinguishing marks on the various lighthouses and life-saving stations, and the places where suitable landings could be made in case of emergency.

As the time became shorter before the arrival of the target ships, the excitement grew.

Our bombs began to come in—the three hundred pounders, the six hundred pounders, and, last, the eleven hundred pounders. We had had some concrete bombs made the same size, shape and weight as the two thousand pounds. With these we had tested the bomb carriers on the airplanes and the mechanism for dropping them, as to insure their proper functioning. We took up a few of the bombs and dropped them to see if everything worked satisfactorily. Not one of these bombs failed us in any way. Their shapes made them fall straighter than any bombs we had ever seen used in Europe or in this country, and their fuses were the best we had ever seen. Still, our two thousand pound bombs did not arrive and as the months shortened into weeks and the weeks into days before the tests were to take place, we grew a little nervous at their non-delivery. At last we found that these monster weapons were on their way and learned one cause why they had been so late. It seems that the steel bomb cases had barely been finished two weeks before the test. It took several days to install the fuses and then the half ton of TNT had to be poured into each one of them in a molten condition. No one had known before that it took such great masses of TNT a very long time to cool. In the ordinary summer temperature it would have taken ten days or two weeks before they would have been ready for shipment, in which case they would have been too late, so, to overcome this, our resourceful Ordnance Department packed each one in ice so that within a couple of days they were on their way. They reached us just in the nick of time and were stored in our ammunition dumps with sand bags piled around them to localize any explosion in case one went off. This would have done little good, however because, if a single one had detonated, probably the whole airdrome with all of its equipment would have been destroyed together with most of the personnel at that place.

The First Provisional Air Brigade was now ready to attack any warships or fleet of warships which could have been sent against that part of the coast.

The personnel was experienced with all of the difficulties incident to using the great bombs and knew how to obtain the best results from them. We also had the best planes that we could get hold of, but they were not at all suitable for work at sea, as they had been designed for work in Europe. Some of the little pursuit planes had only sufficient gas to get out to the target battleships and back again, but their pilots were determined to go even though they might have to land in the sea and be rescued by one of the patrol vessels. The First Provisional Air Brigade was also supplied with a squadron of seaplanes, equipped for rescue purposes, with doctors, first aid equipment, and means for carrying patients. These, however, did not prove very successful because seaplanes, when required to land in heavy waves, usually smash in their bottoms and often sink more quickly than the ordinary airplane buoyed up by the air in its wings. The seaplane squadron was carefully trained in the work for which it was intended, and wherever it had smooth water to land in, did good work.

In our large lighter-than-air hangar we had four small dirigible airships. These had the ability of staying in the air from twenty-four to thirty hours and of making a speed of about sixty miles per hour. They could operate by night or by day. They, also, were trained in rescue work so that if forced landings in water occurred, they were able to go down near the water, drop rope ladders down to the swimmers, and haul them up to safety. This was practiced at different times in the middle of Chesapeake Bay. In addition to their rescue work, they were trained for reconnaissance service, and, because they had very powerful radio telegraph installations on board, they could be heard for long distances, much further than the airplanes. Their use was particularly efficient at night when they themselves could not be seen but when they could easily distinguish shipping on the surface of the water, either by seeing the ship directly or by dropping the large calcium flares which produce lights of several hundred thousand candle power, that illuminate great stretches of the ocean. Ordinarily, they had little trouble at night in picking up seacraft on account of the phosphorescent wake and the white waves thrown up by the bows and sterns of the vessels.

We had photographic planes equipped with both still and motion picture cameras so as to make a complete record of every shot. We had a completely organized meteorological service and the means of transmitting weather information to all of our airplane squadrons and of predicting weather from twenty-four to thirty hours ahead of time. Cloud flying, rain flying, and flying in storms were practiced and well understood by all. . . .

At last the day arrived when the target warships were put into position and we were given orders to stand by for the first attack.

We were now to be given a chance to prove whether aircraft could actually sink the latest types of battleships. If this were successful, it would mean eventually that aircraft would control all traffic on the seven seas and that, as they would eventually be able to destroy and attack all communications on land, the outcome of these maneuvers would cause an entire rearrangement of the elements of national defense which each country possessed at that time.

III

THE UNITED STATES AIR FORCE
PROVES THAT AIRCRAFT
DOMINATE SEACRAFT

The stately Atlantic fleet, consisting of eight battleships, several cruisers, many destroyers and auxiliary vessels, hospital ships and tenders, moved into the Chesapeake Bay and anchored in the Lynnhaven Roads. The appearance of these great vessels was majestic. The fleet had been assembled to watch and observe the bombing tests, so that all could see what happened. Many considered this trial to be utterly useless, because they reasoned that it was entirely impossible to sink, or even injure, a battleship. That, neither could a battleship be hit by an aerial bomb, and, if it were hit, could it be damaged to any great extent. These people little knew the great accuracy of aerial bombing, which at the present time, at battle ranges, is perhaps the most accurate method of hurling missiles. Also on account of the tremendous proportional amount of explosives carried in the bombs they constitute the most powerful weapon of their kind ever devised by man.

On the other hand, the officers and men of the First Provisional Air Brigade were certain that their efforts would be crowned with success. They were eager to have their theories put to the test.

The first trial took place on June 2, 1921, against the ex-German submarine U-117. It was anchored on the target grounds, about seventy-five miles off the Capes, in an awash condition. The day was perfect and the line of the destroyers placed at ten mile intervals across the Chesapeake Bay and from the Capes out to the target ships, looked like little beetles in the molten sea as we sped over them.

The first air units to attack this submarine were three flying boats of the Naval Air Service, commanded by Lieutenant Thomas. They flew close together in a "V" shaped formation, and each dropped one bomb for sighting purposes, as they passed over the target. The practice was perfect and each missile either hit the submarine or struck within a few feet of it. Making a turn, they came back dropping three bombs each, or a total of nine bombs. These bombs weighed one hundred and eighty pounds each. The center of impact of this volley struck the submarine squarely, split her in two and down she went.

None, except the air people, had expected such a rapid termination of the first experience. Had she been fired at with cannon no such result could have been obtained—she would have been hit above the water line and would have had to fill up with water gradually before she would have gone down. These bombs tore her all to pieces above the water, below the water, and along the water line. Some of the skeptics began to be convinced that there was something to air bombing. It was a very severe jolt for those who still adhered to the old theories.

This was not all: The vessel that was directing the target practice, which remained about a mile and a half away from the submarine, had her condenser system so badly damaged that she steamed into the Chesapeake Bay that night at only three knots an hour. If these small bombs could produce such an under-water shock as to affect a warship's condenser system a mile and a half off, what could the big bombs do?

The discussions waxed stronger than ever, and the Congressmen, naval officers, press representatives, and guests on the Naval Transport Henderson spent the night in terrific arguments. These arguments, however, were soon to have their answer.

A couple of days later, the Army Air Service was given as a target the "ex-German Torpedo Destroyer G-102." She was one of the large type boats of this class, employed so successfully by the Germans. Our Air Brigade moved out with all its different parts in exactly the same way that it would have attacked any sea force, equipped with airplane carriers and airplanes. First came the pursuit ships, eighteen of them, flying in three flights, so that they could attack, underneath, up above, or on the same level, any enemy pursuit ships which might contest their progress. They not only had their machine guns, but each plane carried four twenty-five pound bombs to be used against the ship's super-structure, anti-aircraft guns, searchlights, and personnel, so as to sweep the deck clear and interfere with her navigation. Should one of these small bombs be dropped down the funnel into the boiler rooms and detonate, it would cause the boiler to explode, and, of course, blow up the vessel.

The pursuit pilots thought they would be able to sink this vessel alone with their twenty-five pound bombs, but I hesitated a long time before allowing them to go so far to sea, as their old airplanes had only a two hours supply of gas. They insisted on being allowed to go, however, so that they could carry out their allotted part in the maneuvers.

Following the pursuit aviation, went the light weight bombardment squadrons of DH two seaters, each plane equipped with four one hundred pound bombs. These bombs alone were sufficient to sink a destroyer or any unarmored ship, and in case a battleship was attacked, they could at least clear the decks of any exposed personnel, smash up the communicating and radio systems, and probably bend the battleship's propeller shafts and rudders, so that even a heavily armored vessel could not be worked after an attack with these light bombs.

Following the light weight bombers, came the heavy Martins, a dozen of them, each equipped with six three hundred pound bombs. They sped along in their "V" formation about two miles behind the DH squadrons. It was the first time in aeronautical history that an attack had been made in this way. Every element of a large air force was there. First the pursuit aviation to take care of the opposing aviation, and, after having conquered it, to attack with their machine guns and bombs the decks of the war vessels. Next the light weight bombardment to scatter and destroy the auxiliary vessels of the battleships, such as cruisers, destroyers, and submarines, and, last, the heavy weight bombers to sink and destroy the battleships themselves.

We had been allotted this destroyer to attack in any way we saw fit, not with restricted conditions as was the case with the other vessels, so I took this occasion to have the whole air brigade take part so that all could see that the plans that we had worked out were correct, which they proved to be.

I accompanied every bombing mission of the airplanes over the sea in my control ship the "Osprey," a two seater DH plane, with sufficient gas in it to fly for five hundred miles. On that day Lieutenant Johnson accompanied me in a brand new Thomas Morse single seater pursuit airplane. It was able to go about one hundred and seventy miles an hour. I used him as a courier, signalling to him what I wished to be done. He would go and return with the information in a very short time in this very fast plane.

As we approached the target vessel we could see the whole Atlantic Fleet formed in a circle around it. We wound our way in and out of great banks of cirrocumulus clouds behind which we could have concealed our approach very easily had it been actual war. As the pursuit squadron arrived over the target, they formed into a large "V," preparatory to attacking with bombs, as it was assumed that the hostile pursuit aviation had been defeated in the air battle. Captain Baucom, leading them, gave the signal for the attack and one after another in regular cadence dove for the destroyer, coming straight out of the heavens for three thousand feet. Straight toward the destroyer they went until within two hundred feet of it when they let go one of their bombs. The airplanes followed each other at about thirty second intervals, so that there was a continuous stream of bombs against the target. It had been decided beforehand that a certain number of bombs should be fired at the decks, a few exploded in the water alongside, and some hits made down the funnels in the expectation that these small bombs alone might sink the vessel. The attack was beautiful to watch; the accuracy of the bombing was remarkable, practically every bomb went where it was directed. The decks of the destroyer were punctured and swept from end to end. Lieutenant Alsworth put one bomb straight down one of the funnels, which undoubtedly would have blown up the boilers. Every one was surprised at the great accuracy of this bombing.

Under cover of the pursuit attack the light weight bombardment airplanes with their hundred pound bombs moved up. The method for attack found to be the best was to fly one airplane behind the other at a distance of about two hundred yards, so as to bring a succession of bombs falling at the target with only a few seconds interval between them. In this way, one airplane could correct from the other's fire in front. Also, it would be impossible for a vessel to escape by changing its course or dodging, because it would be seen from the airplane succeeding in the column and its fire would be corrected accordingly. We had taken up so much time in the pursuit attack that I feared the fuel would run short in the two seaters, so I called off this attack and ordered the Martin bombers to finish the destroyer. They moved up at once, directly into the wind, led by Captain Lawson, who so greatly distinguished himself in all of the bombing. Behind him stretched the squadron of twelve great airplanes. In less time than it takes to tell it their bombs began churning the water around the destroyer. They hit close in front of it, behind it, opposite its side and directly in its center. Columns of water rose for hundreds of feet into the air. For a few moments the vessel looked as if it was on fire, smoke came out of its funnels and vapors along its decks. Then it broke completely in two in the middle and sank down out of sight.

The demonstration was absolutely conclusive. While it was not particularly difficult to sink the vessel itself, those who thought any anti-aircraft guns could keep off an air attack, saw that it was now impossible because under cover of pursuit and light weight bombardment aviation, the larger bombers could move in with little danger. All our methods and systems of bombing had proven to be correct. The bombs themselves never failed to explode. The accuracy was remarkable and the spirits of every man ran high. We had, however, stretched our cruising ability out at sea to the limit with some of the old airplanes that we possessed. Many of the planes of the pursuit squadron barely got back to the shores of the coast where they landed along the beach. All the airplanes we had except the Martin bombers were obsolescent war machines entirely unsuited for this work. There were no injuries and no forced landing in the water, and due to the excellence of our mechanics very little trouble was experienced with the engines. This again surprised the onlookers, who had expected the airplanes to fall into the water and that disaster might attend our efforts. . . .

That night all of our men had returned safely to Langley Field after their first great experience in bombing. The rejoicing was tremendous. They knew now that unless something most unusual happened, it would be proven for all time that aircraft dominated seacraft.

The next operation scheduled was to search for and find a battleship that was supposed to be located anywhere between the mouth of the Delaware River and the mouth of the Chesapeake Bay, and then to bomb it with sand loaded bombs. It was to be under steam and controlled by radio telegraphy. Its speed was only six knots an hour under these circumstances. This was such a simple problem that there was no use of sending any airplanes out over the water for that purpose, particularly as we had so few of them and as this test would give us very little practical benefit. So some of the dirigible airships were sent out and promptly found the ship, which was the Iowa, and sent back news of its whereabouts. Seacraft are not only very easy to find, but their type and character are also as easy to determine from the air.

The air bombs had now sunk the unarmored ships, that is, the submarine and destroyer. These tests did show conclusively that planes could sink merchantmen, transports, or any kind of a vessel not protected by armor.

Our next target was to be the cruiser Frankfurt, a beautiful vessel. It had considerable side-armor, deck-armor, excellent watertight compartments and bulkheads, and every perfection of a modern vessel of that class. The tests were to be conducted with varying sizes of bombs and after each attack with a specified number of bombs which was not intended to sink the ship, an inspection would be made by officers of the navy to see what damage had been inflicted. These tests started on July 18th, and, of course, the interest grew as they went on. First one hundred pound bombs were tried, and then three hundred pound bombs. The three hundred pound bombs, undoubtedly, would have sunk the ship had not this part of the test been called off by the navy. The vessel was then thoroughly inspected and the damage resulting noted. At last came our chance to attack the cruiser with the six hundred pound bombs and again Captain Lawson led his squadron to the ship. At that time the Board of Inspection was so slow that they kept us flying around way out at sea about an hour before Captain Lawson had to signal that unless he was allowed to attack within fifteen minutes, he would have to return to shore on account of lack of gas. At last came the order to go ahead. Captain Lawson deployed his bombers into single column and immediately went for the target. The bombs fell so fast that the attack could not be stopped before mortal damage had been done to the ship. The control vessel made the signal to cease bombing as the good ship was toppling over, so quick was the effect of the bombs.

Many amusing things occurred. At the first direct hit of a bomb on the Frankfurt's deck, fragments of steel were thrown over the water for over a mile. The crews of the observing battleships had crowded to the rails to watch but as these pieces of steel came nearer and nearer to them, they rushed to the other side of the vessel for protection. It made one think what might happen in case a real attack was made against naval vessels in war, whether the crews could be held to their posts in view of almost certain destruction. As Captain Lawson's bombs fell tremendous columns of water shot up. Some fell in tons on the deck of the ship, sweeping it clear. It was the first time we had used our six hundred pound bombs at sea, and they worked splendidly. From the time the cruiser Frankfurt received her mortal blow, she sunk rapidly toward the port side, then slid down bow on. She was soon out of sight and again it was proven that our air bombs could destroy a cruiser as no other weapons could. . . .

At last the time came for the bombing of the Ostfriesland. This was our real test. If we could not sink this great ship the efforts against the other smaller vessels would be minimized and the development of air power against shipping might be arrested, at least for the time being. No foreign air service had been able to obtain battleships as targets, as such action had always been strenuously opposed by their navies. Ours was the first to get them through an Act of our Congress. About the fifteenth of July we began the test, firing bombs of small calibre against the Ostfriesland. This bent up the equipment on her decks and caused some other damage, enough to put her out of business but not to sink her. We knew full well that the very large bombs, eleven hundred pounders and two thousand pounders, would be necessary to sink her and that the little bombs, from our standpoint, were very largely a waste of time. We had to kill, lay out and bury this great ship in order that our people could appreciate what tremendous power the air held over battleships.

At last we were allowed to take out our eleven hundred pound bombs on the 20th of July. We, however, were ordered to drop only one of these at a time, instead of two at a time. An impact of two of these in any place near the ship would probably have sunk her. It was desired, however, to observe the effect without sinking the ship. This attack was made by a flight commanded by Lieutenant Bissell, and was a perfect exhibition of airmanship. . . .

Arrived at the target Lieutenant Bissell's flight of five planes deployed into column and fired five bombs in extremely rapid succession, in fact, it looked as if two or three bombs were in the air at the same time. Two of these bombs hit alongside and three hit on the deck or on the sides, causing terrific detonations and serious damage. Fragments of the battleship were blown out to great distances. Spouts of water hundreds of feet high shot into the air. We felt the jolts and noise of the explosives in the air in our planes three thousand feet above where the bombs hit.

Immediately the Navy Control Vessel made frantic signals for the attack to stop. Lieutenant Bissell had turned his flight and was ready to finish her, as he had five additional bombs left. He had injured the ship so severely that if she had been equipped with her crew, her ammunition, and had had steam in her boilers, she probably would have been destroyed. That night she listed so badly that two thousand tons of water were let in on the other side to keep her straight up so that she would not roll over. Just as Bissell's attack was ceasing, we saw a storm driving in from the north. We had received no intimation of this from our weather service. It was a typical severe thunder squall, prevalent at this time of the year in that locality. The dirigible airships that had been watching the maneuvers taking photographs, and ready to rescue any planes which might have to make a forced landing, proceeded to the north at once and escaped. Lieutenant Bissell's flight broke through it toward Langley Field. . . .

Bright and early next morning Lawson was ready to take out his squadron loaded with the two thousand pound bombs for the final chapter in our tests. It was now felt we could destroy the Ostfriesland; some thought we should be restrained from doing it because it would lead people to believe that the navy should be entirely scrapped, as a thousand airplanes could be built for the price of one battleship. Others thought it should be done because air power had brought an entirely new element into warfare on the water, and if the United States did not draw the proper lessons from it, other nations would and we would be at a great disadvantage. Those of us in the air knew that we had changed the methods of war and wanted to prove it to the satisfaction of everybody.

Finally the time came for us to attack the Ostfriesland with the two thousand pound bombs, and Captain Lawson's flight went to sea. The great ship was down a little by the stern, drawing about forty feet of water; she had sunk considerably after Bissell's attack on the preceding day. Lawson circled his target once to take a look at her and make sure of his wind and his altitude. He then broke his airplanes from their "V" formation into single column and attacked it. Seven airplanes followed one another. Four bombs hit in rapid succession, close alongside the Ostfriesland. We could see her rise eight or ten feet between the terrific blows from under water. On the fourth shot Captain Streett, sitting in the back seat of my plane, stood up and waving both arms shouted: "She is gone!"

When a death blow has been dealt by a bomb to a vessel, there is no mistaking it. Water can be seen to come up under both sides of the ship, she trembles all over, as if her nerve center had been shattered, and she usually rises in the water, sometimes clear, with her bow or stern. In a minute the Ostfriesland was on her side; in two minutes she was sliding down by the stern and turning over at the same time; in three minutes she was bottom-side up, looking like a gigantic whale, the water oozing out of her seams as she prepared to go down to the bottom, then gradually she went down stern first. In a minute more only the tip of her beak showed above the water. It looked as if her stern had touched the bottom of the sea as she stood there straight up in a hundred fathoms of water to bid a last farewell to all her sister battleships around her.

We had been anxious to sink the submarine and destroyer, but I had felt badly to see as beautiful a ship as the Frankfurt go down. She rode the water like a swan. The Ostfriesland, however, impressed me like a grim old bulldog, with the vicious scars of the battle of Jutland still on her. We wanted to destroy her from the air but when it was actually accomplished, it was a very serious and awesome sight. Some of the spectators on the observing vessels wept, so overwrought were their feelings. I watched her sink from a few feet above her, then I flew my plane above the transport Henderson, where the people who had observed the tests were waving and cheering on the decks and in the rigging.

Contrary to the popular opinion, that great vortices in the water are formed as a ship sinks, there were none in this case. She slid to her last resting place with very little commotion. Thus ended the first great air and battleship test that the world has ever seen. It conclusively proved the ability of aircraft to destroy ships of all classes on the surface of the water.

Later that same summer we were given another battleship to practice on. It was the Alabama. She was towed into about thirty-five feet of water near Tangier Sound in the Chesapeake Bay. Again Captain Lawson's invincible squadron attacked the battleship. This time we went in to sink her as quickly as possible and being in shallow water, the effect of our bombs was greater. The first two thousand pound bomb did its work, she sank to the bottom in thirty seconds. Six other bombers coming behind Lawson struck her with their projectiles and within four minutes she was a tangled mass of wreckage unrecognizable as the fine ship which had been there before. We tried out various weapons against her before she was sunk. Phosphorus bombs gave a magnificent spectacular display, the lapping flames completely enveloping the ship. We put thermite, the greatest producer of heat known, on her decks and covered her with smoke clouds dropped from the airplanes. We attacked her at night and made direct hits with our bombs in the darkness. . . .

At the end of 1921 the American Air Service had conclusively demonstrated what could be done by air forces against seacraft. During the following year, 1922, all the World's flying records were captured by the United States—speed, altitude, long distance, and the hours of time that an airplane could stay aloft. In 1923 and '24 we sank more battleships, flew across the American Continent from daylight to dark, and then our airplanes circled the earth, having established an airway clear around it. Whenever an airway can be established, there aircraft can go. The means of bringing their fuel to them, such as railroads, automobiles, boats or other aircraft are merely their auxiliary means of transportation.

In spite of these splendid performances of individuals, which have led the way for the world in the development of this most important art and science, and benefit to commerce and civilization, we, today, compared to our resources and ability are falling back constantly.

V

How Should We Organize Our National Air Power? Make it a Main Force or Still an Appendage?

"Where there is no vision the people perish." This old Biblical quotation is more applicable to the development of aviation and air power than to any other undertaking.

We are at the turning of the ways in the development of our air power and the people, who are the judges of what should be done, should weigh the evidence on the subject carefully. In order to be successful in anything, it is necessary to concentrate one's mind, one's time and one's money on it in such a way as to get the greatest good with the least effort. In doing this with aviation, vision is a most important matter because its great possibilities lie ahead and not behind us. At this juncture, the United States is faced with the alternative of progressing in its aeronautical organization and consolidating its air activities under one responsible head, or going on with its effort split up between other services that have a major function apart from aeronautics.

Aviation is very different from either armies or navies in its economic aspect. Every military airplane can be used in time of peace for some useful undertaking not necessarily connected with war. Every pilot employed in civil aviation can be used in case of war and is ninety per cent efficient at least in time of peace. Every mechanic used in civil aviation is one hundred percent efficient in time of war. In time of peace, the bulk of the effort and thought of a nation in an aeronautical way may be applied to civil and commercial development of aeronautics and this same effort and thought can be shifted at once to military purposes. There is no reason, for instance, why the air forces in time of peace should not be employed in mapping the country, patrolling the forests to prevent forest fires, carrying the mail, eliminating insect pests from cotton, fruit trees and other vegetation, and in making an aeronautical commercial transportation survey of the country to determine what can be carried economically and at a profit through the air instead of on boats, railroads, and by automobiles, and in working out new commercial air routes throughout the world. The Government, for instance, in time of peace should maintain only a small percentage of its total aerial strength on strictly military duty; the rest could be used on civil work for the greater part of the time and assembled for a month or so each year to perform maneuvers and military training.

The great countries of the world are using their vision and are straining every effort to establish their aeronautical position so that the future will not see them hopelessly distanced by their rivals.

So far as national defense is concerned, they have carefully studied the whole problem as affected by aviation, so that they will get a maximum benefit from each dollar of money expended and from each man hour of work put in. From a military standpoint, the airmen have to study the effect that air power has on navies and what their future will be. They know that within the radius of air power's activities, it can completely destroy any surface vessels or war ships. They know that in the last war, surface ships, battleships, cruisers and other seacraft, took comparatively little active part except as transportation and patrol vessels. No battleship sunk another battleship and of the hundred and thirty-four warships sunk or destroyed during the war, the submarines sunk sixty-two British warships and eight large French and Italian ships. No American battleship saw any fighting in the last

war, not even those in European waters. Aircraft have great difficulty in attacking and destroying submarines at sea. They are
very hard to detect, dive with great rapidity and are very difficult
to see under water. The effect of air power on submarines is
probably less than on any other target, whether on water or land.
The best offense against them is to destroy their bases and fuel
stations. It is necessary to consult the best available information
about them as they will be the future means of operating on the
seas. Existing records show that submarines sunk, either by torpedoes or mines, the battleship, Audacious; they sunk the
cruiser, Hampshire, with Lord Kitchener on board; they sunk the
cruisers, Cressy, Aboukir and Hogue in a few minutes. From that
time on, the British battleships were either tied up in their ports
behind torpedo nets and screens of destroyers and submarines or
they were ziz-zagging their course at great speed for a few hours
on the high seas. It is stated that the submarines sunk two battleships in the Dardanelles and drove the Allied fleets into Mudros
harbor. Men even landed from a submarine in Turkish territory
and blew up a bridge by setting an explosive charge off on it.

A modern battleship, according to the old system of naval
thought, may cost somewhere between fifty and seventy million
dollars; it may require, on an average, one cruiser costing
between twenty and thirty million dollars, four destroyers costing three or four million dollars each, four submarines, a certain
amount of air power to protect it, and, in addition to this, great
stores for maintaining the personnel of more than a thousand
men and dock yards and supply facilities to keep them up. So
that every time that a battleship is built, the nation constructing
it is binding itself to about one hundred million dollars or more
of expenditure and a certain amount per year to keep it up. Battleships have required heretofore complete replacement every
few years to prevent their becoming obsolete.

As battleships and surface craft are helpless against aircraft
unless they themselves are protected by air power and, as their
influence on the destruction of seagoing trade is secondary to

that of the submarines, nations are gradually abandoning battle-ship construction. Three are keeping it up: England, Japan and the United States.

England is entirely dependent for existence on her sea-borne trade; Japan, also, is dependent almost entirely on her sea-borne trade. Where England and Japan would have to protect their commerce in the Seven Seas or starve, America could entirely dispense with her sea-going trade if she had to, and continue to exist and defend herself. Where, therefore, a nation might have to expend a tremendous amount of effort and treasure on the main-tenance of its sea-borne trade at great distances from home, it would be better for one not so dependent on sea-borne trade to put its national defense money and effort into active offensive equipment designed directly to defeat the enemy instead of dissi-pating its power in an indecisive theater.

The airman looks at the development of a country's military effort somewhat as follows. National defense consists roughly of four phases: First, the maintenance of domestic tranquillity in the country itself so that the preparation of active fighting mate-rial can go on unhindered. An army on the ground to insure tranquillity and an air force in the air to prevent hostile air raids can take care of this. Second, the protection of the coasts and frontiers. An air force can do this and fight any hostile aircraft or destroy hostile warships while its home country is policed and protected on the ground by a land force. Third, the control of sea communications. This can be done by aircraft within their radius of action and otherwise by submarines. Surface craft have a sec-ondary value for this. Fourth, the prosecution of offensive war across or beyond the seas. This may be carried out primarily under the protection of air power, assisted by submarines and an army. A succession of land bases held by land troops must be occupied and the enemy must be attacked directly through the air. Floating bases or aircraft carriers cannot compete with air-craft acting from land bases. So that, in future, surface transports escorted by war vessels such as carried the American troops to Europe cannot exist in the face of a superior air force. Only when complete dominion of the air has been established can a war of invasion across the seas be prosecuted under present conditions. Air power, therefore, has to be employed as a major instrument of war, no matter whether a land force or a sea force is acting on the surface of the earth. . . .

Submarine officers think our next national emergency will find them fighting on our most advanced front from the day hostilities begin. It is conceivable and probable that there will be a long period of hostilities before any surface fleets come into action. The weaker surface fleet would certainly retreat to the protection of its air power in the radius of aircraft action of its own coast. The superior fleet menaced by submarines and long distance aircraft could not long exist on the high seas and would be of little service there under such conditions. A fleet action in the old sense may never occur again. Undoubtedly, submarines will be developed into aircraft carriers in addition to their other uses.

A modern organization of a country's military power, therefore, indicates that aircraft will be used over both land and sea for combating hostile air forces, demolishing ships on the sea and important targets on the land. Submarines will be used in and on the seas for controlling sea lanes of communication and assisting air power. Armies will be used on land for insuring domestic tranquillity, holding operating bases for aircraft and seacraft and, in a last analysis, together with air power against hostile armies. What might be termed "battleship sea power" is fading away. Only a few nations still maintain it. If an attempt is made to use it in future, it will be so menaced by aircraft from above and submarines from underneath that it will be much more of a military liability than an asset. To this extent has the advent of air power and the use of submarines wrought a change in methods of war.

In the future, therefore, surface navies based on battleships, cannot be the arbiters of the communications over the ocean.

The tremendous cost of these craft and their upkeep will be applied to more efficient and more modern methods of defense. Fighting airplanes can be built in production with their engines for from fifteen to seventy-five thousand dollars, or an average of about twenty-five thousand. Therefore, so far as construction is concerned, at the price of a battleship and its accessories, that is: one hundred million dollars, an average of four thousand airplanes can be built for the price of a battleship.

The United States is now allowed a fleet of eighteen battleships. On this basis, seventy-two thousand airplanes could be built. In any national emergency that we can visualize, the country certainly does not need over three or four thousand airplanes at the decisive point; these can be built and maintained for a relatively small proportional cost and still have great use in civil and commercial aviation in peace time. The cost of the battleships and their accessories is not all. The Navy Yards cost tremendous amounts. In the United States alone there are some twenty of these, whose value aggregates one billion three hundred million dollars. The cost of upkeep and depreciation of these amounts to a vast annual sum. Into many of these Navy Yards a wounded battleship drawing forty feet of water cannot go as there is not enough water on the sills of the dry docks.

If the defense of the coast is intrusted to aircraft and the Navy's coast defense functions are modified, many of these stations can be dispensed with.

In order to carry on offensive operations, a surface navy has to have tremendous naval stations and bases, thousands of miles away from their own country in some cases. These take the forms of dry docks, fuel stations, oil and ammunition depots and shops which cost millions of dollars and are quite vulnerable to air attack. The amount of money and effort put into these might be applied to better use for aircraft and submarines.

So far as land forces are concerned, airplanes will reduce the cost of coast fortifications. As they are able to attack seacraft at long distances from the coast, they not only will keep surface seacraft entirely away from cannon range of the coast but they will eliminate the necessity for many of the great seacoast cannon. Every time a large seacoast cannon is installed on its concrete foundation, it costs half a million dollars. In the ten years preceding 1920, the United States expended about one billion eight hundred million dollars on coast defenses of different kinds. The present land system of fortifications has changed little from the system employed during the Revolutionary War, which was to have all estuaries, ports, or harbor entrances garnished with cannon so as to keep away all hostile surface ships. Part of the money and effort saved from some of these expenditures could be put into more mobile cannon to be used with an active army, or into aircraft to keep the enemy away from the coast and frontiers. With a well organized air force, it is hard to visualize how an enemy could gain a footing on land in a country such as the United States.

Constant development must be kept up in civil and commercial aviation as well as in military aviation, and again accurate vision is required to see what will take place several years hence. The older services such as the Army and Navy to which aviation was attached at first, were entirely incapable of visualizing aviation's progress, particularly in its civil and commercial application which must work hand in hand with its military use.

Another very important consideration is the budget. So long as the budget for the development of aircraft is prepared by the Army, Navy or other agency of the Government, aviation will be considered as an auxiliary and the requisite amount of money, as compared with the older services, will be subject to the final decision of personnel whose main duty is not aviation. This has resulted in an incomplete, inefficient, and ultimately expensive system of appropriating money.

Of equal importance is the question of the personnel, of the people who have to act and actually fly in aviation. We now have an air-going personnel as distinguished from a sea-going and land-going class. In military aviation, in time of peace, the Air Service in the United States loses nearly half of the total number of deaths in the Army per year; in time of war, the number of casualties among the flying officers is proportionally great. We therefore need an entirely different system of training, education, reserves, and replacements, from that of the other services.

As important as anything else is the placing of one man in charge of aviation who can be held directly responsible for the aeronautical development of the whole country and, next, an air representative on councils of national defense, who has co-equal power with that of the representatives of the Army and of the Navy. Not only does this give proper weight to aeronautics, both in peace and in war, but the Army and Navy have always, and will always, deadlock under certain issues where they have equal representation. The introduction of a third service would tend to break this. Eventually, all military power of the Government should be concentrated under a single department which would have control over all national defense, no matter whether it be on land, on the sea, or in the air. In this way, overhead might be cut down, definite and complete missions assigned to air, land and water forces, and a more thorough understanding of the nation's needs would result. . . .

VI

The Effect of Air Power on the Modification and Limitation of International Armaments

The rapidly increasing efficiency of the airplane and the submarine gives us the opportunity to move towards a new limitation of armaments.

Both of these implements of national defense are essentially defensive in their nature as distinguished from offensive military arrangements designed for aggression across and beyond the seas.

They will cause new economies in national expenditures. For example, more than 1000 airplanes can be built and maintained for the outlay required for a single battleship.

Airplanes have a great application in time of peace in useful civil and commercial pursuits. The same airplanes can do this work that are suitable for duty in war and for national defense. In fact all aircraft developments, the factories that make them, the airways that are established for civil aviation and the civilian pilots and crews, are distinct military assets, and can bring in a return in time of peace, thereby reducing the national expenditure necessary in their maintenance if they were kept solely and exclusively for war.

In the case of the submarine, the cost of construction, ton for ton, is about equal to that of other vessels. Their size, however, ranges from 1500 tons to 2500, or less than one-tenth of that of battleships and cruisers. Their efficiency in offensive operations on the sea against any other vessel, either on the surface of the water or below its surface, is constantly increasing. The best defense against submarines is other submarines.

In case of war at the present day, submarines would be the greatest controlling element on the water of the sea lanes of communication, while aircraft above the water would control communication within their radius of operations. The theory of battleship sea power is becoming obsolescent and should be discarded at an early date.

Leaving out of consideration civil, commercial and economic methods of carrying on competitions between the nations and viewing the military side of international disputes alone, it is entirely practical to make up-to-date appraisal of what modern military forces consist of and what they are actually worth. As long as it was a question of land power and sea power, that is, armies and navies, the matter was well understood because they had been continued and applied for centuries. The variation in their use has been very small and has consisted almost entirely in improving instruments and equipment but not methods. The action of armies and navies on one plane or dimension—that is, on the surface of the ground or the surface of the water—is slow in execution as compared to operations in the air. They also require tremendous and expensive organizations for their maintenance and upkeep on account of the great number of men and the vast amount of equipment which they need. The advent of air power has completely changed this. The relations of armies to navies and navies to armies are now very different from what they were, while both bear an entirely new relation to air power from that which they formerly bore to each other. Even if hostile armies and navies come into contact with each other, they are helpless now unless they can obtain and hold military supremacy in the air. Air power holds out the hope to the nations that, in the future, air battles taking place miles away from the frontiers will be so decisive and of such far-reaching effect that the nation losing them will be willing to capitulate without resorting to a further contest on land or water on account of the degree of destruction which would be sustained by the country subjected to unrestricted air attack.

Air power carries out its military missions, competes in battles in the air and attacks ground and water establishments without participation in its conflicts by either armies or navies. A striking thing about air power, also, is that in time of peace military air power may be employed for useful purposes such as mapping the country, carrying the mails, patrolling against forest fires, aids to agriculture in eliminating insect pests such as locusts and boll weevils, farm surveying, life saving, and an infinite number of other things. No other military formations which the countries possess have such an economic application. From a military standpoint, air power is the only agency that is able to defend the country from hostile air attack and is the principal defense against hostile sea attack along a coast. No defense from the ground is capable of stopping air raids over a country. Along the coast line air power is a positive and absolute defense against any hostile surface ships, as it can sink or destroy any vessels that ever have been built or that can ever be constructed. This feature of the application of air power will constantly increase in its relative ability rather than decrease. Air power, however, has very little effect on submarines and undersea boats. Consequently, naval operations in the future will be conducted by submarines to an increased extent.

The battleship is so expensive and difficult to maintain and so vulnerable to aircraft and submarines that it will be eliminated eventually. Sea power as expressed in battleships is almost a thing of the past. Battleship fleets can no longer control the sea lanes of communication. This attribute has passed to aircraft and undersea boats. The tremendous power of submarines is just beginning to be understood by the people, as the facts and figures relative to their use were concealed largely for political purposes during and even since the War. During the War the Germans maintained at sea only about thirty submarines. These thirty submarines sank eleven million tons of allied shipping. They sank six million six hundred ninety-two thousand six hundred and forty-two tons of British shipping and in nine months of the War, during 1918, they sank one million six hundred sixty-eight thousand nine hundred and seventy-two tons of British shipping. Forty percent of all British shipping was destroyed by these few submarines, which reduced the British Isles to the verge of starvation. The Germans never employed over ten thousand men in the handling of their submarine forces, whereas the allies employed over a million men in counter submarine operations and spent hundreds of millions of dollars for equipment. All of these measures were comparatively ineffective. . . .

When war between two powers separated by oceans occurs in the future all sea lanes leading to the hostile power will be planted with mines by submarines. The surface of all oceans will be districted and organized in geographic squares. To each square submarines will be assigned and a constant patrol will be kept, no matter whether there be warships or commercial ships of the opposing side crossing the seas. The submarines' power is sufficient to destroy any surface vessels including battleships or other war craft. Nations, therefore, will put their money and effort into submarines instead of battleship fleets because the submarine operations are more economical in financial expenditure, in numbers of men employed, and in effectiveness. They, however, are largely a defensive element. They cannot transport troops across the seas as can surface vessels. At present surface craft only may be used for this purpose and also to act as airplane carriers for transporting planes to hostile shores and launching them. As airplane carrying vessels are of no use against hostile air forces with bases on shore, and as they can only be of use against other vessels or hostile fleets that are on the surface of the water, and as these fleets will be supplanted by submarines, there is little use for the retention of airplane carriers in the general scheme of armaments.

Air power has caused a decided change in applying armed forces both defensive and offensive.

In the case of an insular power or continental power, separated by oceans and seas from a possible enemy, it is difficult to see under modern conditions how such a country could be invaded by hostile land forces, or how a surface navy could compromise the country's independence. This is so because air forces can destroy any surface ships that approach the coast of a nation. Submarines also can plant the coast with mines so as to make it practically an impossibility for hostile shipping to land armed forces.

Future invasions into the heart of an enemy country, therefore, will be made by air craft.

In the former conception of national defense, the principle was held that to invade a nation the piercing of its lines of resistance was necessary. If the nation lay across the sea its line of battleships had to be pierced, destroyed and overcome to gain access to the shores. Again, the line of the armies had to be pierced to gain access to the interior. This condition no longer exists in its entirety and is decreasing relatively every day. Air craft do not need to pierce the line of either navies or armies. They can fly straight over them to the heart of a country and gain success in war.

To gain a lasting victory in war, the hostile nation's power to make war must be destroyed—this means the manufactories, the means of communication, the food products, even the farms, the fuel and oil and the places where people live and carry on their daily lives. Not only must these things be rendered incapable of supplying armed forces but the people's desire to renew the combat at a later date must be discouraged.

Aircraft operating in the heart of an enemy's country will accomplish this object in an incredibly short space of time, once the control of the air has been obtained and the months and even years of contest of ground armies with a loss of millions of lives will be eliminated in the future.

Much, if not most, of the present equipment for making war is obsolete and useless and can be replaced by much more economical and useful arrangements and agencies. Nations nearly always go into an armed contest with the equipment and methods of a former war. Victory always comes to that country which has made a proper estimate of the equipment and methods that can be used in modern ways. Air power has introduced new considerations which should be weighed carefully in estimating their effect on the possibility of the limitation of armaments. When the actual value or uselessness of the various branches of national armaments is realized and the conditions affecting their use are fully understood by the people, it will be an entirely practical proposition to limit them. People hesitate to give up arrangements for insuring their own safety.

In countries that are susceptible to constant altercations with their neighbors every man, every woman and almost every child knows what the underlying principles of their national defense are, and they freely and unhesitatingly give their services, their money and their time towards protecting their homes, their institutions and their governments because they have been taught the necessity of this by repeated examples during practically every generation of their existence. They cannot maintain their lives in peace and tranquillity without protection. In other countries far removed from possible aggression, the people have turned for provision for their security to professional organizations created for that purpose and have ceased to interest themselves personally in these matters because they consider the possibility of war so remote. These rely entirely on the advice of professional soldiers and sailors. Usually nations of this kind are the ones that suffer more terribly in casualties, financial outlay and disaster when war takes place, because the conservatism of these permanent military services always tend to perpetuate their existing systems and institutions and resist changes and innovations.

They always fear to change, to do away with or eliminate anything which has long been a part of their organization or system. Unless the public and the legislatures periodically inspect and overhaul the professional organizations maintained for national security, increased expenditures, adherence to obsolete and useless principles of defense, and an inexact knowledge of military conditions are always the result. Contests between nations consist of many things beside actual armed conflicts. They start with competitions of various kinds, usually commercial, and are carried on in different ways by the nations involved depending upon their means of transportation and communication, their wealth and their diplomatic aptitude.

Armed forces usually are called in only as a last resort and when all other means of coercion have failed. The maintenance of armed forces by a nation may be regarded as a direct symptom of the country's punitive psychology. A very accurate estimate may be made as to how and in what manner the policies of a state are to be enforced by the size of its organized armament and the distribution of its forces.

Within the last generation great changes have taken place in the internal organization of states and in their relations to each other. A constantly increasing influence in the policies of a State is being wielded by the common people as distinguished from the ruling class or an aristocracy, as was formerly the case. This condition has been brought about through two principal agencies. First, the general education of everyone which makes it possible for most of the people to read, write and transmit their ideas from one to another. This encourages freedom of speech and a discussion by the people of the nation's policies, both national and international. Second, the development of electrical communication which puts every part of the world in constant touch with every other part and makes possible an instantaneous distribution of the thoughts and ideas of individuals to an increasingly literate people.

Secret diplomacy in its old application is difficult to carry on today because it is next to impossible to conceal warlike preparations.

The nations understand each other better than has ever been the case before. The factors which have contributed decidedly to the understanding of one people by another have been the constantly increasing rapidity of transportation both on the land and over the water, the railroad and the steamship. The facility with which voyages now can be made around the world is not only increasing commerce between the nations, but the travel of individuals between the hemispheres. There is no part of the civilized world that cannot be reached at present in a fraction of the time that was required fifty or a hundred years ago. Within the last decade the advent of air transportation has added a decidedly new element in the relations of nations to each other.

The older means of transportation, vessels and railways, have followed the parallels of latitude, through the Temperate Zone. The new means of transportation through the air will follow the meridians, that is, the shortest routes, straight across the poles in the north and south—the most direct lines from place to place. To illustrate this, we may take for example a line of communication from New York to Peking, China. At present the route by sea and land goes across the United States to the Pacific Coast, from there via the Hawaiian Islands, Japan, and the littoral of Asia to Peking. It takes from four to five weeks for the voyage along that line in railways and steamships. By going directly across the top of the earth from New York via Lake Athabasca, Canada; Nome, Alaska; Khabarovsk on the Amur River in Siberia, and thence to Peking, the trip may be made by air in from sixty to eighty hours. Meridian routes may be used from North America, to South America, across the Antarctic continent to Australia and Africa, respectively, which would bring New York in touch with Australia in about 100 hours, and Africa in about 130 to 140 hours.

Cold is no impediment to air transportation but is a decided help because it freezes up the lakes and covers the ground with snow, both of which make landing for aircraft easy on the surface of the earth. Cold also renders the holding of moisture by the air difficult. This prevents the formation of fogs and clouds which lead to storms, heavy winds and uncomfortable conditions for flying. Aircraft should be designed to give great comfort to the passengers and security to any cargoes carried. Air transportation and air power, therefore are creating a totally new element in the relations of nations; this is principally a military one so far but soon its economic aspect will be even greater.

As physical means are employed by nations to impress their will on an adversary only when other means of adjusting a dispute have failed, air power will be called on as the first punitive element. The virtual extension of frontiers completely over a nation, which air power has brought about is entirely different from the old frontiers that consisted of coast lines, rivers, or mountain barriers, when armies and navies were the only factors concerned in military power. Now air forces may attack any town or hamlet no matter whether these be on the shores of the ocean, the crests of the mountains, or the inland regions of the countries subject to international dispute. This factor alone will cause nations in dispute to consider long and carefully the questions involved before resorting to an armed contest.

As conditions are at present no nations will willingly give up a reasonable organization for the defense of its territory, the maintenance of its institutions and the furtherance of its civilization either by civil, commercial or military means. On the other hand, due to the increased radius of operation of modern vessels and sea craft the conditions for the maintenance of bases on foreign shores are not as necessary as they were a century ago. Modern commercial vessels can go around the earth on one charge of fuel. Motor ships with internal combustion engines burning heavy oil are able to go with their full cargo for 25,000 miles. Each employs an incredibly small number of men to handle it. One of these ships of 15,000 tons requires a total crew of only about 25 men. The maintenance of militarily defended sea craft bases distant from the home country no longer has the strategic importance it used to. They often serve as means of irritation and fear to the nations that consider themselves menaced by them. It seems probable, therefore, that nations at the present time will be willing to enter into conversation regarding military establishments designed entirely to take the offensive across the seas and away from their own territories, especially where these have little or no defensive value. Many of the institutions and establishments still maintained by the nations for offensive military use across the seas have little or no actual value and have become obsolete and useless. Their maintenance requires excessive taxation and personal services in the building up of industries and classes which cannot be used for anything except war.

The three elements of national defense which nations will not give up until their protection is assured by some means which has not yet been tried successfully, are air forces, armies and submarines.

Surface navies, particularly battleships and other surface craft, are rapidly losing their importance as they can only be used for offensive operations across the sea and have little or no defensive value. They are the most expensive equipment in the military scheme.

What is keeping them up as much as anything else and largely preventing open and free discussion of their uses are the propaganda agencies maintained by navies for perpetuating the existing systems. Not only do they resist any change which will take away from the battleship its primary importance in sea dominion, but they tend to minimize and depreciate the ability of air power and submarines. Propaganda has a great effect on the public mind. As the people are the ultimate judge of what national defense should be, as expressed by their legislatures, it is necessary that the exact facts be submitted to them without restraint or evasion.

Heretofore armies and navies have had such well defined spheres of operation that they have been left largely to themselves to organize and carry out their own plans. Air power has changed this, and if air power is not given a sufficient voice in the national councils to be able to compete with the voice of the land and of the sea it cannot exert the influence commensurate with its power. This fact, among others, has led the various nations to give to air power an organization coequal with the army and navy and tend to group all means for national defense under one general head who can be responsible for all the armament of a state. This organization tends to distribute the duties of defense in accordance with the particular requirements of the case to armies, navies and air forces, to prevent any one arm from being expanded inordinately or from getting a dominant political position before the people and the legislatures by means of propaganda which may not exhibit a nation's exact needs.

There are three ways, therefore, of bringing on a discussion as to the limitation of armaments.

First, to show what is useless and can be eliminated in the national defensive armaments.

Second, to show what is of a purely defensive nature for the protection of the country itself and not necessary for prosecuting offensive war beyond the seas.

Third, what governmental scheme of national defense is the best suited to a balanced organization, so that air, land and water will each be represented, provided for and understood, and to bring about a full and exact publication of all arrangements and expenditures for the national defense.

The effect of air power on the armies is not as decided as it is on navies. Armies will still be used very much as they have been heretofore, primarily for insuring tranquillity in the countries themselves, for maintaining the constitution and the laws when other means fail, and last, for use against other armies. It is difficult to see in this country in particular, how armies will ever be used against other armies in the defense of the country if an adequate air force exists, because to get to this country hostile countries must come either through the air or across the waters. In either case an air force is an efficient and positive protection. An army can neither oppose an air force in the air nor a navy on the water. As everything begins and ends on the ground and as armies are the manifestation of the man power of a State in a military sense, they must hold the land bases from which air forces or sea forces act.

The people in most countries are so busy with their vocations that they have comparatively little time to look into the exact conditions of national defense. This is particularly so with nations that are far removed from an apparent possibility of future conflicts. They entrust their defense to professional bodies known as armies and navies, and pay comparatively little attention to what arrangements they make for national defense, providing they do not spend too much money or become too resistant to public opinion. This nonchalance always results in armies and navies if continued too long. It is manifested in the retarded development of modern equipment and the slow adoption of the latest instruments, and in a disregard of changed conditions of education, enlightenment and progress among people, which tends to settle international conflicts by other means than by war. The personnel of these permanent establishments often tend to become uniformed office holders instead of public servants entirely engaged in furthering the betterment of their nation.

As a preliminary step in developing the whole theory of the limitation of armaments, it is believed at this time that it is practical to do away entirely with the surface battleship, the airplane carrier, certain naval bases and dock yards, and many useless and expensive organizations of ground coast defenses. To bring this about, frank discussion, a truthful exposition of facts, and the widest publicity are needed. Our last conference for a limitation of armaments was greatly facilitated by the absolute proof that aircraft could destroy surface seacraft and battleships. Since the last conference in 1921 air power has made such strides that its effect is still more appreciated, and further limitations are now practicable. . . .

VIII

THE MAKING OF AN AIR FORCE PERSONNEL

Men and machines have to be harnessed up and driven as a team to make up air power. The selection and training of the persons who are to fly the machines and those that are required to keep them up is the most important consideration. The next is to obtain and distribute the actual airplanes and the equipment that are necessary for use in the air.

Without knowledge on the part of the personnel of their work, neither proper air units nor suitable material can be devised or created for the flyers. If persons are put in authority that are not trained air officers, with long service as pilots and observers, they cannot know the kinds of airplanes which should be given their men and the material which should accompany them to keep them up.

All countries have attempted at first to put men in the control of aviation who knew little about it just because they had high military rank. These officers always attempted to conceal their ignorance of the subject from others, and have surrounded themselves with advisers that knew little more about aviation than themselves so as to maintain greater control over their subordinates. The result of this procedure always comes quickly and is manifested in worthless and dangerous machines for the pilots, an inadequate system of training, no real air system for reserve officers, and no appreciation of what the conditions of a future war will be. Everything depends primarily on the creation and development of a specialized air personnel, capable of actually handling their duties in an efficient manner making a class of real air men.

An air force's duty is in the air and not on the ground. People who are unused to or unfamiliar with air work are incapable of visioning what air power should be, of training the men necessary for work in the air, or of devising the equipment that they should have. The greatest deterrent to development which air forces combat in every country is the fact that they have had to be tied up to armies and navies where senior officers, unused to air work, were placed in the superior positions at the beginning of the organization of the air forces. In practically all cases these affected to treat flying men as aerial chauffeurs, where as a matter of fact, they are the most highly organized individual fighting men that the world has ever seen.

Airplanes are not merely a means of transportation, they are fighting units. Air forces fight in line against other air forces. They use their own tactics, and have a highly specialized method of maneuvering in three dimensions. The air man's psychology of war depends on the action of the individual, he has no man at his elbow to support him; no officers in front to lead him, and no file closers behind him to shoot him if he runs away as is the case in a ground army. The whole system is entirely different from that of troops on the ground where mob psychology has to be used in directing the men in combat. To cover up their ignorance in these matters, these older ground officers have always hedged back to the fact that administration was the main thing in the conduct of air forces. Administration is merely the orderly conduct of correspondents in affairs. It has nothing to do with the actual handling or leading of fighting forces. It is merely a necessary nuisance. The best administrators usually are the old sergeants or clerks that have been long in the service. An excellent administrator could be obtained and hired for certain fixed wages in civil life. An airman cannot be. He must be of suitable personal characteristics, self reliant, bound to overcome any and all obstacles in front of him, and well versed in his profession from the ground up.

Another thing that one frequently hears is that the air game is a young man's game. This is not the case when one considers that it is a life's work. Even in a ground army, a general would no longer be capable of carrying a musket and pack in the ranks nor making the long marches on foot that he used to when twenty years of age.

An officer has to come up through each grade to his position, and in addition he has to learn about all the branches of the service in the army to be a general. It is the same way in the air force. One starts as a pilot, learns how to fly the machine, then learns how to handle a greater number of machines as rank and experience increases, and last, to handle whole forces of all branches of aviation, including their supply and upkeep.

It takes much longer to train upper officers in an air force than it does in a ground army or navy. To begin with, every boy has the background of an army and navy even in his primary school. He is marched round, and has some instructions in military movements. He hears his parents talk about wars, and studies about them in the school histories. He goes to the sea in ships as well as in boats, and also reads about sea combats. He is more or less familiar with both. The modern boy is the first of his kind to know about the air. He is just beginning now to get a background of the air, but, unfortunately, air battles and air history of the European war have not yet been written. The ground troops were so busy with their own work, as they always will be, that they knew practically nothing of the great air operations that took place miles behind the enemy front or sometimes miles behind our own front. Air forces act in such an incredibly large space. They are capable of going one or two thousand miles a day so that the whole country becomes a frontier—a horizontal frontier,—with the ground being one element and a blanket of air all over it the other element. It is not a vertical frontier like the coast, a river line or mountain barrier. Speed of locomotion is tremendous in the air. It is ten times as fast as the average steamship, four times as fast as the average railway train, and nearly a hundred times as fast as the foot soldier. Furthermore, an air force fights in three dimensions, on the same level, from up above and from underneath. It can go wherever there is air and this air is about seven miles deep. In other words, fighting air craft can mount to 35,000 feet. The control of all the different branches of the air service in this medium of air is a most complicated and difficult undertaking. The technical part of it alone is more complicated than that of any other service. More than seventy-five different professions are necessary to be known by the personnel handling the aircraft to keep them in repair and in serviceable condition.

In the actual fighting of the aircraft, moral qualities are required that were never before demanded of men. In the first place, they are all alone. No man stands at their shoulder to support them. They know that if a flaming bullet comes through their gasoline tank it immediately becomes a burning torch and they are gone. They know that if a wing is torn off there is the same result. They know that a dozen fatal things may happen anytime, and that if they fall two hundred or twenty thousand feet, existence is at an end. A man on the ground may be wounded and yet may be saved, as he falls a foot or two to the ground. In spite of all these things, the airman has to push his attack without other thought than the destruction of the enemy. Human beings that are endowed with these characteristics are not to be found without careful selection and elimination. . . .

X

The Defense Against Aircraft

It was proved in the European war that the only effective defense against aerial attack is to whip the enemy's air forces in air battles. In other words, seizing the initiative, forcing the enemy to the defensive in his own territory, attacking his most important ground positions, menacing his airplanes on the ground, in the hangars, on the airdromes and in the factories so that he will be forced to take the air and defend them. To sit down on one's own territory and wait for the other fellow to come, is to be whipped before an operation has even commenced. . . .

When seizing the initiative and carrying the air war into the enemy's country is not possible or practicable, the only other method of defense against aircraft is the use of guns and cannon from the ground, combined with the action of defensive pursuit aviation. The air is so vast and extends so far that the shooting of airplanes out of the sky, with cannon from the ground, is almost impossible of achievement, especially when the planes are almost always protected by clouds, by the glaring sun or by darkness. Once airplanes have beaten the hostile aircraft in air battles, nothing can stop their operations.

To begin with, the airplanes have to be seen or heard. Clouds, the night, storms and the sun itself conceal airplanes from view. Nowadays, large propellers are being used which make little noise and the engine itself can be muffled as well as that on an automobile, so that it is becoming more difficult to hear a flying airplane. This was not the case in the war when the gearing of the engine to slow down the total number of the propeller's revolutions was not practicable because the gears were not sure enough in their action. Consequently, the small propellers, in whirling through the air, made as much if not more noise than the engines themselves. This is the reason noiseless airplanes were not used during the European war. Aircraft then could be located, at times easily, by sound ranging systems on the ground. Now it would be very difficult.

Before the true attack on a city or locality develops, many feints are made. Airplanes are sent from various directions to draw out the enemy's means of defense. Thousands of rounds of shells from the antiaircraft guns are wasted in the air by the defenders. The gun crews kept up at night constantly firing are soon worn out; their eyes become blinded by the incessant flashes. The whole arrangement of ground protection against aircraft, sound ranging, searchlights and guns cannot stand up under intelligent air attack and is incapable of serious effect on airplanes.

In addition to anti-aircraft guns, a network of wires was raised by balloons around important places in the World War so as to form an entanglement into which airplanes would fly. The wires were intended to cut off wings, damage propellers and otherwise bring airplanes down. Airplanes forthwith were equipped with steel-cutting wires projecting in front of them which would cut through any of the barrages. The airplanes also found the supporting balloons and shot them down, thereby completely nullifying the wire barrages. I never saw an airplane brought down by this device.

In a modern war, bombardment aircraft would be equipped with the aerial torpedo and with gliding bombs. With these they can stand off for many miles and hit a target as large as a city practically every time. A gliding bomb depends on gravity for its impelling power. They have been constructed so that they will go about a mile for every one thousand feet of altitude. An airplane 10,000 feet up could project one of these ten miles. They can be directed toward their objective, by gyroscopic control, or by radio telegraphy. The aerial torpedo of course will go as far as its charge of gasoline will carry it. It can also be directed and controlled by radio. . . .

Any system of defense against aircraft from the ground alone is fallacious and money put into it, if not spent along carefully considered lines, is merely thrown away.

Ground armies, unfamiliar with the action of air power, are constantly setting up the claim that anti-aircraft artillery is capable of warding off air attack. This is absolutely not in keeping with the facts, and a doctrine of this kind is a dangerous thing to be propagated, because it inclines people to think that they have security from this source whereas they have not. It is, of course, more difficult to protect a warship at sea with anti-aircraft artillery than it is to protect localities on land because the vessel is a movable platform.

Aside from the method of attacking an enemy's air force when it is at a distance, which is the only real means of keeping aircraft away, the next best way of meeting an attack is to organize a given locality such as New York, for instance, with the following system. . . . The average bombardment formation of about a hundred airplanes will move at an altitude of about 15,000 feet and at a speed of from a hundred to a hundred and thirty-five miles an hour. It will keep together until it approaches its objective so that the leader may be able to maintain control of the individual airplanes, to concentrate the attack and to allow them to return to their initial airdromes so that they can be quickly refueled, re-ammunitioned and continue the attack. If hostile aircraft are enabled by the lack of offensive action at a distance to come directly over a city and engage in combat with our own aircraft, it is manifest that, if anti-aircraft artillery fires into the air, it is just as apt to hit its own aircraft as that of the enemy, as they will be close together in combat. Many of these actions will take place at night, in the clouds or in the direction of the sun.

It takes our own defending pursuit aviation at least twenty minutes to take to the air and rise to 15,000 feet after having received the order. Usually we allow half an hour. They should be up there a few minutes before the hostile formation arrives so as to be entirely ready to launch a concentrated attack against the enemy. This requires that the hostile formation be picked up at least a hundred miles away so as to enable our own people to make up their minds as to the strength, disposition, probable intentions and number of the enemy in order to take proper counter measures. It cannot be told with certainty from what direction the opposing aircraft are coming; therefore it is necessary to completely surround the locality to be defended with observation and listening posts both in the air and on the ground.

Listening posts are not enough, because modern airplanes do not necessarily make a noise; therefore, surveillance aviation has to be kept constantly in the air where they can not only see but hear the enemy aircraft. . . .

The complete air defense of a locality requires: First, that there be a circle of listening and reporting posts, extending for at least a hundred and fifty miles out from the area to be defended. These should be supplemented by aerial observation posts and surveillance aircraft. Second, there should be an organization of pursuit aircraft, the type that rises rapidly and maneuvers easily. Third, there should be several circles of searchlights in groups of forty or fifty each. In Europe I always liked groups of thirty lights, twenty of which were fixed in position so as to illuminate an area in the sky and ten of which were movable so as to try to pick up the opposing aircraft and follow them. The fixed lighted area was always that in which the maximum danger was to be expected. These would be flashed on and off as the hostile aircraft came over the area to be defended while the movable lights searched for and tried to follow the planes. Fourth, there should be anti-aircraft guns and cannon. All of these elements should be under one control, that of the air commander or the one charged with the whole of the air defense of the locality. He should have a large control board arranged like a map showing each part of the defense area in detail, and the whole marked in squares covering a distance on the ground corresponding to five minutes' flight of an airplane. A system of electric lights should be so arranged under this map so that the direction of flight, the speed, number and type of the hostile aircraft could be projected easily on the board. The anti-aircraft defense system should have an independent and separate telephone, telegraph, radio and courier system to every element in the command so as to instantaneously communicate with them about any arrangement desired. If the air communication system is used by other troops its efficacy is lost. An instant's delay in an air operation may nullify the whole thing because planes move so quickly. By a system of this kind every element for the air defense of a locality is brought into play, and coordinated with every other part. It is an extremely complicated, expensive and difficult arrangement to install, but it was the only method possible to use during the European war to ward off air attack. It unquestionably had the effect of keeping aircraft up at a considerable altitude so as to escape the attack of pursuit airplanes. Machine guns, cannon, or any missile throwing weapons would not do this because of the ineffectiveness of anti-aircraft fire, and because sometimes it is easier to fly down close to the ground to avoid fire from the ground than it is to keep up high in the air. The idea of being able to defend any locality whatever against airplanes with anti-aircraft guns, cannon or any other arrangements from the ground alone is absolutely incapable of accomplishment. . . .

During the past year a great many statements have been made that the anti-aircraft artillery is improving and that the results now would be different from those that occurred during the war.

This is most decidedly not the case. The improvements made, which amount to little, are nothing in comparison with the improvements made in airplanes, in their speed, their ability to climb high in the air, to make little noise and to conceal themselves from view. Anti-aircraft positions can be attacked directly by airplanes so as to nullify their fire and may be covered by smoke clouds or gas clouds. Airplanes themselves may shoot them up with machine guns or with bombs dropped in their vicinity either by the gliding method or directly.

The average anti-aircraft gun costs anywhere from twenty to thirty thousand dollars. They will fire about twenty shots a minute with each shot costing from twenty to thirty-five dollars. The life of these guns is from about fifteen hundred to two thousand rounds when they must be replaced.

If a locality is defended from the air passively, and tied up to one place in much the way that a seacoast artillery gun is, an attacking air commander of ability, seizing the power of initiative, can arrange his air raids, make feints and confuse the enemy, so as to be able to launch his main attack practically when and where he desires without much loss to himself.

The only defense against aircraft is by hitting the enemy first, just as far away from home as possible. The idea of defending the country against air attack by machine guns or anti-aircraft cannon from the ground, is absolutely incapable of being carried out.

XI

CONCLUSIONS

The development of air power has forced a complete reorganization of all the arrangements for national defense.

The rapidity and sureness of electrical communication all over the world make it possible to combine the use of all the elements entering into national defense in a manner impossible of accomplishment heretofore.

The influence of air power on the ability of one nation to impress its will on another in an armed contest will be decisive. Aircraft of certain classes are now able to traverse the air all over the world no matter whether they be over the sea or over the land.

Consequent upon this, the mission of each branch of the national defense must be clearly stated and its powers and limitations thoroughly understood in order to combine its action with the other branches to insure the maximum effect.

Before the coming of air power, the national defense elements consisted of land power and sea power. At that time, all operations over the sea were assigned to the Navy. Everything on or over the land was assigned to the Army. There was a little overlapping of duties between these services immediately along the coasts, but this was not a serious proposition.

Now, however, air forces operating from land bases can control the surface of the sea and the air over it up to their operating distance from the coast. Within that distance a navy no longer has the paramount interest. Therefore the Navy's mission so far as coast defense is concerned, has ceased to exist and its mission must be beyond the zone of aircraft activity.

The land organization of a navy for coast defense and the land establishments incident to it can be dispensed with. The money and effort heretofore put into these should now be placed in air defense organization.

The mission of land power and the army will remain very much the same. The modifications necessary will consist largely in concentrating gun power around the major units of infantry and giving them their maximum mobility. Coast artillery, except at points that can be affected by gun fire from submarines, has become superfluous and the money and effort put into this should be transferred to air power.

Air power, however, must be assigned a definite mission in its particular sphere of activity. This mission should be the responsibility for the complete air defense of the nation. Without a mission of this kind being specifically prescribed, the aeronautical effort of the country will be dissipated between the land, water, and other services, so that maximum efficiency *cannot be obtained.*

All of the great countries of the world are now organizing their air power for striking their adversaries as far away from their own countries as possible, whether the enemy be in the air, on the water, or on the land. This policy is adopted so as to make the home country free from the interference of hostile forces by keeping the fighting at a distance from the frontiers or coasts.

The underlying principle in the organization of air power is the creation of an air force capable of the greatest radius of action practicable under the conditions limited by personnel, material, and armament.

Next in the air force in order of importance is the organization of certain local air units destined for the protection of extremely important centers of power. The City of New York serves as all example of a locality of this kind. Such local defense units should combine all means and methods used for defense against aircraft, both in the air and on the ground.

Third, in order of importance, are the auxiliary air units assigned to military organizations in the air, on the water, and on the land. This class of air unit, ordinarily, is called observation aviation. Like all auxiliaries, it should be cut down to the lowest point commensurate with the efficiency.

Therefore, in the organization of our air power we should consider:

1. The air force.
2. Local air defense units.
3. Auxiliary air units.

Two and three, in addition to their other duties, should be trained to assume the offensive.

The system of command of military air power should consist in having the greatest centralization practicable. An air force now can move from one to two thousand miles within twenty-four hours. Military elements on the land or water can move only a fraction of this. If, for instance, we take an air sector from the Chesapeake Bay to and including Maine, approximately eight hundred miles in length, which can be covered by an air force in eight hours or less, several sectors of defense would have to be organized by the ground troops for this distance. To assign air force units to any one of these ground organizations would result in the piece-meal application of air power and the inability to develop the maximum force at the critical point. Therefore, all air force units should be directly under the orders of the Commander in Chief of the military power of the country.

Local air defense units destined for the protection of a locality likewise should be under the control of the supreme commander and also in close liaison with the ground troops in their vicinity.

Auxiliary air units should be under the command of the military elements to which they are assigned, subject to the general control as to training, sector, depth of reconnaissance, methods, and supply by the air force.

The establishment and control of airways and the seizure of aviation bases in offensive operations, in which the air force has a dominant interest, should be under air force control. The air force also should have the decision about the recruitment and training of all air force personnel, the procurement of all aircraft, all flying material, armament and accessories.

Air power is the most rapidly developing element in the makeup of nations. Accurate vision is required to keep abreast of the times and programs must be adopted on the basis of what will happen from seven to ten years hence. Failure to estimate properly what will occur will result in serious consequences in case of war.

Considering our possible emergencies in the future, the following Air Force should be provided for:

Within the continental limits of the United States there should be an offensive air force of one air division of twelve hundred planes to be operated as a unit, and two separate brigades, one along the Atlantic Coast and one along the Pacific Coast, of six hundred airplanes each. The force should consist of two-thirds pursuit and one-third bombardment (included in the bombardment aviation should be some attack aviation, if this continues to be an element in our organization).

There should be a local defense unit of one hundred planes and accessories to defend the City of New York, to be used as a model on which defense against aircraft organizations for other places could be based when required.

There should be a local defense unit of one hundred airplanes at Panama. The airways should be organized throughout the United States, Porto Rico, the West Indies Islands, Cuba, Mexico, and Central America to Panama, so that air force units could be dispatched to the most important point for the defense of that area.

The Hawaiian Islands, due to their remoteness from the continent, should be equipped with an air force of three hundred airplanes, two-thirds of which should be pursuit and one-third, bombardment. In addition to the air force units, there should be a unit for the local defense of the Island of Oahu of one hundred pursuit planes and accessories for defense against aircraft.

Due to the strategic position of the Philippine Islands, there should be no air force or local defense units maintained because the locality could not be defended in case of war. The aeronautical organization there should consist merely of two general service squadrons of twenty-five two-seater airplanes each. These should be organized for use against local uprisings, for reconnaissance, and in developing the airways of the Islands.

Alaska should be provided with an air force of three hundred planes, two hundred pursuit and one hundred bombardment. These should have their headquarters in time of peace in the vicinity of Fort Gibbon, opposite the mouth of the Tanana River on the Yukon. The airways should be organized, with the consent of Canada, from the United States to Alaska as far as Nome and Cape Prince of Wales, and also down the Alaskan Peninsula and the Aleutian Islands to the Island of Attu.

Of the force in the continental United States, there should be about fifteen per cent of officers and enlisted men maintained permanently with the organizations and the rest in Reserve. The general overhead, engineering and supply services should be permanent. In Panama, the units should remain at half strength; in the Hawaiian Islands, they should be at full strength; in the Philippines, at full strength; and in Alaska, at half strength. The number and strength of both the local defense and auxiliary units for observation purposes should be varied from time to time in accordance with the needs of the organizations which they are designed to serve.

The greatest necessity exists for the creation of an air personnel as distinguished from an Army or Navy personnel. The Air Service suffers annually nearly half of the total deaths in the

Army: in 1921, 42%; 1922, 43%; 1923, 47%; 1924, 41%. In war, the proportion of fatalities among the commissioned personnel is even greater. This requires an entirely different system of replacement of personnel from that followed in the Army or Navy, a different Reserve system, and an entirely different system of entrance into the service, promotion, and retirement.

The Air Service navigating personnel should be drawn from the younger elements in our population that are well educated, of an athletic disposition, and fit physically for the duties. Upon entrance into the service, they should be guaranteed a certain promotion, based on years of service. Those who distinguish themselves should be placed in command of organizations and be given the temporary rank which the duties and responsibilities of the position require. Those that are retired for reasons not due to their own fault, should be given retired pay commensurate with their years of service. A system of this kind would guarantee a career to the individual and would also provide a suitable personnel for the various units in the Air Service.

Unity of command is essential to air forces. These can not be operated efficiently in time of war if scattered and assigned to ground or water organizations.

The system of education of air officers primarily as officers of the ground army is wrong. It tends to promote timidity of operation, lack of foresight as to air needs, and lack of ability to lead air troops. Air personnel should be educated and brought up essentially at air institutions of learning. Liaison with other branches of the service should be reciprocal and the personnel of the ground army should be instructed in the duties of air forces by air officers instead of by ground officers. This is a very serious defect in our system which will continue to grow worse because our officers are now educated primarily on the ground and secondarily in the air.

The present system of budget control for the Air Service is destructive of the development of air power. Air forces have no relation to ground forces any more than a navy has. Air forces must be designed primarily to attain victory in the air against a hostile air force and then to destroy enemy establishments, either on the land or on the water. Air power should have an entirely separate budget from the Army and Navy.

Under the conditions that exist today where military aeronautics are a part of the Army and Navy, aviation cannot obtain the consideration necessary to meet its requirements of building up its offensive aviation for wresting control of the air from an enemy, because the basic principle is followed that an army must be built up on infantry and a navy on battleships.

Unity of tactical instruction is necessary. At the present time, none exists between the air forces of the army or of the navy.

In practically all of the civilized countries of the world there is unity of command in the air forces. They are handled by general officers of the air forces. The separate and independent fighting air units are directly under the tactical and strategical command of the Commander in Chief of the respective countries. In sharp distinction to this, there is no single command in the U. S. aviation, nor is there actually any air force in the United States.

The time has passed when any one service can be thrown off to work out its own salvation without respect to the others, as has been the case very largely in the past with the armies and navies. Air, land and water must be hitched together under one general command and direction to provide for an efficient defense.

As a result of many years of service and an intimate knowledge of the aeronautical organization of each of the great powers I am convinced that our inefficient national military aeronautics, our undeveloped civil and commercial aeronautics, and our curtailed and interrupted experimentation in aeronautics are a direct result of the lack of

1. A department of aeronautics to handle the whole air question, co-equal with the Army and Navy.

2. A definite aeronautical policy.

3. An organization, both military and civil, to fit the aeronautical policy.

4. A method of providing suitable personnel for all air undertakings.

5. A single system of procurement and supply for all air undertakings.

6. A system of instruction and inspection for all air elements.

Until these fundamental principles for the creation of air power are put into effect, the air power of the United States will continue to flounder in the slough of aeronautical despond.

ENDNOTES

INTRODUCTION TO BOOK FOUR

1. Richard E. Neustadt and Ernest R. May, *Thinking in Time: The Uses of History for Decision Makers* (New York: The Free Press, 1986), pp. 257-266, 251, and 254. The ability to look at distant futures "with a clear sense of the long past from which those futures would come" (ibid., p. 248). Key questions are those "that shed light almost regardless of the answers" (ibid., p. 269).

2. Michael Howard, "Military Science in an Age of Peace," *RUSI, Journal of the Royal United Services Institute for Defence Studies* 119, no. 1 (March 1974): 4.

3. Ibid., p. 7.

4. Alfred Thayer Mahan, *The Influence of Sea Power Upon History, 1660-1783* (Boston: Little, Brown, and Company, 1890); Julian S. Corbett, *Some Principles of Maritime Strategy* (London: Longmans, Green, 1911); Giulio Douhet, *The Command of the Air,* trans. Dino Ferrari (New York: Coward-McCann, 1942); and William Mitchell, *Winged Defense: The Development and Possibilities of Modern Air Power—Economic and Military* (New York: G. P. Putnam's Sons, 1925).

5. John B. Hattendorf and Lynn C. Hattendorf, *A Bibliography of the Works of Alfred Thayer Mahan* (Newport: Naval War College Press, 1986). *The Influence of Sea Power Upon History* was the first of Mahan's four-part series on naval warfare between 1660 and 1815. That volume as well as *The Influence of Sea Power Upon the French Revolution and Empire, 1793-1812* (Boston: Little, Brown, and Company, 1892) originated as lectures, which Mahan at their inception intended for eventual publication in book form (Philip A. Crowl, "Alfred Thayer Mahan: The Naval Historian," in *Makers of Modern Strategy from Machiavelli to the Nuclear Age,* ed. Peter Paret [Princeton: Princeton University Press, 1986], p. 449 and Jon Tetsuro Sumida, *Inventing Grand Strategy and Teaching Command: The Classic Works of Alfred Thayer Mahan Reconsidered* [Baltimore: The Johns Hopkins University Press, 1997], pp. 5-6).

6. Phillip S. Meilinger, "Giulio Douhet and the Origins of Air Power Theory," in *The Paths of Heaven: The Evolution of Air Power Theory,* ed. Phillip S. Meilinger (Maxwell AFB, Ala.: Air University Press, 1997), pp. 1-8; Irving B. Holley, Jr., "Doctrine and Technology as Viewed by Some Seminal Theorists of the Art of Warfare from Clausewitz to the Mid-Twentieth Century," in *Emerging Doctrines and Technologies: Implications for Global and Regional Political-Military Balances,* ed. Robert L. Pfaltzgraff, Jr., Uri Ra'anan, Richard H. Shultz, Igor Lukes (Lexington, Mass.: D.C. Heath and Company, 1988), pp. 22-23; Richard H. Kohn and Joseph P. Harahan, "Editors' Introduction," in Giulio Douhet, *The Command of the Air,* trans. Dino Ferrari (Washington, D.C.: Office of Air Force History, 1983), pp. vii-viii; and Edward Warner, "Douhet, Mitchell, Seversky: Theories of Air Warfare," in *Makers of Modern Strategy: Military Thought from Machiavelli to Hitler,* ed. Edward Mead Earle (Princeton: Princeton University Press, 1943), pp. 487-488.

7. Warner, "Douhet, Mitchell, Seversky," p. 488 and Alfred Hurley, *Billy Mitchell: Crusader for Air Power* (Bloomington: Indiana University Press, 1975), pp. 1, 12, and 29-36.

8. Donald M. Schurman, *Julian S. Corbett, 1854-1922: Historian of British Maritime Policy from Drake to Jellicoe* (London: Royal Historical Society, 1981), p. 7.

9. The two earlier works: *Drake and the Tudor Navy: With a History of the Rise of England as a Maritime Power,* 2 vols. (London: Longmans, Green, 1898) and *Successors of Drake* (London: Longmans, Green, 1900); see also Eric J. Grove, "Introduction," in Julian S. Corbett, *Some Principles of Maritime Strategy* (Annapolis: Naval Institute Press, 1988), pp. xiv-xv; Liam J. Cleaver, "The Pen Behind the Fleet: The Influence of Sir Julian Stafford Corbett on British Naval Development, 1898-1918," *Comparative Strategy* 14, no. 1 (January-March 1995): 49; and Donald M. Schurman, *The Education of a Navy: The Development of British Naval Strategic Thought, 1867-1914* (Chicago: University of Chicago Press, 1965), pp. 147, 149.

10. Mahan, *Influence,* p. 21; Bernard Brodie, *Strategy in the Missile Age* (Princeton: Princeton University Press, 1959), p. 78; and Walter Millis, *Arms and Men: A Study in American Military History* (Brunswick, N.J.: Rutgers University Press, 1986), p. 155.

11. This did not mean that Mahan believed that the art and science of command could be reduced to a mechanistic use of Jomini's principles; see Sumida, *Inventing Grand Strategy,* pp. 4 and 109-113, who demonstrates that "Jomini's influence on Mahan was important but limited" (ibid., p. 23). Mahan did not become familiar with Clausewitz until long after he had written his first book—possibly 1908, certainly by 1910. But both Mahans, father and son, like Clausewitz, always placed more emphasis on the art rather than the science of command, particularly in their thoughts on uncertainty in war and limitations of theory. In

later years, Mahan came to believe that both Jomini and Clausewitz were valuable guides to warfare (Schurman, *Education,* p. 78; Sumida, *Inventing Grand Strategy,* pp. 110-111 and 113; and Crowl, "Alfred Thayer Mahan," p. 462).

12. Crowl, "Alfred Thayer Mahan," p. 450; see also Millis, *Arms and Men,* p. 155; Russell F. Weigley, *The American Way of War: A History of United States Military Strategy and Policy* (Bloomington: Indiana University Press, 1973), p. 174; and Barry M. Gough, "The Influence of History on Mahan," in *The Influence of History on Mahan: The Proceedings of a Conference Marking the Centenary of Alfred Thayer Mahan's "The Influence of Sea Power Upon History, 1660-1783,"* ed. John B. Hattendorf (Newport, R.I.: Naval War College Press, 1991), p. 17.

13. John B. Hattendorf, ed., *Mahan on Naval Strategy: Selections from the Writings of Rear Admiral Alfred Thayer Mahan* (Annapolis: Naval Institute Press, 1991), p. x. Mahan spent the time between the notification in 1884 and the assumption of his duties at the Naval War College reading a vast amount of secondary sources, much of it at a branch of the New York Public Library. For the various naval reform groups and their motivation between the Civil War and the publication of Mahan's first book, see Mark Russell Shulman, *Navalism and the Emergence of American Sea Power, 1882-1893* (Annapolis, Md.: Naval Institute Press, 1995); Peter Karsten, *The Naval Aristocracy: The Golden Age of Annapolis and the Emergence of Modern American Navalism* (New York: The Free Press, 1972); and Benjamin L. Apt, "Mahan's Forebears: The Debate Over Maritime Strategy, 1868-1883," *Naval War College Review* 50, no. 3 (summer 1997): 86-111. On specific ties between Mahan and navalist colleagues, see Walter R. Herrick, Jr., *The American Naval Revolution* (Baton Rouge: Louisiana State University Press, 1966), p. 47; on Laughton, see Schurman, *Education,* pp. 83-109.

14. Robert Seager II, *Alfred Thayer Mahan: The Man and His Letters* (Annapolis, Md.: Naval Institute Press, 1977), p. 199; see also ibid., pp. 202-203 and Hattendorf, *Mahan,* p. xi.

15. Quoted in Millis, *Arms and Men,* p. 162; See also David MacIsaac, "Voices from the Central Blue: The Air Power Theorists," *Makers of Modern Strategy from Machiavelli to the Nuclear Age,* p. 631; Kohn and Harahan, "Editors' Introduction," p. ix; Brodie, *Strategy,* pp. 71-72; and Hurley, *Billy Mitchell,* p. 139.

16. Seager, *Man and Letters,* p. 215; see also Schurman, *Corbett,* pp. 19 and 32. At a later date, Corbett privately considered Mahan's work as "shallow and wholly unhistorical" (penciled marginalia in Mahan's *Great Britain, Germany and Limited War,* in Grove, "Introduction," p. xxx).

17. For both versions of the "Green Pamphlet," see Grove, "Introduction," pp. 305-345.

18. Ibid., p. 307; see also Schurman, *Corbett,* p. 51, who points out how much of Corbett's 1907 history of England in the *Seven Years War* was informed by Clausewitzian thought as opposed to the 1904 study of the Mediterranean.

19. Hattendorf, *Mahan*, pp. xvii-xviii; see also John Gooch, "Maritime Command: Mahan and Corbett," in *Seapower and Strategy*, ed. Colin S. Gray and Roger W. Barnett (Annapolis, Md.: Naval Institute Press, 1989), pp. 29-30 and Schurman, *Corbett*, pp. 5 and 185.

20. Millis, *Arms and Men*, p. 161; Weigley, *American Way*, p. 178; Sumida, *Inventing Grand Strategy*, pp. 2 and 6; and Schurman, *Education*, pp. 3 and 5, who points out that the British army, primarily dependent upon horsepower and foot power up until 1914, still worked in an environment that the navy perceived as equivalent to the age of sail.

21. MacIsaac, "Voices," p. 629.

22. Millis, *Arms and Men*, p. 251 and Hurley, *Billy Mitchell*, pp. 36-37.

23. Hurley, *Billy Mitchell*, pp. 25-26 and George H. Quester, *Deterrence Before Hiroshima: The Airpower Background of Modern Society* (New York: John Wiley & Sons, Inc., 1966), p. 52. On the *Bolling Mission*, which interviewed strategic bombing enthusiasts in all allied countries, see Hurley, *Billy Mitchell*, pp. 31-32. Mitchell probably met Douhet during his trip to Italy as part of his European trip that began in December 1921 and may have become familiar with the key points from *The Command of the Air*. Mitchell never alluded to Douhet's possible influence on his thinking. At the very least, Alfred Hurley points out, Mitchell became aware of Douhet's principal thoughts in 1922. Mitchell later remarked that he had had "frequent conversations" with Douhet (Hurley, *Billy Mitchell*, pp. 75 and 146).

24. Brodie, *Strategy*, p. 71; see also Hurley, *Billy Mitchell*, p. 27.

25. Henry Harley Arnold, *Global Mission* (New York: Harper, 1949), p. 52. "I was sure that if the war lasted," Mitchell concluded after the armistice in referring to strategic bombardment of the German heartland, "air power would have decided it" (Isaac D. Levine, *Mitchell: Pioneer of Air Power*, rev. ed. [New York: Duell, Sloan and Pearce, 1958], p. 148).

26. Hurley, *Billy Mitchell*, pp. 32 and 35 and Holley, "Doctrine," p. 26.

27. Douhet, *Command*, pp. 196 and 282; see also Michael S. Sherry, *The Rise of American Air Power: The Creation of Armageddon* (New Haven: Yale University Press, 1987), pp. 27 and 29; and I. F. Clarke, *Voices Prophesying War, 1763-1984* (London: Oxford University Press, 1966), p. 166.

28. B. H. Liddell Hart, *Paris, or The Future of War* (New York: E. P. Dutton, 1925), pp. 33-34; original emphasis (ibid., p. 37). See also Weigley, *American Way*, p. 236 and Sherry, *Rise*, pp. 21 and 24.

29. Douhet, *Command*, p. 25; see also Sherry, *Rise*, pp. 26 and 28.

30. Liddell Hart, *Paris*, p. 42.

31. J. F. C. Fuller, *Reformation of War* (London: Hutchenson and Co., 1923), p. 150; see also Quester, *Deterrence*, p. 56.

32. Millis, *Arms and Men*, pp. 251-252.

33. Quester, *Deterrence*, p. 71.

34. Millis, *Arms and Men*, p. 258. Given the conditions and technology of the time, Walter Millis concludes that the Morrow Board findings "may have

been the best answer" (ibid., p. 257). Ironically, the board was headed by Dwight Morrow whose daughter would marry Charles Lindbergh, the great popularizer of aviation because of his 1927 transatlantic flight.

35. Corbett, *Principles,* p. 26.

36. Douhet, *Command,* p. 181.

37. Ibid., p. 185.

38. Mitchell, *Winged Defense,* p. 16; see also Sherry, *Rise,* pp. 28-29.

39. Mahan, *Influence,* pp. v-vi; but note that Mahan qualified this by point-ing out that "it would be absurd to claim for it an exclusive influence" (ibid., p. 21). See also Sumida, *Inventing Grand Strategy,* p. 27 and Crowl, "Alfred Thayer Mahan," p. 450.

40. Mahan, *Influence,* pp. 63-64.

41. Sumida, *Inventing Grand Strategy,* pp. xi-xii and Hattendorf, Mahan, p. ix.

42. Gooch, "Maritime Command," p. 31; see also Sumida, *Inventing Grand Strategy,* p. 102; and Paul M. Kennedy, *The Rise and Fall of British Naval Mas-tery* (New York: Charles Scribner's Sons, 1976), p. 3, who while noting Mahan's impreciseness in dealing with the concept of sea power, perceives it clearly mov-ing from just the short-term, tactical aim of discharging troops across the oceans to a longer term, grand strategic objective that includes control of mercantile trades and routes.

43. Interview with Col. James Holcomb, October 1998; Millis, *Arms and Men,* p. 162; Seager, *Man and Letters,* p. 207; and Margaret Tuttle Sprout, "Mahan: Evangelist of Sea Power," *Makers of Modern Strategy: Military Thought from Machiavelli to Hitler,* p. 418.

44. The British victories in the Seven Years War, Corbett pointed out in an earlier work in 1907, were the result of "the ordered combination of naval, mili-tary, and diplomatic force" (*England in the Seven Years War: A Study in Combined Strategy,* vol. 1 [London: Longmans, Green, 1907], p. 8). See also Schurman, *Education,* p. 165; and Barry D. Hunt, "The Strategic Thought of Julian S. Cor-bett," in *Maritime Strategy and the Balance of Power: Britain and America in the 20th Century,* ed. John B. Hattendorf and Robert S. Jordan (New York: St. Mar-tin's Press, 1989), p. 111.

45. Julian S. Corbett, *The Successors of Drake* (London: Longmans, Green, 1900), p. vii. Corbett was also influenced at this time by his study of Mahan's works (Schurman, *Education,* p. 156).

46. Julian S. Corbett, *England in the Mediterranean,* vol. 1 (London: Long-mans, Green, 1904), pp. 150-175.

47. Julian S. Corbett, *The Campaign of Trafalgar* (London: Longmans, Green, 1910), p. 415.

48. Corbett, *Principles,* pp. 13-14.

49. Gooch, "Maritime Command," p. 41.

50. Corbett, *Principles,* p. 55.

51. Ibid., p. 90.

52. Gooch, "Maritime Command," p. 40.

53. Douhet, *Command,* p. 180.

54. Ibid., p. 24.

55. Ibid., p. 61.

56. Ibid., p. 188; see also Quester, *Deterrence,* p. 54; and Brodie, *Strategy,* p. 99.

57. Douhet, *Command,* p. 181. Brodie, Strategy, p. 37, took Douhet to task for not understanding that war must follow policy. Meilinger, "Giulio Douhet," pp. 24-25, points out that Brodie missed the point. Douhet was a cynic about human nature who believed that policy in future wars would be just as irrational as it had been in the Great War and thus resistent to fine-tuning strategy.

58. Douhet, *Command,* p. 55.

59. Ibid., p. 18.

60. Ibid., pp. 196-197; see also ibid., p. 202: "Whatever its arms, the side which decides to go to war will unleash all its aerial forces in mass against the enemy nation the instant the decision is taken, without waiting to declare war formally. . . ." But in the article, "The War of 19—," book 4 of the 1942 compilation of *The Command of the Air,* which is not included in this volume, Douhet depicts the Germans in this hypothetical conflict as permitting the French to strike first in order to secure favorable "world public opinion" for the aerochemical "reprisals" by the German Air Force (ibid., p. 372). See also ibid., p. 353; Brodie, *Strategy,* p. 100; and Meilinger, Giulio Douhet, p. 16.

61. Douhet, *Command,* p. 117; Holley, "Doctrine," p. 25; Brodie, *"Strategy,"* pp. 93-95; and Meilinger, "Giulio Douhet," p. 13.

62. Mitchell, *Winged Defense,* p. 199; see also Sherry, *Rise,* pp. 30-31; and Weigley, *American Way,* p. 228.

63. William Mitchell, *Our Air Force: The Key to National Defense* (New York: Dutton, 1921), p. xix.

64. Sherry, *Rise,* pp. 28-29 and Hurley, *Billy Mitchell,* p. 76.

65. Arnold, *Global Mission,* p. 159; see also Hurley, *Billy Mitchell,* pp. 90-92; and Sherry, *Rise,* p. 38.

66. Hurley, *Billy Mitchell,* p. 92. "The fact is that General Mitchell welcomed the court-martial," Gen. Ira C. Eaker noted in 1981, "as it gave additional publicity to his cause, which was of course to obtain a separate Air Force" (Timothy E. Kline, "Where Have All the Mitchells Gone?" *Airpower Journal* 11, no. 3 (fall 1997); 75.

67. Emphasis added, Mitchell, *Winged Defense,* p. xiv. See also ibid., pp. 126-127; Quester, *Deterrence,* p. 57; and Weigley, *American Way,* pp. 232-233, 236, and 515.

68. William Mitchell, *Skyways: A Book on Modern Aeronautics* (Philadelphia: J. B. Lippincott Company, 1930), pp. 255-256; see also ibid., p. 262; and Warner, "Douhet, Mitchell, Seversky," p. 498.

69. Schurman, *Education,* pp. 74 and 182; Gooch, "Maritime Command," p. 26; Crowl, "Alfred Thayer Mahan," p. 454; Hattendorf, *Mahan,* p. xii; and Sumida, *Inventing Grand Strategy,* p. 7. Mahan, of course, was not a trained scholar

and was preoccupied with mastering the subject and making it digestible to students. "It is a military exercise that yielded some scholarly insights: not a scholarly search that yielded some military results" (Gough, "The Influence of History on Mahan," p. 106).

70. Grove, "Introduction," p. xv. Referring to Mahan's dependence on secondary sources, Corbett wrote in 1916, "the wonder is that Mahan could build as well as he did on a foundation so insecure" (Hunt, "Strategic Thought," p. 110).

71. Schurman, *Education,* p. 184.

72. Both quotes in Sumida, *Inventing Grand Strategy,* p. 3. See also Schurman, *Education,* p. 81, who points out that Mahan's style and use of primary sources improved throughout his long writing career after his initial effort; Holger H. Herwig, "The Influence of A. T. Mahan Upon German Sea Power," *The Influence of History on Mahan,* p. 70, who sees the book as consisting of "a rather plodding chronology of British sail from the Second Dutch War to the Surrender at Yorktown," which demands close examination "for the few nuggets that it contains"; and Hattendorf, *Mahan,* p. xvi, for a contemporary newspaper review of Mahan's style:

> It is cold, it is heavy, it is unrhythmical; it is without any quality of beauty. But as a historian, he compels admiration—he has such a grasp upon his subject; his cold, clumsy, telling phrases go home deeply. His "nuts of knowledge" are heavy round shot.

73. Grove, "Introduction," p. xxv; see also Schurman, *Education,* pp. 149-150; and Adm. J. C. Wylie, "Mahan: Then and Now," *The Influence of History on Mahan,* p. 40, who concludes that Corbett has "perhaps more graceful prose than Mahan." "There are times when the reader stands amazed at the magnificent edifice erected to assist his understanding," Schurman writes of Corbett's historical works from 1898 to 1910, "and there are other times when the connection between cause and effect appear too elusive to really convince. Corbett's charm, and his difficulty as an historian, lie in the way he exercised this considerable talent" (Schurman, *Corbett,* p. 197).

74. Douhet, *Command,* p. 103.

75. "It is always dangerous," Douhet commented, "to keep looking backward when marching forward. . . ." (Brodie, *Strategy,* p. 79); see also Sherry, *Rise,* p. 27; and Meilinger, "Giulio Douhet," p. 27.

76. Holley, "Doctrine," p. 27; see also Sherry, *Rise,* p. 27.

77. Warner, "Douhet, Mitchell, Seversky," p. 487; MacIsaac, "Voices," p. 626; Meilinger, "Giulio Douhet," pp. 14-15; and Brodie, *Strategy,* p. 77, who believes that "writing was decidedly not Mitchell's forte."

78. Douhet, *Command,* book 4, pp. 293-394; and Sherry, *Rise,* pp. 25 and 52.

79. Hurley, *Billy Mitchell,* p. 97; see also Schurman, *Education,* p. 183; and Warner, "Douhet, Mitchell, Seversky," p. 497.

80. Mitchell, *Winged Defense,* p. 139.

81. Hurley, *Billy Mitchell,* p. 139; see also ibid., p. 40.

82. On Mahan's influence, see, for example, Schurman, *Education,* pp. 79 and 82; Gooch, "Maritime Command," p. 36; Sumida, *Inventing Grand Strategy,* p. 107; and Seager, *Man and Letters,* p. 218. On Mahan's didactic purpose as a navalist, see Crowl, "Alfred Thayer Mahan," p. 468; Karsten, *Naval Aristocracy,* p. 337 who sees Mahan as "a simple navalist first and everything else thereafter;" Seager, *Man and Letters,* p. xi, who concludes that "as a propagandist for sea power . . . he was a genius;" and Millis, *Arms and Men,* p. 161 who believes that "Mahan's major impulse was simply to produce an argument for more naval building." But see Sprout, "Evangelist," p. 425, who perceives Mahan's views concerning an American naval program as moderate, since he did not accept the territorial expansion that appeared to be inherent in his concept of sea power. In 1890, for instance, Mahan did make a key exception when he wrote of creating a navy "which, if not capable of reaching distant countries, shall at least be able to keep clear the chief approaches to its own" (Mahan, *Influence,* p. 87).

83. Crowl, "Alfred Thayer Mahan," p. 473; and Sprout, "Evangelist," p. 423. The book appeared at a time when naval races were beginning to heat up in Europe; it is thus impossible to separate the influences that the book had on intensifying those races from the degree to which the influence of naval consciousness furthered the immense popularity of the book (Schurman, *Education,* p. 60). See also Crowl, "Alfred Thayer Mahan," p. 474, who sees Mahan's role in Germany's fleet expansion as one of "marginal influence" and Herwig, "Influence of Mahan," p. 69, who points out that Mahan's enthusiastic German reception rested primarily on his general advocacy of sea power, rather than upon the specific "lessons" that he had drawn from his study of Britain's history in the age of sail.

84. Crowl, "Alfred Thayer Mahan," p. 445. Moreover, except for a few minutes at Port Royal, South Carolina, on 7 November 1861, Mahan had never heard a shot fired in anger (Seager, *Man and Letters,* p. xi).

85. Schurman, *Education,* p. 175.

86. Grove, "Introduction," p. xi; see Cleaver, "Pen," p. 49.

87. Appendix D, "Lord Nelson's Memorandum," in Corbett, *Trafalgar,* vol. 2, p. 498. In that book, Corbett had criticized the risks Nelson had taken, prompting one journalist to note Corbett's generally "unhealthy" influence on his War Course students (Schurman, *Corbett,* p. 123). See also Grove, "Introduction," p. xxiii; Schurman, *Education,* p. 183; and Corbett, *Principles,* part 1, chapter 2, pp. 28-37.

88. Winston S. Churchill, *The World Crisis 1915* (New York: Charles Scribner's Sons, 1929), p. 318; see also Hunt, "Strategic Thought," p. 112.

89. Grove, "Introduction," p. xliv; and Schurman, *Corbett,* pp. 193, 171, and chapters 9 and 10; see also Schurman, *Education,* pp. 150 and 183.

90. Brodie, *Strategy,* p. 75; see also ibid., p. 76. On the resistance to Douhet on moral and practical grounds by Italian advocates of air support and

interdiction campaigns, see James S. Corum, "Airpower Thought in Continental Europe Between the Wars," *Paths of Heaven*, pp. 160-161. In the interwar period, each major European air power conducted debates between those who believed in strategic bombing by an independent air force and those who saw airpower's primary role as support for land and naval forces (ibid., p. 176).

91. Warner, "Douhet, Mitchell, Seversky," p. 496. There is little evidence that Douhet attempted to spread his concepts of airpower outside his own country. He wrote for Italian professional journals in a language not widely shared by military thinkers. And although he probably attempted to influence the Bolling Mission during that group's visit to Italy in World War I, his primary goal at that time was to bring the United States into the war as an ally (Meilinger, "Giulio Douhet," pp. 32 and 36). See also ibid., pp. 17-18. The Germans, of course, were receptive to new ideas, but Douhet's philosophy never fully penetrated the Luftwaffe which focused on air-land tactical support. Douhet appears to have had little or even no influence in Britain between the wars. In any event, *The Command of the Air* was never required reading in that period at the Royal Air Force Staff College (ibid., pp. 32-33).

92. Arnold, *Global Mission*, p. 149; see also MacIsaac, "Voices," p. 635; Weigley, *American Way*, p. 240; and Brodie, *Strategy*, pp. 73-74, who points out that Douhet had different positions on fighter escorts at different times and generally gave the impression that such escorts were desirable, but not necessary. In the 1930s, many of the ideas gestating in various air forces around the globe were similar to those of Douhet's. But to draw specific lines of influence is almost impossible because of the efforts of many people in many nations at the time to come to grips with what the airplane could accomplish (Meilinger, "Giulio Douhet," pp. 33-34).

93. Sherry, *Rise*, p. 37; see also ibid., p. 33. On Mitchell's impact on the Air Corps Tactical School, see Peter R. Faber, "Interwar U.S. Army Aviation and the Air Corps Tactical School: Incubators of American Airpower," *Paths of Heaven*, pp. 212-216. On Mitchell's link to Progressivism, see Mitchell, *Winged Defense*, p. x: "The time has come when aviation must be developed for aviation's sake and not as an auxiliary to other existing branches. Unless the progressive elements in our makeup are availed of, we will fall behind in the world's development."

94. Hurley, *Billy Mitchell*, p. 105.

95. As pointed out earlier concerning the *status quo* aspects of the legislation, no separate air arm or Department of National Defense would emerge. But the 1926 law did call for a minor buildup of the two service air arms for a period of five years (ibid).

96. Article of 1 May 1926 entitled "When the Air Raiders Come" (Hurley, *Billy Mitchell*, pp. 111-112).

97. MacIsaac, "Voices," p. 632; Hurley, *Billy Mitchell*, p. 57; and Samuel F. Wells, "William Mitchell and the *Ostfriesland*: A Study in Military Reform," *The Historian: A Journal of History*, 26, no. 4 (August 1964): 538-562. The aerial

bombing of the battleships, Mitchell commented, "clearly demonstrated" that the expenditure of large funds was a waste for the U.S. Navy "where certain superannuated gentlemen known as admirals dictate the practical workings and policies. . . ." (Holley, "Doctrine," p. 27). Admiral Moffett was as frustrated as Mitchell with the Washington bureaucracy; but, unlike Mitchell, he learned to work effectively within institutional boundaries (William C. Rynecki, "Transformational Leaders and Doctrine in an Age of Peace: Searching for a Tamer Billy Mitchell," *Airpower Journal* 12, no. 1 (spring 1998: 22-36). On Moffett's relationship with Mitchell, see William F. Trimble, *Admiral William A. Moffett: Architect of Naval Aviation* (Washington, D.C.: Smithsonian Institution Press, 1994), p. 93.

98. Arnold, *Global Mission,* p. 121; see also ibid., pp. 158-159: "The public enthusiasm . . . was not for air power—it was for Billy."; Sherry, *Rise,* pp. 36-37; Hurley, *Billy Mitchell,* pp. 134-135; and Mark A. Clodfelter, "Molding Airpower Convictions: Development and Legacy of William Mitchell's Strategic Thought," *Paths of Heaven,* p. 104.

99. Mahan, *Influence,* p. 7.

100. Schurman, "Mahan Revisited," *Maritime Strategy and the Balance of Power,* p. 95; see also John B. Hattendorf, "Alfred Thayer Mahan and his Strategic Thought," *Maritime Strategy and the Balance of Power,* p. 86; and John B. Hattendorf, "Recent Thinking on the Theory of Naval Strategy," *Maritime Strategy and the Balance of Power,* pp. 144-145.

101. Douhet, *Command,* p. 30.

102. Mitchell, *Winged Defense,* p. 127.

103. I. B. Holley, "Reflections on the Search for Airpower Theory," *Paths of Heaven,* p. 583; see also Meilinger, "Douhet," *Paths of Heaven,* pp. 29-30.

104. On reservations concerning Mahan's assertions concerning the superiority of sea power over land power, the importance of commerce, colonies, and shipping, and the universality of his historical findings, see Kennedy, *Rise and Fall,* pp. 6-8. On Mackinder's geopolitical challenge and the importance in that challenge of the railway, ironically a British invention, see ibid., chapter 7, pp. 177-202, particularly pp. 183 and 195. See also Schurman, "Mahan Revisited," *Maritime Strategy and the Balance of Power,* pp. 98 and 106; Hattendorf, "Recent Thinking on the Theory of Naval Strategy," *Maritime Strategy and the Balance of Power,* p. 137; John B. Hattendorf and Robert S. Jordan, "Conclusions: Maritime Strategy and National Policy: Historical Accident or Purposeful Planning," *Maritime Strategy and the Balance of Power,* p. 354; Gooch, "Maritime Command," pp. 36-37; and Gough, "The Influence of History on Mahan," pp. 19-21.

105. Holley, "Reflections on the Search for Airpower Theory," p. 597; Tony Mason, *Air Power: A Centennial Appraisal* (London: Brassey's, 1994), pp. 272 and 278; Phillip S. Meilinger, "Giulio Douhet and Modern War," *Comparative Strategy* 12, no. 3 (July-September 1993): 321-328; and Sherry, *Rise,* pp. 31-32.

106. Mason, *Air Power,* pp. 273-274; Hurley, *Billy Mitchell,* p. 140; and Quester, "Mahan and American Naval Thought Since 1914," p. 178; see also

Howard, "Military Science," p. 4: "The military profession is . . . also a bureaucracy, and bureaucracies accommodate themselves with great difficulty to outstanding original thinkers."

107. Mitchell, *Winged Defense,* p. 18.

108. Benjamin S. Lambeth, "Bounding the Air Power Debate," *Strategic Review* 25, no. 4 (fall 1997): 42; and Clodfelter, "Molding Airpower," p. 108.

109. Lambeth, "Bounding Air Power," p. 49; see also Mason, *Air Power,* p. 273.

INTRODUCTION TO MAHAN: *The Influence of Sea Power Upon History*

1. Jon Tetsuro Sumida, *Inventing Grand Strategy and Teaching Command: The Classic Works of Alfred Thayer Mahan Reconsidered* (Baltimore: The Johns Hopkins University Press, 1997), p. 25. See also Robert Seager II, *Alfred Thayer Mahan: The Man and His Letters* (Annapolis, Md.: Naval Institute Press, 1977), pp. 197, 199, and 205. Most reviewers, in fact, did not appear to have read past the first chapter (ibid., p. 211). "In short, the theoretical issues must have attracted the armchair strategists, not the nuts and bolts" (Barry M. Gough, "The Influence of History on Mahan," in *The Influence of History on Mahan: The Proceedings of a Conference Marking the Centenary of Alfred Thayer Mahan's The Influence of Sea Power Upon History, 1660-1783,* ed. John B. Hattendorf [Newport, R.I.: Naval War College Press, 1991], p. 9).

2. But see his caveat in terms of sea power that "it would be absurd to claim for it an exclusive influence" (Alfred Thayer Mahan, *The Influence of Sea Power Upon History, 1660-1783* [Boston: Little, Brown, and Company, 1890], p. 21).

3. Ibid., pp. 1, 25-26, 28, and 29-89; see also Sumida, *Inventing Grand Strategy,* p. 27; Seager, *Man and Letters,* pp. 206-207; and Margaret Tuttle Sprout, "Mahan: Evangelist of Sea Power," in *Makers of Modern Strategy: Military Thought from Machiavelli to Hitler,* ed. Edward Mead Earle (Princeton: Princeton University Press, 1943), p. 418. On earlier arguments on these subjects, see Peter Karsten, The *Naval Aristocracy: The Golden Age of Annapolis and the Emergence of Modern American Navalism* (New York: The Free Press, 1972), pp. 277-317; and Seager, *Man and Letters,* pp. 205-208.

4. Mahan, *Influence,* pp. 33-35 and 38; see also Sprout, "Evangelist," p. 426; Sumida, *Inventing Grand Strategy,* p. 82; and Seager, *Man and Letters,* pp. 206-207.

5. Mahan, *Influence,* pp. 29-89; see also Sprout, "Evangelist," pp. 426-428; and Seager, *Man and Letters,* p. 207.

6. Mahan, *Influence,* p. 28.

7. Ibid., p. 82.

8. Ibid.

9. Ibid., p. 83.

10. Ibid., p. 67.

11. Ibid., p. 76; see also Sumida, *Inventing Grand Strategy,* p. 30. Mahan was careful to point out that only very few great sea power states in history, such as Carthage and Spain, were despotic in nature (Seager, *Man and Letters,* p. 207).

12. Mahan, *Influence,* pp. 7-10.

13. Sumida, *Inventing Grand Strategy,* pp. 42-43.

14. Mahan, *Influence,* p. 200.

15. Sumida, *Inventing Grand Strategy,* pp. 30-31, who points out that in these last six chapters, Mahan uses approximately 40 percent of the text to address 4 percent of the chronology.

16. Ibid., p. 32.

INTRODUCTION TO CORBETT: *Some Principles of Maritime Strategy*

1. On the Fisher reforms, the "Syndicate of Discontent," and the reaction to Corbett's book on Trafalgar, see Donald M. Schurman, *Julian S. Corbett, 1854-1922: Historian of British Maritime Policy from Drake to Jellicoe* (London: Royal Historical Society, 1981), chapters 4 and 7; Eric J. Grove, "Introduction," in Julian S. Corbett, *Some Principles of Maritime Strategy* (Annapolis: Naval Institute Press, 1988), p. xvi; and Barry D. Hunt, "The Strategic Thought of Sir Julian S. Corbett," in *Maritime Strategy and the Balance of Power: Britain and America in the Twentieth Century,* eds. John B. Hattendorf and Robert S. Jordan (New York: St. Martin's Press, 1989), pp. 112-113 and 120-121. On the committee of inquiry, see Hunt, "Strategic Thoughts," p. 113; and Schurman, *Corbett,* p. 128.

2. Julian S. Corbett, *Some Principles of Maritime Strategy,* (London: Longmans, Green, 1911), p. 2; see also Hunt, "Strategic Thought," p. 122; and Grove, "Introduction," p. xxiv.

3. Corbett, *Principles,* p. 3.

4. Ibid.

5. Ibid., pp. 23-24.

6. Ibid., p. 25.

7. Ibid., p. 33.

8. Ibid., p. 41.

9. Ibid., p. 52.

10. Ibid., p. 55.

11. Ibid., pp. 54-55.

12. Ibid., pp. 57 and 63.

13. Ibid., pp. 62-63; see also ibid., p. 59. Modern critics have addressed the ideal circumstances for Wellington's campaign, particularly under modern conditions of land transportation and communication, which could allow the continental enemy to neutralize, destroy, or even ignore the land threat from the sea (Hunt, "Strategic Thought," p. 126). But Corbett had also pointed out that even

if the ideal conditions of the Spanish threats could not be duplicated, there were still options ranging from coastal deception or diversion operations to the direct reinforcement of land forces that had a great deal of strategic and psychological value (Corbett, *Principles,* p. 64).

14. Corbett, *Principles,* p. 73.

15. Ibid., p. 81.

16. Ibid., pp. 81-82.

17. Ibid., p. 213.

18. Ibid., p. 269; see also Corbett's discussion of emerging torpedo and submarine technology in a section not included in this volume: "The improved value of submarines only deepens the mist which overhangs the next naval war" (ibid, p. 233).

19. Donald M. Schurman, *The Education of a Navy: The Development of British Naval Strategic Thought, 1867-1914* (Chicago: University of Chicago Press, 1965), p. 181.

20. Hunt, "Strategic Thought," p. 131 and Grove, "Introduction," p. xxxvii.

21. Ibid., p. 132 and Grove, "Introduction," p. xxxviii.

22. Emphasis added; Hunt, "Strategic Thought," p. 131 and Grove, pp. xxxix-xl.

23. Hunt, "Strategic Thought," p. 119.

24. Schurman, *Corbett,* p. 196.

INTRODUCTION TO DOUHET: *The Command of the Air*

1. The 1942 translation only contains about half of the first edition. A 93-page appendix concerning principles of flight and technical details of aircraft was not translated for the 1942 book. The appendix is contained in a 1958 translation that the Italian Air Force considers the official translation. It does not contain the other articles by Douhet that compose parts 2, 3, and 4 of the 1942 edition (Giulio Douhet, *The Command of the Air,* trans. Sheila Fischer [Rome: Rivista Aeronautica, 1958]). See also Phillip S. Meilinger, "Giulio Douhet and the Origins of Air Power Theory," in *The Paths of Heaven: The Evolution of Air Power Theory,* ed. Phillip S. Meilinger (Maxwell AFB, Ala.: Air University Press, 1997), pp. 8, 17-18, and 34.

2. The first two chapters of "The Probable Aspects of the War in the Future" address the broad strategic issues of World War I, despite the fact that he had once exclaimed: "In the name of charity, let us forget the last war" (Bernard Brodie, *Strategy in the Missile Age* [Princeton: Princeton University Press, 1959], p. 79). See also Giulio Douhet, *The Command of the Air,* trans. Dino Ferrari (New York: Coward-McCann, 1942), pp. 143-208 and 209-292; Meilinger, "Giulio Douhet," pp. 18 and 35-36; and Edward Warner, "Douhet, Mitchell,

Seversky: Theories of Air Warfare," in *Makers of Modern Strategy: Military Thought from Machiavelli to Hitler,* ed. Edward Mead Earle (Princeton: Princeton University Press, 1943), p. 489.

3. Douhet, *Command,* p. 220.

4. Ibid., pp. 293-394; see also Brodie, *Strategy,* p. 72; and Meilinger, "Giulio Douhet, pp. 18-19.

5. Original emphasis; Douhet, *Command,* p. 294.

6. Ibid., p. 207. At one point, Douhet did concede that aerial bombardment could "certainly never hope to attain the accuracy of artillery fire" (Ibid., p. 14). In "The War of ——," he went well beyond his "unit of destruction" in claiming that five hundred tons of bombs could destroy a major city (Ibid., p. 393).

7. Meilinger, "Giulio Douhet," p. 22.

8. Douhet, *Command,* p. 50.

9. Brodie, *Strategy,* p. 91. On this point, it was a "kind of intellectual hiatus" for Douhet (Ibid).

10. H. G. Wells, *The War in the Air* (New York: The Macmillan Co., 1908). See also Michael S. Sherry, *The Rise of American Air Power: The Creation of Armageddon* (New Haven: Yale University Press, 1987), pp. 8 and 26; Warner, "Douhet, Mitchell, Seversky," p. 486; and I. F. Clarke, *Voices Prophesying War, 1763-1984* (London: Oxford University Press, 1966), pp. 100-101.

11. Douhet, *Command,* p. 61.

12. Original emphasis; ibid., p. 55.

13. Ibid., p. 128.

14. Ibid., p. 276.

15. Ibid.

16. See Warner, "Douhet, Mitchell, Seversky," p. 494, who believes that Douhet failed to deal adequately with the evolution of technology in this regard; but also see Douhet, *Command,* pp. 45 and 65-66, in which Douhet emphasizes the need for armor, all-metal construction, and the use of superchargers and pressurized cabins; Brodie, *Strategy,* p. 96; and Meilinger, "Giulio Douhet," p. 15.

17. Douhet, *Command,* p. 9; see also ibid., pp. 342-383, in which Douhet begins to concede that at least tactical defense might be possible. All of the attacking German battleplanes in the initial wave in "The War of ——" are shot down by enemy pursuit. But, Douhet emphasizes that those losses are compensated by the succeeding waves of bombers who penetrate the enemy air space to achieve victory. On the reflection of the "bomber will always get through" mentality in the popular culture of the 1930s, see Meilinger, "Giulio Douhet," p. 20; and Clarke, *Voices Prophesying,* p. 170, who describes, as an example, the popularity of the 1931 book, *The Gas War of 1940,* which depicts great fleets of bombers destroying London.

18. Meilinger, "Giulio Douhet," pp. 26 and 29.

INTRODUCTION TO MITCHELL: *Winged Defense*

1. Alfred Hurley, *Billy Mitchell: Crusader for Air Power* (Bloomington: Indiana University Press, 1975), p. 100. See also the foreword to William Mitchell, *Winged Defense: The Development and Possibilities of Modern Air Power—Economic and Military* (New York: G. P. Putnam's Sons, 1925), p. viii, in which Mitchell also admits that the book "has been thrown together hastily."

2. Mitchell, *Winged Defense,* pp. xi and xiii.

3. Ibid., p. 101.

4. Ibid., p. ix.

5. William Mitchell, *Our Air Force: The Key to National Defense* (New York: Dutton, 1921), pp. 15 and 37.

6. Mitchell, *Winged Defense,* p. 214; see also ibid., p. 16; and Mark A. Clodfelter, "Molding Airpower Convictions: Development and Legacy of William Mitchell's Strategic Thought," in *The Paths of Heaven: The Evolution of Airpower Theory,* ed. Phillip S. Meilinger (Maxwell AFB, Ala.: Air University Press, 1997), pp. 94-96.

7. Mitchell, *Winged Defense,* pp. xvi and 12. Even the title, *Winged Defense,* demonstrated Mitchell's sensitivity to the country's mood of isolation. And in fact in chapters 4 and 5 of the book, which are not included in the reading, Mitchell emphasized how the airplane could be used peacefully in a domestic setting, whether it was spraying agricultural crops and patrolling the border for illegal immigrants, or performing geological mapping and carrying the mail; see also Clodfelter, "Molding Airpower," p. 100.

8. Mitchell, *Winged Defense,* p. 12.

9. Ibid., p. 10.

10. Ibid., pp. 16-17; see also ibid., p. 19; and Michael S. Sherry, *The Rise of American Air Power: The Creation of Armageddon* (New Haven: Yale University Press, 1987), p. 30.

11. Mitchell, *Winged Defense,* pp. 5-6; see also ibid., pp. 126-127, in which Mitchell was still not willing to make the full acknowledgment and instead writes of using strategic bombardment to destroy the enemy's power to make war and "the places where people live and carry on their daily lives."

12. Mitchell, *Winged Defense,* pp. ix, 9, 123 and chapter 10.

13. Clodfelter, "Molding Airpower," p. 90.

14. Ibid.; and Mitchell, *Winged Defense,* p. 19.

15. Clodfelter, "Molding Airpower," p. 100; and Russell F. Weigley, *The American Way of War: A History of United States Military Strategy and Policy* (Bloomington: Indiana University Press, 1973), p. 228, who concludes of Mitchell in this regard, that "the navy obfuscation of his accomplishments justified his own oversimplifications."

16. Clodfelter, "Molding Airpower," p. 94.

17. Mitchell, *Our Air Force,* p. 168.

18. William F. Trimble, *Admiral William A. Moffett: Architect of Naval Aviation* (Washington, D.C.: Smithsonian Institution Press, 1994), p. 93.

19. Irving B. Holley, Jr., "Doctrine and Technology as Viewed by Some Seminal Theorists of the Art of Warfare from Clausewitz to the Mid-Twentieth Century," in *Emerging Doctrines and Technologies: Implications for Global and Regional Political-Military Balances,* eds. Robert L. Pfaltzgraff, Jr., Uri Ra'anan, Richard H. Shultz, Igor Lukes (Lexington, Mass.: D.C. Heath and Company, 1988), p. 28.

20. Mitchell, *Winged Defense,* pp. 62, 123, and 136. But see also Clodfelter, "Molding Airpower," p. 93, who points out that even as late as his court-martial in 1925, Mitchell argued for the construction of more carriers capable of carrying either one hundred bombers or an equal number of pursuit planes.

21. Mitchell, *Winged Defense,* p. 21. As early as 1922, the secretary of war had ruled that Mitchell was to submit his articles for official clearance (Hurley, *Billy Mitchell,* pp. 79-80).

22. Henry Harley Arnold, *Global Mission* (New York: Harper, 1949), p. 122. In the years after the court-martial, Mitchell became an even harsher critic of the other services. "We must relegate armies and navies to a place in the glass case of a dusty museum, which contains examples of the dinosaur. . . ." (Holley, "Doctrine," p. 27; and Clodfelter, "Molding Airpower," p. 107). In 1934 one army general heading up that service's War Plans Division, remarked that "for many years the General Staff of the Army has suffered a feeling of disgust amounting at times to nausea over statements publicly made by General William Mitchell and those who follow his lead" (Clodfelter, "Molding Airpower," p. 106).

23. Hurley, *Billy Mitchell,* p. 98.

24. Mitchell, *Winged Defense,* pp. xv and xviii.

25. The cartoons were added, "supposedly without Mitchell's knowledge." Hurley, *Billy Mitchell,* p. 100. But see Clodfelter, "Molding Airpower," pp. 102 and 113, who points out that Mitchell was unaware that the cartoons would be published in the book. In any event, his wife was upset that the cartoons lampooned Secretary of War John W. Weeks, seriously ill at the time of the *Winged Defense* publication. As a result, Mitchell publicly apologized to Secretary Weeks on 5 September 1925 for any disrespect the cartoons might have implied.

26. Hurley, *Billy Mitchell,* p. 101.

27. Arnold, Global Mission, pp. 119-120. For Coolidge, Mitchell was a "God-d—d disturbing liar" (Eugene M. Emme, "The American Dimension," in *Air Power and Warfare: Proceedings of the Eighth Military History Symposium, USAF Academy, 1978,* ed. Alfred F. Hurley and Robert C. Ehrhart [Washington, D.C.: Government Printing Office, 1979], p. 67). The Morrow Board's accommodating recommendations included new nomenclature (Air Service to Air Corps) and formal representation on the War Department General Staff. All this may have been part of a preemptive attempt to mitigate the political impact of Mitchell's impending court-martial (Benjamin Foulois, *From the Wright Brothers to the Astronauts* [New York: McGraw Hill, 1968], pp. 199-200).

28. The fact that Mitchell never referred to the court-martial in any future writings, treating it as a closed subject, is possible proof that he deliberately created the entire controversy (Hurley, *Billy Mitchell,* p. 107).

29. William Mitchell, *Skyways: A Book on Modern Aeronautics* (Philadelphia: J. B. Lippincott Company, 1930), pp. 29 and 32; Edward Warner, "Douhet, Mitchell, Seversky: Theories of Air Warfare," in *Makers of Modern Strategy: Military Thought from Machiavelli to Hitler,* ed. Edward Mead Earle (Princeton: Princeton University Press, 1943), p. 499; and Weigley, *American Way,* p. 236, who concludes: "There were two Billy Mitchells, the Mitchell of 1917-26, whose theories were closely tied to technology and to tactical as well as strategic knowledge, and the post-1926 apostle of the war of swift decision against the enemy's vital centers."

30. Mitchell, *Skyways,* pp. 262-263.

31. Clodfelter, "Molding Airpower," p. 101; and George H. Quester, "Mahan and American Naval Thought Since 1914," in *The Influence of History on Mahan: The Proceedings of a Conference Marking the Centenary of Alfred Thayer Mahan's "The Influence of Sea Power Upon History, 1660-1783,"* ed. John B. Hattendorf, (Newport, R.I.: Naval War College Press, 1991), p. 190, who notes also of Douhet that his "paragraphs about the proper approach to control of the air sometimes read as if they had been copied from Mahan with the word 'air' simply substituted over and over again for 'sea'." In his introduction to the 1943 edition of *Makers of Modern Strategy,* Edward Mead Earle acknowledged that the inclusion of only two Americans, Mahan and Mitchell, in the volume was "small representation for a people which has been preoccupied with war, to a greater or lesser degree, since the first colonists landed on our shores." The reason, he explained, was "that our significant contributions to warfare have been in the fields of tactics and technology" (Edward Mead Earle, "Introduction," *Makers of Modern Strategy,* p. ix).

ABOUT THE EDITOR

Dr. David Jablonsky (Colonel, Retired) is the Professor of National Security Affairs in the Department of National Security and Strategy at the U.S. Army War College, Carlisle, Pennsylvania. He is a graduate of the U.S. Army Command and General Staff College and the U.S. Army War College. He holds a BA in European history from Dartmouth College, a MA in international relations from Boston University, and a MA and Ph.D. in European history from Kansas University. Dr. Jablonsky has held the Elihu Root Chair of Strategy and the George C. Marshall Chair of Military Studies at the War College. He is the author of four books: *Hitler and The Verbotzeit: The Nazi Party in Dissolution, 1923-1925; Churchill, The Great Game and Total War; Churchill and Hitler: Essays on the Political Military Direction of Total War;* and *Paradigm Lost? Transitions and the Search for a New World Order.* His military decorations include the Silver Star and the Purple Heart.

STACKPOLE
BOOKS

Roots of Strategy Series

ROOTS OF STRATEGY

Sun Tzu's *The Art of War*
Vegetius's *The Military Institutions of the Romans*
De Saxe's *My Reveries Upon the Art of War*
Frederick the Great's *Instructions for his Generals*
Napoleon's Maxims

ROOTS OF STRATEGY – Book Two

Du Picq's *Battle Studies*
Clausewitz's *Principles of War*
Jomini's *Art of War*

ROOTS OF STRATEGY – Book Three

von Leeb's *Defense*
von Freytag – Loringhoven's *The Power of Personality in War*
Erfurth's *Surprise*

Available at bookstores, military exchanges or directly from Stackpole Books
5067 Ritter Road
Mechanicsburg, PA 17055
1-800-732-3669
www.stackpolebooks.com